The Causes and Consequences of Income Tax Noncompliance

Jeffrey A. Dubin

The Causes and Consequences of Income Tax Noncompliance

Springer

Jeffrey A. Dubin
Anderson School of Management
Global Economics and Management
C505 Box 951481
Los Angeles, CA
90095-1481
USA
e-mail: jeffrey.dubin@anderson.ucla.edu

ISBN 978-1-4419-0906-0 e-ISBN 978-1-4419-0907-7
DOI 10.1007/978-1-4419-0907-7
Springer New York Dordrecht Heidelberg London

Library of Congress Control Number: 2011941618

Cover design: eStudio Calamar, Berlin/Figueres

Printed on acid-free paper

Springer is part of Springer Science+Business Media (www.springer.com)

Acknowledgments

This study has benefited from the assistance of several individuals. James Lin of Pacific Economics Group provided valuable research assistance on both phases of the IRS criminal investigations research. Patrick Travers, Operations Research Analyst, IRS CI Research, Debbie King (Director of IRS CI Research), Alan Plumley (Economist and Technical Advisor in IRS Office of Research) and Colleen McGuire (Senior Associate, ICF Consulting) all deserve thanks for their assistance during the CI period of this research. Jim Alm receives my thanks and recognition as the editor of Public Finance Review. Jim was instrumental in the publication of some of the new research in 2007 at PFR and an original supporter of DGW research published at the NTJ where he apparently served as a referee.

At UCLA, I was assisted by two research assistants: Sophie Park (Ph.D. candidate, economics) and Aravind Moorthy (Ph.D. candidate, economics). Sarah-Eve Pelletier and Hersh Kashyap provided clerical assistance. Special thanks also go to Julie A. Lee for her help assembling the book and for editorial assistance.

I also thank Gillian Greenbough and Jon Gurstelle at Springer for their assistance and patience and for their invitation to submit another monograph. The UCLA Anderson School of Management (Global Economics and Management) graciously provided financial support that allowed me to hire the UCLA research assistants and clerks.

I of course thank my wife Jackie and sons Andrew and Ethan for their love and support.

All errors in this manuscript remain my own.

Contents

Chapter 1
Introduction

Recent estimates from the Internal Revenue Service (IRS) indicate that the annual tax gap (i.e., the difference between the taxes owed and taxes paid on a timely basis) was $345 billion for tax year 2001.[1] Of this amount, IRS Enforcement activities and late payments recovered about $55 billion, leaving a net tax gap of $290 billion. According to the IRS, roughly $197 billion of the tax gap was attributable to individual taxpayers, nearly triple the level estimated in 1985.[2] While the tax gap has grown, the IRS's ability to audit and enforce the tax code has diminished. For instance, in 2002, the IRS had roughly 13,000 revenue and tax agents devoted to examination. This number decreased from the 18,000 revenue and tax agents employed in 1995. Next to these numbers, the Criminal Investigation Division of the IRS (CI) appears small. In 1970, CI had approximately 2,500 agents. By 1998, the number of CI agents had increased to approximately 3,000 agents. Without doubt, a major shift in tax enforcement has occurred during the last three decades. Greater attention and reliance is placed on computer matching of information reports and on correspondence audits. On the other hand, fewer individuals are audited or sentenced for tax violations. Due to the increases in the tax gap, it is important to reassess the role played by examination in taxpayers' voluntary compliance.

This book presents an empirical analysis of the federal and state revenue collection process and specifically the causes of taxpayer noncompliance, which have occurred as a consequence of limited IRS tax enforcement and audit examination. The methods are empirically based and utilize historical information assembled between 1977 and 2004. The econometric technique relies on an aggregate macro time-series analysis of federal and state individual income tax and a separate analyses of the additional taxes and penalties that result from IRS

[1] See "IRS Updates Tax Gap," IR-2006-28, February 14, 2006.

[2] The tax gap attributable to individual taxpayers was estimated to be $70 billion in 1988 the date of the last complete Taxpayer Compliance Measurement Program (TCMP) audit. Recent estimates of the tax gap are based on the audits of 46,000 individual income tax returns from 2001 conducted as part of the National Research Program (NRP). The NRP reported a noncompliance rate of 16.3% of true tax liability, 80% of which was due to under-reported income.

J. A. Dubin, *The Causes and Consequences of Income Tax Noncompliance*,
DOI: 10.1007/978-1-4419-0907-7_1, © Springer Science+Business Media, LLC 2012

enforcement and examination. This work extends the empirical contributions of Jeffrey Dubin, Michael Graetz, and Louis Wilde made nearly 30 years ago that culminated in the article published by these authors in the National Tax Journal (Dubin et al. 1990). There are important differences in the present analysis. First, the DGW analysis examined the period between 1977 and 1986. I update the current analysis to the period 1987–2004 using new econometric methods. Second, DGW analyzed the role of IRS audits on voluntary compliance. This study reports the results of integrating IRS criminal investigations into the tax compliance paradigm. Finally, this study extends the original DGW study to examine state individual tax collections as well as federal individual tax collections. Along the way, new econometric specifications are examined and the role of media coverage as it affects compliance is studied.

Some of these results have been previously reported. In this regard, Dubin (2007) published the first results that include the role of IRS criminal investigations on taxpayer noncompliance. Dubin (2007) presented an abbreviated version of some of the research reported in this book. The present study (especially Chaps. 7 and 8) and Dubin (2007) were made possible by the support of the IRS under two contracts to analyze the role of IRS criminal investigations.[3] However, the research presented in this monograph goes significantly beyond Dubin (2007) and includes more recent data (the period from 2002 to 2004) and a new analysis of state income tax compliance.

The book is organized as follows. Chapter 2 discusses the tax gap—how much revenue is lost due to noncompliance. In this chapter the various definitions of the tax gap are considered, the estimated levels of the tax gap, and the methods used by the IRS and others to measure the tax gap are discussed. Next in Chap. 3, I consider recent patterns in IRS enforcement and audit examination. With respect to IRS enforcement, the chapter discusses the role of the IRS Criminal Investigations (CI) division. This chapter presents a picture of declining IRS audit and criminal enforcement over the last three to four decades. A main theme of this book is that the decline in IRS enforcement and examination has resulted in specific and general taxpayer noncompliance and a corresponding increase in the tax gap. However, these trends are potentially reversible.

In Chap. 4, I present a summary of recent economic theory and related empirical studies. The purpose of this chapter is not to review the extensive publication history in this subject area but instead to provide nonspecialists with some pertinent background and additional studies to review. In Chap. 5, I present a detailed discussion of the DGW methodology. The basic approach used in this monograph relies heavily on DGW and consequently it is important to fully appreciate their models and estimation methods.[4]

---

[3] The original research was sponsored in part by the IRS under the project: IRS Criminal Investigation Research—Empirical Analysis of the Impact of CI Activities on Taxpayer Compliance, TIRNO-00-D-0039. The IRS CI project was itself a response to a review of the IRS CI Division by Judge William Webster. Chapters 7 and 8 are based in part on this research.

[4] Chapter 5 significantly relies on DGW (1990).

In Chap. 6, I present a detailed review of the data employed in this monograph. The chapter discusses trends in socio-economic, compliance, revenue, and enforcement factors especially comparing the period 1987 to present with the original period of the DGW study (1977–1986). Given new and alternative variables to measure enforcement and media coverage, the chapter presents an in-depth analysis of this new data and sets the stage for the empirical analysis that follows. Chapter 7 presents the results on IRS enforcement activities and taxpayer noncompliance. This chapter concentrates on the period 1987 through 2001. It also presents the results of simulations using the estimated models including the restoration of audit levels to historical levels and the doubling of CI enforcement activities. It presents a cost-benefit analysis of alternative enforcement levels.

Chapter 8 extends the results of Chap. 7 to further explore the marginal impacts of increased enforcement. It adopts simulations of increased enforcement activities that are well within the IRS's current ability to accomplish and presents the cost and benefits of these activities. The principal focus in this chapter is a further understanding of the role of IRS criminal investigations. Chapter 9 presents the results of extending the data period from 2001 to 2004. This chapter reconsiders the role of state and marginal tax rate, the role of media and publicity, and provides further estimates of the marginal benefits and costs of increased enforcement. The extension of the data period to 2004 from that previously studied in Dubin (2007) (ending in 2001) reveals significant structural changes that have occurred in tax administration in these more recent years.

Next in Chap. 10, I present the results on state tax administration and the first estimates of the role of federal enforcement on state tax collections including estimates of the spillover benefits. This chapter makes an even stronger case for increases in examination to reduce the tax gap at the federal and state levels. Chapter 11 presents conclusions and directions for additional research.

I have attempted in this monograph to keep the mathematical presentation to a minimum. The statistical methods used in the various chapters are mentioned for interested readers. However, most readers will easily understand the empirical analysis even with only a limited understanding of linear regression modeling.

This book represents certain facets of over 30 years of research I have conducted in the area of tax administration. As a researcher, this continues to be a fertile and important area of research. Hopefully, it also demonstrates that the cooperation of the IRS is crucially important to foster progress in tax noncompliance research. It is my hope that this study will encourage additional efforts in the understanding of specific and general deterrence.

Chapter 2
The Tax Gap

Introduction

How much tax revenue is lost due to noncompliance? The IRS and other researchers attempt to answer this question by estimating the difference between taxes owed and those actually paid. The result is known as the tax gap.

The tax gap consists of three categories of noncompliance: (1) *underreporting*, which is the amount of lost revenue from filed tax returns that underreport the amount of taxes owed; (2) *underpayment*, which is the difference between amounts that were reported to be owed, and amounts actually paid for correctly filed tax returns; and (3) *nonfiling*, which is the amount of tax revenue lost from returns that were never filed. The total amount of lost revenue for each of these three categories is determined by aggregating estimates of loss across the five major categories of tax: individual income, corporate income, employment, estate, and excise (see Table 2.1).[1] The gross tax gap is defined as the sum of estimated noncompliance losses across types of tax and types of noncompliance.[2]

Table 2.1 reports estimates of the gross tax gap in 2001.[3] For that tax year, the IRS estimated that just under 84% of all taxes owed were paid on time. The IRS expected to recover approximately $55 billion of the gross tax gap through late payments, audits, and other enforcement, leaving a net tax gap for 2001 of $290

---

[1] GAO Report, Testimony of Michael Brostek, Director Strategic Issues, Before the Subcommittee on Federal Financial Management, Government Information, and International Security, Committee on Homeland Security and Governmental Affairs, U.S. Senate, October 2005, "Tax Gap: Multiple Strategies, Better Compliance Data, and Long–Term Goals Are Needed to Improve Taxpayer Compliance".

[2] Tax payments are sometimes made late, potentially many years after the taxes were owed. To account for this, I use the term gross tax gap for the total amount of money that was not paid in a timely manner, and net tax gap for the final annual disparity between taxes owed and those paid after late payments are tallied. The generic term "tax gap" usually refers to the gross tax gap.

[3] More recent estimates of the gross tax gap are not available.

J. A. Dubin, *The Causes and Consequences of Income Tax Noncompliance*,
DOI: 10.1007/978-1-4419-0907-7_2,

Table 2.1 IRS's tax year 2001 gross tax gap estimates by type of noncompliance and type of tax
Dollars in billions

	Type of tax					
Type of noncompliance	Individual income tax	Corporate income tax	Employment tax	Estate tax	Excise tax	Total ($)
Underreporting	$197	$30	$54	$4	No estimate	285
Underpayment	23	2	5	2	1	34
Nonfiling	25	No estimate	No estimate	2	No estimate	27
Total	$244	$32	$59	$8	$1	345

Source IRS
Note Figures may not sum to totals due to rounding

billion. Table 2.1 was prepared by the US Treasury. It shows the tax gap by source and the certainty, attached to their estimates.

As one can see from Table 2.1, underreporting, at $285 billion, represents the overwhelming majority of the gross tax gap, and most of that comes from under reporting of individual income tax. In fact, individual income tax underreporting accounted for well over half (57%) of the total annual tax gap. Before we examine the practical policy implications of the tax gap, let us first take a look at the methodologies used to calculate the tax gap itself.

Measuring the Tax Gap

The main challenge in estimating the size of the tax gap is determining the amount of taxes that were owed. Researchers studying the US tax gap have typically turned to data gathered by two IRS programs: the Taxpayer Compliance Measurement Program (TCMP), which conducted audits of a random sample of taxpayers from 1968 to 1988, and the National Research Program (NRP), which resumed the work of the TCMP in 2001 and continues to be active. The Taxpayer Compliance Measurement Program was a series of special audits that the IRS conducted every three years. TCMP audits randomly selected about 50,000 individual taxpayers. By their nature, TCMP audits were extremely comprehensive and exhaustive with an effort made to examine the entire tax return against third-party reports and individual's tax records. The data collected from these audits was analyzed using a statistical technique known as discriminant function analysis (DIF). The goal of the analysis was to identify the characteristics of returns that are likely to yield additional revenue if audited. The higher the DIF score associated with a return the more likely that an audit of the return would yield additional revenue above a threshold amount. The primary use of DIF score was to select returns for routine audits. A second goal was to develop an understanding of the magnitudes of underreported income sources, over reported deductions, and noncompliance levels as part of the effort to measure the tax gap. Routine audits are considerably less detailed than TCMP or NRP audits and typically focus on a fairly narrow range of return items. The National Research Project replaced the TCMP but the goals were essentially identical.

Although these programs provide data on the additionally owed tax that could be recovered from audited taxpayers, they fall short of providing the amounts that taxpayers truly owed. Routine audits are not likely to uncover all of the taxes that taxpayers do not pay or some amounts will generally remain undetected. However, several models have been proposed to infer the size of the true tax gap. Of the three categories comprising the tax gap, underpayment is the simplest to calculate. To do so, the IRS aggregates the observable differences between taxes reportedly owed and taxes actually paid. To determine the underreporting and non-filing portions of the tax gap, each of which present their own unique challenges, the IRS uses different statistical models to estimate the amounts of taxes owed by individuals in each category.

The IRS Non-Filing Tax Gap Model

The model used to impute the aggregate non-filing tax gap is best understood through the IRS data collection process for non-filing individuals. The IRS first draws a random sample from the pool of individuals who did not file tax returns. Next, the IRS attempts to locate each of the individuals. Each of the successfully located individuals is then evaluated to determine whether he or she owed taxes; those who owed taxes are described as *delinquent*. Among delinquent individuals, only some of the returns can be secured because others require some further action to process. Finally, a random sample of the located, delinquent, and secured returns is drawn for research purposes, containing data on the amounts assessed for each line item of each return.[4]

In 1988, the IRS reported non-filer data based on the Taxpayer Compliance Measurement Program (TCMP) audits. A probability sample of over 23,000 individuals who were potential nonfilers was selected. The probability sample was based on age, prior filing history, and other characteristics. Of these the IRS located 18,689 returns (and did not locate 4,597 returns). Of the 18,689 located returns, the IRS concluded that 4,796 were delinquent but that 13,928 were, in fact, not required to file. The IRS then secured TCMP data on 3,456 of 4,750 delinquent returns and examined a random sample of 2,198 of these for tax noncompliance.

In order to estimate the non-filing gap, the model imputes the aggregate taxes owed by all nonfilers from the final sample of examined returns by weighting each of the returns in the sample according to the portion of the aggregate population

[4] "Federal Tax Compliance Research: Individual Income Tax Gap Estimates for 1985, 1988, and 1992." IRS Publication 1415 (Rev. 4–96).

that it represents.[5] The weighting process allows the probability of a return being located to depend on the amount of taxes owed, and also for the probability of being secured to depend on the amount of taxes owed, through the following procedure.

First, a probit model is estimated by maximum likelihood to determine the relationship between the probability that an individual is located and the known characteristics of the individual.[6] The characteristics used for each individual are age, marital status,[7] whether a return was filed the previous year, and whether returns were filed more than a year ago. Next, using the coefficients from this estimation, the ex-ante probabilities of being located are computed for all individuals who were actually located. The inverse of each ex-ante probability is used as a weight for the located individual, allowing that person to represent a portion of all (located and unlocated) potential nonfilers.[8] The IRS uses a similar process to weight secured and examined returns, so that they represent all (secured and unsecured) delinquent returns. The IRS uses a probit model to estimate the probability of each delinquent return being secured and examined, and uses the coefficients from this estimation to compute ex-ante probabilities of each *actually* secured and examined return being secured and examined. They use the inverses of the ex-ante secured probabilities as weights for each return.[9]

The IRS non-filing tax gap model estimates reported taxes due among nonfilers by multiplying the amounts reported in the sample by the weights based on location probability and the weights based on secured probability. While these estimates provide tax amounts from the sample that are weighted to represent the population of potential nonfilers, it does not account for any amounts underreported by individuals in the sample, or take into account any amounts of their tax liability that they have already paid. Hence, the final estimate of the aggregate non-filing gap is based on the sum of the reported taxes and underreported taxes, less any amounts prepaid. Underreported taxes are determined following the procedure described in the next section.

In sum, the IRS approach to imputing the non-filing gap presumes that individuals who were located and whose returns were secured may not represent a random sample of the population of potential nonfilers, but only insofar as the individual characteristics—such as age, marital status, and filing history—of those whose returns are secured and located differ from those of the population. The approach therefore relies on the assumption that *located* (*secured*) individuals of a given age, marital status, and filing history owe amounts similar to those owed by

---

[5] The methodology is analogous to adjusting for nonresponse in survey sampling.

[6] The probit model is a maximum likelihood probability model wherein probabilities are determined using the cumulative normal distribution.

[7] This information is based on prior returns filed.

[8] These location probability weights are further adjusted based on whether each individual filed a married joint return, under the assumption that the returns for these individuals are twice as easy to locate.

[9] For further detail see IRS Publication 1415 (rev. 4–96).

unlocated (*unsecured*) individuals with the same characteristics. In addition, the model maintains the assumption that those returns identified as delinquent constitute the entirety of the actually delinquent returns.

The IRS Underreporting Tax Gap Model

The primary strategy of the underreporting gap model is the same as that of the non-filing gap model: the model imputes the underreported taxes of individuals in the population of taxpayers by matching their characteristics to individuals whose underreported taxes are known. The challenge in the underreporting model is, of course, determining the actual amounts of underreported taxes for individuals in the sample. While the TCMP (and later the NRP) provide samples of individuals who have been audited, the amounts of taxes owed that IRS examiners detect for each individual in each sample are only lower bounds for the actual amounts owed, since examiners cannot efficiently determine all sources of income with certainty in the course of an audit.

To compensate for this, the IRS uses a set of multipliers for each line item of a tax return, which is used to modify the amounts detected. The multipliers are based on a study conducted in 1976 that compared the amounts that individuals owed based on documents collected in the Information Reporting Program (IRP)[10] with amounts detected by IRS auditors without the aid of IRP documents. The study found that, for every dollar of unreported income detected by auditors, another $2.28 went undetected. This result has been used to justify a multiplier of 3.28 for the detected portion of many income line items for which IRP documents are not available, under the assumption that the detection of non-IRP income items is as accurate as the detection of income items for which IRP documents existed in the 1976 study.[11] Income items verified with IRP source documents do not require augmenting multipliers, since those amounts are presumed to be accurate. For instance, state income tax refunds detected outside the IRP program are not augmented via the multiplier procedure.

Once the IRS determines the underreported income amounts for taxpayers in the TCMP sample, they impute the aggregate underreported income for the population based on a statistical matching procedure utilizing key returns characteristics including income, primary income source, age, filing status, and itemization.[12] Then, they estimate the marginal tax rate for each line item and

[10] IRP documents include wage and income statements collected by the IRS from employers, banks, and other institutions that provide individuals with income.

[11] Several income items, such as tip and informal income, use different multipliers based on surveys or other data. For a discussion of these items, see IRS Publication 1415 (Rev 4–96), and Ho and Wong (1994).

[12] This methodology is referred to as model assisted survey sampling in the sampling literature. For further details on the statistical matching procedure, see Ho and Wong (1995).

calculate the aggregate underreported tax, which is associated with the underreported income.[13]

In sum, the underreporting model uses multipliers for undetected income, although the multipliers were derived from a study on income items for which IRP documents existed. If taxpayers are less likely to underreport income for items that have supporting documents (due to the likelihood of detection, for example), then these multipliers could understate the true amount of underreported income for non-IRP income items.

The Detection-Controlled Estimation Model

The detection-controlled estimation model[14] is a somewhat different model for estimating the tax gap and, more generally, other quantities that may be only partially detected. Detection-controlled estimation allows for undetected (or fractionally detected) noncompliance by specifying two equations. The first equation refers to the propensity of the individual to evade taxes, while the second equation refers to whether an evasion was detected. Since the observable data only include detected evasions, the two equations are not separately identifiable. However, with certain assumptions about the "quality" of the IRS examiner present at each audit instance, i.e. the differential ability of a specific examiner to detect tax evasion, the model can be estimated to determine the probability and extent of tax evasion.

This model differs from the IRS tax gap estimation model, which determines the probability and extent of underreporting, and allows each line item in a tax return to have a unique detection probability. Instead, it assumes a homogenous detection probability per return, but exploits the possibility that different IRS examiners have different likelihoods of detecting evasion. Despite these differences, results from detection-controlled estimation and the IRS model are similar.

Policy Implications of the Tax Gap

The annual US tax gap represents a substantial percentage of the US annual budget deficit. The GAO estimates that this percentage is approximately 81–84%.[15] With predictable demographic trends, the rising cost of health care, and diminished federal revenue continuing to increase US deficits, decreasing the tax gap could

---

13 Marginal tax ratios are calculated for specific line items by recomputing total taxes due on the individual's tax returns after income adjustments are made.

14 This model was developed by Jonathan Feinstein. See Feinstein (1990).

15 Ibid.

help mitigate these persistent fiscal challenges. Also while knowing the size of the tax gap can alert policymakers to the issue of noncompliance—including which types of noncompliance are increasing, decreasing, or newly emergent—addressing the tax gap itself requires a deeper understanding of what's behind the numbers. Thus it is crucial to understand how and why taxpayers are not compliant. Understanding the factors behind noncompliance can help the IRS to determine which enforcement programs are working and where to most effectively direct their resources. For instance, it is essential for the IRS to determine whether taxpayers are noncompliant intentionally or unintentionally. This will help focus both their enforcement activities (e.g., audits and criminal investigations) and non-enforcement activities (e.g., clarifying forms and instructions to help taxpayers avoid mistakes) more efficiently. Intentional and unintentional noncompliance result to some degree from the complexity of the tax code. A significant source of this complexity is the ever-growing number of deductions, exemptions, and credits, collectively known as "tax expenditures." The number of these preferential provisions has almost tripled in the last 30 years.[16] An example of an expenditure than can lead to both intentional and unintentional noncompliance is the Earned Income Tax Credit (EITC). The EITC allows qualified low-income taxpayers to receive tax credits based on their income and number of children. Given that children must live with the filer for at least half the year, it is easy to see how some taxpayers could inadvertently include a non-qualifying child, while others could do so intentionally. The complexity produced by tax expenditures renders the tax code virtually incomprehensible to the average taxpayer, and provides countless opportunities for tax evasion. Thus, an essential part of any plan to reduce the tax gap must include improved taxpayer education and customer service as a way to decrease unintentional filing errors. Additionally, the use of technology (e.g., a new phone system and electronic filing) has streamlined customer interaction, reduced costs, and improved data analysis. Meanwhile, increased withholding and use of information returns—for payments to independent contractors, payments to corporations, or for capital gain income—would likely decrease underreporting and, therefore, decrease the tax gap, even if it imposes a burden on business and taxpayers.

While tax code simplification, education, increased withholding, and greater reporting will no doubt improve the tax gap, the IRS must also combat the detrimental effects of lost funding and lower enforcement levels. In the next chapter we will take a closer look at the punitive side of IRS enforcement and its effect on taxpayer noncompliance. In the next chapter we will take a closer look at the punitive side of IRS enforcement and its effect on taxpayer noncompliance.

[16] GAO, "Multiple Strategies, Better Compliance Data, and Long-Term Goals Are Needed to Improve Taxpayer Compliance," GAO-06-453T (Washington, D.C.: February 15, 2006).

Chapter 3
Recent Patterns in IRS Enforcement

Introduction

As discussed in Chap. 2, the tax gap remains a significant concern to policymakers who would prefer the gap be close both because of fairness to the vast majority of taxpayers who voluntarily pay their taxes in full and as a means to deter further tax cheating and raise tax revenues. The primary purpose of this chapter is to discuss the two principal forms of IRS enforcement: Auditing and Criminal Enforcement. A central purpose of the empirical studies reported in later chapters is to develop an understanding of the linkage between enforcement and levels of taxpayers' noncompliance. We begin with a discussion of the role of IRS audits.

Audit Enforcement

The IRS performs at least one type of compliance check—verifying calculations on tax returns, requesting additional information, or checking third party reporting with income reported by taxpayers—on virtually every tax return filed. A small percentage of these checks are considered audits. In 1999, the IRS performed 620,000 audits on the 125 million returns filed.[1] An audit examination may involve a simple issue resolved through the mail to complex, face-to-face analyses of returns on a line-by-line basis.

The IRS calculates the audit rate as the proportion of audits completed in a fiscal year compared to the number of tax returns filed the previous calendar year. The audit rate has been steadily declining for years—dropping about 70% just

[1] "IRS Audit Rates: Rate for Individual Taxpayers Has Declined But Effect on Compliance Is Unknown." United States General Accounting Office, GAO.

DOI: 10.1007/978-1-4419-0907-7_3,

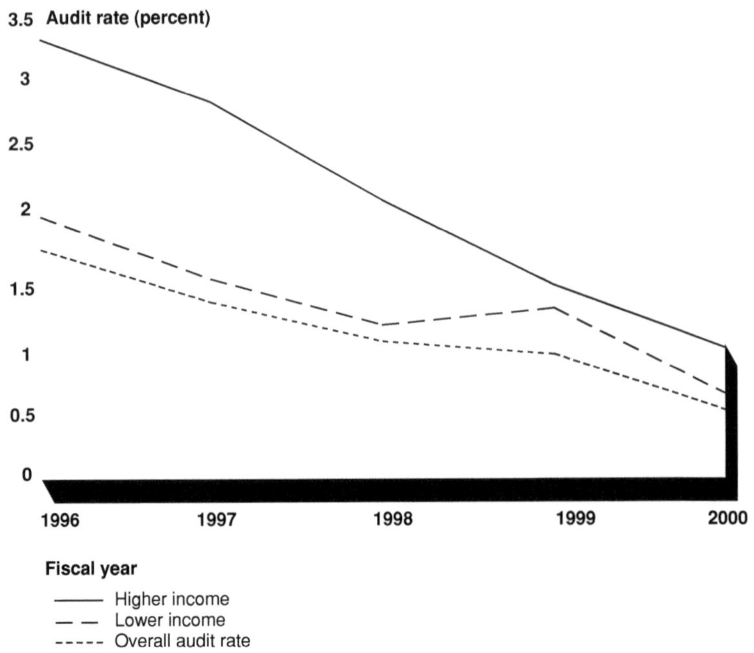

Fig. 3.1 Audit rates for lower income and higher income individuals. *Note 1* Lower income includes individuals reporting income less than $25,000 and higher income includes individuals reporting income of $100,000 or more. *Note 2* The overall audit rate falls below the other two lines because it also includes audits of other individuals, such as those reporting moderate income on their tax returns. *Source* GAO analysis of IRS data

between 1996 and 2000, from 1.67 to 0.49% . As can be seen in Fig. 3.1,[2] this decline occurred across income levels. As we will shortly see this trend has continued in recent years.

The IRS provides three primary reasons for this decline in audit rates. First, as a result of changes in priorities that shift personnel to assist taxpayers *before* they file their returns, the number of auditors declined by more than half. Second, many of the remaining auditors were used to assist taxpayers rather than perform audits. Third, new rules and regulations for additional written communications with taxpayers during their audit dramatically increased the time it took to perform each audit.

While there is concern regarding the impact of the decline in audit rates on voluntary compliance, the IRS is hesitant to presume a causal link between audit rates and compliance. First, the IRS does not have reliable information on voluntary compliance rates. Second, there may be an impact on compliance of

[2] GAO Report to Chairman, Subcommittee on Oversight, Committee on Ways and Means, House of Representatives, April 2001, "IRS Audit Rates: Rate for Individual Taxpayers Has Declined But Effect on Compliance is Unknown".

Table 3.1 Audit staffing levels for individual adults

	Fiscal year					Change	
Type of auditor	1996	1997	1998	1999	2000	Number	Percent
Revenue agents	2,441	2,121	1,751	1,407	1,116	−1,325	−54
Tax auditors	1,173	1,045	797	621	461	−712	−61
Tax examiners	[a]	1,515[b]	1,772[c]	1,740	1,715	200	13
Total	[b]	4,681	4,320	3,768	3,292	[c]	

[a] IRS was not able to provide examiner data for fiscal year 1996
[b] Tax examiner totals for fiscal years 1997 and 1998 are IRS estimates
[c] Only covers change from fiscal year 1997 to 2000
Source GAO analysis of IRS data

recently expanded non-audit programs, such as math and consistency checks and comparison of third party reporting (e.g., W-2 forms) and income reported by taxpayers. For example, in 1997 IRS reclassified more than 700,000 audit cases as simply "math error" cases, as the only issues were missing or incorrect Social Security numbers. Efforts like these may lower the audit rate without affecting compliance. Finally, recent improvements in taxpayer assistance may have compensated for any negative impact of reduced auditing on voluntary compliance.

The IRS conducts audits either by correspondence or face-to-face—either in the field or at an IRS office—and there are three types of auditors: tax examiners, tax auditors, and revenue agents. Tax examiners conduct correspondence audits, which usually focus on a single line item on simpler tax returns. Tax auditors conduct office audits, which involve more complex issues than can be addressed by correspondence. IRS revenue agents conduct field audits, which involve either complex returns and/or business income.

As a consequence of tight budgets and shifting priorities, the number of IRS auditors has decreased dramatically in recent years. One exception to this trend is the position of tax examiners, which actually saw a 13% increase in personnel from 1996 to 2000, compared with revenue agents and tax auditors, which decreased by 54 and 61%, respectively, during this same period (see Table 3.1).[3]

We also see that auditors spend less time auditing, compared with non-direct audit activities such as taxpayer assistance and training as they have in the past. For example, between 1996 and 2000, revenue agents increased the amount of time spent on taxpayer assistance by more than 300% (from 1.0% of available staff years to about 4.4%), while tax auditors increased their taxpayer

[3] GAO Report, Testimony of Michael Brostek, Director Strategic Issues, Before the Subcommittee on Federal Financial Management, Government Information, and International Security, Committee on Homeland Security and Governmental Affairs, U.S. Senate, October 2005, "Tax Gap: Multiple Strategies, Better Compliance Data, and Long-Term Goals Are Needed to Improve Taxpayer Compliance".

assistance workload by almost 800% (from 1.4% of available staff years to 12.3%).

Tax auditors and revenue agents also spent significantly more time in training during this period. While the number of tax auditors decreased 61%, the training time per auditor increased 95%. Revenue agents saw their training time increase more than 225%. Additionally, due to requirements of the Internal Revenue Service Restructuring and Reform Act of 1998, along with other factors, the time it took to conduct each audit has increased dramatically. For example, field audits took 37% longer, office audits took 56% longer, and correspondence audits took more than 150% longer.

IRS officials have stated that the new law required additional correspondence with the taxpayer and third parties, and provisions to protect taxpayers required additional review work by auditors. The IRS also saw many experienced auditors promoted to higher-grade positions, and IRS officials suggest that the resulting decrease in auditor experience may have also increased the time per audit examination leading to fewer total audit examinations. As we will see below, the dramatic decline in audits has led to a direct and causal increase in taxpayer noncompliance.

Criminal Investigation Enforcement

In 1919, six U.S. Post Office inspectors moved to the newly formed Intelligence Unit of the Bureau of Internal Revenue to investigate the increasing incidence of tax fraud. In 1979, the Intelligence Unit changed its name to Criminal Investigations (CI). Over the years, CI grew into an elite group of financial investigators, maintaining a greater than 90% conviction rate for federal tax prosecutions, including such famous cases as those of gangsters Al Capone and Mickey Cohen, former Vice-President Spiro Agnew, baseball legend Pete Rose, rock and roll star Chuck Berry, and hotel queen Leona Helmsley.

Today, CI employs almost 3,000 special agents who investigate criminal tax, money laundering, and narcotics and terrorism-related financial crimes. From 2002 to 2007, the number of federal criminal tax investigations increased almost 50%, with CI conducting about 4,600 investigations in 2007.

The Criminal Investigation (CI) division—the "criminal law enforcement arm of the IRS" (www.IRS.gov)—has focused its activities for some time on narrowing the tax gap. Tax gap investigations include both tax and money laundering cases that involve tax issues. Tax gap investigations normally do not include illegal activity associated with narcotics or counterterrorism-financing investigations. Tax-related investigations encompass all Title 26 violations (tax evasion, failure to file, filing of false returns, fraudulent returns, or aiding or providing assistance to fraudulent returns), as well as tax violations that fall under Title 18 USC §286, 287, 371 (conspiracy to defraud the Government or commit offense or false claims).

CI also has jurisdiction over Title 31 cases (currency reporting violations). CI tax investigations are so-called legal source tax crimes because they encompass all cases involving tax violations where income is derived from legal activity, including questionable refund schemes, return preparer cases, excise tax cases, employment tax cases, and frivolous filers and non-filers. CI also investigates illegal source financial crimes and narcotics and terrorism-related financial crimes.

The CI is the only Federal agency with the power to investigate potential criminal violations of the U.S. Tax Code. CI's tax cases sometimes result from referrals by the IRS's civil arm. During an audit or tax investigation, a case might be referred to the CI for criminal investigation. However, audits are not the sole source for tax-related cases. CI may investigate a tax case initiated by a special agent in the field, a referral from another agency (FBI, Customs, or the US Attorney or Department of Justice), informants (as part of the Grand Jury process), or as a result of refund fraud-related activity.

While the IRS can investigate and audit tax returns and recommend civil penalties, CI has the exclusive responsibility and authority to investigate tax fraud and to recommend prosecution for willful and egregious tax code violations. CI's role as a tax crimes agency expanded in 1970 under the Bank Secrecy Act (BSA) and has been further expanded over the last 30 years to include narcotics investigations and money laundering violations. Money laundering cases often result from the recordkeeping requirements established in the BSA.

Money laundering activity and tax activity can be closely related. Money laundering activity (i.e., activity involving illegal income sources) is often a precursor to tax evasion. As such, it is sometimes difficult to determine whether a case is primarily tax-related or not. CI has been able to classify its cases in terms of whether they are primarily tax or money laundering-related. CI has further classified cases according to whether they are both tax and money laundering cases, tax cases only, money laundering cases only, or neither.

CI summarizes its activities in different ways. First, CI reports its cases by the Title and Section of law for which there is a violation or an alleged violation. For Fiscal Year 1999, for example, CI reports cases recommended for prosecution as follows: 1,068 for Title 26 violations; 1,988 for Title 18 violations; and 64 for Title 31 violations. Of these 3,120 cases, CI further classifies 1,959 cases as fraud-related and 1,161 cases as narcotics-related.

A criminal investigation case proceeds in several steps. Generally, cases subject to investigation are either recommended for prosecution or are dropped. If a case is recommended for prosecution, then the Department of Justice (DOJ) or U.S. Attorney may proceed with the case, and the U.S. Attorney either issues an indictment or declines to prosecute. Indicted individuals may be acquitted, have their cases dismissed, or be convicted. If a conviction is obtained, then the individual is sentenced. Cases recommended for prosecution represent the outcomes of CI procedures and protocols. Such cases may or may not be processed by the DOJ depending on the nature of the case or resource constraints at the DOJ. In most cases where there is an indictment, defendants will be found guilty and will be sentenced. At this point in the process, the sentence is given and the media

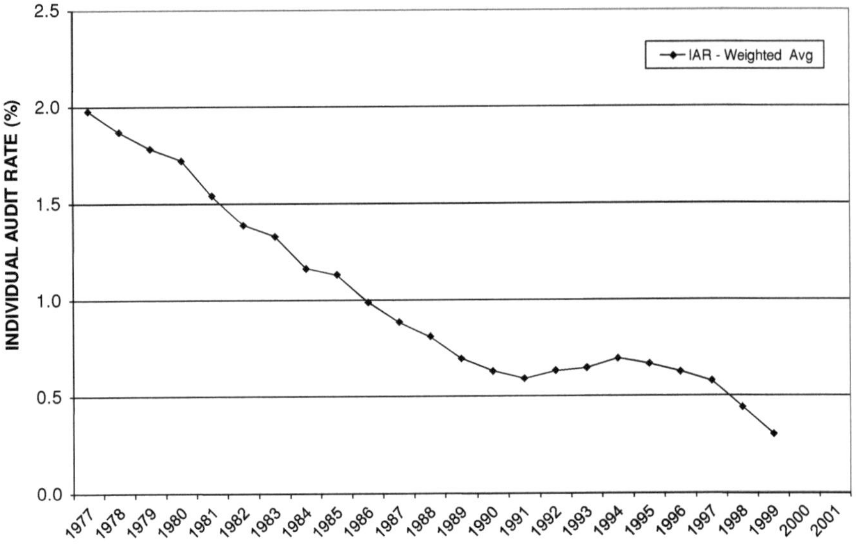

Fig. 3.2 Individual audit rate

attention paid to the case is measured. The impact on compliance can be experienced whenever publicity is received. This may include the coverage of an issued search warrant, indictment, plea, or conviction. Media coverage acts as a form of indirect contact with the general public and provides the greatest amount of exposure for CI activities.

Trends in Tax Enforcement

With some understanding of the two principal enforcement mechanisms, we can next examine how each has changed over time. As we will see, the audit rate for individuals has decreased significantly over several decades while criminal enforcement measured through criminal sentences received by tax evaders has remained more constant. However, the pattern for CI enforcement is more complex as the mix of cases between tax and money laundering has shifted over time.

The decline in the individual audit rate is shown in Fig. 3.2 where the examination data shown comes from the Annual Reports of the Commissioner of Internal Revenue Service. In Fig. 3.2 I have aggregated the information reported at the state and district level to annual figures. The audit rate is shown by state in Fig. 3.3 at average levels for the time period between 1977 and 2001. Apparently there is significant variation in the audit rate for individuals depending on their state of residence.

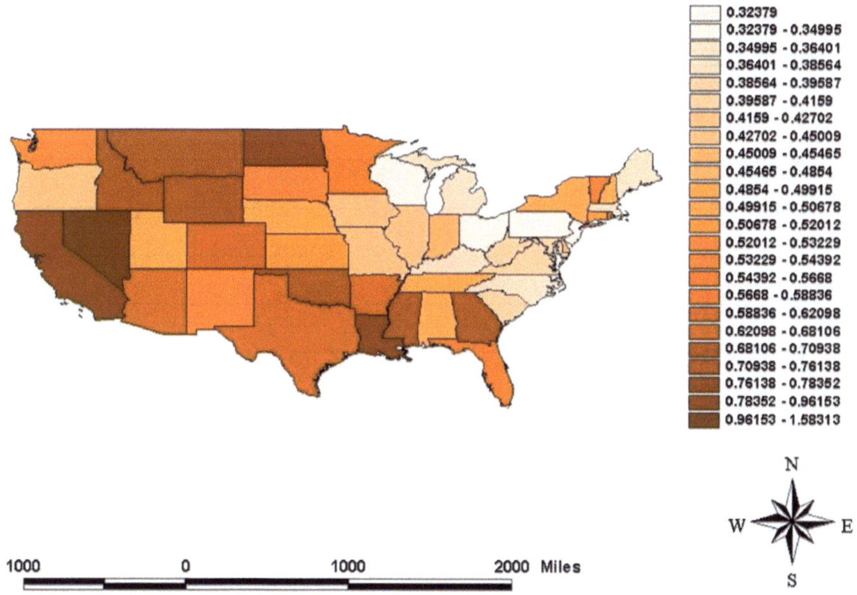

Fig. 3.3 Indiviudal audit rate (%)

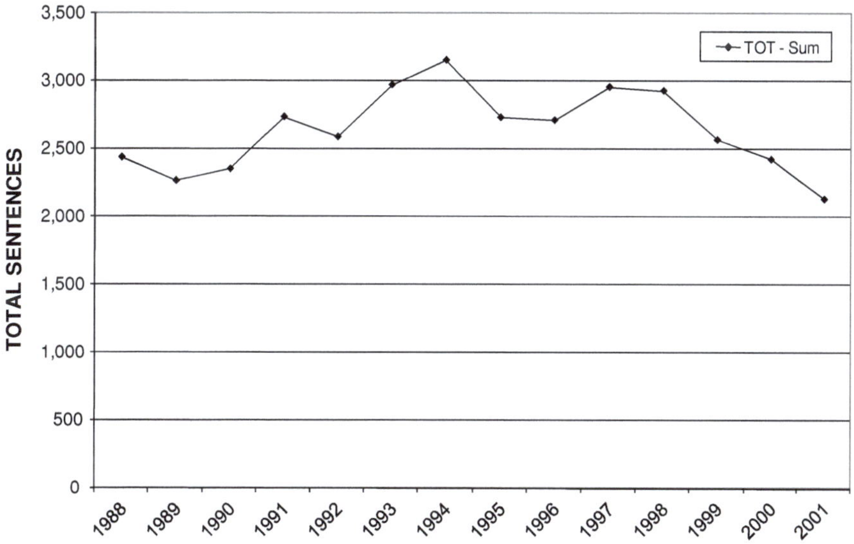

Fig. 3.4 Total sentences

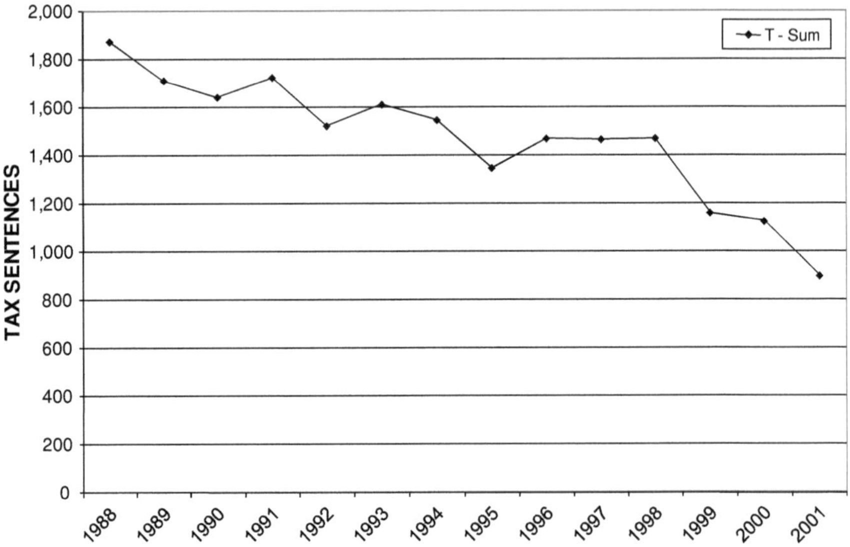

Fig. 3.5 Tax sentences

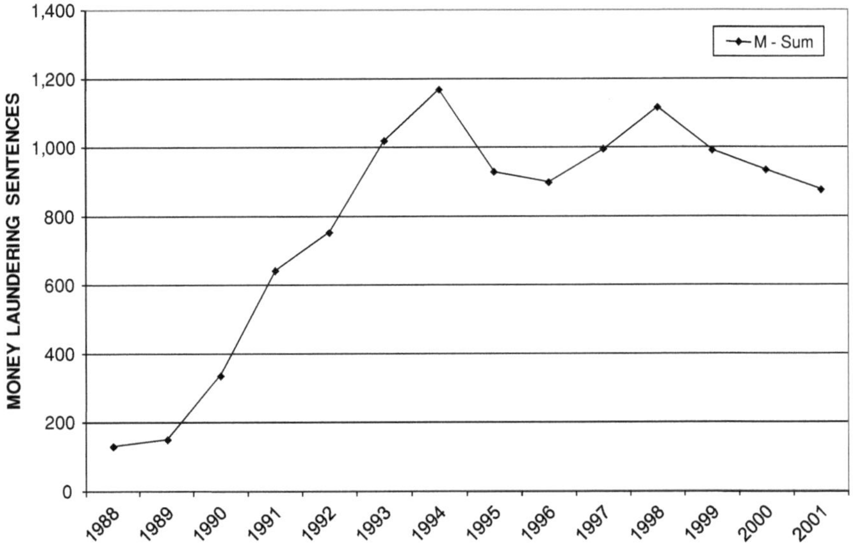

Fig. 3.6 Money laundering sentences

A less obvious picture emerges for CI enforcements. In Fig. 3.4, I display the total sentences that resulted from CI investigations for the period 1988 to 2001. For the same period, Figs. 3.5 and 3.6 show the tax, and money laundering-cases

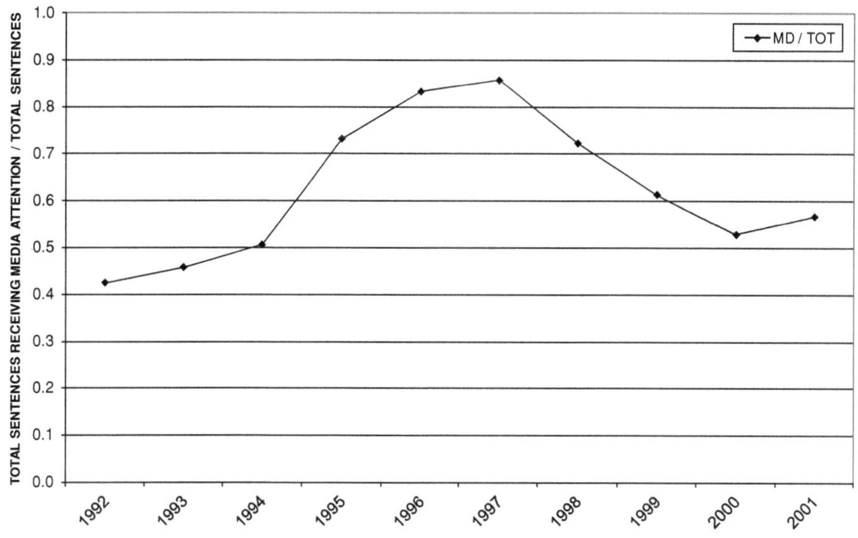

Fig. 3.7 Total sentences receiving media attention/total sentences

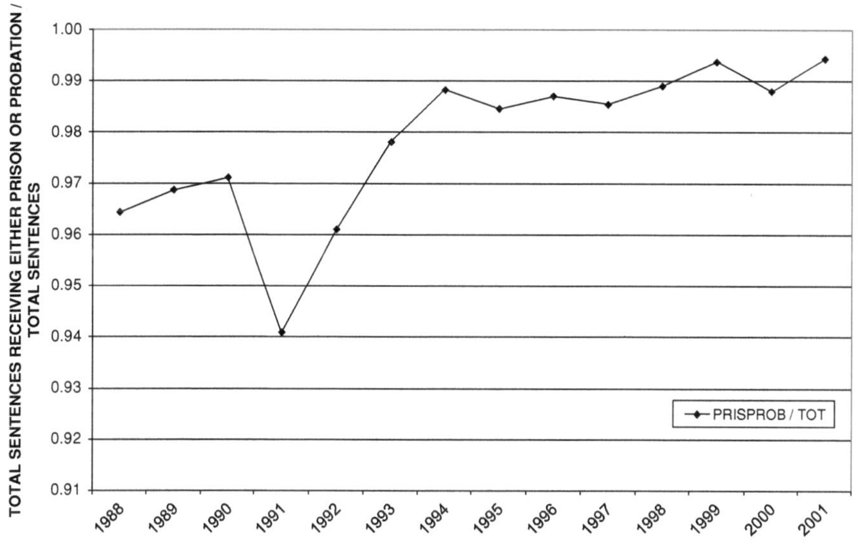

Fig. 3.8 Total sentences receiving either prison or probation/total sentences

respectively. A trend, which I discuss further below, is not in the decline in tax, related CI investigations in favor of a greater number of money laundering cases.[4]

[4] The Graphs are based on historical data provided by CI.

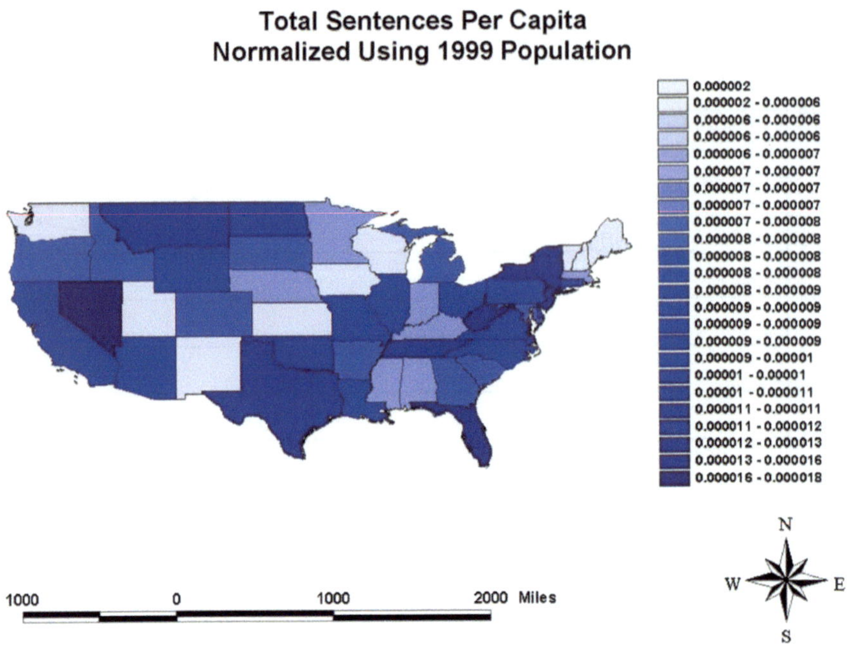

Fig. 3.9 Displays the total CI sentences per capita. Among states, some significant variations are apparent

Figure 3.7 displays the percentage of CI sentenced cases that received some form of media attention. There is little pattern to media coverage of IRS CI activities at least in the 1992 through 2001 period for which this data was available.

Figure 3.8 displays the percentage of cases that received prison or probation (as compared to monetary fine) among sentenced cases. Between 1988 and 2001, the proportion of sentenced cases reverse a stricter form of punishment increased. Finally, Fig. 3.9 displays the total CI sentences per capita. Among states, some significant variations are apparent.

The econometric models, developed below, use the variation in time and across states of IRS enforcement activities in conjunction with individual collections information (tax revenues collected per return filed) to identify the relationship between enforcement and tax compliance. The econometric models are used to control for factors other t—han enforcement, which also determine tax revenues such as demographic and economic trends and differences across states that affect tax revenues.

Chapter 4
Economic Theory and the Literature

Introduction

The economic analysis of crime began in 1968 with Becker's classic article "Crime and Punishment: An Economic Approach." While Becker mentioned tax evasion as an area of application for his general model, Allingham and Sandmo (1972) and Srinivasan (1973) provided the analysis. Generally, this approach treats noncompliance as a rational individual decision based upon probabilities of detection and conviction and levels of punishment. In Allingham and Sandmo's model, the taxpayer's actual income is exogenously given and known by the taxpayer but not the IRS.

A constant proportional tax is applied to reported income, the amount of which is chosen by the taxpayer. With some exogenous and constant probability, the taxpayer is "audited". If she is discovered to be underreporting income, a penalty proportional to the amount of undeclared income, at a rate higher than the proportional tax rate, must be paid. The taxpayer chooses a level of reported income so as to maximize his or her expected utility of net wealth. The Allingham and Sandmo model assumes that a taxpayer with income I decides to evade an amount E of income. By not reporting the amount E, taxable income is reduced to the level $I - E$. With an assumed probability p, the taxpayer evades taxations on the full amount. On the other hand, if caught (with probability $(1 - p)$) taxpayer will pay taxes in full and incur a penalty (or fine) assumed to be proportional to the taxes evaded tE. Hence, income after taxes in the first scenario is $I - t(I - E) = I - tI + (tE)$ and income after taxes in the second scenario is $I - tI - F(tE) = I(1 - t) - F(tE)$ where F is the fine per dollar of taxes evaded. The expected utility for the taxpayer is $pU[I(1 - t) + tE] + (1 - p)U[I(1 - t) - F(tE)]$.

Within the Allingham and Sandmo model, a decrease in the probability of evasion (declining audit rates or criminal prosecution) makes a larger evasion level E a better strategy. Hence tax noncompliance increases when the likelihood of audit declines and vice versa. Importantly, in this model, the likelihood of

J. A. Dubin, *The Causes and Consequences of Income Tax Noncompliance*,
DOI: 10.1007/978-1-4419-0907-7_4, © Springer Science+Business Media, LLC 2012

successful tax evasion is associated with the optimal level of noncompliance among all taxpayers whether or not they are even in fact audited. This is called the "spillover or ripple benefit of enforcement" and is also termed the "general deterrence effect" in the literature. Even this simple model produces ambiguous results. For example, the effects of increases in income or the tax rate on reported income depend on properties of the taxpayer's utility function (i.e., relative risk aversion). However, an increase in the probability of detection and conviction or an increase in the penalty rate increases compliance even in this simple model.

In the main, the theoretical economics literature on tax compliance consists of extensions and refinements of Allingham and Sandmo's model. In most cases, however, the modifications produce more ambiguous results, not fewer. For example, making labor supply decisions endogenous obviates even the conclusion that increases in the probability of detection and conviction increase compliance.[1] Extensions to the Allingham and Sandmo's model have attempted to move beyond the decision theoretic framework characteristic of the early tax compliance literature. Of particular interest are the principal agent models of Border and Sobel (1987) and Reinganum and Wilde (1985) and the game theoretic model of Graetz et al. (1986). In these approaches the IRS is allowed to act strategically, conditioning its audit rules on the information it receives from taxpayers. Thus the models yield predictions about the nature of the equilibrium audit rule used by the IRS as well as the equilibrium reporting rule used by taxpayers. This has important consequences for our empirical work where we need to treat audit rates and CI enforcement levels endogenously.

Whether the IRS should be included as a strategic actor in theoretical models of tax compliance is of more than technical interest. In empirically assessing the deterrent effects of audits, it is critical whether the IRS audit selection process depends on taxpayer compliance behavior. If it does, then any empirical specification meant to explain taxpayer compliance behavior, which treats audit rates exogenously maybe seriously biased unless appropriate econometric methods are employed.

While models that incorporate the IRS as a strategic player in the tax compliance game, such as Graetz et al. (1986) make precise predictions about the nature of both equilibrium auditing and income reporting rules, I focus on the narrower question of the deterrent effects of audits and enforcement in this monograph.[2]

---

[1] For a general model which incorporates labor supply decisions, see Sandmo (1981). See also Witte and Woodbury (1983) or Cowell (1985).

[2] Our treatment is therefore a "limited information" approach but is nonetheless appropriate because it produces a consistent and unbiased estimate of the effect of IRS audits and enforcement on taxpayer compliance.

Data Used to Study Tax Noncompliance

Andreoni et al. (1998) and Slemrod and Yitzhaki (2002) provide summaries of the tax compliance literature.[3] As discussed by these authors, the IRS has made few data sources that can be used to study tax compliance available to researchers. With respect to non-experimental and non-survey data for the United States, there continues to be limited data. There are essentially two data sources. The first data source is the Taxpayer Compliance Measurement Program (TCMP) data. These data have been analyzed by Dubin and Wilde (1988) Witte and Woodbury (1985), and Beron et al. (1992) for tax year 1969. These papers were important empirical studies on audit effects and compliance because they demonstrated the endogeneity of audit rates and positive compliance effects from audits in certain audit classes. Subsequently, Dubin, Greatz, Udell, and Wide (DGW) (1992) used the 1979 TCMP data to study tax return preparation decisions by taxpayers. Recently, Mete (2002) combined TCMP surveys conducted by the IRS for several tax years to study the interaction between taxpayers, the IRS, and political ideology.

The second data source is based on time-series cross-sectional information available by state and year. Measures of audit activity, taxes assessed, and taxes collected are taken from the Annual Reports of the Commissioner of the IRS. For instance, Dubin et al. (1990) used IRS audit data and taxpayer information measured at the state level over a 10-year period to analyze taxpayer noncompliance. Ali et al. (2001) also relied on data taken from the Annual Reports. Their analysis was based on annual data from 1980 through 1995 (i.e., 16 observations at the National level). Giles and Caragata (2001) presented an aggregate analysis similar to DGW (1990). Their study analyzed the ratio of the hidden economy to Gross Domestic Product (GDP) and the ratio of tax revenues to GDP.[4]

Plumley (1996) extended the analysis in Dubin et al. (1990). His time-series cross-section analysis covered the period from 1982 to 1991, whereas the DGW study used data from 1977 to 1987. Importantly, Plumley was the first to show that CI activities (measured as criminal convictions obtained per million people) were significant and positively related to compliance.[5] However, few studies have focused on the role of criminal investigation enforcement and taxpayer noncompliance and none other than Dubin (2007) has simultaneously considered the dual enforcement roles of audits and criminal investigations.

---

[3] See also the compendium Why People Pay Taxes: Tax Compliance and Enforcement, Joel Slemrod, ed. The University of Michigan Press: Michigan: Ann Arbor, 1992.

[4] The similarity to DGW is due to using proxy evasion measures for the economy rather than direct evasion measures. Another similarity is using a time-series data source as opposed to a purely cross-sectional data source, such as the 1969 TCMP. However, DGW (1990) combined both cross-sectional and time-series information in their empirical analysis.

[5] Plumley modified some of the DGW reporting and compliance equations using: (i) income and offsets rather than tax collected; and (ii) tax return filings relative to expected filings rather than to population. Plumley introduced refinements to the DGW audit rate measure (based on start rates versus closure rates) and considered new factors for taxpayer burden and CI enforcement activity.

Empirical Findings

Empirical studies of tax compliance can be broadly categorized as studies that use TCMP or NRP data, macro-economic time-series data, survey data, or experimental data. As described above, the taxpayer compliance measurement program collected a stratified random sample of about 50,000 federal income tax returns. It contains information on a taxpayer's tax return and the IRS auditors' assessment on each line item on the return. While TCMP (and more recently NRP) data is one of the most reliable sources of information about tax noncompliance, it lacks socioeconomic and demographic information for individual taxpayers. As a result, some researchers employed survey data (in which samples of taxpayers were surveyed regarding their compliance levels) but these studies found that survey results tend to overstate the degree of tax compliance. Due to these imperfections, other researchers turned to building their own data using laboratory experiments. However, laboratory experiments were often unrealistic and could not replicate tax compliance behavior, which is mainly influenced by social, moral, and emotional factors.

One of the earliest studies using TCMP data was conducted by Clotfelter (1983) He studied the relationship between tax compliance, income, and the marginal tax rate. Using a tobit model of tax evasion, he found that after-tax income and the marginal tax rate have significant positive effects on tax evasion. However, as the relationship between marginal tax rates and tax evasion drew contradicting conclusions among researchers, further studies were conducted in order to sort out the effects of socioeconomic factors and tax rates on tax evasion. Among those studies are Slemrod (1985), Witte and Woodbury (1985), Beron et al. (1992), and Dubin and Wilde (1988).

Later studies explored the relationship between the likelihood of audit and tax evasion. Witte and Woodbury (1985) conducted an econometric analysis of tax compliance behavior based on seven different taxpayer income classes. They found a positive and significant relationship between voluntary compliance and the probability of audit. In addition to audit rates, they found that higher tax withholding increases tax compliance while itemizing deductions tends to decrease compliance. They also examined attitudinal variables but found no uniform effect on all taxpayer classes. Audit rates were not treated endogenously in their study.

As the probability of audit may depend on the taxpayer's compliance level, Dubin and Wilde (1988).treated the audit probability as an endogenous variable. After controlling for potential endogeneity and misspecification, Dubin and Wilde Dubin and Wilde (1988) found a significant positive relationship between compliance behavior and audit rate.

Beron et al. (1992) reanalyzed the earlier studies and confirmed that the audit rate is, in fact, endogenous; however, the endogeneity decreases the magnitude of the effect the audit rate has on compliance level. In contrast to Beron, Tauchen and Witte, Dubin, Graetz, and Wilde (1990) found that audit rate not only has positive direct effects but also positive indirect (spillover) effects. As a taxpayer is more vulnerable to being audited, he is more likely to comply with taxes. However, other taxpayers knowing that the IRS is generally employing higher audit rates are also more likely to comply.[6]

Although these studies disagree on the exact magnitude that the audit rate has on the level of compliance, they agree that there is a positive relationship between the probability of being audited and the level of tax compliance. Until recently, no study had simultaneously examined the role of audits and enforcement on taxpayer behavior. The empirical approach used in this treatise follows DGW (1990). The DGW method can determine both specific and general deterrence effects of criminal investigations, as well as the effects of audit rates on taxpayer compliance. Although the general deterrence effects provided by audits have been widely acknowledged, the IRS has never reported the "spillover" benefits of audit. Spillover benefits are the increase in collections from taxpayers, whether or not they are audited, who report more taxes in response to in increased likelihood of an audit. DGW's principal innovation was to directly estimate taxes due, rather than first attempting to construct a noncompliance measure and then extrapolating from noncompliance to revenue.

Mikesell (1985) noted the significance of specific versus general compliance in revenue streams such as sales tax. Mikesell reviewed the extant literature on compliance with sales tax by firms that collect and report taxes. He noted that the main focus of such studies was optimal audit strategy as it affects potential yield from examination. Similar to our approach, Mikesell observed that the majority of sales tax yield occurs through "compliance ripples" or general deterrence effects generated by audit. Mikesell estimated his model using a single year of data for the forty-two states with a sales tax. His approach measures a sales tax base as a function of various socio-economic factors including personal income, tourism, and tax rates. Mikesell fitted econometric models including and excluding the direct revenue from enforcement. His econometric specification does include a sales tax audit rate. However, he does not control for potential endogeneity of the audit rate. Nonetheless his approach is similar to DGW, who first attempted a parallel study of individual income taxation. Alm, Blackwell and McKee (2004) analyzed the gross receipts tax in New Mexico. Their analysis differs from mine as it is specifically cross-sectional and limited to one state. Their focus is on compliance which is measured directly among audited forms (compliance of firms with respect to sales tax reporting). Their estimation does control for audit selections although there is no methodology in their analysis to measure general deterrence effects. We examine the DGW model in greater detail in the next chapter.

[6] In addition to this spillover effect of audit rate, they also found that there is a positive relationship between education and tax compliance.

Chapter 5
The Dubin Graetz Wilde Model

Introduction

In this chapter we review the model of Jeffrey Dubin, Michael Graetz, and Louis Wilde published 25 years ago. The importance of this work is twofold. First, the DGW model was the first and remains the only empirical methodology to separate and measure the direct and indirect effects of audit rates on tax compliance. Second, the DGW approach forms the basis of the empirical research presented in subsequent chapters. The results reported in Chaps. 7 and 8 extend the period to 2001 from 1986. Importantly, this extended period represents significant structural changes in tax administration including the Tax Reform Act of 1986 and the continued erosion of tax enforcement.

DGW Model

The primary purpose of the DGW model was to investigate empirically the overall role of audits in the federal revenue collection process. Surprisingly, this had never been done. Although the general deterrence effects of audits have been widely acknowledged, the IRS has never put forth any estimates of the "spillover" benefits of audits (the increase in collections from taxpayers, whether or not they are audited, who report more taxes due in response to an increase in the likelihood of an audit). Before DGW, only the direct revenues obtained from audits (additional taxes and penalties) had been estimated.

The principal innovation in the DGW study was to directly estimate taxes due rather than first attempting to construct a measure of noncompliance, and then extrapolating from noncompliance to revenue. This approach is consistent with the theoretical literature in which taxpayers decide on an optimal level of noncompliance. In particular, DGW is based on two models, both of which are estimated using a state level time-series cross-section data set for the years 1977–1986.

J. A. Dubin, *The Causes and Consequences of Income Tax Noncompliance*,
DOI: 10.1007/978-1-4419-0907-7_5,

One model specifies reported taxes per return filed as a function of audit rates and a variety of socio-economic factors. The other model specifies returns filed per capita as a function of the same variables. This decomposition allows a separation of the effects of underlying explanatory variables into a "reporting effect" and a "filings effect".

DGW Model Specification

The DGW analysis generates estimates of the effects of federal audit rates on reported taxes per return, reported taxes plus additional tax and penalty from audit per return, and returns filed per capita. DGW begins by specifying a model in which reported taxes per return depends on the state income tax rate, the audit rate, per capita income, and various other socio-economic variables. DGW then specifies a second model, which relates federal returns, filed per capita to the same variables. DGW then repeated the analysis using reported tax plus additional tax and penalty from audit (per return) as a dependent variable in the first model. This approach allows DGW to estimate the spillover effects from increases in the audit rate.

Much of the analysis in DGW is based on data reported in the *Annual Report of the Commissioner of Internal Revenue* for the years 1977–1986. These reports include district-level data on Internal Revenue Service collections, number of returns filed, amount and number of refunds, number of examinations, total additional tax and penalties recommended after examination, and budgets. The data is further broken down by "class of tax"—individual, corporate, estate, gift, etc. As discussed below, the Commissioner's reports remain an important source of data in our updated analysis.

DGW use the following five primary variables from the annual reports: total tax returns filed; number of individual income tax returns filed; number of individual income tax returns examined; additional tax and penalty recommended after examination for individual income tax returns; and costs incurred by the Internal Revenue Service.

Using these five primary variables plus reported taxes as given in the *Statistics of Income*, DGW constructed five secondary variables:

ALR Reported individual income tax plus additional tax and penalty recommended after examination divided by the number of individual income tax returns filed, in 1972 dollars—assessed liability per return;

RTR Reported individual income tax divided by the number of individual tax returns filed, in 1972 dollars—reported taxes per return;

RCAP Total individual income tax returns filed divided by total population-returns per capita;

AUDIT Total individual income tax returns examined divided by total individual income tax returns filed—the individual audit rate;

BPR Total IRS budget divided by total returns filed in 1972 dollars divided by the total returns filed in 1972 dollars—budget per return.

DGW also use a number of socio-economic variables taken from a variety of sources:

STAXR Total state individual income tax paid as a percentage of total state personal income—the average state income tax rate;
PERED Percent of the adult population with at least a high school education;
PER65 Percent of the adult population over age 65;
UR The unemployment rate;
INCOME Income per capita, in 1972 dollars;
PMAN Percent of the work force employed in manufacturing;
PSERV Percent of the work force employed in the service industry;
HOUSES Households per capita;
FARMS Farms per capita;
WELFARE The number of households on welfare divided by the total number of households.

The DGW models for individual income tax and returns filed per capita were specified to depend on the audit rate and the socio-economic variables listed above. The IRS budget level was used as an instrument for the audit rate as discussed below.

DGW Hypothesis

Variables primarily related to the tax base are *PER65*, *HOUSES*, and *WELFARE*. Variables related to both the tax base and the compliance behavior of taxpayers depend on the audit rate and the socio-economic variables listed above. The IRS budget level was used as an instrument for the audit rate as discussed below are *UR*, *INCOME*, and *STAXR*. Variables primarily related to the compliance behavior of taxpayers are *PERED*, *PMAN*, *PMAN*, *PSERV*, *FARMS*, and *AUDIT*.

DGW provides a detailed discussion of the theoretical underpinnings of this model. In brief, with respect to variables that are primarily related to the tax base, DGW expected a negative coefficient on *PER65* since taxpayers over 65 years of age are allowed special tax reductions. An increase in the number of households per capita (*HOUSES*) was expected increase reported taxes per return since it implies fewer exemptions. Finally, an increase in the percent of households on welfare (*WELFARE*) was expected to increase reported taxes per return as it effectively eliminates a portion of the lower tail of the distribution of income.

DGW uses three variables that are related both to the tax base and to the compliance behavior of taxpayers. In general, this leads to ambiguous predictions.

For example, states with higher unemployment rates may have unsound economies and thus yield lower reported taxes per return. On the other hand, if most unemployed taxpayers have relatively low income, then reported tax per return should rise as a portion of the lower tail of the distribution of income is eliminated. Changes in real income per capita also have confounding effects on reported tax per return. In general, higher income taxpayers have increased opportunities to evade, but there is a strong direct relationship between real income per capita and reported taxes per return. In fact, DGW expected the latter effect to be quite large, leading to a positive coefficient on (*INCOME*). Finally, since state income taxes are deductible, an increase in the average state income tax rate should decrease reported taxes per return. On the other hand if states attempt their own tax enforcement, and share information yielded by their enforcement activities with the IRS, and if states with higher income taxes do more enforcement, then an increase in average state income tax rates should increase reported taxes per return. Since the former is likely to dominate the latter, DGW expected a negative coefficient on *STAXR*. In Chap. 9 I revise the treatment of state income taxes significantly.

DGW employed variables that are primarily related to the compliance behavior of taxpayers. Some of these variables reflect opportunities to evade while others reflect IRS enforcement activity. The percent of the adult population with at least a high school education was thought to be positively related to tax noncompliance, presumably because more educated individuals are better able to play the "tax lottery". The employment distribution variables directly measure opportunities to evade. Thus DGW expected that the percent of the work force employed in manufacturing industries (*PMAN*) should be positively related to the reported taxes per return since taxpayers working in manufacturing industries presumably have little income other than that reported on W2 or 1099 forms. Meanwhile, the percent of the work force employed in service industries (*PSERV*) should be negatively related to the reported taxes per return since some service sectors are thought to be closely connected with the "underground economy". Farms were thought to have low levels of voluntary compliance so DGW expected a negative coefficient on farms per capita (*FARMS*).

Finally, DGW expected that increases in the federal audit rate (*AUDIT*) would increase taxpayer compliance and thus reported taxes per return. However, as audit rates presumably respond to compliance levels, the federal audit rate was treated as an endogenous factor. Endogeneity occurs when elements of the taxpayers' income and tax status, which are known by the taxpayer and observed by the IRS, induce below average compliance and simultaneously induce greater audit rates. In this case, the correlation leads to inconsistent estimates of the parameters using ordinary least squares regression. Consistent estimation requires the use of "instruments" which are correlated with audit rates but not with the unobservables. The IRS budget per return filed, BPR, filled this role in the DGW analysis. I continue to rely on this factor as an instrument while adding new instrumental variables as I discuss in Chap. 7.

DGW expected that these considerations apply whether reported taxes per return (*RTR*) or assessed liability per return (*ALR*) is used as the dependent variable. However, as discussed by DGW, changes in variables related to the compliance behavior of taxpayers which reduce taxpayer noncompliance should increase reported taxes per return but decrease additional taxes and penalties per return, leaving the expected effect on assessed liability per return, in principle, ambiguous.

DGW's choice of independent variables for the "filing effect" equation was closely related to their choice of independent variables for the reporting effect equations. This is discussed in more detail in the original article.

The Compliance Principle and Tax Base

With respect to variables that relate to the compliance behavior of taxpayers, there is one principle that applies to nearly all. This principle arises from the observation that taxpayers confront three options: to file a return and report honestly, to file a return and underreport taxes, or not to file a return at all. Anything that reduces the benefits or increases the costs of filing a return and underreport will increase the likelihood that a taxpayer chooses one of the other two options, to file a return and report honestly or not to file a return. DGW called this the *compliance principle.* It generally applies to variables that relate to the compliance behavior of taxpayers, but it may be masked by other more direct effects.

With respect to variables that relate to the tax base, there is also a rather clear general principle at work. Any change which increases the tax base will tend to increase returns filed per capita as more taxpayers find themselves with incomes above the minimum required for filing. DGW called this the *tax base principle.*

DGW applied the Compliance Principal and Tax Base Principal to develop a set of hypotheses regarding the direction of expected effects for socio-economic control variables. For instance, an increase in the percent of the adult population over 65 years of age was expected to decrease returns filed per capita since more taxpayers in this age group are likely to fall below the minimum requirements for filing. An increase in the number of households per capita was expected to increase returns filed per capita. Finally, an increase in the percent of households on welfare reduces returns filed per capita as fewer individuals can be expected to have an income level above the minimum required for filing.

DGW expected a positive relationship between the percent of the adult population with at least a high school education and returns filed per capita for two reasons. First, the compliance principle implied that because more educated taxpayers find it easier to exploit opportunities to evade they are also more likely to file returns. Second, more educated taxpayers at the lower end of the income distribution are more easily able to comprehend the federal income tax laws and to comply with them. With respect to employment distribution variables, the compliance principle suggests that the percent of the work force employed in manufacturing industries should be negatively related to returns filed per capita and that the percent of the work force employed in service industries should be positively related to returns filed per capita. On the other hand, DGW predicted a positive relationship between the percent of the work force employed in manufacturing industries and reported taxes per return. Those employed in manufacturing industries have little income other than that reported on W2 or 1099 forms. Given the extent of withholding of taxes and information matching for such income, DGW expected that taxpayers employed in manufacturing industries should file tax returns and report honestly on their returns. Meanwhile, the relationship between farms per capita and returns filed per capita is more difficult to predict. DGW expected that farms per capita to have little or no effect, other things equal, on returns filed per capita.

Finally DGW expected the compliance principle to apply very strongly to the federal audit rates i.e. because increases in the federal audit rate decrease the benefits and increase the costs of filing a return and underreporting taxes due, DGW expected an increase in the audit rate to decrease returns filed per capita. DGW also employed three variables that are related both to the tax base and to the compliance behavior of taxpayers: the unemployment rate, real income per capita, and the average state income tax rate. Despite a potentially complex relationship between the unemployment rate and the compliance behavior of taxpayers, DGW expected that an increase in the unemployment rate would decrease returns filed per capita since it decreases the number of taxpayers with incomes above the minimum required for filing. An increase in real income per capita should have a strong positive effect on returns filed per capita since both the compliance effect and tax base effect work in the same direction; that is, taxpayers with higher income have more opportunities to evade and thus should file more often, and they are also more likely to have incomes above the minimum required for filing. DGW expected that an increase in the average state income tax rate to decrease returns filed per capita. This is because the compliance principle implies that states with higher average state income tax rates, who are the most likely to have enforcement programs of their own, are also the most likely to have taxpayers who fail to file at both the state and federal level. On the other hand, the tax base effect is relatively neutral with respect to average state income taxes since state income taxes are deductible at the federal level but do not by themselves affect the minimum requirements for filing. These issues are taken up further below.

Conclusions

The DGW model corroborated the central role of audit rates in the revenue collections process. DGW found that after treating audit rates as endogenous factors, the decline in audit rates had caused increased noncompliance but a larger number of returns to be filed per capita. Dubin, Graetz, and Wilde were the first researchers to separate the direct and indirect effects of audit examination on tax compliance.

They concluded that the spillover effects of audits produce six out of every seven dollars of additional revenue. In the next chapter, we investigate how tax compliance has experienced further structural shifts since 1986 and specifically how the explanatory factors selected in the DGW model may have different effects in the two decades that followed the original DGW study.

Chapter 6
The Data

Introduction

In this chapter, I review the data considered in my analysis. The data employed is a compilation of annual tax enforcement, criminal investigation, socioeconomic, and political statistics for each US state from 1977 to 2001. The tax collections and examination variables rely on data reported in the Annual Report of the Commissioner of Internal Revenue, IRS Data Book, and IRS Statistics of Income Bulletin. I begin with a graphical analysis of several variables used in the statistical models, as well as other factors collected and considered in the course of this study. I present these graphs for the period beginning in 1977 and ending in 2001. In some cases, the graphs contain data for a shorter period of time if the underlying factors were not available for the full period. I discuss, in turn, the socioeconomic factors, the audit examination factors, the CI activity factors, and a few factors that were not used in this study.

Socioeconomic Factors

The percentage of families on welfare (*PWELFAM*) declined slightly during the 1970s and 1980s, falling from 4.70 to 4.08%, before rising to its peak of 5.17% in 1994. From 1995 to 2001, the percentage of families on welfare declined to 2.03%. This decline, shown in Fig. 6.1, may have been due to welfare reform enacted in the Personal Responsibility and Work Opportunity Reconciliation Act of 1996 (Personal Responsibility Act).[1] Welfare cases necessarily fell when fewer individuals qualified for welfare under the PRA.

---

[1] In the appendix to this chapter, I present a geographic representation of the same figures discussed in the chapter. Note that the US maps are for the period 1997–2001 and not every figure have been presented.

J. A. Dubin, *The Causes and Consequences of Income Tax Noncompliance*,
DOI: 10.1007/978-1-4419-0907-7_6, © Springer Science+Business Media, LLC 2012

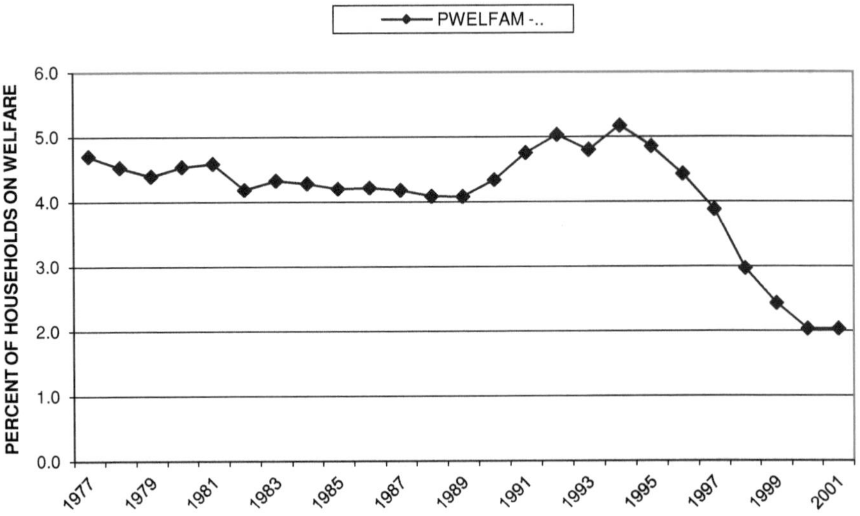

Fig. 6.1 Percent of households on welfare

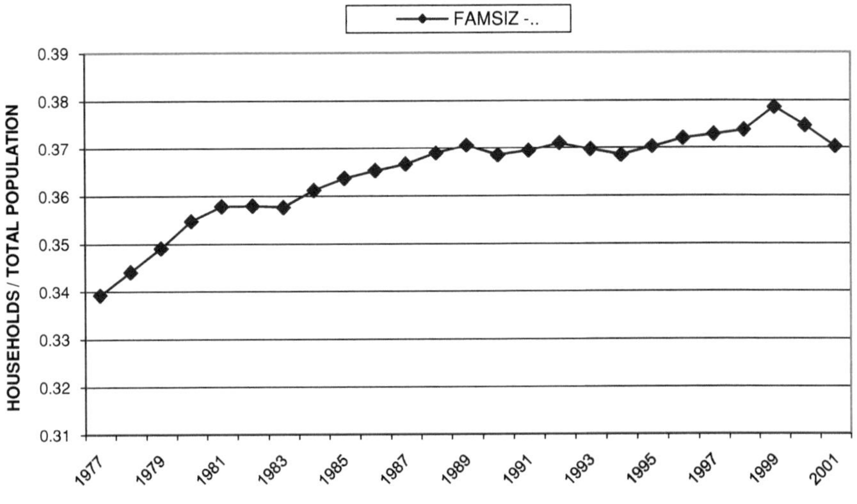

Fig. 6.2 Households/total population

Households per capita (*FAMSIZ*) show a modest rise from 0.34 in 1977 to nearly 0.38 in 1999. This change indicates that average family size has declined from 2.94 to 2.63 persons per family. I show this relationship in Fig. 6.2.

The number of farms per household (*FRMFAM*) continued to show a decline during the analysis period, reflecting fewer farms in the United States and a larger

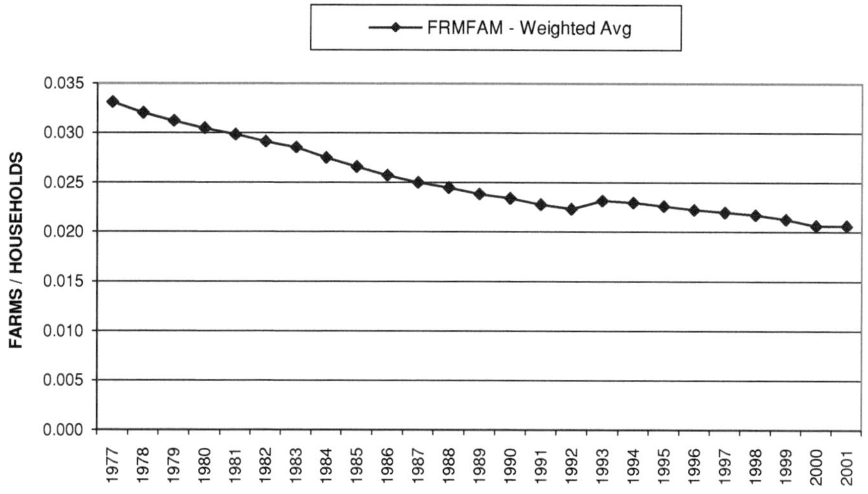

Fig. 6.3 Farms/households

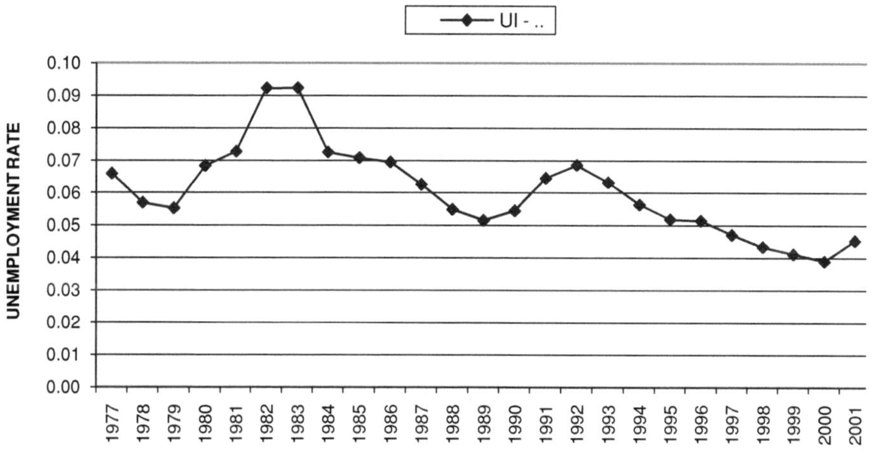

Fig. 6.4 Unemployment rate

number of households. The decline was from 3.30 farms per hundred families to just over 2.06 farms per hundred families. I show this decline in Fig. 6.3.

Unemployment rates (*UI*) varied notably during the late 1970s and 1980s. Reaching a peak in the early 1980s (at 9.23%), unemployment has generally declined with the exception of the recession in the early 1990s and the most recent increase in unemployment that has occurred in the last few years. I show this trend in Fig. 6.4.

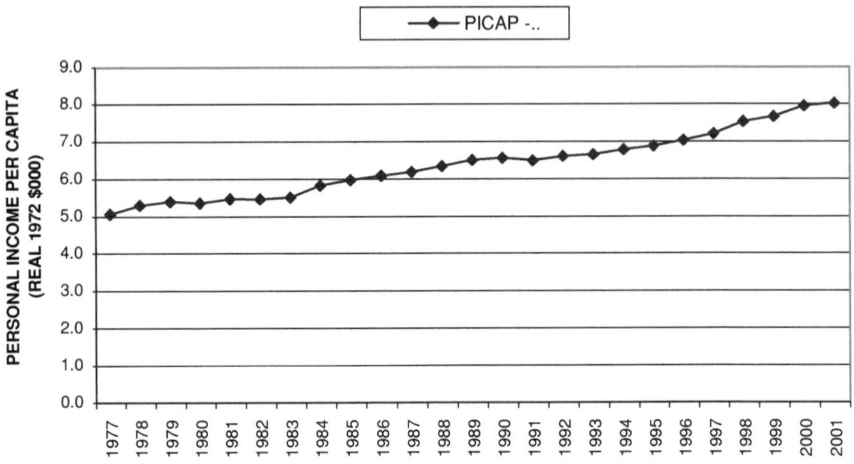

Fig. 6.5 Personal income per capita (real 1972 $000)

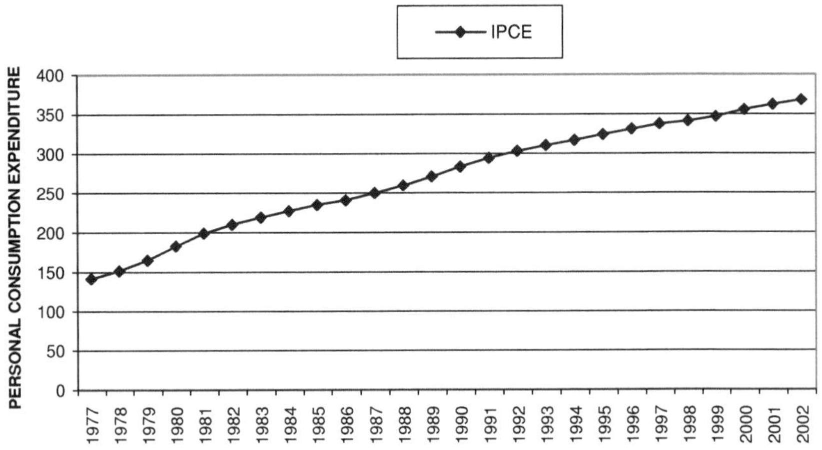

Fig. 6.6 Personal consumption expenditure

Personal income in real terms (*PICAP*) has risen steadily from 1977 to 2001. Average real income per capita rose from $5,066 to $8,017. I show this increase in Fig. 6.5.

During this 25-year period, inflation was present. The personal consumption expenditure price deflator (*IPCE*) indicates a 156% rise in prices over the 25-year period, an average of 6.2% per annum. I show this increase in Fig. 6.6.

State tax rates (*STAXR*) rose on average from 4.06% in 1977 to 4.52% in 1984. From the mid-1980s forward, the state tax rate grew to 4.74% and remained fairly steady at this level in the late 1990s. I show this trend in Fig. 6.7.

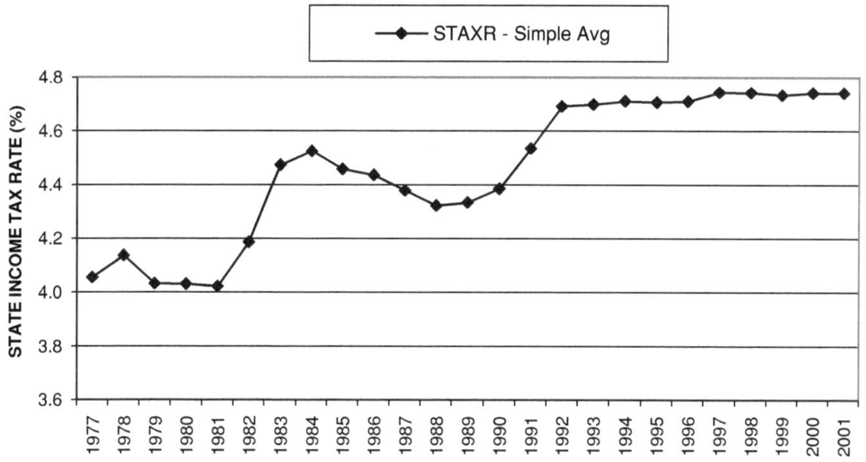

Fig. 6.7 State income tax rate (%)

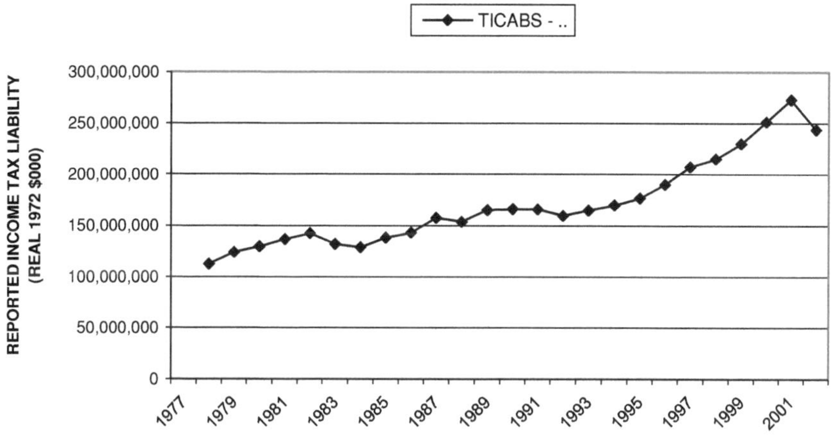

Fig. 6.8 Reported income tax liability (real 1972 $000)

Total tax liability reported by individuals during the previous fiscal year (*TICABS*) grew steadily during this period as well but showed a small decline in 2002. I show this trend in Fig. 6.8.

Using the reported total tax liability, I created the reported liability per individual tax return filed (*RTR*). This factor remained fairly constant (in real terms) between 1977 and 1992. From 1992 to 2000, reported tax liabilities increased by 48.8% (4.88% per annum) before experiencing a drop in 2001. I show this trend in Fig. 6.9.

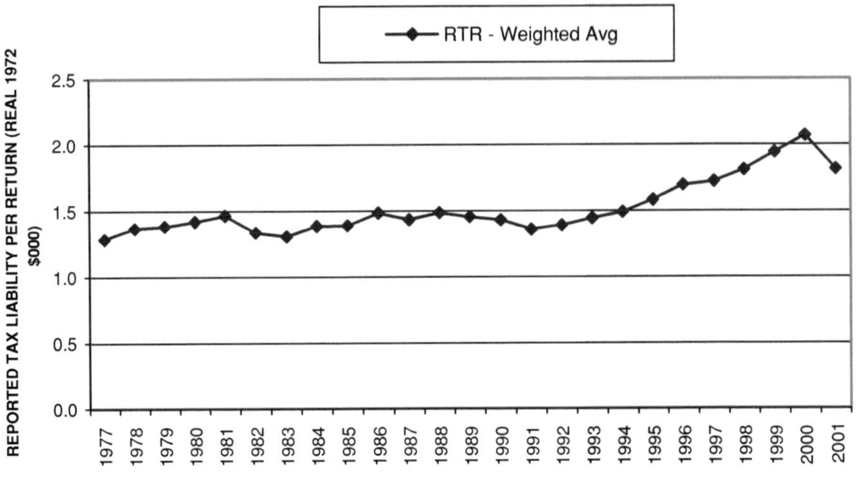

Fig. 6.9 Reported tax liability per return (real 1972 $000)

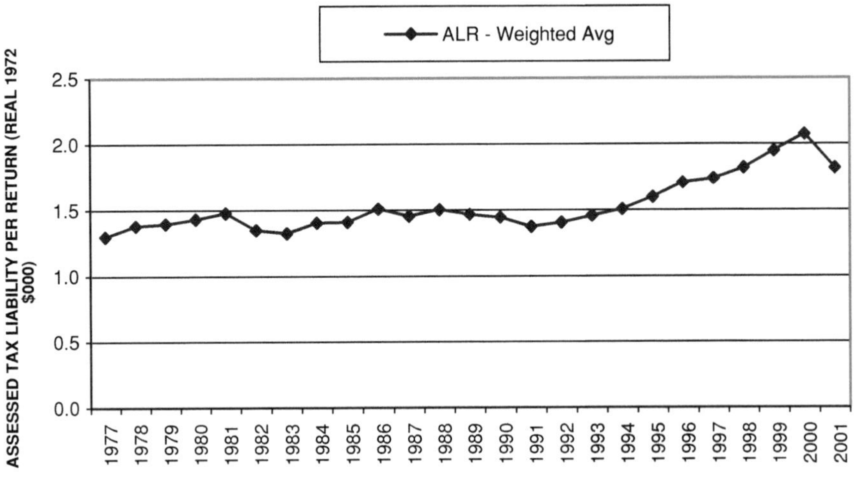

Fig. 6.10 Assessed tax liability per return (real 1972 $000)

Combining reported tax liabilities and additional taxes and penalties resulting from examination yields assessed liabilities per return (*ALR*). The pattern in ALR was similar to that of reported tax liability per return. Therefore, the observed increase was not a result of dramatic changes in additional taxes and penalties, as I discuss further below. Assessed liabilities per return increased from $1,298 per return filed to $2,075 by 2000 (in 1972 dollars). Reported liability per return and assessed liability per return were of similar magnitude. I show this relationship in Fig. 6.10.

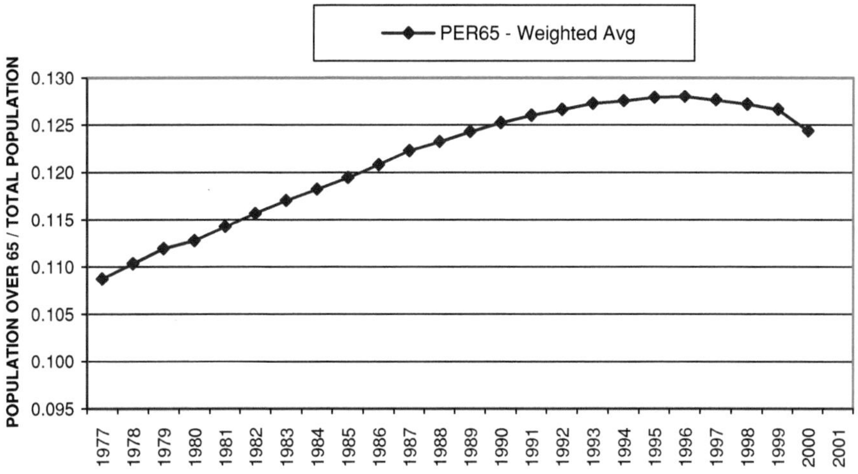

Fig. 6.11 Population over 65/total population

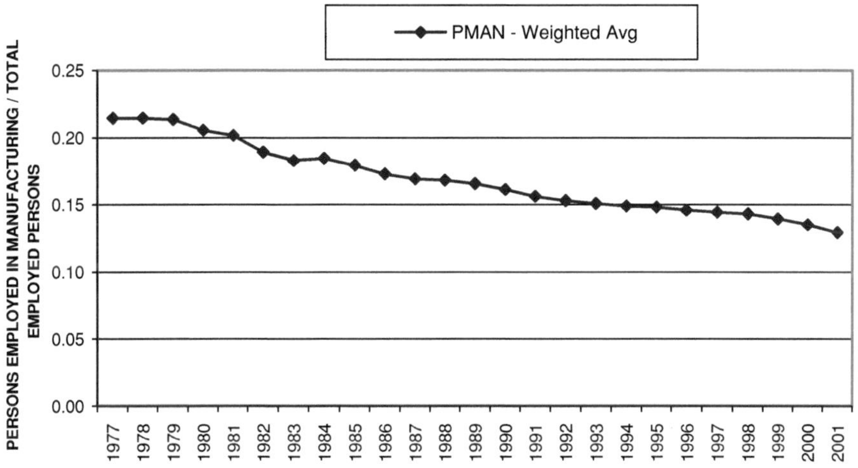

Fig. 6.12 Persons employed in manufacturing/total employed persons

The percentage of the population over age 65 (*PER65*) showed a relatively modest growth during the period. I show this increase in Fig. 6.11.

The percentage of employed individuals in manufacturing (*PMAN*) declined from just over 21.45% in 1977 to roughly 12.94% by 2001. I show this decline in Fig. 6.12.

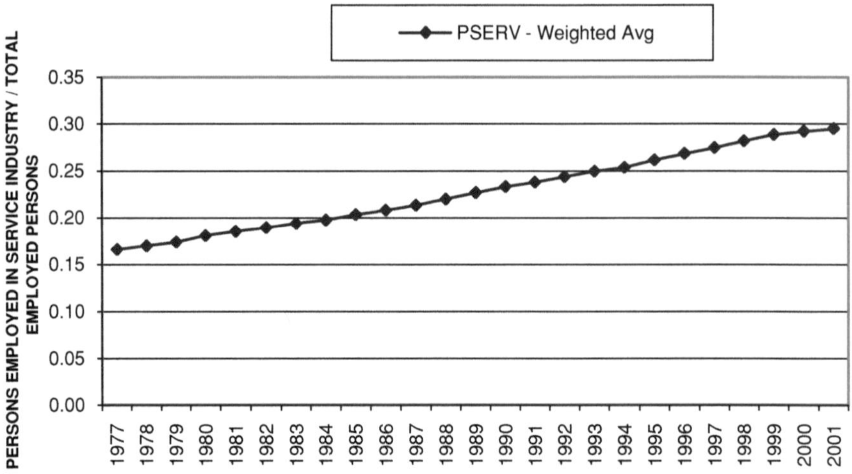

Fig. 6.13 Persons employed in service industry/total employed persons

The percentage of employed individuals in service industries (*PSERV*) increased from 16.61% in 1977 to nearly 29.49% in 2001. I show this increase in Fig. 6.13.

This pattern continues the trends described in the original DGW study. However, as described more fully below, the importance of manufacturing and service industry employees may have changed as compliance and collections associated with these sectors has shifted since the original 1977–1986 study of DGW.

Audit and Examination Factors

Statistics on examination coverage variables such as numbers of returns examined, additional taxes and penalties recommended after examination, and costs incurred by the IRS, were broken down by district office and service center in the IRS Data Book and Annual Report. In states where there were multiple districts, I performed an aggregation to derive state-level figures for those factors. The IRS Reform Act reorganized the entire district system and required many district offices to be responsible for the tax returns filed by multiple states. As a result, most of the district-level statistics from 1997 to 2001 included services provided to multiple states. Since only state-level data is used in the analysis, I took the 1996 allocation of examinations, additional taxes, and cost incurred for each state among the other states in the newly defined districts and extrapolated the annual figures for 1997–2001 based on the 1996 percentages. For states with multiple districts, the district-level data is aggregated to the state level.

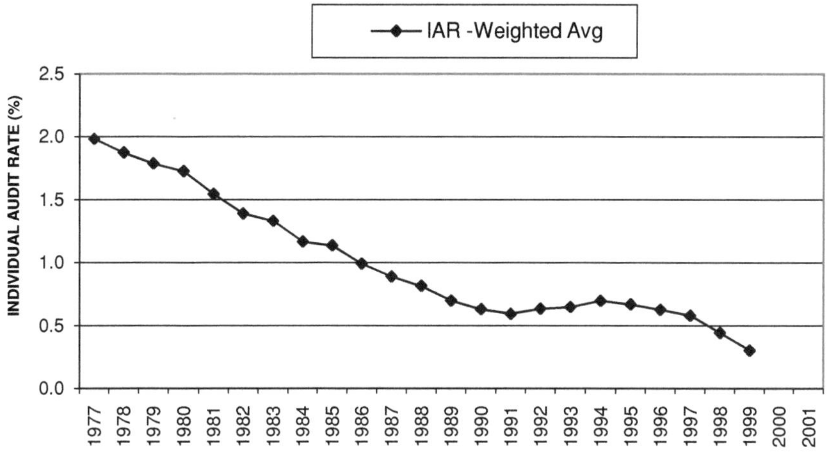

Fig. 6.14 Individual audit rate (%)

The role played by audit examination on compliance was important for my analysis and for the original DGW study. The dramatic decline in the individual audit rate (*IAR*) between 1977 and 1987 was followed by an equally staggering decline during the subsequent 15 years. Indeed, audit rates fell from 1.98% in 1977 to 0.59% by 1991. The decline continued through the end of the analysis period, where the IAR was only 0.3% in 1999. I show this decline in Fig. 6.14.

The IRS indicates that this decline in audit rates has been partially offset by automated programs such as the CP2000 program and other correspondence audits. I examine this proposition below.

Meanwhile, individual returns filed per capita (*RCAP*) grew steadily over the 25-year period by 18.44, or 0.74% per annum. I show this growth in Fig. 6.15.

With respect to instrumental variables, I extended the budget per return variable used in the DGW study and added some new instruments. First, the IRS budget per individual return filed was estimated and published by the IRS through 1999. The budget (in real 1972 dollars) reached its peak of $5.29 per return in 1988. The growth was likely a consequence of the Tax Reform Act of 1986 (TRA). The TRA was a major shift in United States tax policy. Tax rates were cut, the tax base was broadened, IRA rules were changed, and the tax laws were generally simplified. However, the budget per return subsequently underwent a significant decline between 1993 and 1999, dropping from $5.18 to $3.69, ultimately falling to levels lower than those in any of the previous years in the analysis. Given the importance of this factor as an instrument for IRS audit levels, I extended this figure for the 2000 and 2001 period at 1999 levels. This approximation is revealed in Fig. 6.16. There is little consequence from this approximation when budget per returns filed is used as an instrumental variable.

Next, the IRS provided a measure of the total available resources devoted to examinations (*DIR_EXAM*). This percentage further refines the budget variable

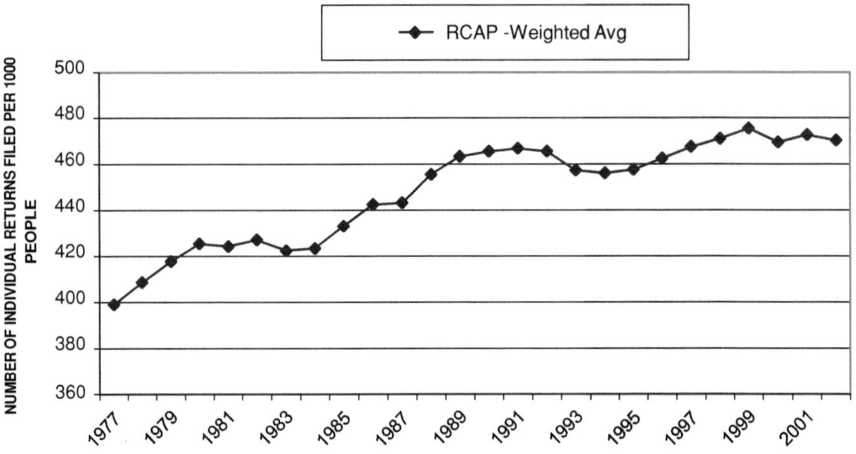

Fig. 6.15 Number of individual returns filed per 1,000 people

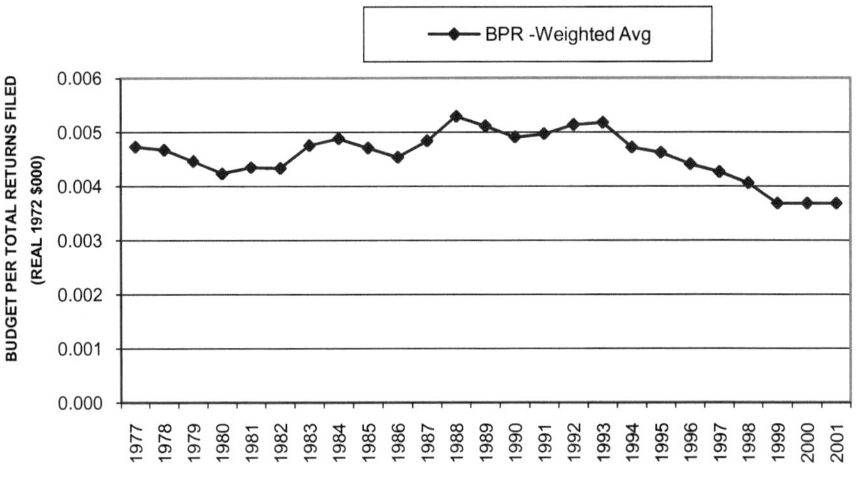

Fig. 6.16 Budget per total returns filed (real 1972 $000)

described above; it should be highly correlated with audit activity but nevertheless exogenously set by the IRS in any fiscal period as it corresponds to the planned examination activity. As discussed by Plumley (1996), the direct examination measure provides the percentage of all examiners' time allocated to the direct examination of tax returns. Plumley argues that this factor is a reasonably exogenous measure of audit activity. Beginning in 1980 with a simple state average of 64.4%, the direct examination percentage fell to 41.1% by 1988. While the percentage of time devoted to examinations rose somewhat through 1997 (to 54.1%),

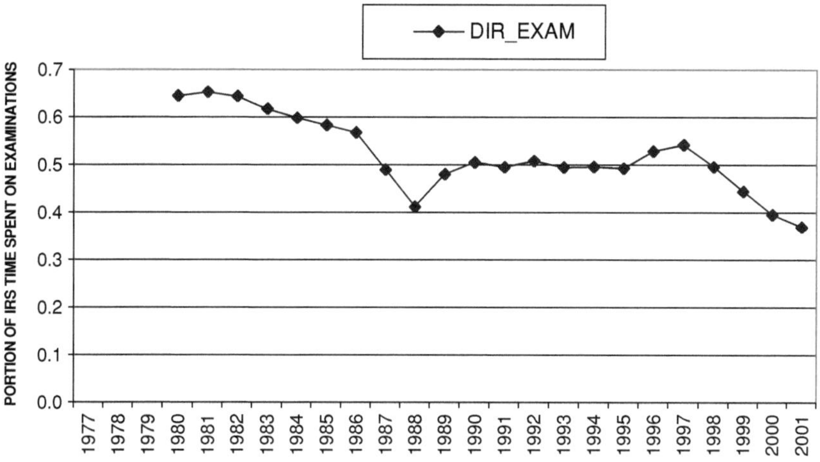

Fig. 6.17 Portion of IRS time spent on examinations

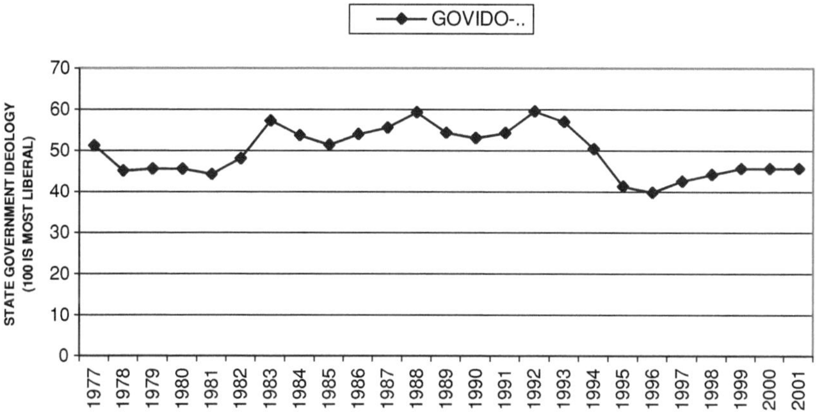

Fig. 6.18 State government ideology (100 is most liberal)

the pattern from 1997 to 2001 had been to reduce direct examination time (measured at 36.9% in 2001). I show this reduction in Fig. 6.17.

In some models, I needed additional instruments, as I discuss further below. Following Mete (2002), I assembled several political factors that could be used as potential instruments. Based on correlations with the audit rate, I ultimately focused on four potential instruments: (1) political party of the state governor (*GOVR*); (2) a measure for state government liberalism (*GOVIDO*); (3) the ratio of Democrats to Republicans in the House (*HRATIO*); and (4) the ratio of Democrats to Republicans in the Senate (*SRATIO*). I show these relationships in Figs. 6.18, 6.19, 6.20, and 6.21, respectively.

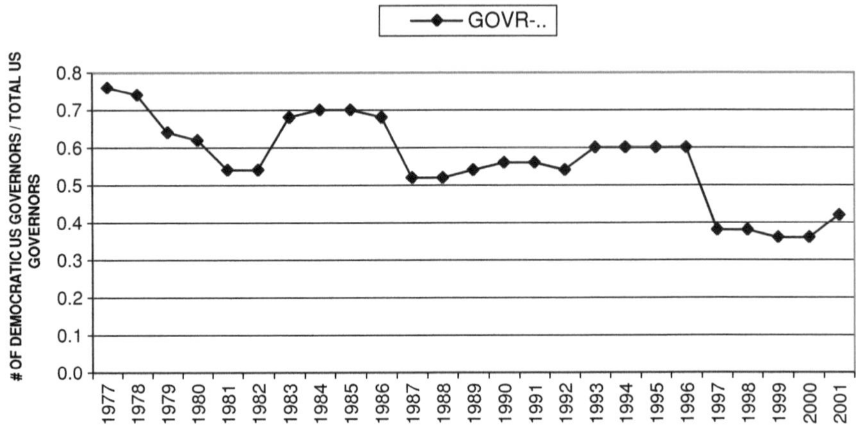

Fig. 6.19 Democratic governors/total US governors

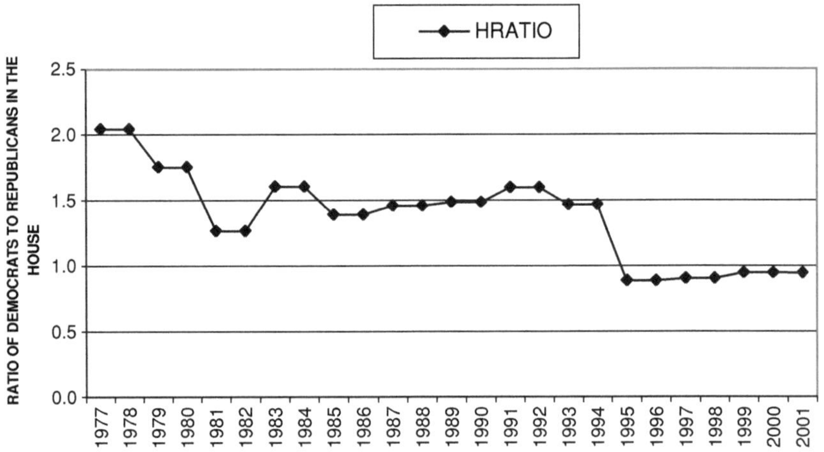

Fig. 6.20 Ratio of democrats to republicans in the house

Mete (2002) provides the rationale behind these factors and discusses how they are expected to correlate with the audit rate. Mete argues that Republicans prefer lower levels of enforcement for all forms of regulation than do Democrats. Additionally, Mete argues that Republicans provide less support for increasing government spending and enforcement activities than Democrats. Therefore, the undesirable effects of tax enforcement on citizens may be worse for Republican politicians. In sum, Mete expects the audit rate to be higher under Democratic control. Thus, a higher proportion of Democrats in Congress or a more liberal

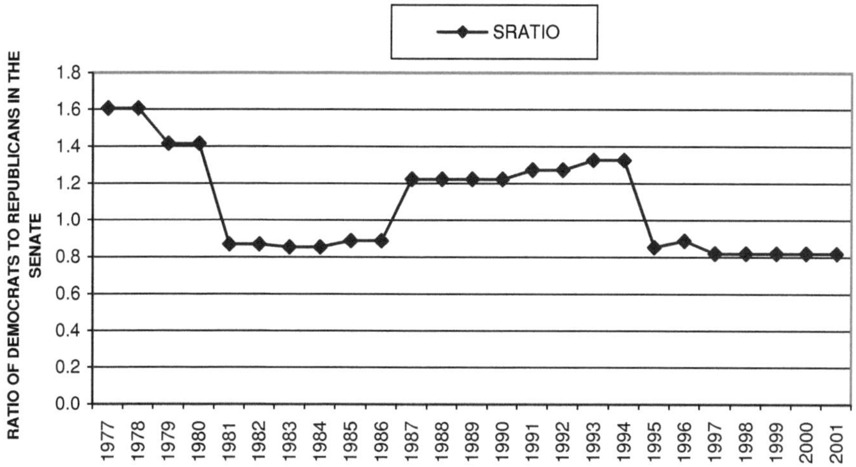

Fig. 6.21 Ratio of democrats to republicans in the senate

ideology score should lead to generally higher audit rates. Based on the empirical results, I ultimately selected the instrument based on government liberalism and used it in conjunction with IRS budget per return filed and the direct examination percentage. I then used these instruments in a subset of models that simultaneously considered three examination factors.

I treated CI activities as exogenous both on theoretical and empirical grounds. First, CI activity is largely a result of cases discovered and selected for examination that arise independently of tax gap or noncompliance issues. Second, my specification tests for endogeneity of the CI enforcement factors did not reveal endogenous behavior. Pragmatically, each CI factor potentially requires at least one instrument, and instruments are difficult to collect and justify in aggregate studies. DGW used a measure of information returns filed as an instrument in some of their models, but this factor was not available at the state level in any meaningful year for the time period covered in this study.

As part of this study, the IRS provided several new factors to examine tax enforcement. These factors refine the IAR used in DGW but are limited to a subset of the analysis period (from 1993 forward). The first factor measures examinations of individual tax returns conducted by revenue agents (*AUDR1*). Revenue agents are required to have extensive accounting knowledge. They are qualified to audit all tax returns and provide a more thorough audit. Revenue agents typically audit more complex issues that involve higher income levels or greater deductions. Revenue agents conduct their audits in person rather than through the mail. As with the audit rate defined in the DGW study, I express the revenue agent audit rate as a fraction of individual returns examined. Figure 6.22 shows that revenue agent audits have declined significantly between 1994 and the present. The rate of these audits fell from 0.313 to 0.065% during the period.

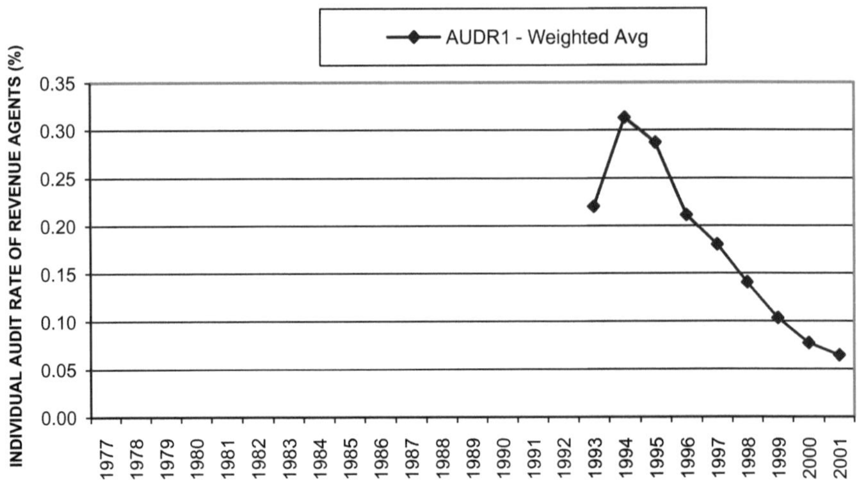

Fig. 6.22 Individual audit rate (revenue agents)

The second examination factor represents the tax agents' audit activity. Tax auditors or tax agents generally have less tax knowledge than revenue agents. They typically audit individual non-business returns and Schedule C returns (sole proprietorships). Relative to revenue agent audits, tax audits are less complex and involve lower income and expense levels. A tax audit is typically conducted in an IRS office, as opposed to a revenue agent audit, which takes place at the taxpayer's (or his/her representative's) business or residence. Expressed as a fraction of individual returns filed, tax audits (*AUDR2*) also show a dramatic decline over the last decade. The rate of these audits fell from roughly 0.428 to 0.086% by the end of the period. I show this decline in Fig. 6.23.

Statistics on the number of examinations and additional taxes and penalties were not published in the data book after 1999 and 1997, respectively. In order to have the two variables span the entire period, I substituted the data obtained directly from the IRS for the published data in the post-1993 portion of the dataset. The sum of audits performed by both revenue agents and tax auditors tied out closely to the number of audits reported in the Data Book. Therefore, I used the factor (*AUDR12*) to extend the DGW explanatory factor in later years. I used the same approach for additional taxes and penalties. In the years where the variable new data and published data overlap, the correlation between the original and updated versions of the audit variable is 0.92. Similarly, the correlation between the two versions of the additional tax variable is 0.97. The resulting variable is denoted *IAR2* and extends the DGW factor *IAR* for recent years where the IRS data books no longer report audit rates by state. Figures 6.24 and 6.25, respectively, show the overlap of *IAR* and *AUDR12* and the *IAR2* factor over time.

Finally, the IRS provided a measure of correspondence audits. These audits are done through the mail, as the name implies, and represent a modern extension of

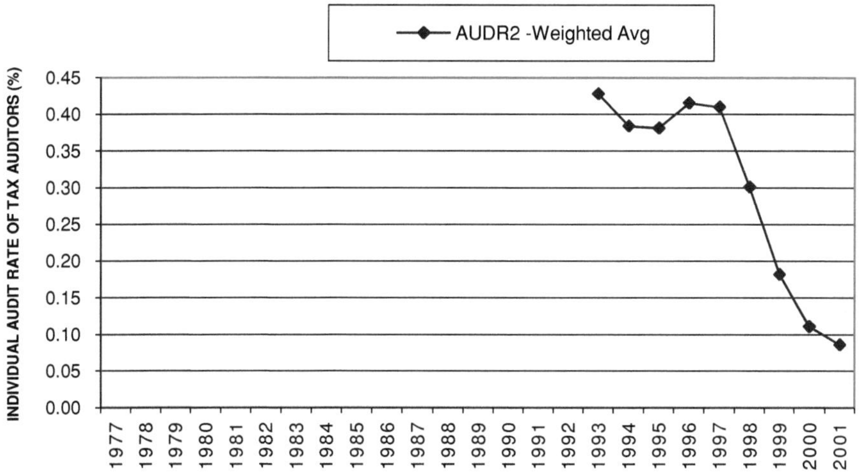

Fig. 6.23 Individual audit rate (tax auditors)

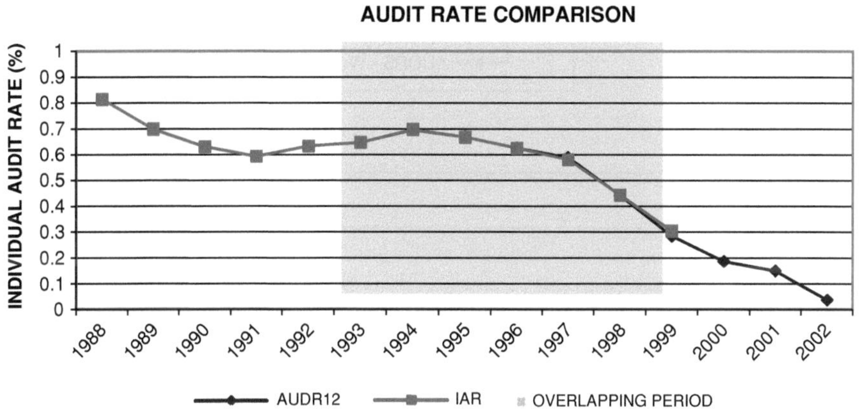

Fig. 6.24 Individual audit rate—comparison

the CP2000 program (DGW 1990). I attributed service center audits to the state in which the taxpayer resided. Normalizing by individual returns filed yields the third audit factor (*AUDR5*). As shown in Fig. 6.26, correspondence audits have increased from 0.261% in 1993 to 0.962% in 1996. In recent years, however, the rate of correspondence audits has declined after significant fluctuation. The 2001 measurement shows an average rate of just 0.395%.

Corresponding to these audit rates, the IRS provided measures of the additional taxes and penalties recommended as a result of examination. These are *ADDT1*, *ADDT2*, and *ADDT5* and correspond to the three audit rates *AUDR1*, *AUDR2*, and

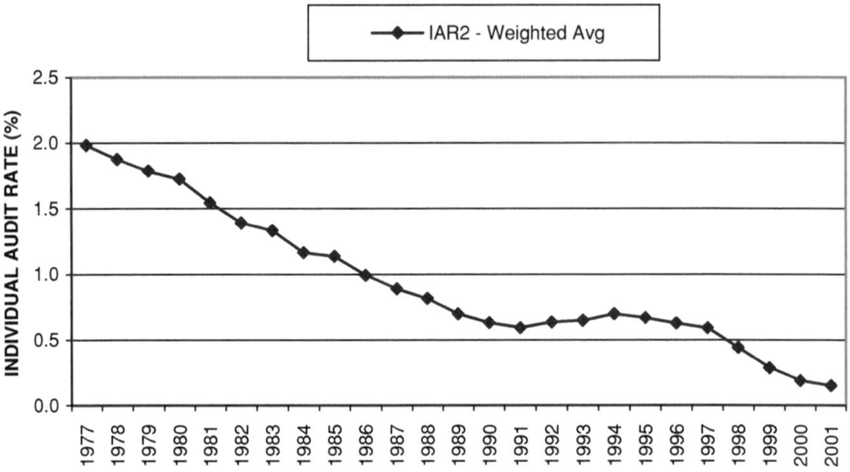

Fig. 6.25 Individual audit rate (IAR2)

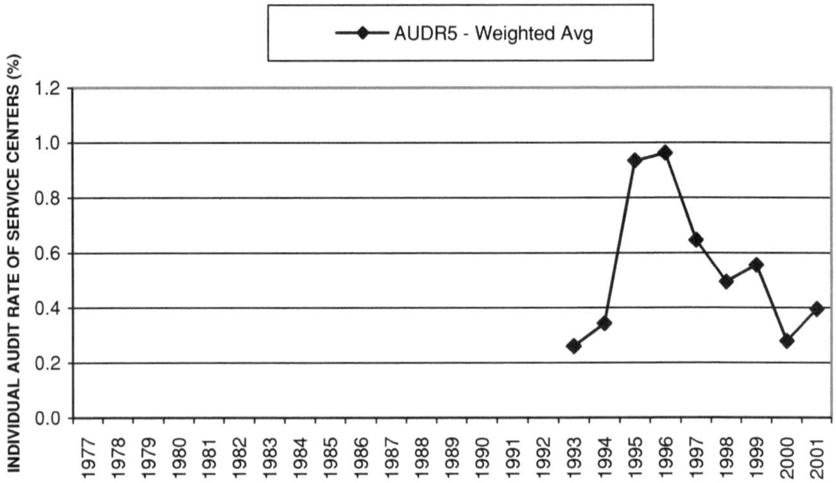

Fig. 6.26 Individual audit rate (service centers)

AUDR5. I combined the additional taxes and penalties recommended that result from face-to-face audits to form *ADDT12*. This factor is comparable to the additional tax and penalty variable used in the DGW study, and I used it to extend that figure for those recent years during which the IRS no longer published the information by state (*IAT2*). As shown in Figs. 6.27, 6.28, 6.29, 6.30 and 6.31, there has been a significant decline in additional taxes and penalties recommended

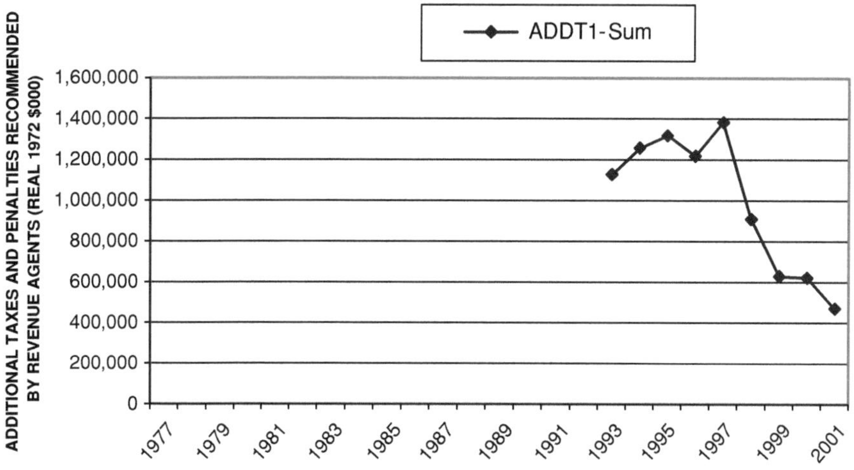

Fig. 6.27 Additional taxes and penalties (revenue agents)

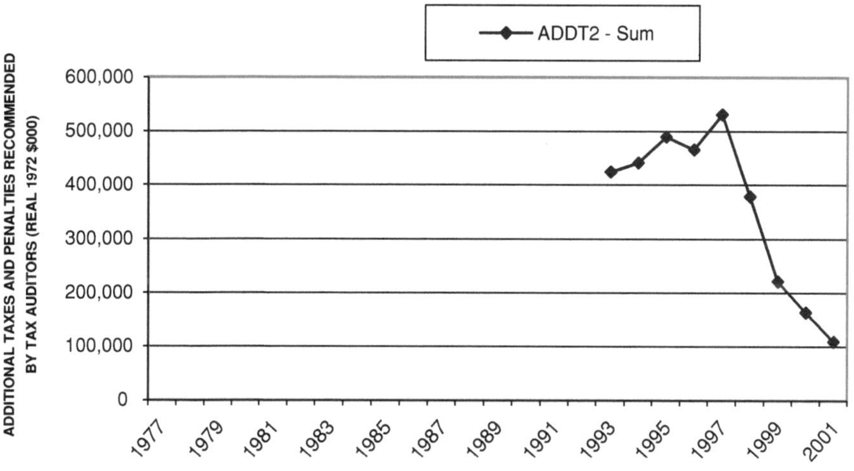

Fig. 6.28 Additional taxes and penalties (tax auditors)

during the 1993–2001 period. In real terms, this represents a reversal of the trend that had occurred during the period from 1977 to 1986.

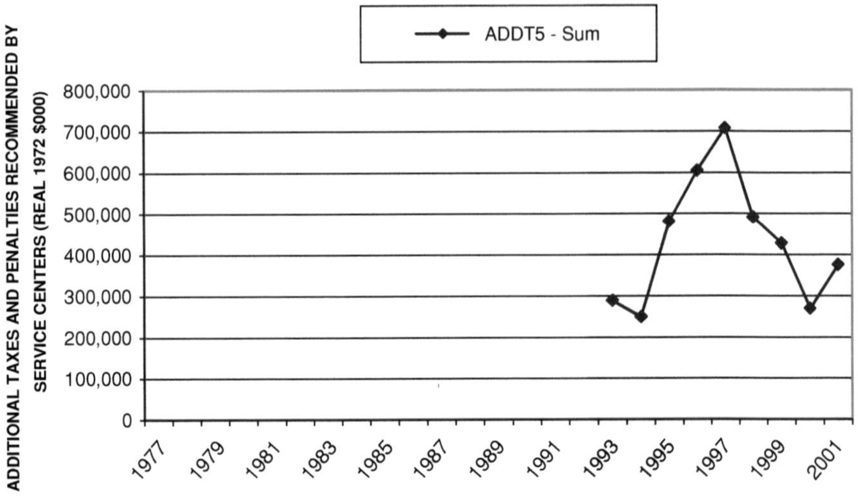

Fig. 6.29 Additional taxes and penalties (service centers)

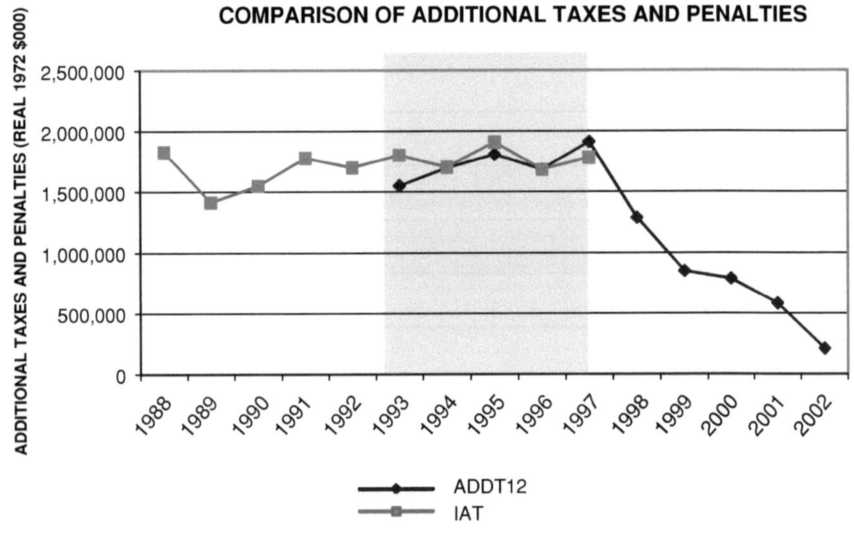

Fig. 6.30 Additional taxes and penalties (real 1972 $000)—comparison

IRS Criminal Enforcement Factors

Next, I review the data provided by the CI. The CI provided detailed information about sentenced cases and cases recommended for prosecution, including media coverage and sentence type (typically probation or prison). Figure 6.32 shows the

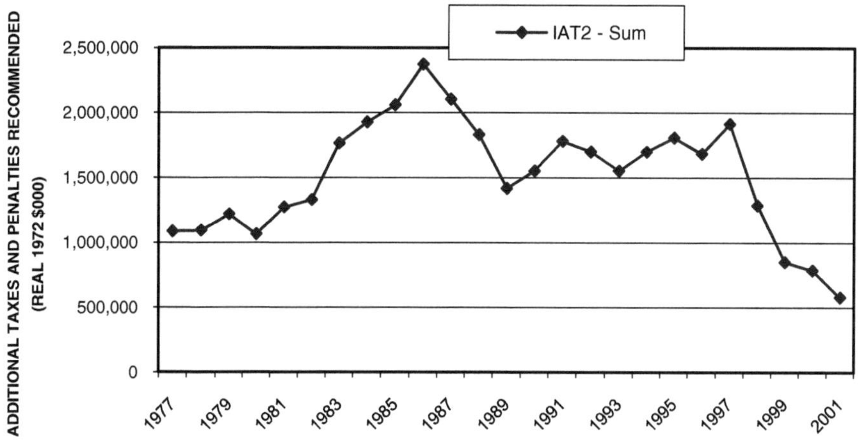

Fig. 6.31 Additional taxes and penalties recommended (real 1972 $000)

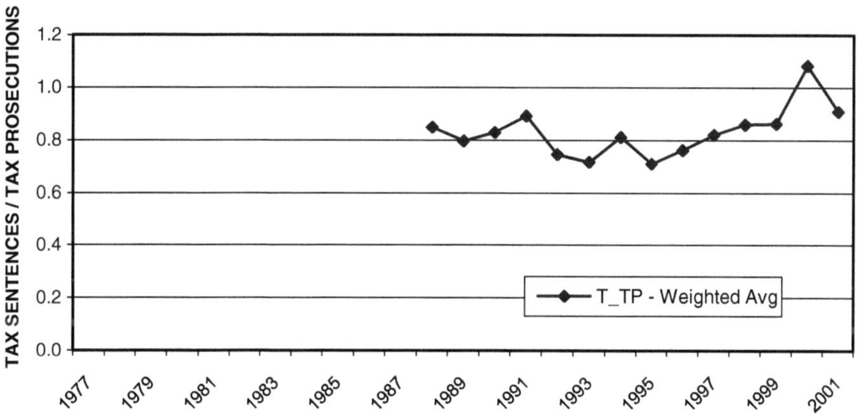

Fig. 6.32 Tax sentences/tax prosecutions

percentage of tax cases receiving sentencing among all tax cases recommended for prosecution for the time period 1988–2001. Thus, 82.3% of tax cases recommended for prosecution resulted in a conviction and sentencing. As seen in Fig. 6.32, this percentage fluctuated over time.[2]

Figure 6.33 shows the percentage of money laundering cases receiving sentencing among all money laundering cases recommended for prosecution. Thus,

[2] Total sentences can be greater than total prosecutions for certain years since a sentence can occur in a different fiscal year from the year of prosecution for that same crime.

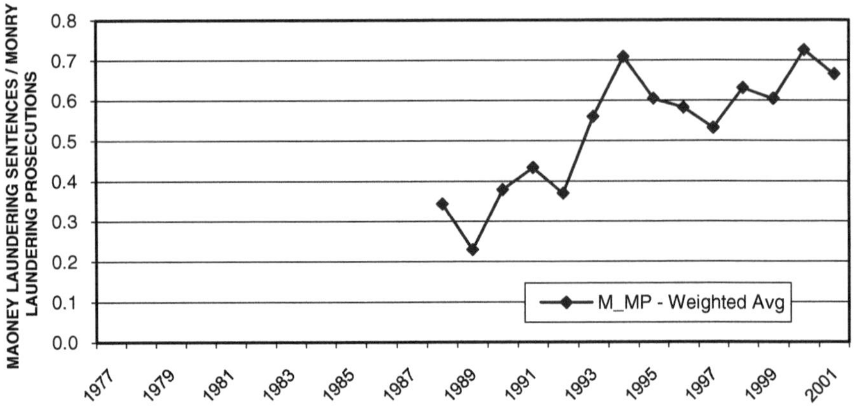

Fig. 6.33 Money laundering sentences/money laundering prosecutions

56.5% of the cases recommended for prosecution resulted in a conviction and sentencing. As seen in Fig. 6.33, the percentage is generally increasing over time.

Sentences from IRS criminal investigations were classified into categories and subcategories in the dataset. The sentence counts were first broken down by the crime that was committed and then further distinguished by the sentence's punishment (prison or probation) and by whether news of the case was released through any form of media (radio, television, print). My analysis begins by decomposing all CI cases that were sentenced. Sentenced cases can arise as a result of a pure tax investigation, a pure money laundering investigation, a combination of both tax and money laundering investigations, or something not related to either tax or money laundering. The preponderance of CI cases had either tax or money laundering aspects. In addition, sentenced cases may or may not have received media coverage. Finally, sentenced cases may have received recommendations for prison, probation, or some other fine or penalty. There are many ways in which to classify individual CI cases. Finding the empirical classifications that have significance with respect to tax compliance is a significant goal of this study.[3]

The money laundering cases provided are not considered tax gap cases, except for a few cases that were both tax and money laundering-related. I allocated these cases to both the tax and money laundering category. It is natural to consider how such cases can affect taxpayer compliance. The most plausible mechanism is

[3] It may be argued that every CI case is different from every other case. Of course, the specifics of a given case may make it a more or less representative case for CI and could affect the perceptions formed by the public. Indeed, the amount of media coverage may be completely different for different cases, even though each receives some media coverage. These issues are masked, to some degree, by aggregate econometric studies. They may be relevant if they create errors in measurement, which can attenuate measured statistical significance, or if they lead to biases in aggregation. I proceeded using counts of cases as the relevant proxy as previous studies have done empirically with audit examinations rates.

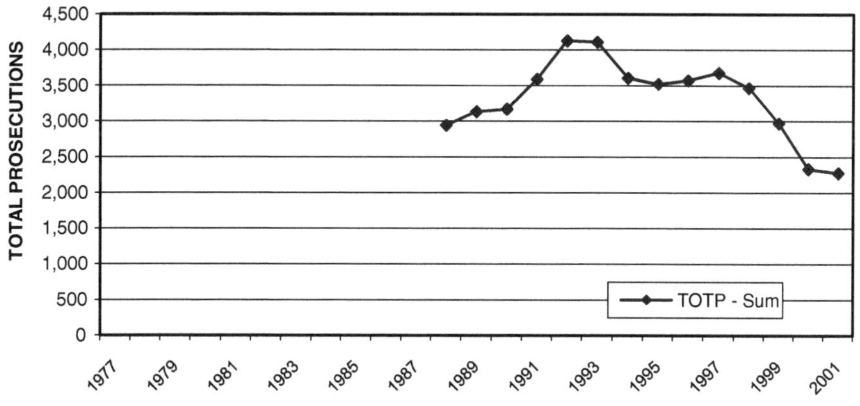

Fig. 6.34 Total prosecutions (sum of TOTP)

through publicity. It is possible that a CI-related activity that receives media attention may influence some taxpayers to be more tax compliant. It is possible that media coverage of money laundering cases and the sentences received by the individuals under indictment convey the mission of the CI division and emphasize its role in tax matters. Econometric analysis is limited in its ability to discern the mechanism by which CI sentenced cases or cases recommended for prosecution affect compliance. Econometric analysis can identify the correlation of this effect and measure its statistical significance. Also, to the extent that media variables are measurable for a reasonable time period, analysis of media attention provides a direct test of the CI message mechanism. Ultimately, it is an empirical question and one that I investigate in this report.

Total CI cases recommended for prosecution (*TOTP*) ranged from 2,937 cases per annum in 1988 to 4,126 cases in 1993. *TOTP* fell to 2,271 cases in 2001. I show this decline in Fig. 6.34.

Annual counts of CI tax cases recommended for prosecution (*TP*) reached 2,255 in 1993 but then fell dramatically to 991 cases by 2001. I show this decline in Fig. 6.35.

Money laundering prosecutions (*MP*) grew rapidly, from 385 cases in 1988 to 2,042 cases in 1992, nearly equaling the number of tax prosecutions for the same year (2,047). Interestingly, annual counts of money laundering prosecutions became greater than tax prosecutions beginning in 1997, and they have remained that way every year since. I show this trend in Fig. 6.36.

Total CI sentenced cases (*TOT*) ranged between 2,133 and 3,157 during the period from 1988 to 2001. There is some evidence of a recent decline in the total cases performed by CI (Fig. 6.37). Tax cases conducted by CI (*T*) have declined fairly steadily from 1988 to 2001 and declined from 1,876 cases per annum in 1998 to 899 cases in 2001 (Fig. 6.38). Conversely, money laundering cases (*M*) have risen from 132 cases per year in 1998 to a high of 1,170 cases per annum

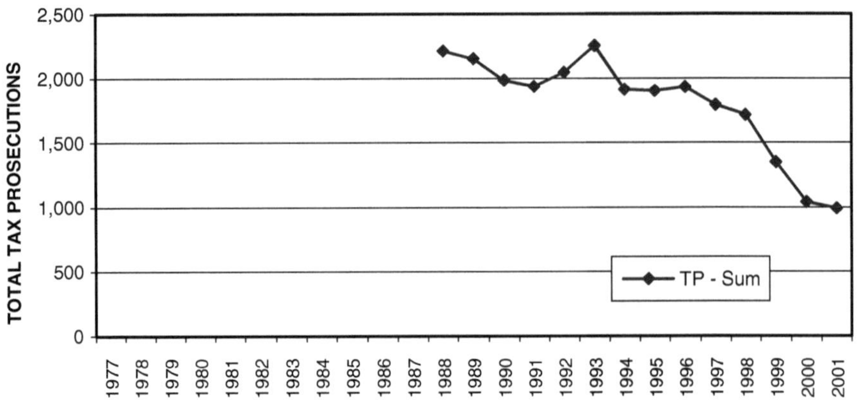

Fig. 6.35 Total tax prosecutions (sum of TP)

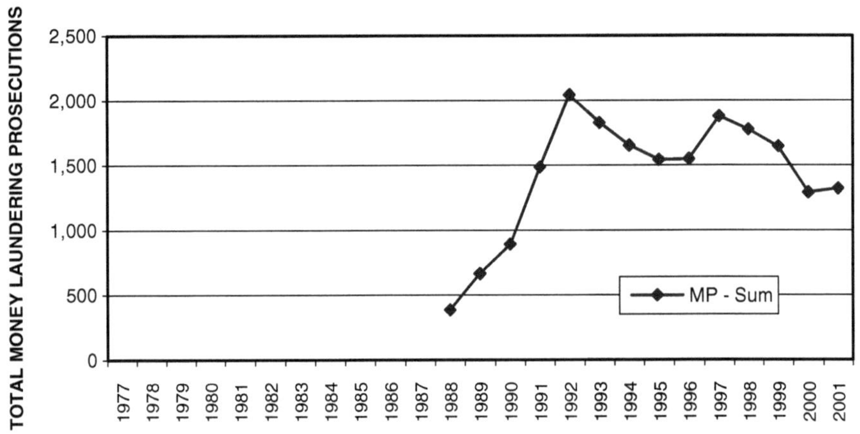

Fig. 6.36 Total money laundering prosecutions

in 1994. There are approximately 900 such cases conducted per year at present. I show this trend in Fig. 6.39.

On a percentage basis, these patterns are quite dramatic. The number of CI tax cases as a percentage of total CI cases (*T_TOT*) fell from 76.9% in 1988 to 42.2% in 2001. I show this decline in Fig. 6.40. Meanwhile, money laundering cases rose from just 5.4% of all CI cases (*M_TOT*) to 41.2% by 2001. I show this increase in Fig. 6.41. As the percentages reveal, a small number of cases conducted by CI are classified neither as money laundering nor tax cases. Similarly, there are a few cases that have aspects of both money laundering and tax. I have included such cases as both money laundering and tax cases. The amount of double counting is, however, insignificant.

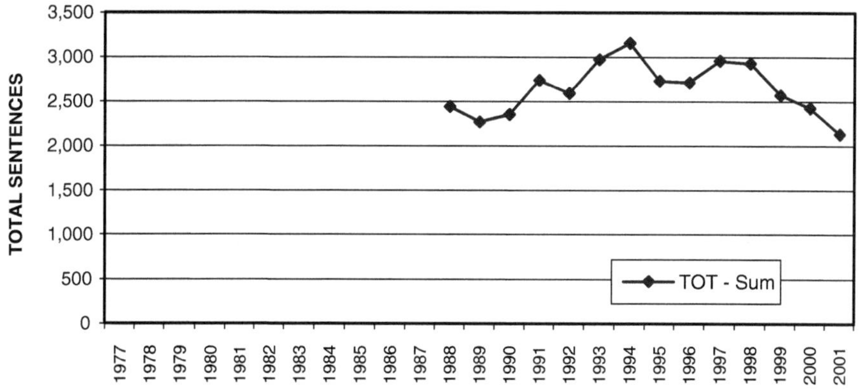

Fig. 6.37 Total sentences (sum of TOT)

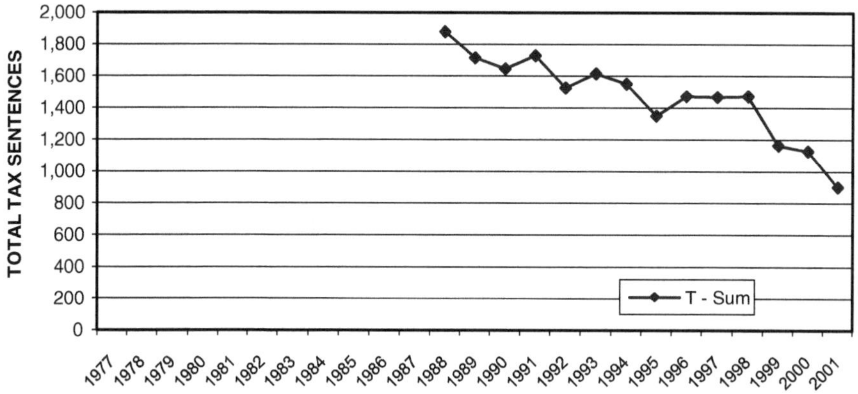

Fig. 6.38 Total tax sentences

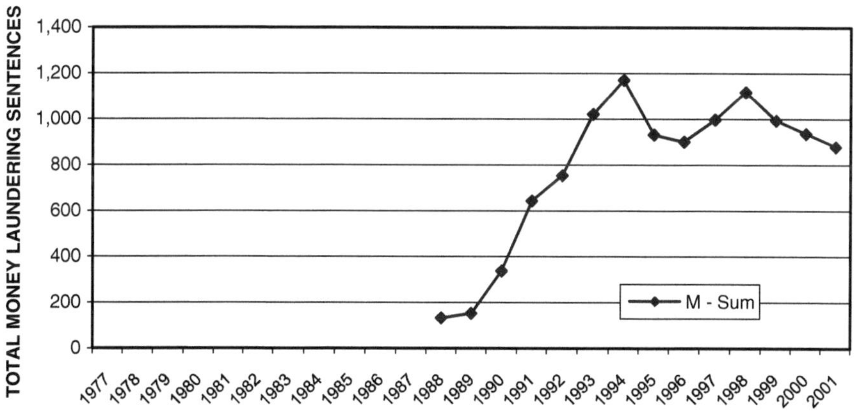

Fig. 6.39 Total money laundering sentences

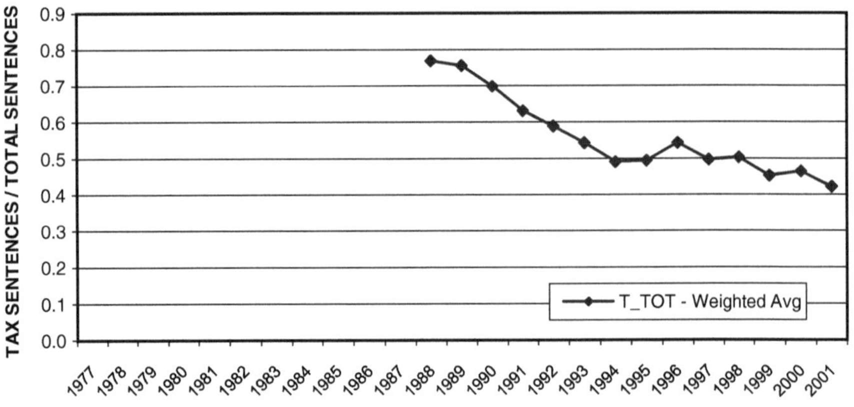

Fig. 6.40 Tax sentences/total sentences

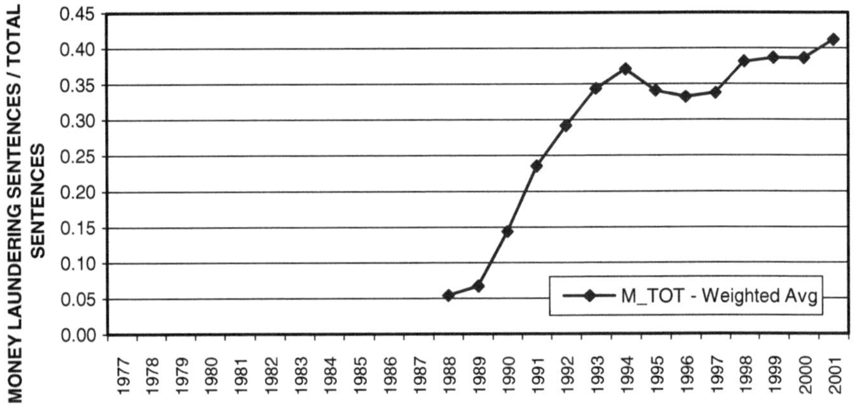

Fig. 6.41 Money laundering sentences/total sentences

I next turn to tax-only case disposition. Similar to tax and money laundering cases, an individual who is sentenced may receive prison time, probation, both prison and probation, or neither (typically a fine of some kind). Unlike the situation with tax and money laundering sentences, where few cases were sentenced for both tax and money laundering violations, most tax cases have both prison and probation components. For instance, in the 50 states and for the years 1998–2001, there were 21,604 tax sentences. Only 507 cases received neither prison nor probation, while 11,719 cases received both. There were 11,660 tax sentences resulting in prison sentences, but only 2,941 of these cases were prison-only sentences. The overlap in money laundering sentenced cases was similar.

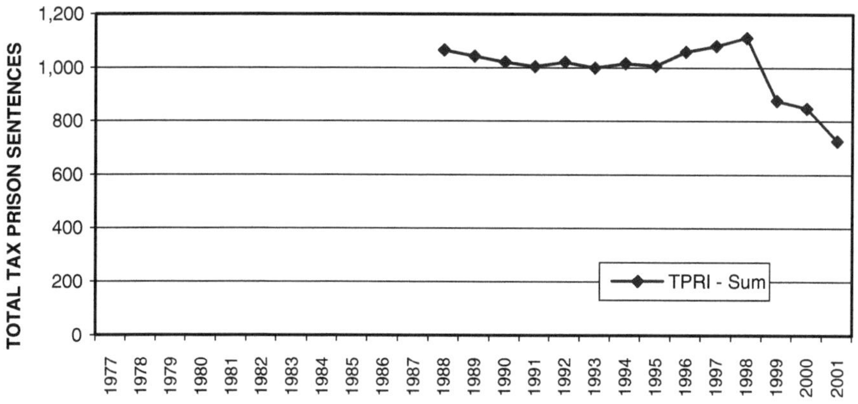

Fig. 6.42 Number of tax prison sentences

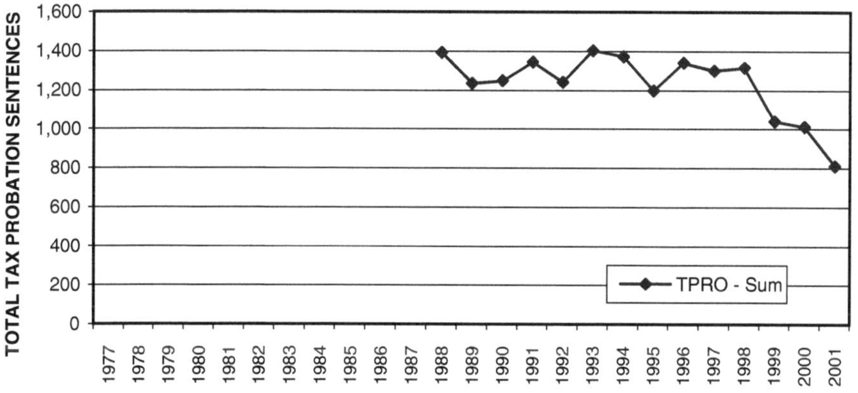

Fig. 6.43 Number of tax probation sentences

Of 11,865 sentenced money laundering cases, 164 received neither prison nor probation, while 7,789 received both sentence types.

With respect to the way cases are disposed, I see that tax cases that received prison sentences (*TPRI*) averaged 1,037 per annum from 1989 to 1998. After 1998, there was a decline in this level to 726 cases per annum in 2001. I show this decline in Fig. 6.42. The number of tax cases that received probation (*TPRO*) fluctuated around 1,300 cases per annum from 1988 to 1998. In 2001, the amount declined to 811 cases per annum. I show this decline in Fig. 6.43. Money laundering cases receiving prison sentences (*MPRI*) increased dramatically from 80 cases per annum in 1988 to 1,041 cases per annum in 1994. There was an average of 863 cases per annum in the subsequent years from 1995 to 2001, with 785 cases per annum in 2001. I show this trend in Fig. 6.44. Money laundering cases

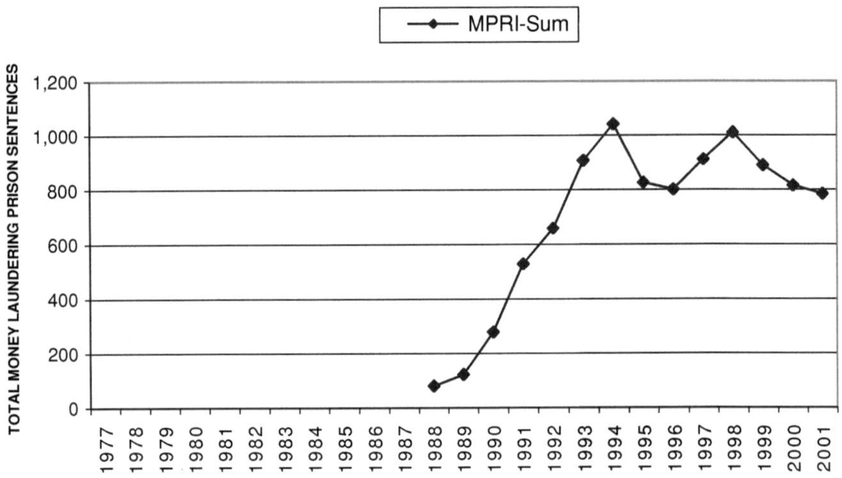

Fig. 6.44 Number of money laundering prison sentences

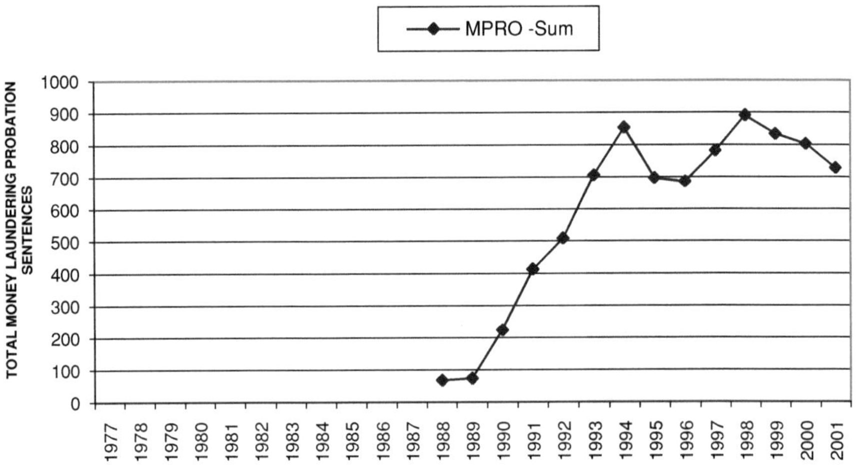

Fig. 6.45 Number of money laundering probation sentences

receiving probation (*MPRO*) followed a very similar pattern, rising from 68 cases per annum in 1988 to 727 cases per annum by 2001. I show this rise in Fig. 6.45.

Media attention for tax cases rose between 1992 and 1997. It then fell starting in 1998, continuing to decline through 2001.[4] I show this trend in Fig. 6.46. Media

[4] The media variable I obtained provided the number of cases that received media attention and the type of media coverage given (i.e. newspaper, television, or radio). However, the data did not reveal the amount of media attention a case received.

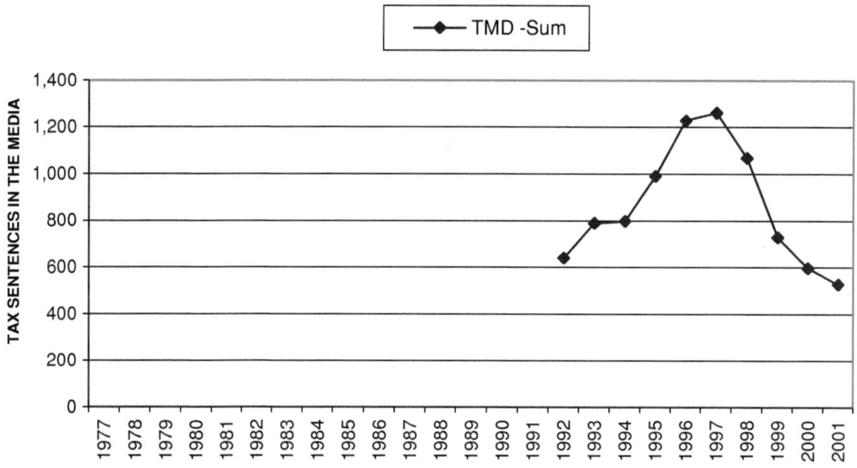

Fig. 6.46 Tax sentences in the media

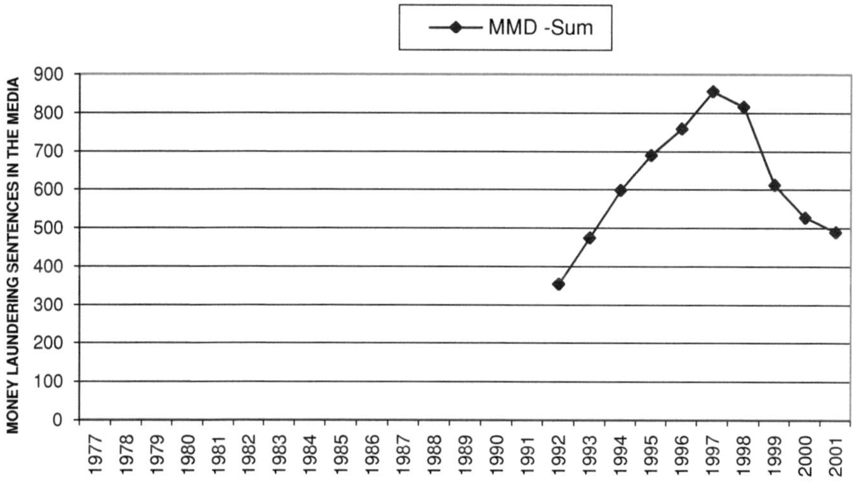

Fig. 6.47 Money laundering sentences in the media

attention for money laundering cases followed a similar pattern, peaking in 1997. This trend is seen in Fig. 6.47.

Cases receiving media attention (*MD*) rose from 1,102 in 1992 to 2,539 per annum in 1997. However, more recently, the coverage of CI cases in the media has declined to 1992 levels (when such figures were first tracked by the CI division). I show this trend in Fig. 6.48.

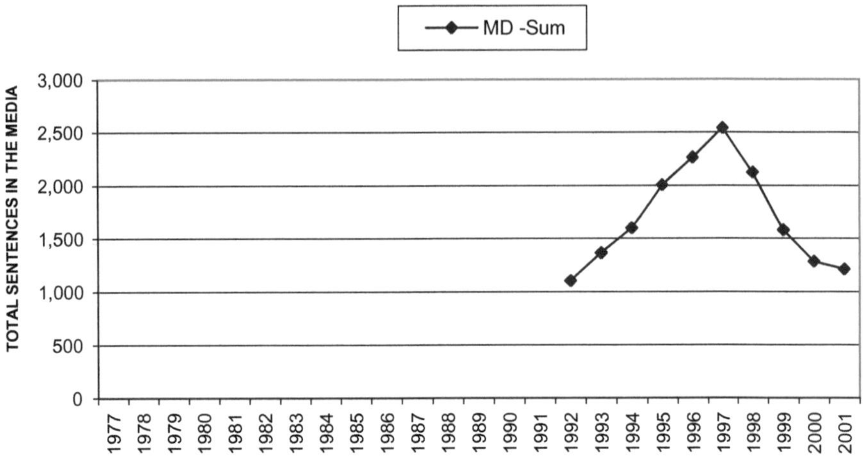

Fig. 6.48 Total sentences in the media

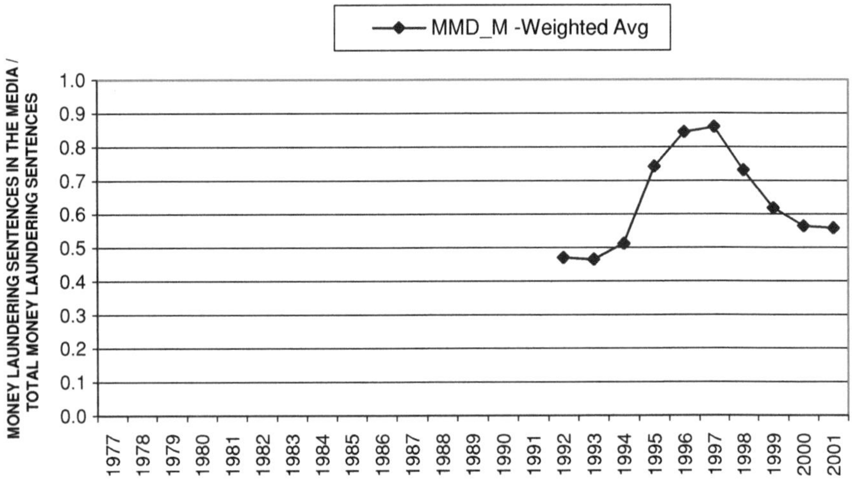

Fig. 6.49 Money laundering sentences in the media/total money laundering sentences

Money laundering cases receiving media attention as a percentage of all money laundering cases (*MMD_M*) rose and fell with general media interest. I show this relationship in Fig. 6.49.

Tax cases receiving media attention as a percentage of all tax cases (*TMD_T*) showed a similar pattern. I show this trend in Fig. 6.50. Not much distinguishes the pattern in these two factors.

Tax cases receiving media attention as a percentage of all media cases (*TMD_MD*) and money laundering cases receiving media attention as a percentage

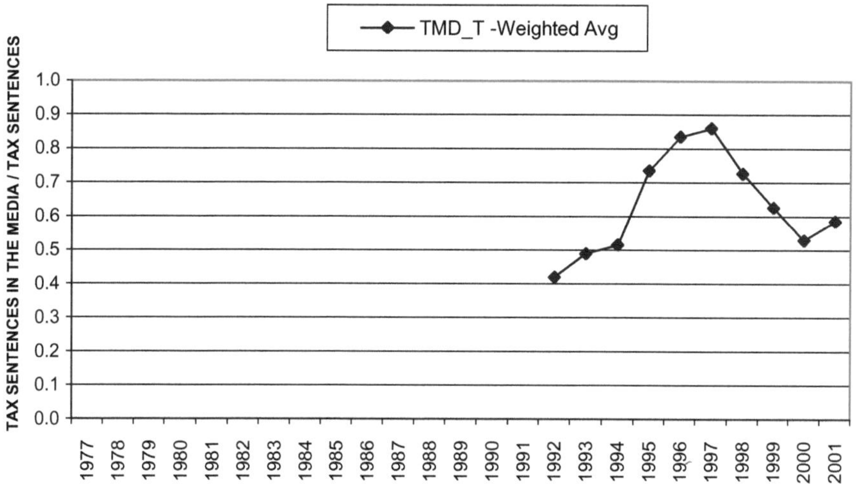

Fig. 6.50 Tax sentences in the media/tax sentences

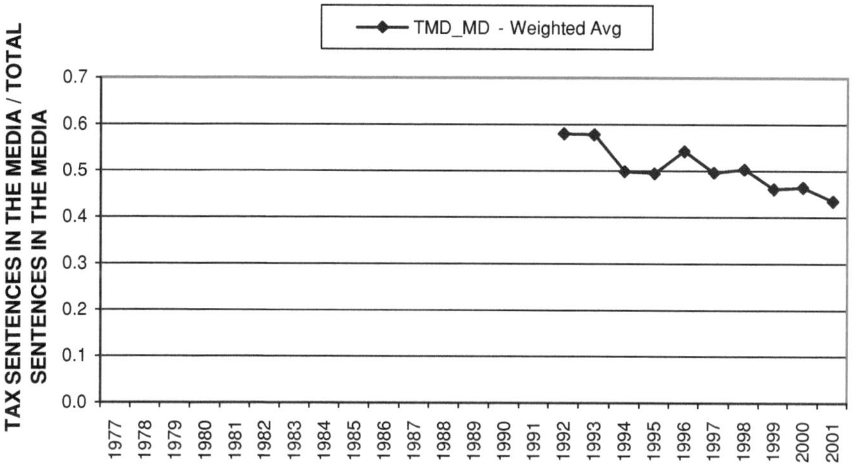

Fig. 6.51 Tax sentences in the media/total sentences in the media

of all media cases (*MMD_MD*) show some modest variation, with money laundering cases receiving a growing percentage of coverage by the media. I show this relationship in Figs. 6.51 and 6.52, respectively.

These two categories do not exclusively exhaust media attention, but the residual coverage is very small in percentage terms. Media cases generally, as a percentage of all CI cases (*MD_TOT*), reveal the same bell-shaped trend as did

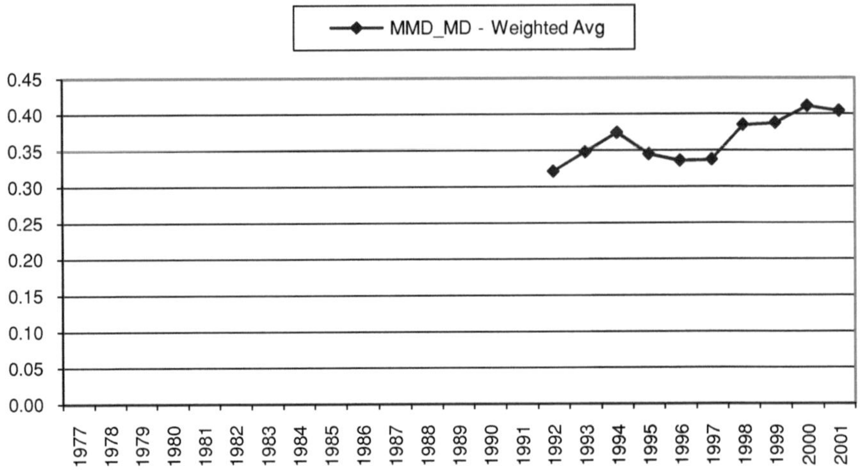

Fig. 6.52 Money laundering media sentences/total media sentences

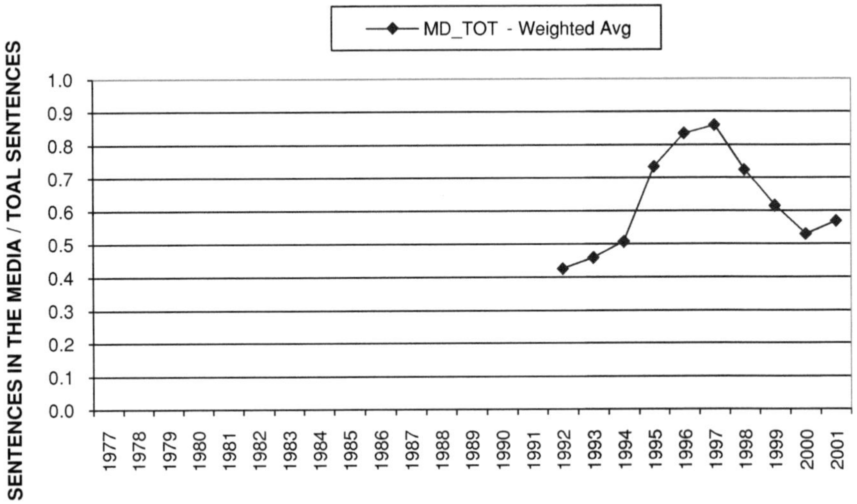

Fig. 6.53 Sentences in the media/total sentences

aggregate media cases. I show this trend in Fig. 6.53. Given the relative constancy of the CI cases and the pattern of media coverage, this is not a surprising outcome.

With respect to sentencing, the patterns are more dramatic. The percentage of all money laundering cases where the defendant received a prison sentence (*MPRI_M*) has grown from 60.6% in 1988 to 87.4% in 1992. During the last decade, this rate has grown further to 91.5% of money laundering cases in 1997. I show this growth in Fig. 6.54. This growth cannot be attributed to mandatory

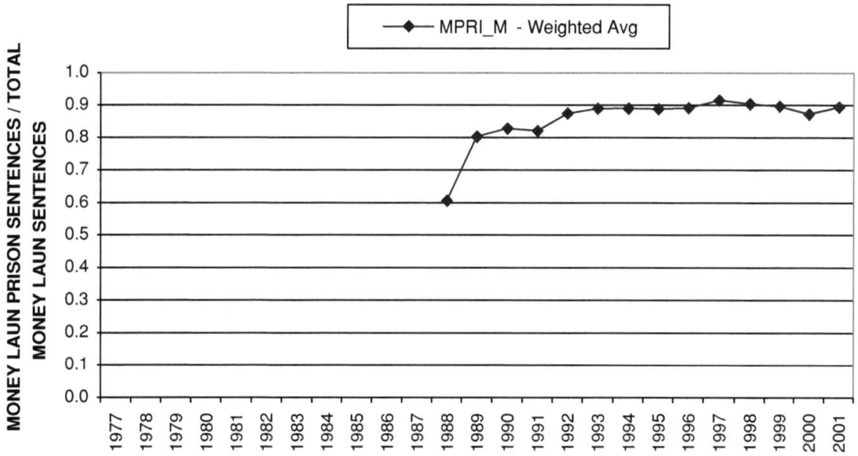

Fig. 6.54 Laun prison sentences/total money laun sentences

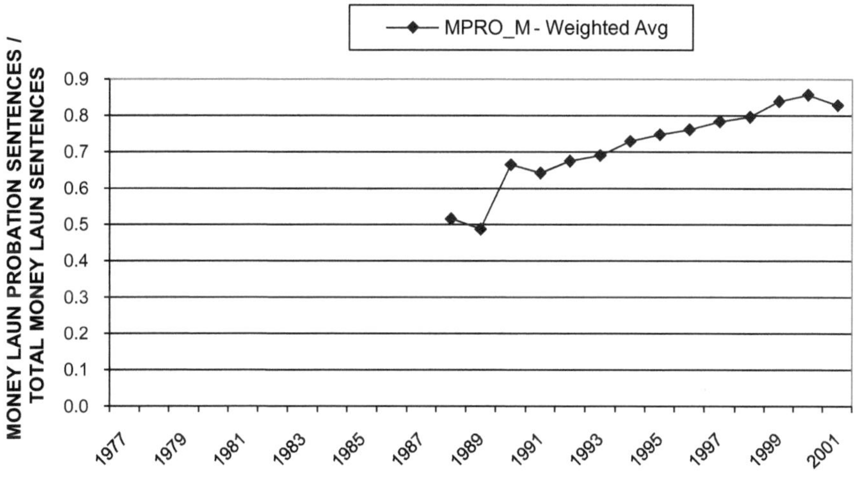

Fig. 6.55 Laun probation sentences/total money laun sentences

sentencing guidelines in place during this period and must reflect an increase in efficiency of the CI in choosing cases.

Similarly, the percentage of CI money laundering cases receiving probation (*MPRO_M*) grew from 51.5% in 1988 to 85.7% in 2000. I show this increase in Fig. 6.55.

The CI division has also managed to improve its sentencing rate for prison and probation among its tax cases. The percentage of CI tax cases receiving prison

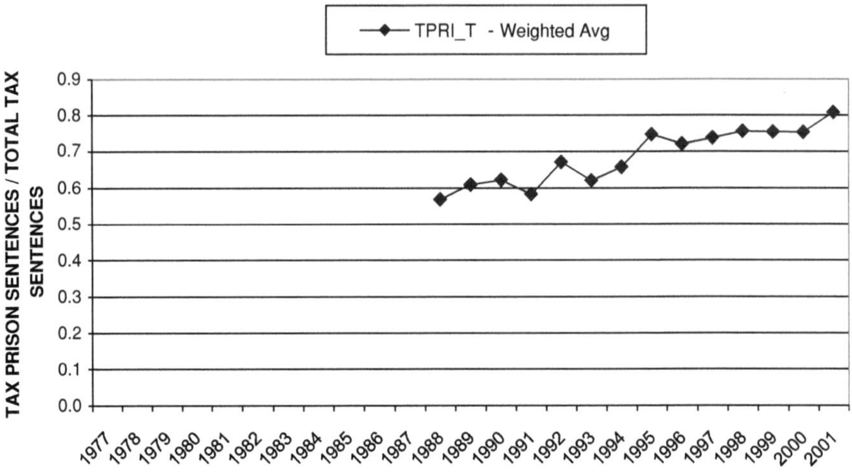

Fig. 6.56 Tax prison sentences/total tax sentences

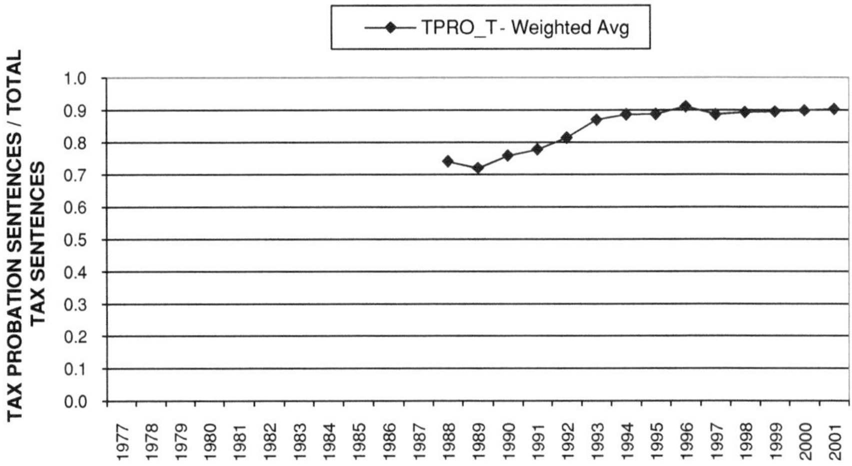

Fig. 6.57 Tax probation sentences/total tax sentences

sentences (*TPRI_T*) rose from 56.8% in 1988 to 80.8% in 2001. I show this increase in Fig. 6.56.

Similarly, the percentage of tax cases receiving probation among all CI tax cases (*TPRO_T*) rose from 74.1% in 1988 to 90.2% in 2001. I show this increase in Fig. 6.57.

I can compare the trends in CI sentencing activity to the period from 1978 to 1988. Dubin et al. (1990) analyzed several factors related to CI activity in their

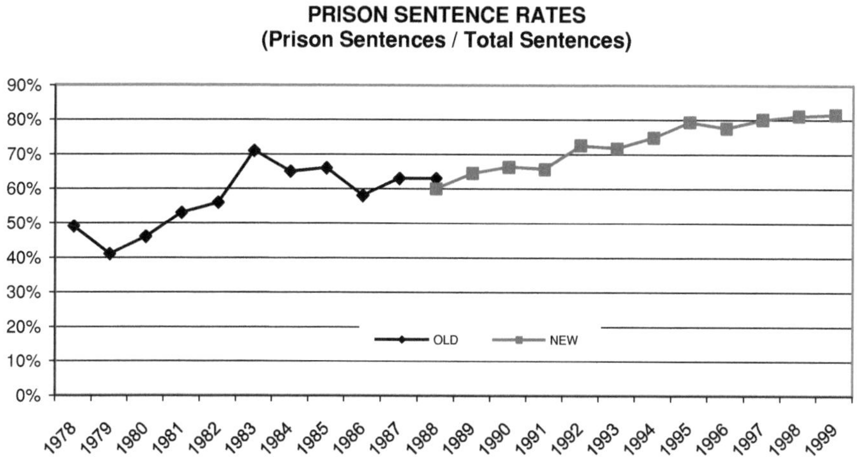

Fig. 6.58 Prison sentence rates (prison sentences/total sentences)

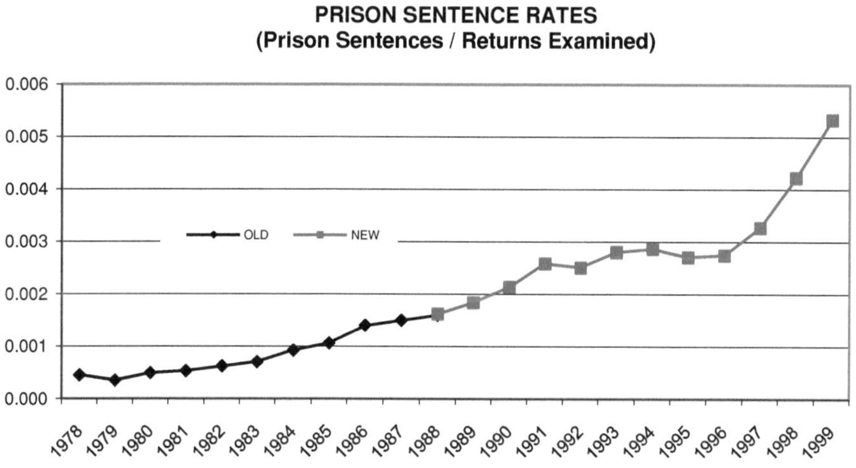

Fig. 6.59 Prison sentence rates (prison sentences/returns examined)

article, "The Changing Face of Tax Enforcement 1978–1988." DGW examined a factor for prison sentence rates defined as the number of CI cases receiving prison sentences to total sentences. Ignoring a few cases, this is simply $(MPRI + TPRI)/TOTAL$. Figure 6.58 shows how the trend seen in the 1978–1988 time period has continued, with an increasingly large percentage of cases receiving a prison sentence.

This trend is also reflected in the rate of prison sentences received as compared with individual returns filed. Dramatic increases in prison sentences may also be

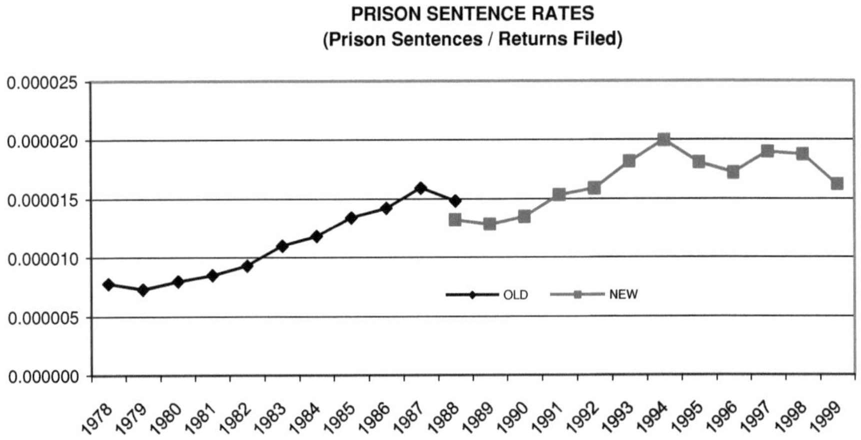

Fig. 6.60 Prison sentence rates (prison sentences/returns filed)

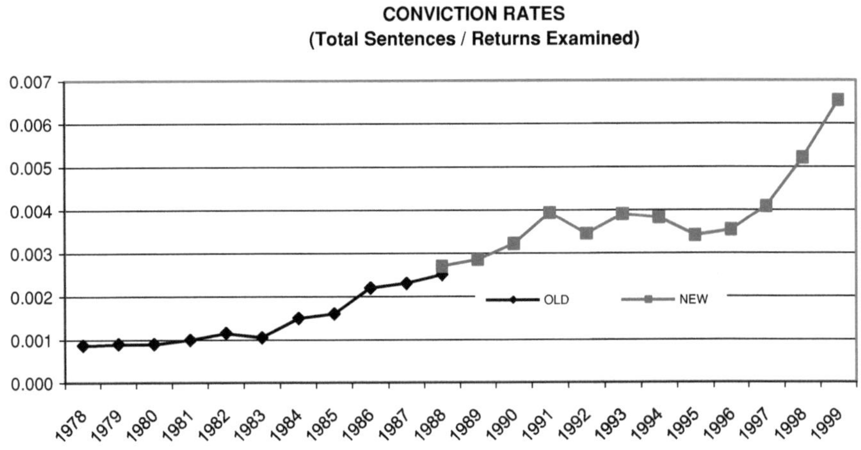

Fig. 6.61 Conviction rates (total sentences/returns examined)

seen when comparing the number of cases receiving prison sentences to the number of returns examined. However, Fig. 6.59 also makes clear that the prison sentence rate is more than 100 times smaller than the audit examination rate for individuals Fig. 6.60.

Conviction rates have also increased in comparison to the 1978–1988 period. Here, I define the conviction rate as the total number of CI cases that are sentenced as compared to returns examined. Figure 6.61 demonstrates the rapid increase in conviction rates for the CI division. However, as noted by DGW, the sentences at issue may not be a result of cases that are selected for tax examination.

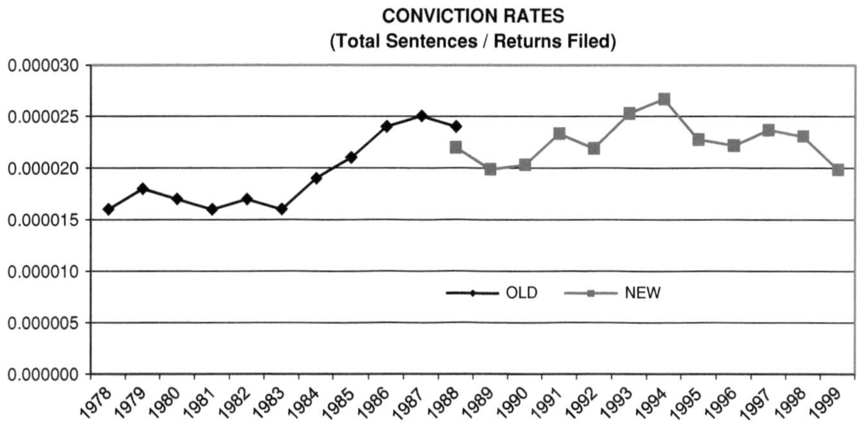

Fig. 6.62 Conviction rates (total sentences/returns filed)

Total sentences as compared to returns filed shows a slight increase, but the magnitude of the rate is again quite small compared with audit activity in general. I show the trend in this factor in Fig. 6.62.

With a detailed review of the data accomplished we proceed in the next chapter to the estimation of the econometric models.

Appendix

Geographic Representation of Selected Variables from this Chapter

See Figs. 6.1, 6.2, 6.3, 6.4, 6.6, 6.8, 6.10, 6.11, 6.12, 6.14, 6.15, 6.16, 6.17, 6.19, 6.40, 6.41, 6.53, 6.54, 6.55, 6.56 and 6.57.

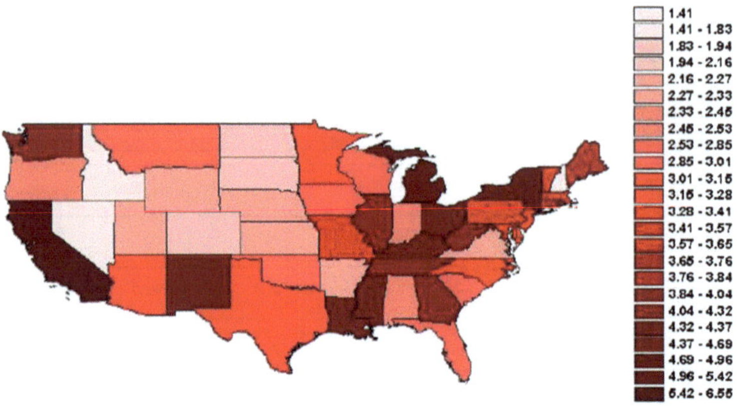

Fig. 6.1 Percentage of families on welfare

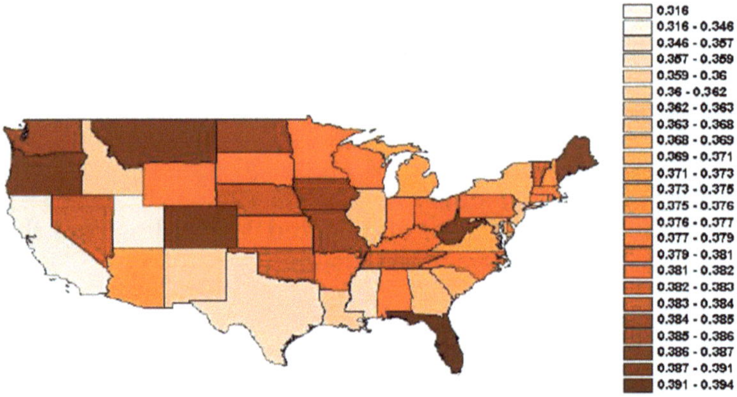

Fig. 6.2 Number of households per capita

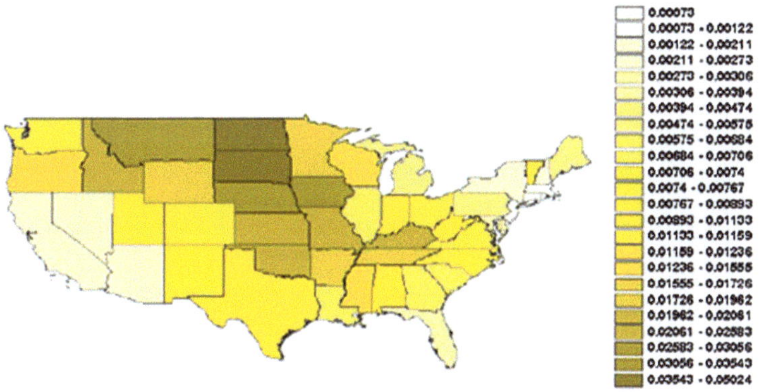

Fig. 6.3 Number of farms per household

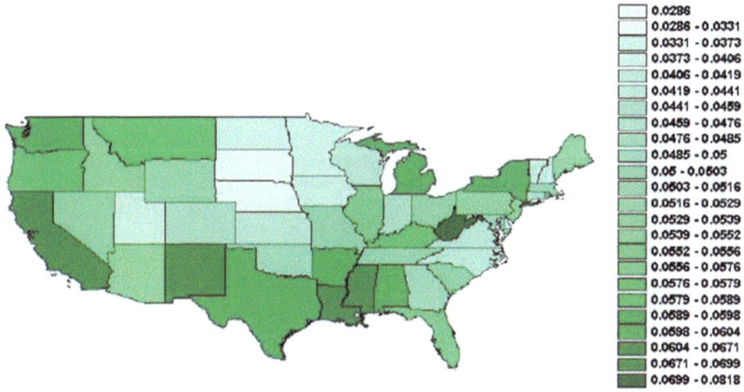

Fig. 6.4 Unemployment rate

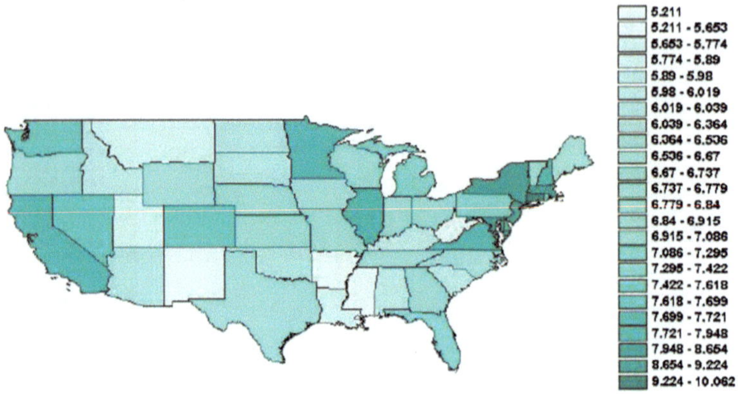

Fig. 6.6 Personal income per capita

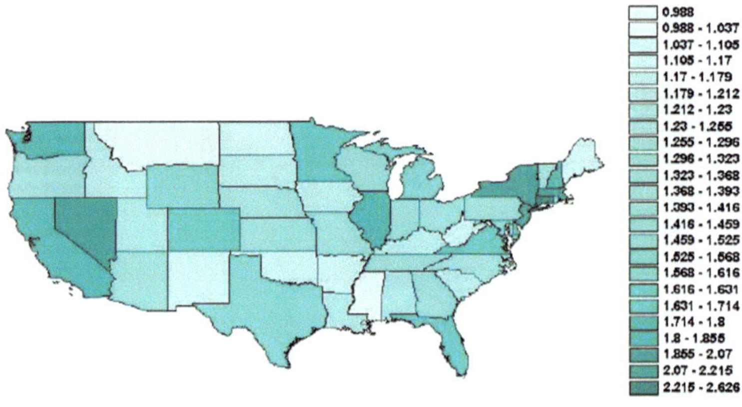

Fig. 6.8 Reported tax liability per return ($000's)

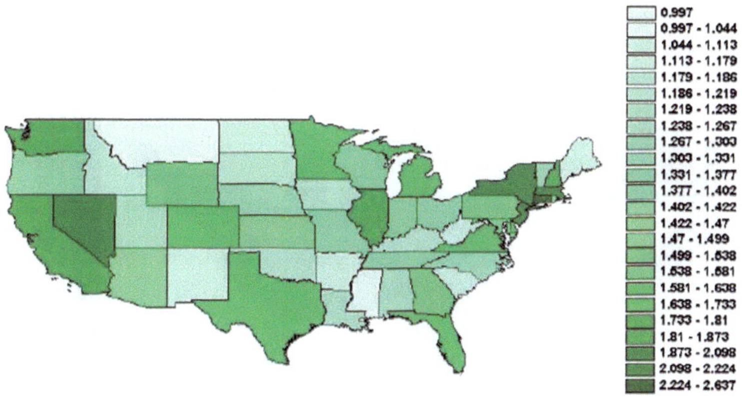

Fig. 6.10 Assessed tax liability per return ($000's)

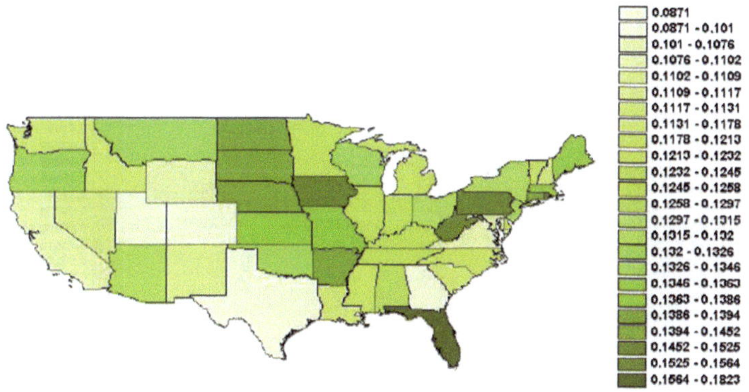

Fig. 6.11 Population over 65/total population

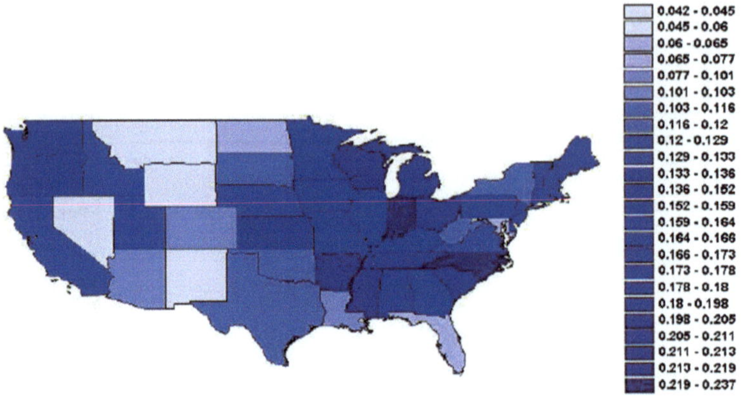

Fig. 6.12 Proportion of the labor force in manufacturing

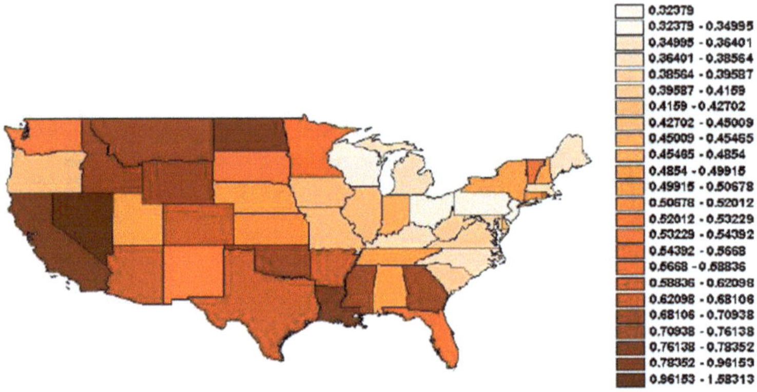

Fig. 6.14 Individual audit rate (%)

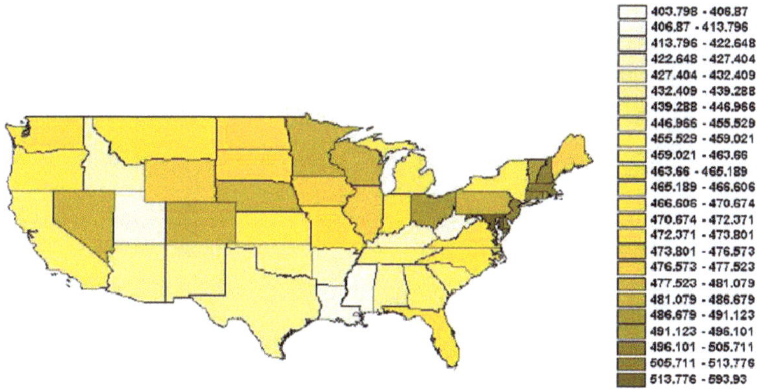

Fig. 6.15 Returns filed per capita (per 1,000 persons)

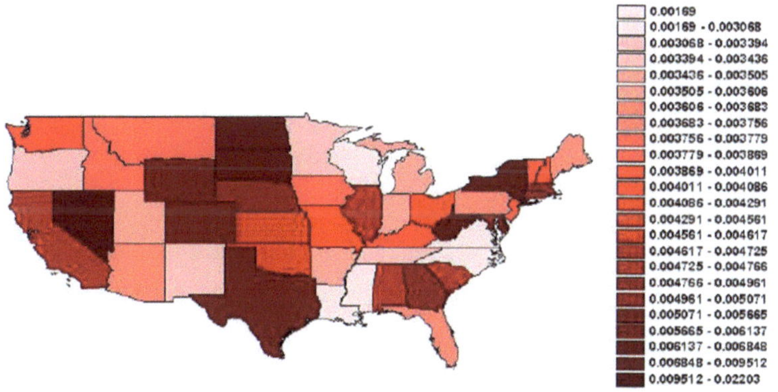

Fig. 6.16 Budget per return ($000's)

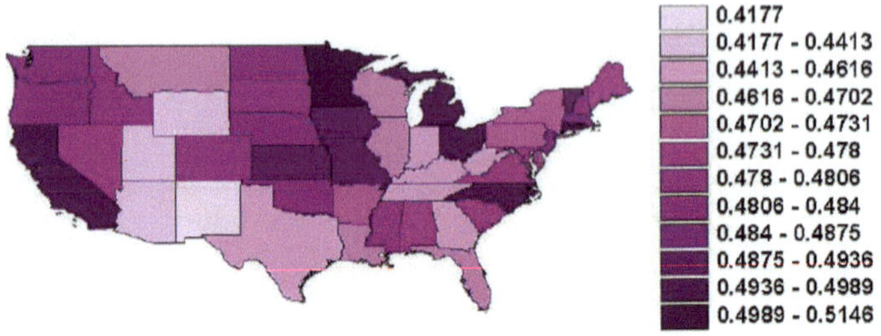

Fig. 6.17 Direct examination time

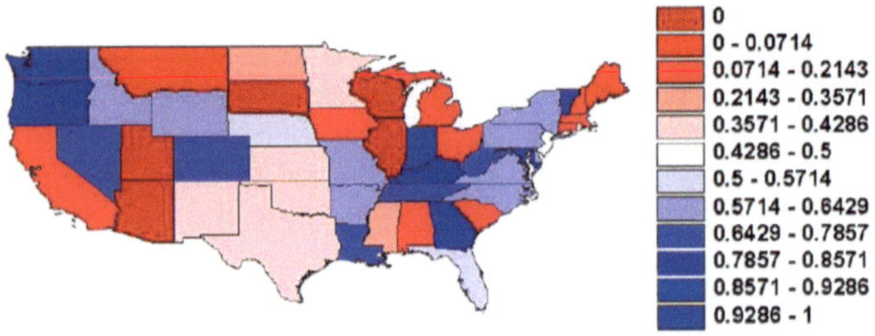

Fig. 6.19 Political party of governor (1 = Democrat)

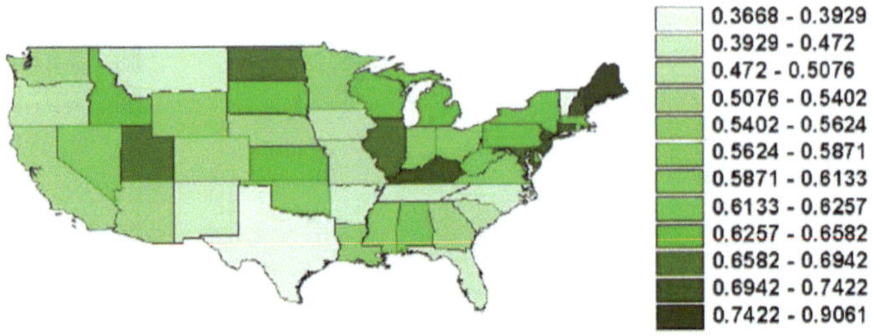

Fig. 6.40 Proportion of tax sentences to total sentences

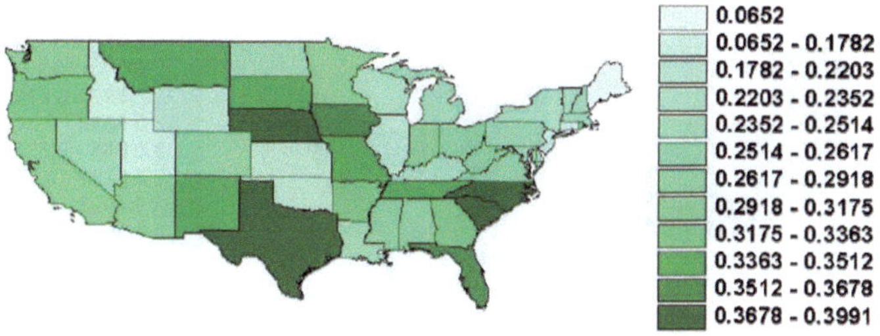

Fig. 6.41 Proportion of money laundering sentences to total sentences

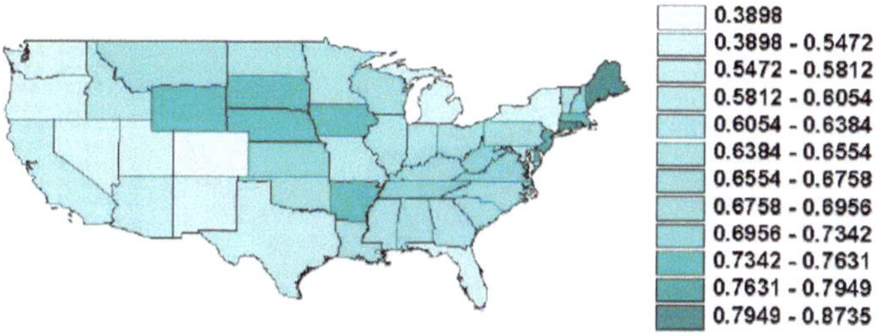

Fig. 6.53 Proportion of total sentences receiving media exposure

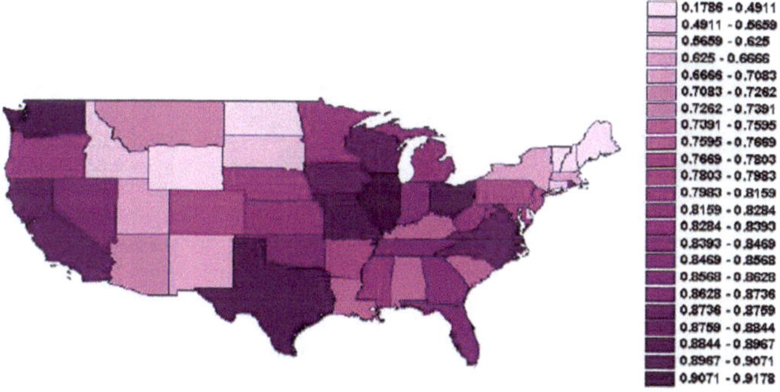

Fig. 6.54 Money laundering cases resulting in prison/total money laundering cases

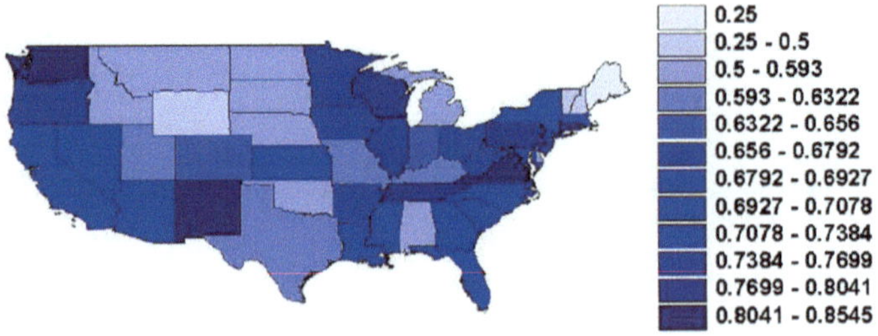

Fig. 6.55 Proportion of money laundering sentences resulting in probation

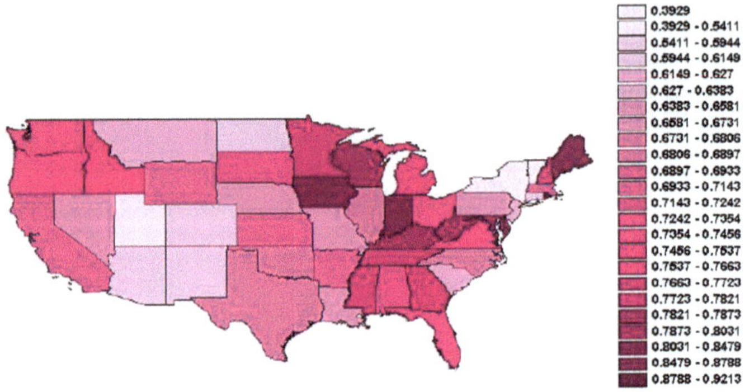

Fig. 6.56 Tax cases resulting in prison/total tax cases

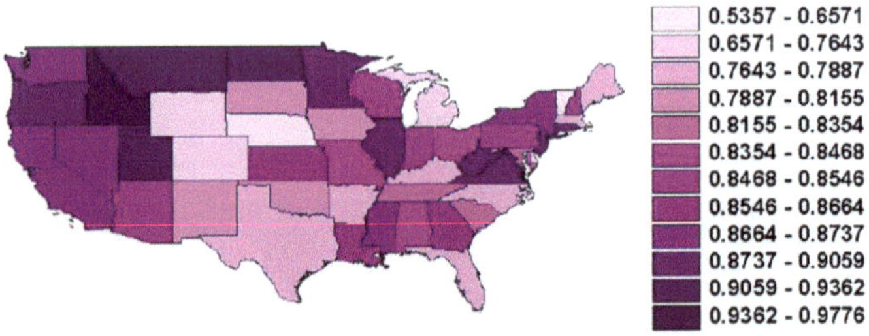

Fig. 6.57 Proportion of tax sentences resulting in probation

Chapter 7
IRS Criminal Enforcement Activities and Taxpayer Noncompliance

Introduction

This chapter's purpose is to answer several basic questions. First, does CI have a measurable effect on voluntary compliance, which includes both civil and criminal tax laws? Second, if CI does have a measurable effect on voluntary compliance, what mix of CI investigations has the greatest influence on voluntary compliance? CI investigates two broad categories of cases: tax violations and money laundering violations. A subsidiary inquiry is whether either or both types of cases have an effect on voluntary compliance with the tax laws. Third, does media attention and publicity on IRS audits and criminal investigations increase the compliance effect? Fourth, do convictions that result in prison sentences affect compliance differently from cases that result in probation?

In this chapter, I empirically test whether the IRS's enforcement activities affect taxpayer compliance.[1] I replicate and extend the original DGW analysis to include factors that measure CI activity. The time period covered by the new model is 1988–2001. I reach several conclusions. First, I find that CI activities have a measurable effect on voluntary compliance. I found statistically significant results from my measure of CI sentenced cases on general tax deference. Second, I conclude that the mix of sentenced cases (tax and money laundering) is not a significant determinant of tax compliance, perhaps because the mix has already been optimally set. Third, media attention shows some weak evidence of increasing compliance at least among money laundering cases. It is logical to think that media attention plays an important role in disseminating information to the public. Thus, the significant magnitude of general deterrence results implies that media plays a large role in CI cases. Finally, I find that incarceration

[1] The Webster Report (Review of the IRS' Criminal Investigation Division (William Webster), April 1999, observed that a previous lack of empirical evidence "makes it impossible to prove that the cases CI has investigated previously and is currently investigating either do or do not foster compliance." In this chapter, I provide the empirical evidence that Judge Webster sought.

J. A. Dubin, *The Causes and Consequences of Income Tax Noncompliance*,

DOI: 10.1007/978-1-4419-0907-7_7,

and probation (rather than fines) have the most influence on taxpayers. An emphasis on prison and probation sentences should be encouraged based on these results.

I also performed simulations to determine the direct revenue (spillover) effects of audits and CI activities. I find that the direct effect of doubling the tax audit rate on assessed collections (reported amounts and additional taxes and penalties) is $18.7 billion. Doubling CI tax and money laundering sentences is forecasted to increase assessed collections by $16.7 billion. I estimate the spillover effects from both audit and CI activates to be approximately 94%. Doubling the audit rate or doubling money laundering sentences produced similar increases in total collections. Finally, based on historical cost estimates for the unit costs of audits versus CI case convictions, I find some evidence indicating a beneficial reallocation of resources from audits to criminal investigations.

Model Specification

As discussed above, this chapter's purpose is to update and extend DGW (1990) to analyze the role of CI activities on taxpayer noncompliance. The DGW empirical analysis was based on two models that are both estimated using a state level time-series cross-section. One model specified reported taxes per return filed as a function of audit rates and a variety of socioeconomic control variables. The other model specified returns filed per capita as a function of the same variables.

Dependent Variables

The dependent variables are (1) *ALR* (Assessed Liability Per Return): reported individual income tax plus additional tax and penalty recommended after examination divided by the number of individual income tax returns filed, in 1972 dollars; (2) *RTR* (Reported Taxes Per Return): reported individual income tax divided by the number of individual tax returns filed, in 1972 dollars; and (3) *RCAP* (Returns Per Capita): reported total individual income tax returns filed divided by total population.

Independent Variables

DGW selected explanatory variables for the "reporting effect" equation based on two considerations: the size of the tax base and the taxpayers' compliance behavior.[2] The variables primarily related to the tax base are *PER65*, *HOUSES*, and *PWELFAM*. The variables related to both the tax base and taxpayers' compliance behavior are *UR*, *PICAP*, and *STAXR*. The variables primarily related to the taxpayers' compliance behavior are *PERED*, *PMAN*, *PSERV*, *FRMFAM*, and IAR2.[3]

Compliance factors include variables to measure the nature and extent of CI activities. I treat CI activities as exogenous both on theoretical and empirical grounds. First, CI activity is largely a result of cases discovered and selected for examination that arise independent of tax gap or noncompliance issues. Second, Hausman (1978) specification tests for endogeneity of the CI enforcement factors did not reveal endogenous behavior.

Incorporating Criminal Investigations into the DGW Framework

In principle, the additions to the original DGW study to accommodate criminal investigation factors are straightforward. In fact, the task is far more complex than simply creating and matching various factors from CI and then adding these factors to the basic model. For example, individuals face a complex decision process when dealing with criminal activity. An individual may be deterred from tax evasion, money laundering, or other criminal acts based on the likelihood of being caught. This deterrence possibility has been the empirical paradigm of modern criminal analysis. In this approach, a potential criminal may be deterred from committing a crime due to a sufficiently high probability of being caught and receiving a sufficiently severe penalty. Of course, not all individuals are rational actors with respect to the crimes they commit. However, a rational calculus applied to crime and punishment is a benchmark test and provides policy makers with justification for increasing enforcement levels or changing the enforcement mix. Ultimately, the manner in which individuals respond is an empirical matter. Thus in this approach, I assume that individuals consider the likelihood that they will be detected and punished.

With respect to civil audit examination, a measure such as the audit rate may be significant to a potential tax evader because it measures the probability that the taxpayer will be subjected to an audit. In the current setting, the natural analog to the audit rate is the rate at which CI investigations are commenced or the rate at which prosecutions are recommended. Prosecution rates are, in fact,

---

[2] As discussed in Chap. 5, the effects of these variables on reported taxes per return are based on conventional theoretical considerations.

[3] I expected increases in the federal audit rate (IAR2) to increase taxpayer compliance (and thus reported taxes per return). However, audit rates presumably respond to compliance levels. Therefore, I treat the federal audit rate as an enodogenous factor.

quite small for individual taxpayers. As I noted above, these prosecution rates may be orders of magnitude smaller than the individual audit rate. A compounding factor is that not all cases recommended for prosecution lead to indictments, and not all indictments lead to sentencing. In contrast, the audit rate leads to an audit whether or not a change in the taxpayer's liability is recommended. By focusing on cases sentenced, an exposure measure is produced that is closer to the audit rate but results in a factor that, in relative magnitude to the population at large, is quite small. Additionally, as a matter of general deterrence, it is believed that individuals respond to the probability of detection. The question remains as to how they learn the rates at which they are likely to be caught. Attention by the media would seem to be the most likely forum by which taxpayers become aware of the likelihood that their crimes will be detected. Therefore, those cases that are successfully prosecuted and sentenced and receive some media attention would appear to be most relevant. Finally, taxpayers may be concerned only with the sentences that result in incarceration or probation as compared to monetary fines. Thus, the subset of sentenced cases that result in non-monetary fines may be relevant to taxpayers.

Taxpayers may respond to the probability of an audit in a rational calculus that affects their decision to file a tax return or the degree to which they file an honest and correct return. This theory is known as deterrence theory in the literature. It has also been persuasively argued that taxpayers may react to the actions of other taxpayers, especially as those actions concern notions of fairness and support for their decisions to voluntarily comply with the law. This theory of taxpayer behavior is known as assurance theory (see, e.g. Roth et al. 1989; Scholz 1998; Scholz and Lubell 1998a,b). Models of conformity and social dynamics (see e.g. Durlauf and Young 2001) postulate that the utility of a given decision may in part be determined by the expected actions of others. Models of social dynamics bridge the deterrence and assurance theories of taxpayer compliance. Manski (1993, 1995) has shown that for linear models with aggregate data there is an inherent identification problem that may not allow the theoretical issue to be resolved empirically.[4]

As an empirical matter, many non-exclusive approaches could have significance. Among the choices are: (1) separating tax and money laundering cases; (2) separating media cases from non-media cases; and (3) the sentencing mix. With three types of CI cases (tax, money laundering, and other), media (Yes versus No, or type of coverage), and at least three sentencing outcomes, variables that can be used to measure CI activities quickly expand relative to the available years and geographic locations available for analysis. My approach simplified the relevant

[4] Our finding that CI enforcement levels are significant determinants of taxpayer compliance would reinforce the assurance theory aspects of behavior rather than the deterrence theory. Conversely, the empirical support for significant audit rates found in this study and others suggest that deterrence theory is valid for some types of taxpayer behavior.

set of CI factors as much as possible, while considering specifications and models that would allow a full picture to emerge.

Dynamic Specifications

In this section, we consider several alternative models for dynamic relationships between audit activity, reported taxes due, and additional taxes and penalties. The model of DGW (1990) is a steady-state equilibrium relationship. It is assumed that all effects are in long-run equilibrium. However, as audit rates change, taxpayers are assumed to change behavior and modify their reported taxes due. At first blush, it is reasonable to assume that reported taxes in a given year react to audit rates that prevail in that year. However, the typical IRS audit cycle may not initiate an audit for several years following the filling of a tax return. Taxpayers, in this situation, must react to their expectation of future audit rate levels. Alternatively, the additional taxes and penalties reported in a given tax year may to some degree depend on the audits of tax returns from previous years. Hence, additional taxes and penalties may be some function of past audit rate levels.

Finally, taxpayers may change their reported taxes due in a continuous adjustment to a new target level. There may be the perception, by some taxpayers, that a rapid or discontinuous (abrupt) change in behavior may be a signal to the IRS of an existing or current tax problem. Such taxpayers may adjust their reported taxes based on a mixture of taxes reported in the previous year and the optimal level of taxes due based on existing or current conditions.

To illustrate these three possibilities we adopt some notation for panel models. The DGW (1988) model may be written:

$$Y_{it} = X_{it}\beta + Z_{it}\gamma + \varepsilon_{it} \tag{7.1}$$

where

Y_{it} =	Reported taxes at time t and for state i
X_{it} =	Endogenous factors (audit rates) measured at time t and for state i
Z_{it} =	Exogenous factors (tax rates, family size, age distribution, etc.) measured at time t and state i
ε_{it}=	Random (unobserved) component of the model
β and γ =	Unknown coefficient vectors to be estimated

DGW (1988) adopted this panel data structure using state level and time-series data. They assumed that audit rates were endogenous and further assumed a random error components structure for ε_{it} with:

$$\varepsilon_{it} = \mu_i + \xi_{it} \tag{7.2}$$

where μ_i is a random effect specific to the state and ξ_{it} is a random effect that is time and state specific. This error structure leads to temporal correlation of the observations for each state (due to the persistent and random μ_i) and is optimally estimated using generalized least squares.

An alternative to model (7.1) is that individuals react to expected audit rates which are themselves formed at time period t and are based on the experiences up to time period t of past audit rates. Equation 7.1 becomes:

$$Y_{it} = X_{it}\beta_0 + X_{it-1}\beta_1 + X_{it-2}\beta_2 + Z_{it}\gamma + \varepsilon_{it} \tag{7.3}$$

where expected audit rates for time period t are assumed to be

$$X^*_{it} = X_{it}\ \beta^*_0 + X_{it-1}\beta^*_1 + X_{it-2}\beta^*_2 \tag{7.4}$$

(Three periods are used here as only an example. In reality, individuals may form their expectation based on either longer or shorter time-series.) The key point is that lagged audit rates may be relevant in the basic model.

Alternatively, additional taxes and penalties in a given year may depend on past audits. In this case, a model for reported taxes that includes additional taxes and penalties is also of the form of Eq. 7.3.

Finally, the adjustment of reported taxes based on a new equilibrium level and the past years reported taxes due may be modeled as a classic adjustment model. Suppose taxpayers adjust reported taxes in time t relative to $t - 1$ based on a fraction $(1 - \lambda)$ of the difference between the optimal level at time period t, Y^*_{it} and last year's reported tax level Y_{it-1}:

$$Y_{it} - Y_{it-1} = (1 - \lambda)[Y^*_{it} - Y_{it-1}] \tag{7.5}$$

Rewriting Eq. 7.5, we have:

$$\begin{aligned} Y_{it} &= Y_{it-1} - (1 - \lambda)Y_{it-1} + (1 - \lambda)Y^*_{it-1} \\ Y_{it} &= \lambda\ Y_{it-1} + (1 - \lambda)Y^*_{it} \end{aligned} \tag{7.6}$$

Hence, taxes reported in time period t are a weighted combination of last years taxes due and the current optimal level. Large values of λ (near 1) reflect slow adjustment while small values of λ reflect immediate adjustment to the equilibrium level Y^*. If Y^*_{it} is given by the model of DGW (1988) (reflecting steady state equilibrium), then Eq. 7.6 suggests that the DGW specification be modified to include lagged dependent variables to account for the dynamic adjustments. The final form of this model is:

$$Y_{it} = \lambda Y_{it-1} + X_{it}\beta + Z_{it}\gamma + \varepsilon_{it} \tag{7.7}$$

Estimation of (7.7) is complicated by the endogeneity of Y_{it-1} in the equation. Ordinary least squares estimates are inconsistent, in the panel context, when lagged values are included because these variables are correlated with the current values of the residuals ε_{it} as they are determined in part by the random component μ_i (μ_i determines Y_{it} and Y_{it-1} to the same degree). This situation is similar to the problem of estimating a non-panel dynamic model when the residuals are auto-regressive. Balestra and Nerlove (1966) discussed this model and derived a consistent estimator based on lagged values of the independent variables in Eq. 7.7. An alternative approach to estimation has been to transform the equation of interest (7.7) by first differencing and then using instrumental variables. Applying first-differences to Eq. 7.7 yields:

$$Y_{it} - Y_{it-1} = (X_{it} - X_{it-1})\beta + (Z_{it} - Z_{it-1})\gamma + \lambda(Y_{it-1} - Y_{it-2}) + (\varepsilon_{it} - \varepsilon_{it-1}) \quad (7.8)$$

This transformation removes the individual effect of μ_I from the equation as $(\varepsilon_{it} - \varepsilon_{it-1}) = (\mu_i - \mu_i) + (\varepsilon_{it} - \varepsilon_{it-1})$. The resulting disturbance $(\varepsilon_{it} - \varepsilon_{it-1})$ is a moving average process. Importantly, the correlation between Y_{it-1} and the residual $(\varepsilon_{it} - \varepsilon_{it-1})$ is still present. However, instrumental variables may be used to consistently estimate the coefficients as Y_{it-2}, Y_{it-3}, and $(Y_{it-2} - Y_{it-3})$ are each uncorrelated with the residual $(\varepsilon_{it} - \varepsilon_{it-1})$ but correlated with the term $(Y_{it} - Y_{it-1})$. This procedure is due to Anderson and Hsiao (1981). See also Anderson and Hsiao (1982). These models were extended by Arellano (1989) and Arellano and Bond (1991). In practice the Anderson-Hsiao method (while not fully efficient) performs satisfactorily compared to the generalized method of moments methods of Arellano-Bond [see e.g. Kiviet (1995)].

The dynamic structure of the reporting and response to charges in enforcement levels is feasibly estimated using dynamic panel analysis. Complications include the short panel available for estimation and the endogeneity of lagged dependent variables. Our attempts to measure these effects indicate that a short-term dynamic is most likely at work with the majority of adjustment occurring within two to three years after a change in tax policy. Interestingly, this period of time for adjustment and audit expectation formation naturally corresponds to the audit cycle itself. It is possible, however, that a shorter audit cycle would change the consumer dynamic response. Further, not all additional taxes and penalties that are recommended are assessed and not all assessments are collected. In sum, a change in enforcement levels may take two to three years to be reflected in reported taxes and additional taxes and penalties. The latter component may take still longer to be collected. Any attempt to increase IRS compliance whether through an increase in audit rates or criminal investigations will consequently produce a general deterrence response after a short-term lag.

Empirical Investigation

As discussed, the original DGW model used data for the years 1977–1986. Adding data for later years more than doubled the observations. However, the overall explanatory power of the model fell in this full data period. This change, coupled with changes in the pattern of coefficients for some factors, suggests that the period after 1987 (and therefore the time period considered in the original DGW study) was different from the earlier period in significant ways.

Focusing on the period after 1987, the re-estimated models show some sign changes in socioeconomic factors, including a shift in the roles played by the percentage of employed populations in manufacturing and service industries. Since these effects were previously understood in terms of the possibility for individual noncompliance and opportunities to evade, it is more likely that a change in IRS policy to focus attention on service industry geographies or a change in the relative economic conditions of these two sectors explains the change in predicted compliance.

Several empirical experiments showed that CI factors have statistical significance when considered as counts. However, little significance remains when these counts are expressed as rates. While a theoretical justification may be made for using rates as estimates of probabilities, and while probabilities are motivated by the theoretical criminology and economics literature, the empirical finding is that CI *rates* reveal low correlation with compliance. However, the finding that absolute *counts* matter is interesting and suggests that general deterrence may result from the overall level of CI activity rather than the rate at which these investigations take place. This interpretation affirms the assurance theory of CI activity.

Econometric Results

In Table 7.1, I present the estimated econometric models in a logical progression from the DGW specifications to the final models used in this study.

Model 1 replicates DGW for the period 1977–1986, using newly collected data. I used the instruments and specifications published in the original DGW article. The next model, Model 2, relies on the time period from 1988 to 2001, using IRS source data for the audit rate in later years merged with IRS Data Book audit rates, were available. Notable in this model is the switch in time periods covered and instruments employed. As the table shows, the IRS budget per return filed is a very significant factor in determining the audit rate (see the reduced form equation reported under Model 2 for the variable, *IAR*2). Also, the instrument for exam time devoted to direct examination is significant and positive in the audit reduced form. This finding implies that in districts and time periods with larger resources devoted a priori to examination, the audit rate is higher. This result is clearly logical and was expected. The revised model shows that audit rate effects remain statistically significant under IV-GLS estimation.[5] I previously discussed the changes in sign in some previously significant factors such as the percentage of employed persons in manufacturing and service industries.

Another very significant change in results concerns the effect of audit rates on filings. Previously, DGW had found that an increase in audits would lead to fewer

[5] At the margin, the estimated audit rate effects are approximately ten percent higher in the 1988–2001 period as compared to the 1977–1986 period. This result is expected when there are increasing returns to examination and a general decline in examination rates.

Table 7.1 Estimated econometric models

Variable	Model 1				Model 2				Model 3			
	ALR	RTR	RCAP	IAR	ALR	RTR	RCAP	IAR2	ALR	RTR	RCAP	AUDR12
Constant	0.59	0.55	303.24	0.89	0.24	0.27	180.34	2.14	1.50	1.53	169.02	(0.21)
	(2.94)	(2.77)	(10.18)	(1.57)	(0.70)	(0.79)	(5.13)	(3.37)	(3.55)	(3.65)	(3.49)	(−0.33)
Percent of families on welfare	−0.00023	0.00089	0.67656	0.03000	0.01515	0.01430	−0.47104	0.05970	0.00780	0.00750	−1.65160	0.09530
	(−0.03)	(0.13)	(0.69)	(1.47)	(1.85)	(1.76)	(−0.66)	(4.16)	(0.75)	(0.72)	(−1.49)	(7.97)
State tax rate	−0.0144	−0.0149	−3.4992	−0.047	−0.0042	−0.0041	−2.2240	−0.0120	−0.0250	−0.0260	−0.1850	−0.0180
	(−1.72)	(−1.79)	(−2.87)	(−1.95)	(−0.66)	(−0.64)	(−2.84)	(−0.98)	(−3.02)	(−3.05)	(−0.14)	(−1.45)
Personal income per capita	0.254	0.250	15.149	−0.244	0.338	0.339	11.608	−0.134	0.314	0.315	16.149	−0.084
	(16.88)	(16.79)	(6.76)	(−5.9)	(18.19)	(18.31)	(6.07)	(−4.24)	(16.54)	(16.65)	(7.38)	(−3.17)
Family size	−0.690	−0.679	−105.775	−2.308	−2.220	−2.318	578.597	1.131	−0.355	−0.454	349.885	1.061
	(−1.26)	(−1.23)	(−1.38)	(−1.42)	(−2.18)	(−2.29)	(5.9)	(0.6)	(−0.35)	(−0.45)	(3.13)	(0.72)
Farms per household	−3.98	−3.97	−270.12	−5.19	0.63	0.82	−191.74	3.86	−3.96	−3.79	−87.30	7.12
	(−4.46)	(−4.55)	(−1.92)	(−1.97)	(0.31)	(0.4)	(−0.59)	(1.01)	(−1.62)	(−1.55)	(−0.23)	(1.99)
Percent of adults with high school diploma	−0.16	−0.09	143.64	3.12	−0.68	−0.69	30.17	−1.19	−1.93	−1.94	90.58	0.28
	(−1.08)	(−0.59)	(6.11)	(7.87)	(−4.93)	(−5.04)	(2.5)	(−4.56)	(−6.56)	(−6.63)	(2.85)	(0.64)
Percent of Pop over 65	−0.27	−0.20	−129.67	−0.85	2.58	2.62	−397.95	−7.81	0.57	0.63	−327.82	−4.15
	(−0.56)	(−0.41)	(−1.76)	(−0.61)	(2.32)	(2.36)	(−2.87)	(−4)	(0.45)	(0.5)	(−1.84)	(−2.27)
Percent of employed persons in manufacturing	0.08	0.11	47.40	0.81	−1.00	−1.00	211.38	−0.55	−0.25	−0.25	141.15	−0.28
	(0.49)	(0.66)	(1.81)	(1.68)	(−2.98)	(−2.99)	(5.56)	(−0.86)	(−0.6)	(−0.6)	(2.52)	(−0.44)
Percent of employed persons in service	−1.72	−1.77	211.93	0.88	0.36	0.37	8.76	0.75	−0.43	−0.43	−1.81	0.69
	(−6.32)	(−6.62)	(4.9)	(1.06)	(0.88)	(0.92)	(0.22)	(0.99)	(−0.84)	(−0.85)	(−0.03)	(0.92)
Unemployment rate	−0.95	−0.97	−311.01	−2.88	−3.11	−3.13	−185.50	−0.44	−6.83	−6.84	−171.18	1.94
	(−3.49)	(−3.5)	(−8.67)	(−3.44)	(−5.51)	(−5.59)	(−4.02)	(−0.42)	(−9.33)	(−9.39)	(−2.31)	(1.74)
Dummy (year >1980)	0.069	0.063	−0.853	0.010								
	(5.14)	(4.57)	(−0.5)	(0.25)	–	–	–	–	–	–	–	–

(continued)

Table 7.1 (continued)

Variable	Model 1				Model 2				Model 3			
	ALR	RTR	RCAP	IAR	ALR	RTR	RCAP	IAR2	ALR	RTR	RCAP	AUDR12
Audit rate	0.12	0.11	−14.25		0.15	0.13	16.15					
	(5.05)	(4.59)	(−4.22)	–	(3.42)	(3.13)	(4.44)	–	–	–	–	–
Audit rate (revenue agents)	–	–	–	–	–	–	–	–	–	–	–	–
Audit rate (revenue agents									0.117	0.097	35.625	
+ tax auditors)	–	–	–	–	–	–	–	–	(2.16)	(1.81)	(6.42)	–
Audit rate (tax auditors)	–	–	–	–	–	–	–	–	–	–	–	–
Audit rate (service centers)	–	–	–	–	–	–	–	–	–	–	–	–
Total sentences	–	–	–	–	–	–	–	–	–	–	–	–
Tax sentences	–	–	–	–	–	–	–	–	–	–	–	–
Money laundering sentences	–	–	–	–	–	–	–	–	–	–	–	–
Percent of tax sentences in media	–	–	–	–	–	–	–	–	–	–	–	–
Percent of money laundering sentences in media	–	–	–	–	–	–	–	–	–	–	–	–
Percent of tax sentences resulting in prison	–	–	–	–	–	–	–	–	–	–	–	–
Percent of tax sentences resulting in probation	–	–	–	–	–	–	–	–	–	–	–	–
Percent of money laundering sentences resulting in prison	–	–	–	–	–	–	–	–	–	–	–	–
Percent of money laundering sentences resulting in probation	–	–	–	–	–	–	–	–	–	–	–	–
Info returns not W2 filed/tot				−0.133								
number of info returns filed	–	–	–	(−9.45)	–	–	–	–	–	–	–	–
Direct examination time								1.019				1.229
	–	–	–	–	–	–	–	(5.26)	–	–	–	(8.1)
Budget per return				258.945				24.447				16.094
	–	–	–	(10.89)	–	–	–	(10.19)	–	–	–	(7.97)
State government ideology (100 is most liberal)	–	–	–	–	–	–	–	–	–	–	–	–

(continued)

Table 7.1 (continued)

Variable	Model 4					Model 5						Model 6			
	ALR	RTR	RCAP	AUDR12	AUDR5	ALR	RTR	RCAP	AUDR1	AUDR2	AUDR5	ALR	RTR	RCAP	IAR2
Constant	9.91	9.80	1817.36	(0.33)	(10.99)	0.90	0.95	201.06	0.09	(0.40)	(9.25)	0.20	0.24	188.76	2.13
	(0.26)	(0.26)	(0.22)	(−0.46)	(−1.72)	(0.57)	(0.61)	(0.82)	(0.23)	(−0.88)	(−1.51)	(0.6)	(0.69)	(5.42)	(3.4)
Percent of families on welfare	−0.233	−0.227	−68.993	0.098	0.274	0.067	0.065	7.407	0.043	0.054	0.266	0.01087	0.01026	−0.24503	0.05970
	(−0.21)	(−0.21)	(−0.21)	(7.6)	(2.37)	(1.07)	(1.06)	(0.78)	(6.27)	(6.48)	(2.35)	(1.31)	(1.24)	(−0.34)	(4.09)
State tax rate	−0.1246	−0.1211	−36.35	−0.0210	0.1250	−0.0219	−0.0225	−1.2784	−0.0070	−0.0130	0.1430	−0.0034	−0.0032	−2.3815	−0.0120
	(−0.28)	(−0.28)	(−0.2)	(−1.12)	(0.75)	(−0.81)	(−0.86)	(−0.31)	(−0.78)	(−1.2)	(0.98)	(−0.54)	(−0.52)	(−3.09)	(−1.08)
Personal income per capita	0.326	0.325	30.70	−0.079	0.024	0.255	0.258	2.485	−0.055	−0.027	0.043	0.335	0.336	11.874	−0.131
	(1.4)	(1.45)	(0.36)	(−2.58)	(0.09)	(4.38)	(4.52)	(0.28)	(−3.4)	(−1.4)	(0.16)	(18.35)	(18.46)	(6.26)	(−4.21)
Family size	−16.755	−16.577	−2582.63	1.830	20.874	0.451	0.330	139.855	−0.047	1.630	18.579	−1.754	−1.854	529.818	1.005
	(−0.22)	(−0.22)	(−0.17)	(1.14)	(1.45)	(0.14)	(0.1)	(0.28)	(−0.06)	(1.58)	(1.32)	(−1.74)	(−1.85)	(5.33)	(0.54)
Farms per household	−5.63	−5.12	−660.72	10.70	4.03	−3.58	−3.25	−656.14	1.01	8.15	0.02	0.37	0.54	−130.62	3.81
	(−0.12)	(−0.11)	(−0.08)	(1.93)	(0.08)	(−0.59)	(−0.54)	(−0.67)	(0.39)	(2.6)	(0)	(0.19)	(0.27)	(−0.42)	(1.02)
Percent of adults with high school diploma	−0.79	−0.80	141.47	0.30	−1.66	−1.10	−1.15	353.58	0.57	−0.27	−1.66	−0.73	−0.74	35.84	−1.18
	(−0.12)	(−0.12)	(0.14)	(0.63)	(−0.4)	(−1.19)	(−1.27)	(2.54)	(2.26)	(−0.88)	(−0.4)	(−5.11)	(−5.24)	(2.91)	(−4.4)
Percent of Pop over 65	−7.58	−7.60	−1168.83	−5.61	12.34	1.88	1.94	−64.36	−0.80	−4.35	11.00	2.24	2.30	−388.86	−7.52
	(−0.19)	(−0.19)	(−0.19)	(−2.21)	(0.54)	(0.58)	(0.61)	(−0.13)	(−0.64)	(−2.87)	(0.53)	(2.07)	(2.13)	(−2.86)	(−3.94)
Percent of employed persons in manufacturing	7.60	7.44	2146.70	0.07	−10.29	−1.47	−1.44	−26.51	−0.15	0.14	−10.44	−0.90	−0.90	192.35	−0.60
	(0.21)	(0.21)	(0.21)	(0.09)	(−1.4)	(−0.81)	(−0.81)	(−0.1)	(−0.37)	(0.27)	(−1.53)	(−2.75)	(−2.77)	(5.12)	(−0.96)
Percent of employed persons in service	−9.49	−9.29	−2332.85	0.37	11.58	−0.41	−0.41	−254.88	−0.29	0.82	9.67	0.15	0.16	26.20	0.75
	(−0.22)	(−0.23)	(−0.21)	(0.43)	(1.5)	(−0.23)	(−0.23)	(−0.94)	(−0.63)	(1.5)	(1.29)	(0.37)	(0.4)	(0.65)	(0.99)
Unemployment rate	−13.01	−12.92	−1447.67	1.79	7.82	−6.15	−6.20	−105.68	0.26	1.52	7.88	−3.13	−3.15	−184.41	−0.42
	(−0.46)	(−0.46)	(−0.21)	(1.58)	(0.77)	(−3.53)	(−3.64)	(−0.4)	(0.42)	(2.04)	(0.78)	(−5.55)	(−5.63)	(−3.98)	(−0.39)
Dummy (year > 1980)	–	–	–	–	–	–	–	–	–	–	–	–	–	–	–
Audit rate												0.15	0.13	16.17	
	–	–	–	–	–	–	–	–	–	–	–	(3.48)	(3.19)	(4.44)	–
Audit rate (revenue agents)						−1.3842	−1.3557	−339.36							
	–	–	–	–	–	(−1.19)	(−1.2)	(−1.95)	–	–	–	–	–	–	–

(continued)

Table 7.1 (continued)

Variable	Model 4					Model 5						Model 6			
	ALR	RTR	RCAP	AUDR12	AUDR5	ALR	RTR	RCAP	AUDR1	AUDR2	AUDR5	ALR	RTR	RCAP	IAR2
Audit rate (revenue agents + tax auditors)	0.36	0.34	124.53												
	(0.28)	(0.27)	(0.27)	–	–	–	–	–	–	–	–	–	–	–	–
Audit rate (tax auditors)						0.56	0.52	156.77							
	–	–	–	–	–	(1.54)	(1.48)	(2.9)	–	–	–	–	–	–	–
Audit rate (service centers)	0.78	0.76	254.28			−0.08	−0.08	−0.60							
	(0.22)	(0.22)	(0.2)	–	–	(−0.56)	(−0.56)	(−0.03)	–	–	–	–	–	–	–
Total sentences	–	–	–	–	–	–	–	–	–	–	–	–	–	–	–
Tax sentences												0.00000	−0.00004	0.03478	0.00000
	–	–	–	–	–	–	–	–	–	–	–	(−0.01)	(−0.11)	(0.98)	(0.12)
Money laundering sentences												0.00112	0.00111	−0.08360	0.00000
	–	–	–	–	–	–	–	–	–	–	–	(2.87)	(2.86)	(−2.47)	(−0.24)
Percent of tax sentences in media	–	–	–	–	–	–	–	–	–	–	–	–	–	–	–
Percent of money laundering sentences in media	–	–	–	–	–	–	–	–	–	–	–	–	–	–	–
Percent of tax sentences resulting in prison	–	–	–	–	–	–	–	–	–	–	–	–	–	–	–
Percent of tax sentences resulting in probation	–	–	–	–	–	–	–	–	–	–	–	–	–	–	–
Percent of money laundering sentences resulting in prison	–	–	–	–	–	–	–	–	–	–	–	–	–	–	–
Percent of money laundering sentences resulting in probation	–	–	–	–	–	–	–	–	–	–	–	–	–	–	–
Info returns not W2 filed/tot number of info returns filed	–	–	–	–	–	–	–	–	–	–	–	–	–	–	–
Direct examination Time				1.182	−0.15				0.189	1.015	−0.339				1.028
	–	–	–	(7.68)	(−0.11)	–	–	–	(2.24)	(9.99)	(−0.25)	–	–	–	(5.29)
Budget per return				16.104	−8.307				5.302	10.783	−8.088				24.494
	–	–	–	(8.09)	(−0.46)	–	–	–	(4.84)	(8.19)	(−0.45)	–	–	–	(10.16)
State government ideology (100 is most liberal)									0	0	−0.005				
	–	–	–	–	–	–	–	–	(0.65)	(0.29)	(−1.08)	–	–	–	–

(continued)

Table 7.1 (continued)

Variable	Model 7				Model 8			
	ALR	RTR	RCAP	IAR2	ALR	RTR	RCAP	IAR2
Constant	0.23	0.25	204.67	1.55	1.43	1.47	147.95	−0.001
	(0.7)	(0.77)	(5.86)	(2.6)	(3.6)	(3.7)	(3.4)	(0)
Percent of families on welfare	0.00825	0.00775	−0.48990	0.06330	0.00786	0.00765	−1.56726	0.09710
	(0.98)	(0.93)	(−0.65)	(4.46)	(0.8)	(0.78)	(−1.58)	(8.3)
State tax rate	−0.0055	−0.0054	−2.4248	−0.0120	−0.0253	−0.0254	−0.2042	−0.0170
	(−0.95)	(−0.93)	(−3.16)	(−1.16)	(−3.09)	(−3.1)	(−0.17)	(−1.38)
Personal income per capita	0.329	0.330	12.019	−0.119	0.311	0.312	16.453	−0.080
	(18.99)	(19.1)	(6.38)	(−4.09)	(17.32)	(17.41)	(8.32)	(−3.1)
Family size	−1.527	−1.604	510.856	1.419	−0.954	−1.052	407.125	0.279
	(−1.57)	(−1.66)	(5.1)	(0.8)	(−1)	(−1.1)	(4.05)	(0.19)
Farms per household	−0.24	−0.09	−134.29	4.53	−2.92	−2.71	−23.80	7.16
	(−0.13)	(−0.05)	(−0.44)	(1.34)	(−1.22)	(−1.14)	(−0.07)	(2.01)
Percent of adults with high school diploma	−0.72	−0.74	31.86	−1.06	−1.71	−1.73	89.30	0.29
	(−5.12)	(−5.22)	(2.55)	(−4.01)	(−6.91)	(−7.00)	(3.54)	(0.77)
Percent of Pop over 65	1.90	1.95	−401.06	−7.04	1.28	1.32	−321.31	−4.27
	(1.89)	(1.94)	(−2.98)	(−4.04)	(1.06)	(1.10)	(−2.04)	(−2.4)
Percent of employed persons in manufacturing	−0.78	−0.78	180.60	−0.51	−0.33	−0.33	144.80	−0.08
	(−2.55)	(−2.54)	(4.8)	(−0.9)	(−0.82)	(−0.82)	(2.9)	(−0.14)
Percent of employed persons in service	0.13	0.15	−0.42	1.30	−0.32	−0.30	−41.06	0.91
	(0.33)	(0.38)	(−0.01)	(1.8)	(−0.68)	(−0.64)	(−0.8)	(1.29)
Unemployment rate	−3.13	−3.15	−193.25	0.08	−6.53	−6.55	−89.36	1.31
	(−5.55)	(−5.62)	(−4.14)	(0.08)	(−10.46)	(−10.53)	(−1.46)	(1.36)
Dummy (year > 1980)	–	–	–	–	–	–	–	–
Audit rate	0.14	0.13	17.33		0.10	0.09	31.07	
	(3.28)	(2.98)	(4.75)	–	(2.06)	(1.71)	(6.31)	–
Audit rate (revenue agents)	–	–	–	–	–	–	–	–
Audit rate (revenue agents + tax auditors)	–	–	–	–	–	–	–	–
Audit rate (tax auditors)	–	–	–	–	–	–	–	–
Audit rate (service centers)	–	–	–	–	–	–	–	–

(continued)

Table 7.1 (continued)

Variable	Model 7				Model 8			
	ALR	RTR	RCAP	IAR2	ALR	RTR	RCAP	IAR2
Total sentences	–	–	–	–	–	–	–	–
Tax sentences	−0.00010	−0.00013	0.03410	0.00000	0.00048	0.00047	0.01078	−0.001
	(−0.27)	(−0.37)	(0.95)	(0.27)	(1.17)	(1.15)	(0.26)	(−1.49)
Money laundering sentences	0.00121	0.00120	−0.08378	0.00000	0.00000	−0.00003	−0.04440	0.001
	(3.15)	(3.14)	(−2.46)	(−0.37)	(0.00)	(−0.07)	(−0.92)	(1.25)
Percent of tax sentences in media					−0.044	−0.044	4.248	0.026
	–	–	–	–	(−2.22)	(−2.23)	(2.25)	(0.87)
Percent of money laundering sentences in media					0.025	0.024	3.933	−0.024
	–	–	–	–	(1.54)	(1.49)	(2.51)	(−0.95)
Percent of tax sentences resulting in prison	−0.023	−0.022	3.354	−0.017	–	–	–	–
	(−0.93)	(−0.88)	(1.67)	(−0.38)	–	–	–	–
Percent of tax sentences resulting in probation	0.00046	−0.00059	−1.53718	0.082				
	(0.02)	(−0.02)	(−0.65)	(1.53)	–	–	–	–
Percent of money laundering sentences resulting in prison	−0.038	−0.037	0.200	−0.150				
	(−1.89)	(−1.86)	(0.12)	(−3.95)	–	–	–	–
Percent of money laundering sentences resulting in probation	0.049	0.047	3.896	−0.012				
	(2.31)	(2.2)	(2.25)	(−0.31)	–	–	–	–
Info returns not W2 filed/tot number of info returns filed	–	–	–	–	–	–	–	–
Direct examination time				1.142				1.238
	–	–	–	(5.95)	–	–	–	(8.15)
Budget per return				23.862				15.579
	–	–	–	(9.98)	–	–	–	(8.5)
State government ideology (100 is most liberal)	–	–	–	–	–	–	–	–

DGW2: obsno = 500 years: 1977–1986
DGW_IAR2A: obsno = 700 years: 1988–2001
DGW93_12, 5: obsno = 450 years: 1993–2001
DGW93_1, 2, 5: obsno = 450 years: 1993–200
1DGW_TM1: obsno = 700 years: 1988–2001
DGW_TM3: obsno = 700 years: 1988–2001
DGW_MD1: obsno = 500 years: 1992–2001

returns filed. As discussed in DGW, the relationship between socioeconomic, tax base, and tax compliance factors and the number of returns filed may be quite complex. With respect to variables that relate to taxpayers' compliance, DGW argued that taxpayers confront three options: (1) to file a return and report honestly; (2) to file a return and underreport taxes; or (3) not to file a return. Anything that reduces the benefits or increases the costs of filing a return and underreporting taxes will increase the likelihood that a given taxpayer chooses to file a return and report honestly or not file a return. We called this the compliance principle. DGW argued that the compliance principle would apply to the federal audit rate because increases in the federal audit rate decrease the benefits and increase the costs of filing a return and underreporting taxes due. DGW expected (and found) that an increase in the audit rate decreased returns filed per capita. My results for the post-1987 period seemingly contradict the findings of DGW pre-1988. However, the compliance principle predicts that either returns filed would decline or returns filed would increase with greater compliance. My results indicate that the latter situation is now in effect—increases in the audit rate lead to greater levels of compliance and a greater number of honestly prepared returns.

In Model 3, the audit rate from the IRS Data Books is replaced with the combined rate for revenue agent and tax agent audits. The results indicate that the selected instruments are significant factors in the reduced form for the audit rate and that the estimated audit effect is positive and statistically significant.

In Model 4, I add the factor for correspondence audits to the previous specification. Interestingly, the significance of *AUDR12* (the combined audit rate for revenue agents and tax agents) and of *AUDR5* (the correspondence audit rate) is now lost. There is a large change in the estimated magnitude of the coefficients, which suggests that collinearity issues are present. Pursuing this specification, I then split the combined audit rate for revenue agents and tax agents into separate factors for each type of audit. This model (Model 5) also reveals the insignificance of these separate audit factors.[6] Additionally, in this specification, the revenue agent audit effect is no longer positively associated with compliance. Given that the simplest of these specifications showed a significant and positive audit effect (paralleling results from the longer time periods), the more refined audit models, based on the limited data period available to study, do not provide useful results.

Next, I examine models selected to measure CI effects. In Model 6, I include factors for tax sentences (*T*) and money laundering sentences (*M*). This model demonstrates that money laundering sentences have a statistically significant effect on tax compliance. Model 7 investigates the sentencing form of the explanatory factors from the previous model. Here, I introduce variables for: (1) the percentage of tax sentences resulting in prison time; (2) the percentage of tax sentences resulting in probation; (3) the percentage of money laundering sentences resulting in prison time; and (4) the percentage of money laundering sentences resulting in probation. These factors do not diminish the available degrees of freedom (the

---

[6] This model requires the use of a third instrument as discussed above.

estimates are determined for the same period 1988–2001 as in Model 6). This specification also fails to indicate statistical significance of tax sentences and of the various percentages of such cases that result in prison or probation. However, money laundering cases remain statistically significant in their effects on compliance. Further, the percentage of money laundering cases that result in prison terms raises the compliance level. However, an increase in the percentage of money laundering cases resulting in probation does not increase compliance.[7]

Turning to media, I added factors for the percentage of tax and money laundering cases that result in some form of media attention (*TMD_T* and *MMD_M*) to the specification that included the total number of tax and money laundering sentences. The resulting model is Model 8. Since media information was available only after 1992, this resulted in losing 200 observations (50 states, 4 years). In these models, the basic variables for tax and money laundering sentenced cases become insignificant. These results appear to contradict the findings in the models with more observations. Therefore, I reject their significance.

In Table 7.2, I present a set of final models. Based on the investigations reported above, I aggregate prison and probation cases and consider a factor for the percentage of sentenced cases not receiving prison or probation. The results of these specifications are presented in Table 7.2. I modify Model 7 by replacing the factors for prison and probation rates in tax and money laundering sentences with variables for the percentage of tax and money laundering sentences receiving neither prison nor probation (Model 9). As was the case in Model 7, the variable for counts of money laundering sentences remains statistically significant. In addition, the percentage of money laundering cases receiving neither prison nor probation has a significantly negative effect on compliance. The audit rate effects are also consistently positive and significant.

Model 10 combines the tax and money laundering sentences into a single explanatory factor. This variable reveals statistical significance. However, a variable which measured the effect of the percentage of such cases which are tax or money laundering cases is statistically insignificant. Model 11 adds the sentencing effect and reveals that sentenced cases that receive neither prison nor probation are negatively associated with compliance. Finally, Model 12 combines all CI cases (tax, money laundering, and other) into a single explanatory factor. I find that this factor is also statistically significant in its effect on compliance.

I conclude from these final specifications that CI activity has a statistically significant and demonstrable effect on tax compliance. However, while I have found that sentenced cases that do not receive prison time or probation lead to lower compliance levels, I am not able to find a specific mix of tax and money laundering cases that would raise compliance over existing levels. Additionally, the factor that measured the percentage of CI sentenced cases that receive media

[7] The percentage of tax or money laundering cases not resulting in prison or probation was also not statistically significant in these models.

Table 7.2 Final models

Variable	Model 9				Model 10			
	ALR	RTR	RCAP	IAR2	ALR	RTR	RCAP	IAR2
Constant	0.19	0.22	0.19	1.91	0.14	0.17	0.19	1.87
	(0.57)	(0.66)	(5.42)	(3.24)	(0.43)	(0.52)	(5.33)	(3.06)
Percent of families on welfare	0.00559	0.00521	−0.00056	0.06501	0.00926	0.00866	−0.00027	0.06129
	(0.65)	(0.61)	(−0.73)	(4.71)	(1.12)	(1.05)	(−0.37)	(4.29)
Family size	−1.7768	−1.8732	0.5175	1.0760	−1.7869	−1.8774	0.5684	1.4303
	(−1.78)	(−1.88)	(5.15)	(0.61)	(−1.84)	(−1.93)	(5.72)	(0.8)
Farms per household	−0.369	−0.172	−0.190	5.361	0.511	0.679	−0.213	4.183
	(−0.19)	(−0.09)	(−0.63)	(1.53)	(0.28)	(0.37)	(−0.71)	(1.22)
Percent of adults with high school diploma	−0.711	−0.726	0.038	−1.160	−0.602	−0.615	0.029	−1.124
	(−5.02)	(−5.15)	(3)	(−4.57)	(−4.3)	(−4.42)	(2.3)	(−4.25)
Unemployment rate	−3.10	−3.13	−0.19	−0.10	−3.06	−3.08	−0.19	−0.03
	(−5.49)	(−5.57)	(−3.97)	(−0.09)	(−5.4)	(−5.46)	(−4.03)	(−0.03)
Personal income per capita	0.33	0.34	0.01	−0.11	0.32	0.33	0.01	−0.12
	(18.57)	(18.68)	(6.4)	(−3.86)	(18.53)	(18.63)	(6.33)	(−4.13)
Percent of employed persons in manufacturing	−0.75	−0.76	0.19	−0.91	−0.75	−0.75	0.19	−0.64
	(−2.3)	(−2.33)	(5.12)	(−1.57)	(−2.42)	(−2.43)	(5.09)	(−1.1)
Percent of employed persons in service	0.13	0.14	0.02	0.70	0.37	0.39	0.00	0.98
	(0.32)	(0.35)	(0.54)	(0.98)	(0.94)	(0.99)	(−0.03)	(1.34)
Percent of pop over 65	2.40	2.45	−0.37	−7.35	1.88	1.93	−0.39	−7.03
	(2.23)	(2.29)	(−2.71)	(−4.12)	(1.85)	(1.9)	(−2.88)	(−3.96)
State tax rate	−0.006	−0.005	−0.003	−0.006	−0.0054	−0.0053	−0.0023	−0.0133
	(−0.93)	(−0.89)	(−3.39)	(−0.59)	(−0.93)	(−0.91)	(−2.94)	(−1.24)
Total sentences	–	–	–	–	–	–	–	–
	–	–	–	–	–	–	–	–
Total sentences either tax or money laundering	–	–	–	–	0.0005	0.0005	0.0000	0.0001
	–	–	–	–	(2.23)	(2.14)	(−1.08)	(0.17)
Tax sentences	0.00001	−0.00003	0.00003	0.00012	–	–	–	–
	(0.02)	(−0.08)	(0.84)	(0.19)	–	–	–	–

(continued)

Table 7.2 (continued)

Variable	Model 9				Model 10			
	ALR	RTR	RCAP	IAR2	ALR	RTR	RCAP	IAR2
Money laun sentences	0.00111	0.00110	−0.00008	−0.00024	–	–	–	–
	(2.84)	(2.83)	(−2.47)	(−0.34)	–	–	–	–
Tax sentences/total sentences	–	–	–	–	0.03242	0.03075	−0.00004	−0.14580
	–	–	–	–	(0.89)	(0.85)	(−0.01)	(−2.17)
Money laun sentences/total sentences	–	–	–	–	1.14E−02	9.47E−03	1.43E−03	−2.41E−01
	–	–	–	–	(0.27)	(0.23)	(0.42)	(−3.23)
Tax sentences neither pris nor prob/total tax sentences	3.33E−02	2.76E−02	9.69E−03	−4.31E−01	–	–	–	–
	(0.37)	(0.31)	(1.31)	(−2.71)	–	–	–	–
Money laun sentences neither pris nor prob/total money laun sentences	−3.55E−01	−3.39E−01	−1.82E−02	9.41E−01	–	–	–	–
	(−4.48)	(−4.3)	(−2.76)	(8.61)	–	–	–	–
Money laun pris sentences/money laun sentences	–	–	–	–	–	–	–	–
	–	–	–	–	–	–	–	–
Tax pris sentences/tax sentences	–	–	–	–	–	–	–	–
	–	–	–	–	–	–	–	–
Money laun prob sentences/money laun sentences	–	–	–	–	–	–	–	–
	–	–	–	–	–	–	–	–
Tax prob sentences/tax sentences	–	–	–	–	–	–	–	–
	–	–	–	–	–	–	–	–
Audit rate	0.18	0.17	0.02	–	1.35E−01	1.22E−01	1.66E−02	–
	(3.93)	(3.64)	(4.69)	–	(3.19)	(2.89)	(4.5)	–
Budget per return	–	–	–	22.06	–	–	–	24.51
	–	–	–	(9.49)	–	–	–	(10.22)
Direct examination time	–	–	–	1.05145	–	–	–	1.05
	–	–	–	(5.71)	–	–	–	(5.43)

(continued)

Table 7.2 (continued)

Variable	Model 11				Model 12			
	ALR	RTR	RCAP	IAR2	ALR	RTR	RCAP	IAR2
Constant	0.12	0.15	0.19	1.61	0.21	0.23	0.20	1.55
	(0.38)	(0.46)	(5.44)	(2.85)	(0.64)	(0.7)	(5.75)	(2.61)
	0.00352	0.00316	−0.00058	0.06608	0.00732	0.00680	−0.00047	0.06329
Percent of families on welfare	(0.41)	(0.37)	(−0.73)	(4.93)	(0.88)	(0.82)	(−0.62)	(4.48)
Family size	−1.7491	−1.8335	0.5490	1.5028	−1.7046	−1.7863	0.5508	1.4841
	(−1.83)	(−1.92)	(5.45)	(0.91)	(−1.78)	(−1.87)	(5.57)	(0.85)
Farms per household	−0.341	−0.143	−0.268	5.642	0.226	0.399	−0.218	4.353
	(−0.19)	(−0.08)	(−0.92)	(1.8)	(0.13)	(0.22)	(−0.73)	(1.32)
Percent of adults with high	−0.589	−0.602	0.030	−1.076	−0.633	−0.643	0.026	−1.092
school diploma	(−4.24)	(−4.35)	(2.37)	(−4.33)	(−4.61)	(−4.7)	(2.08)	(−4.27)
Unemployment rate	−3.01	−3.03	−0.20	0.35	−3.03	−3.05	−0.20	0.07
	(−5.3)	(−5.36)	(−4.1)	(0.35)	(−5.37)	(−5.44)	(−4.25)	(0.07)
Personal income per capita	0.32	0.32	0.01	−0.11	0.32	0.33	0.01	−0.12
	(18.93)	(19.02)	(6.52)	(−3.82)	(18.95)	(19.05)	(6.39)	(−4.09)
Percent of employed persons	−0.57	−0.58	0.19	−0.92	−0.75	−0.75	0.18	−0.53
in manufacturing	(−1.88)	(−1.9)	(5.02)	(−1.72)	(−2.47)	(−2.47)	(4.87)	(−0.94)
Percent of employed persons	0.34	0.35	−0.01	0.96	0.29	0.31	−0.02	1.24
in service	(0.86)	(0.91)	(−0.2)	(1.42)	(0.74)	(0.8)	(−0.47)	(1.75)
Percent of pop over 65	1.98	2.02	−0.37	−6.79	1.79	1.84	−0.40	−6.95
	(2)	(2.04)	(−2.75)	(−4.17)	(1.81)	(1.85)	(−2.98)	(−4.05)
State tax rate	−0.008	−0.008	−0.002	−0.008	−0.006	−0.006	−0.002	−0.012
	(−1.37)	(−1.33)	(−3.24)	(−0.86)	(−1.05)	(−1.04)	(−3.05)	(−1.17)
Total sentences	–	–	–	–	0.00046	0.00045	−0.00003	0.00000
	–	–	–	–	(2.32)	(2.24)	(−1.27)	(0.01)
Total sentences either tax or money	0.00055	0.00053	−0.00003	0.00006	–	–	–	–
laundering	(2.29)	(2.19)	(−1.23)	(0.15)	–	–	–	–
Money laun sentences	–	–	–	–	–	–	–	–
	–	–	–	–	–	–	–	–
	–	–	–	–	–	–	–	–
	–	–	–	–	–	–	–	–

(continued)

Table 7.2 (continued)

Variable	Model 11				Model 12			
	ALR	RTR	RCAP	IAR2	ALR	RTR	RCAP	IAR2
Tax sentences/total sentences	0.03836	0.03642	0.00047	−0.14956	–	–	–	–
	(1.05)	(1)	(0.15)	(−2.35)	–	–	–	–
	2.06E−02	1.80E−02	2.58E−03	−2.64E−01	–	–	–	–
	(0.49)	(0.43)	(0.73)	(−3.73)	–	–	–	–
Tax sentences neither pris nor prob/	0.006	−0.001	0.012	−0.468	–	–	–	–
total tax sentences	(0.06)	(−0.01)	(1.59)	(−2.95)	–	–	–	–
Money laun sentences neither pris nor	−3.55E−01	−3.38E−01	−1.85E−02	9.48E−01	–	–	–	–
prob/total money laun sentences	(−4.44)	(−4.26)	(−2.75)	(8.72)	–	–	–	–
Money laun pris sentences/money	–	–	–	–	0.04609	0.04346	0.00418	−0.15003
laun sentences	–	–	–	–	(2.16)	(2.05)	(2.41)	(−3.94)
Tax pris sentences/tax sentences	–	–	–	–	−1.97E−02	−1.82E−02	3.11E−03	−1.94E−02
	–	–	–	–	(−0.79)	(−0.73)	(1.54)	(−0.42)
Money laun prob sentences/money	–	–	–	–	−3.48E−02	−3.40E−02	1.87E−05	−1.25E−02
laun sentences	–	–	–	–	(−1.74)	(−1.71)	(0.01)	(−0.34)
Tax prob sentences/tax sentences	–	–	–	–	0.003	0.002	−0.002	0.081
	–	–	–	–	(0.1)	(0.07)	(−0.68)	(1.52)
Audit rate	0.17	0.15	0.02	–	0.13	0.12	0.02	–
	(3.66)	(3.35)	(4.73)	–	(3.15)	(2.84)	(4.77)	–
Budget per return	–	–	–	22.11	–	–	–	23.95
	–	–	–	(9.57)	–	–	–	(10.04)
Direct examination time	–	–	–	1.08	–	–	–	1.14
	–	–	–	(5.89)	–	–	–	(5.97)

Number of observations: 700

Years of analysis: 1988–2001

attention was also insignificant. At the margin, changes in media attention were not found to have statistically significant effects on compliance.[8]

Simulations

I performed two basic simulations to determine the direct revenue (spillover) effect of audits. Following the methodology established in DGW, I calculated a predicted value for the increase in total assessed liability for a particular year that would have resulted from holding audit rates at their earlier period (higher) levels. I also calculated the effect of this audit rate change on reported liabilities (excluding additional taxes and penalties resulting from IRS examinations). The difference between the two estimates represents the direct revenue effect of the increase in audit rates. DGW estimated that the spillover effects of audits produce six out of every seven dollars of additional revenue.

In these simulations, a change in the audit rate (and later the levels of CI activity) leads to two measurable effects. First, the change in audit rate causes assessed liabilities and reported liabilities to increase. Let d*ALR* denote the change in assessed liability per return for a change in the audit rate of d*IAR*. Similarly, let d*RTR* denote the change in reported tax liability per return for the same change in audit rate d*IAR*. DGW called the change d*ALR* the total revenue effect (since it includes both reported amounts and additional taxes and penalties) and d*RTR* the indirect effect. The direct effect of audits is defined as d*ALR*-d*RTR*. Since *ALR*-*RTR* is a measure of additional taxes and penalties, d*ALR*-d*RTR* is simply the change in additional tax and penalties resulting from the audit change. Consequently, it is the direct effect. DGW defined the spillover measure as the ratio d*RTR*/d*ALR* since it measures the percentage of the total change that occurs from general deterrence as a result of the change in the audit rate.

I considered several experiments. In some cases, I doubled individual components such as the audit rate. Similarly, I considered doubling the number of tax sentences or doubling the number of money laundering sentences. In some cases, I doubled both the number of tax and money laundering cases. For variables measured in percentages (such as the percentage of money laundering cases that received prison sentences), I increased the percentage by 25% absolutely. Noticing in some cases that certain variables had statistically insignificant coefficients, I experimented with the same model but only increased the levels of the significant variables (generally the money laundering components).[9]

---

[8] The shortened time period available to study media effects on the subcomponent of examinations did not allow me to precisely measure these effects. Given the large general deterrence effect found for CI activities, there is indirect evidence of a large media effect, even if the econometric model did not have sufficient data to isolate this result.

[9] For instance, some CI factors appear in the filings equation with negative but insignificant coefficients.

The simulations are provided in Table 7.3. To understand the results, consider the simulation in which audit rates are doubled and the specification adopted is Model 11 discussed above. The first row in Table 7.3 shows that estimated assessed tax collections would rise to $959.1 billion from $940.4 billion in 2001. The change of $18.706 billion is the total revenue effect. The estimates also show that reported tax collections rise by $17.571 billion. This change is the indirect effect of doubling the audit rate. The difference between these two estimated differences is approximately $1.135 billion and represents the direct revenue effect. This amount is 93.9% of the total revenue effect.

Doubling CI activity (tax and money laundering cases) leads to $15.698 billion in increased reported taxes, $16.68 billion in increased per annum assessed tax revenue, and a direct revenue increase of $0.982 billion. Hence, the spillover effect is measured to be approximately 94%. At the point estimates, doubling CI activity or doubling the IRS audit examination rate leads to similar revenue increases and implies similar levels of increased general deterrence. The precision in these estimates are not of the same magnitude as I next explain.

The calculation of confidence intervals for the simulations conducted in our study is complicated for several reasons. First, as audit or enforcement levels are increased, reported taxes increase as the product of increased collections per return and increased returns filed per capita (audit and enforcement effects are present in both equations for these variables).[10] Complications also arise due to the dynamics in the models, the conversion from real to nominal terms, and the adjustment from per capita to total dollars. Our procedure simulates the audit/enforcement experiments using estimated coefficients that are one or two standard errors different from the estimated values.

For simulations in which the audit rate is doubled, I find that a 90% lower bound on the estimated increase in reported taxes is $11.468 billion. A similar lower bound on the estimated increase in assessed tax revenue is $12.578 billion. At the lower bound estimates, the spillover effect is 91.2%. For simulations in which CI enforcement levels are doubled, I find that a 90% lower bound on the estimated increase in reported taxes is $3.348 billion. A similar lower bound on the estimated increase in assessed tax revenue is $4.309 billion. At the lower bound estimates, the spillover effect is at least 77.7%. There are two important conclusions from this analysis. First, the spillover effect of audits and CI enforcement is quite large and generally estimated to be over 90%. Second, an increase in IRS examination activity could have important fiscal impacts and make a large contribution toward reducing

---

[10] The simulations rely on two simultaneous predicted changes in all cases. As discussed, the simulation affects the level of assessed liabilities per return filed or reported liabilities per return filed. However, the simulation also affects the estimated number of returns filed per capita. In conjunction with estimates of population (and after conversion from real to nominal terms), the product of population, predicted returns per capita, and collections per return filed yields the final dollar figures in Table 7.3. Hence, in some cases, the sign on a single variable in a model is not sufficient to understand the overall significance of increasing one or more components in the model.

Table 7.3 Simulations

Model	Variable substitution	Significant varibles	Estimated assessed tax collections			Estimated reported tax collection			Actual reported collections ($millions)	% Of estimated reported difference and estimated reported tax revenue (F/G)	% Of estimated reported difference and actual reported tax revenue (F/E)	% Change in estimated assessed and reported tax revenue (C − F)/F
			Modified amount ($millions)	Original amount ($millions)	Difference (A − B) ($millions)	Modified amount ($millions)	Original amount ($millions)	Difference (D − E) ($millions)				
			(A)	(B)	(C)	(D)	(E)	(F)	(G)	(H)	(I)	(J)
Model 9	IAR2 → 2 × IAR2	IAR2	965,033	945,424	19,609	962,652	944,152	18,500	882,128	2.1	2.0	6.0
	T− > 2 × T		948,345	945,424	2,921	946,322	944,152	2,170	882,128	0.2	0.2	34.6
	M− > 2 × M	M	960,995	945,424	15,571	959,499	944,152	15,347	882,128	1.7	1.6	1.5
	T→ 2 × T M→ 2 × M	M	964,029	945,424	18,605	961,792	944,152	17,640	882,128	2.0	1.9	5.5
	TNEI_T = 0 MNEI_M = 0	MNEI_M	946,515	945,424	1,091	945,208	944,152	1,056	882,128	0.1	0.1	3.3
	TNEI_T = 0		945,286	945,424	-138	944,024	944,152	−128	882,128	0.0	0.0	7.8
	MNEI_M = 0	MNEI_M	946,654	945,424	1,230	945,336	944,152	1,184	882,128	0.1	0.1	3.9
	T→ 2 × T M→ 2 × M TNEI_T = 0 MNEI_M = 0	M, MNEI_M	965,120	945,424	19,696	962,848	944,152	18,696	882,128	2.1	2.0	5.3
Model 10	IAR2 → 2 × IAR2	IAR2	958,328	942,871	15,457	955,887	941,451	14,436	882,128	1.6	1.5	7.1
	TOTTM→ 2 × TOTTM	TOTTM	960,273	942,871	17,402	957,872	941,451	16,421	882,128	1.9	1.7	6.0
	M_TOT→ M_TOT + 0.25 T_TOT→ T_TOT − 0.25		940,981	942,871	−1,890	939,521	941,451	−1,930	882,128	−0.2	−0.2	−2.1
	T_TOT→ T_TOT + 0.25 M_TOT→ M_TOT − 0.25		944,774	942,871	1,903	943,387	941,451	1,936	882,128	0.2	0.2	−1.7
	TOTTM→ 2 × TOTTM M_TOT→ M_TOT + 0.25 T_TOT→T_TOT − 0.25	TOTTM	958,413	942,871	15,542	955,972	941,451	14,521	882,128	1.6	1.5	7.0
Model 11	IAR2 → 2 × IAR2	IAR2	959,064	940,358	18,706	956,602	939,031	17,571	882,128	2.0	1.9	6.5
	TOTTM→ 2 × TOTTM	TOTTM	957,038	940,358	16,680	954,729	939,031	15,698	882,128	1.8	1.7	6.3

(continued)

Table 7.3 (continued)

Model	Variable substitution	Significant varibles	Estimated assessed tax collections			Estimated reported tax collection			Actual reported collections ($millions)	% Of estimated reported difference and estimated reported tax revenue (F/G)	% Of estimated reported difference and actual reported tax revenue (F/E)	% Change in estimated assessed and reported tax revenue (C−F)/F
			Modified amount ($millions)	Original amount ($millions)	Difference (A − B) ($millions)	Modified amount ($millions)	Original amount ($millions)	Difference (D − E) ($millions)				
			(A)	(B)	(C)	(D)	(E)	(F)	(G)	(H)	(I)	(J)
	M_TOT→ M_TOT + 0.25 T_TOT→ T_TOT − 0.25		939,182	940,358	−1,176	937,772	939,031	−1,259	882,128	−0.1	−0.1	−6.6
	T_TOT→ T_TOT + 0.25 M_TOT→ M_TOT − 0.25		941,595	940,358	1,237	940,342	939,031	1,311	882,128	0.1	0.1	−5.6
	TOTTM→ 2 × TOTTM M_TOT→ M_TOT + 0.25 T_TOT→ T_TOT − 0.25	TOTTM	955,899	940,358	15,541	953,507	939,031	14,476	882,128	1.6	1.5	7.4
	TNEI_T = 0		940,252	940,358	−106	938,937	939,031	−94	882,128	0.0	0.0	12.8
	MNEI_M = 0	MNEI_M	941,585	940,358	1,227	940,213	939,031	1,182	882,128	0.1	0.1	3.8
	TNEI_T = 0 MNEI_M = 0	MNEI_M	941,479	940,358	1,121	940,119	939,031	1,088	882,128	0.1	0.1	3.0
	MNEI_M = 0 T_TOT→ T_TOT + 0.25 M_TOT→ M_TOT − 0.25	MNEI_M	942,822	940,358	2,464	941,524	939,031	2,493	882,128	0.3	0.3	−1.2
Model 12	IAR2 → 2 × IAR2	IAR2	959,456	943,935	15,521	956,931	942,443	14,488	882,128	1.6	1.5	7.1
	TOT→ 2×TOT	TOT	961,464	943,935	17,529	959,125	942,443	16,682	882,128	1.9	1.8	5.1
	TPRI_T→ TPRI_T + .25; TPRO_T→ TPRO_T + .25; MPRI_M→ MPRI_M + .25; MPRO_M→ MPRO_M + .25	MPRI_M	944,007	943,935	72	942,535	942,443	92	882,128	0.0	0.0	−21.7
	TPRI_T→ TPRI_T + .25; TPRO_T→ TPRO_T + .25		943,630	943,935	−305	942,189	942,443	−254	882,128	0.0	0.0	20.1

(continued)

Table 7.3 continued

Model	Variable substitution	Significant varibles	Estimated assessed tax collections			Estimated reported tax collection			Actual reported collections ($millions)	% Of estimated reported difference and estimated reported tax revenue (F/G)	% Of estimated reported difference and actual reported tax revenue (F/E)	% Change in estimated assessed and reported tax revenue (C−F)/F
			Modified amount ($millions)	Original amount ($millions)	Difference (A − B) ($millions)	Modified amount ($millions)	Original amount ($millions)	Difference (D − E) ($millions)				
			(A)	(B)	(C)	(D)	(E)	(F)	(G)	(H)	(I)	(J)
	MPRI_M→ MPRI_M + .25; MPRO_M→ MPRO_M + .25	MPRI_M	944,313	943,935	378	942,789	942,443	346	882,128	0.0	0.0	9.2
	TOT→ 2×TOT TPRI_T→ TPRI_T + .25; TPRO_T→ TPRO_T + .25; MPRI_M→ MPRI_M + .25; MPRO_M→ MPRO_M + .25	TOT, MPRI_M	961,563	943,935	17,628	959,242	942,443	16,799	882,128	1.9	1.8	4.9

(continued)

Table 7.3 (continued)

Model	Variable substitution	Significant varibles	Estimated reported tax revenue increase resulting from change (indirect revenue effect) ($)	Estimated assessed tax revenue increase resulting from change ($)	Difference (direct revenue effect) ($)	Indirect revenue effect/total revenue effect (%)
	(A)	(B)	(C)	(D)	D − C	C/D
Model 9	IAR2 → 2 × IAR2	IAR2	18,500,000,000	19,609,000,000	1,109,000,000	94.3
	T→ 2 × T		2,170,000,000	2,921,000,000	751,000,000	74.3
	M→ 2 × M	M	15,347,000,000	15,571,000,000	224,000,000	98.6
	T→ 2×T M→ 2 × M	M	17,640,000,000	18,605,000,000	965,000,000	94.8
	TNEI_T = 0 MNEI_M = 0	MNEI_M	1,056,000,000	1,091,000,000	35,000,000	96.8
	TNEI_T = 0		−128,000,000	−138,000,000	−10,000,000	92.8
	MNEI_M = 0	MNEI_M	1,184,000,000	1,230,000,000	46,000,000	96.3
	T→ 2 × T M→ 2 × M TNEI_T = 0 MNEI_M = 0	M, MNEI_M	18,696,000,000	19,696,000,000	1,000,000,000	94.9
Model 10	IAR2 → 2 × IAR2	IAR2	14,436,000,000	15,457,000,000	1,021,000,000	93.4
	TOTTM→ 2 × TOTTM	TOTTM	16,421,000,000	17,402,000,000	981,000,000	94.4
	M_TOT→ M_TOT + 0.25 T_TOT→ T_TOT − 0.25		−1,930,000,000	−1,890,000,000	40,000,000	102.1
	T_TOT→ T_TOT + 0.25 M_TOT→ M_TOT − 0.25		1,936,000,000	1,903,000,000	−33,000,000	101.7
	TOTTM→ 2 × TOTTM M_TOT→ M_TOT + 0.25 T_TOT→ T_TOT − 0.25	TOTTM	14,521,000,000	15,542,000,000	1,021,000,000	93.4
Model 11	IAR2 → 2 × IAR2	IAR2	17,571,000,000	18,706,000,000	1,135,000,000	93.9
	TOTTM→ 2 × TOTTM	TOTTM	15,698,000,000	16,680,000,000	982,000,000	94.1
	M_TOT→ M_TOT + 0.25 T_TOT→ T_TOT − 0.25		−1,259,000,000	−1,176,000,000	83,000,000	107.1
	T_TOT→ T_TOT + 0.25 M_TOT→ M_TOT − 0.25		1,311,000,000	1,237,000,000	−74,000,000	106.0

(continued)

Table 7.3 (continued)

Model	Variable substitution	Significant varibles	Estimated reported tax revenue increase resulting from change (indirect revenue effect) ($)	Estimated assessed tax revenue increase resulting from change ($)	Difference (direct revenue effect) ($)	Indirect revenue effect/total revenue effect (%)
	(A)	(B)	(C)	(D)	D − C	C/D
	TOTTM→ 2 × TOTTM M_TOT→ M_TOT + 0.25 T_TOT→ T_TOT − 0.25	TOTTM	14,476,000,000	15,541,000,000	1,065,000,000	93.1
	TNEI_T = 0		−94,000,000	−106,000,000	−12,000,000	88.7
	MNEI_M = 0	MNEI_M	1,182,000,000	1,227,000,000	45,000,000	96.3
	TNEI_T = 0 MNEI_M = 0	MNEI_M	1,088,000,000	1,121,000,000	33,000,000	97.1
	MNEI_M = 0 T_TOT→ T_TOT + 0.25 M_TOT→ M_TOT − 0.25	MNEI_M	2,493,000,000	2,464,000,000	−29,000,000	101.2
Model 12	IAR2 → 2×IAR2	IAR2	14,488,000,000	15,521,000,000	1,033,000,000	93.3
	TOT→ 2×TOT	TOT	16,682,000,000	17,529,000,000	847,000,000	95.2
	TPRI_T→ TPRI_T + .25; TPRO_T→ TPRO_T + .25; MPRI_M→ MPRI_M + .25; MPRO_M→ MPRO_M + .25	MPRI_M	92,000,000	72,000,000	−20,000,000	127.8
	TPRI_T→ TPRI_T + .25; TPRO_T→ TPRO_T + .25		−254,000,000	−305,000,000	−51,000,000	83.3
	MPRI_M→ MPRI_M + .25; MPRO_M→ MPRO_M + .25	MPRI_M	346,000,000	378,000,000	32,000,000	91.5
	TOT→ 2×TOT TPRI_T→ TPRI_T + .25; TPRO_T→ TPRO_T + .25; MPRI_M→ MPRI_M + .25; MPRO_M→ MPRO_M + .25	TOT, MPRI_M	16,799,000,000	17,628,000,000	829,000,000	95.3

the tax gap. However, there is no evidence, in our study, that correspondence audits have made up for the decline in face-to-face tax audits. This result may be due to the limited time period during which we were able to measure the correspondence audit rate. Whether an IRS policy shift in enforcement is warranted based on these results depends on the relative costs and benefits of increasing audits and CI enforcement levels. We turn to these issues below.

Conclusions

It is conceivable that the IRS could double its audit rate without doubling its organizational size. Clearly, the IRS has not shrunk in size in the same proportion that audits have declined. Conversely, doubling CI activities might easily necessitate economically and physically doubling the resources devoted to CI. CI has never sentenced a number of cases represented by doubling of its current load. According to estimates reported by Plumley (1996, Table 5, p. 41), the cost for a CI conviction was nearly 80 times more expensive than an audit in 1991. While these unit costs are unlikely to apply to doubling CI activity, we can get some idea of the dollar magnitude of total costs using Plumley's reported figures.

In 1991, Plumley reported a unit cost of $1,298 per audit and a unit cost of $103,064 per CI conviction. These are $1,597 and 126,801 in 2001 after adjusting for inflation. In the same year, there were approximately 202,244 individual audits performed and only roughly 2,000 tax and money laundering sentences. Plumley's estimates of unit costs include overhead, support, and follow-on costs.

Doubling tax and money laundering sentences would cost $254 million (at these unit cost estimates), while doubling the audit rate would cost $323 million. However, doubling the audit rates is predicted to lead to an $18.71 billion increase in per annum reported collections, while doubling tax and money laundering cases was predicted to increase reported tax collection by $16.68 billion per annum (using the point estimates obtained under the final model specification). Hence, an additional dollar allocated to audit would return $58 in general deterrence,[11] while an additional dollar allocated to CI would result in $66.[12] Thus, there is some slight evidence that resources between civil and criminal enforcement at the IRS have been misallocated, with CI's activities receiving too few resources. As this difference is not statistically different from zero, little should be made of the point estimate differences estimated here. Indeed, a 90% lower bound on additional

[11] Plumley's (1996) estimate of the return to audits was similar. He found a marginal indirect revenue to cost ratio of 55.

[12] The elasticity of audit rates with respect to IRS budget, as determined in the reduced form audit equation, implies that the incremental cost of an audit may be twice as large as that assumed here. This would significantly lower (by half) our estimates of the dollar return to doubling the audit rate. Nonetheless, with estimated elasticity's greater than one, the IRS is likely operating in an increasing returns to scale range wherein increased budgets can readily expand the rate of individual audits.

reported collections per dollar expended is $39 for the doubled audit rate simulation but $17 for the doubled CI activities simulation.

However, as I mentioned above, it is unlikely that CI could double its activity level without incurring substantially greater costs than these marginal (per unit) estimates imply. Moreover, the larger the increase in CI activity we simulate through the model, the less reliable the estimates become as we move away from measurable historical experience. Doubling CI activity is very different from doubling the individual audit rate, since CI has never operated at twice its current size. Conversely, doubling the individual audit rate is within the IRS's historical experience.

Still, an increase in the IRS budget of $25 million allocated to CI for additional investigations, prosecutions, and sentencing would not appear to push the envelope of historical experience. Such an amount might be used to increase tax and money laundering cases by roughly 200 per year and would necessitate roughly 250 additional tax agents. This represents a roughly 10% increase in tax and money laundering cases at 2001 levels. But, more important, this increase is within the range of historical CI experience. According to the simulations, general deterrence would rise by nearly $1.7 billion as a result of the $25 million allocation to cases processed by CI. With fixed budgets, a cost savings of this magnitude allocated to prosecutions and sentences could achieve the same result if efficiency and productivity gains could be achieved.

Chapter 8
IRS Criminal Investigation: Measuring the Marginal Monetary Effect of Criminal Investigation Convictions

Introduction

The purpose of this chapter is to estimate the marginal effect of criminal investigations (CI) conducted by the IRS. Specifically, I answer these questions:

- What is the marginal benefit of a CI conviction (conviction includes all legal, illegal, and narcotic source convictions)?
- What is the marginal benefit of a CI conviction resulting in imprisonment versus probation?
- What is the marginal benefit of the three different types of convictions: legal, illegal, and narcotic sources?

The empirical analysis in Chap. 7 was based on two models that were both estimated using a state-level, time-series cross-section. One model specified reported taxes per return filed as a function of audit rates and various socioeconomic factors. The other model specified returns filed per capita as a function of the same variables. The analysis period was 1988 through 2001. We saw that CI activities have a measurable effect on voluntary compliance. Chapter 7 also showed that the mix of sentenced cases (tax and money laundering) is not a significant determinant of tax compliance. Finally, Chap. 7 concluded that incarceration and probation (rather than fines) have the most influence on taxpayers.

Chapter 7 also presented simulations of the direct revenue (spillover) effect of audits and CI activities. We saw that the direct effect of doubling the audit rate on assessed tax collections (reported amounts and additional taxes and penalties) is \$18.7 billion. Doubling CI tax and money laundering sentences were forecasted to increase assessed collections by \$16.7 billion. I estimated the spillover effects from both audit and CI activities to be approximately 94%. Doubling the audit rate or doubling money laundering sentences produced similar increases in total collections. These simulations increase CI activity by relatively large amounts (e.g., doubling the size of CI activity). In the present chapter, I attempt to find the marginal effect of criminal investigations.

J. A. Dubin, *The Causes and Consequences of Income Tax Noncompliance*,
DOI: 10.1007/978-1-4419-0907-7_8,

Econometric Model Selection and Specification

In the current chapter, I first define the "marginal" benefits of CI activity. I interpret the term "marginal" as a change with respect to a small increase. For instance, economists define marginal cost as the incremental cost of producing one more unit of output. If output for a producer is measured continuously, then "marginal" might be defined as an infinitesimal change in output according to the definition used in the calculus. However, it is sensible to measure marginal in this analysis by a small change in CI activity.

Thus, I consider the marginal effects from two perspectives: (1) a five percent change in the level of an explanatory factor; or (2) a relatively small change in activity, such as 10 additional CI investigations per state. I then convert these small effects to the marginal effect of a single unit change by dividing the response measured at either five percent or through 10 additional investigations by the corresponding number of additional investigations (10 or the level that corresponds to five percent). I do not attempt to simulate an increase in one additional conviction because of the possibility of measurement error. My procedure is, therefore, similar to measuring an "arc" elasticity as compared to a "point" elasticity; the latter is defined by the calculus, while the former is a practical implementation or measurement technique.

The next issue is choosing the econometric specification. For simulations and final results, I select a single model from Chap. 7 estimated for the time period 1988–2001. Hence, the projections I report below are in 2001 dollars. This model, as discussed in Chap. 7 uses a measure of total CI sentenced cases for tax and money laundering, as well as the percentages of the latter two categories. This model found that total CI sentenced cases, the percent of cases that are money laundering cases, and the percent of cases resulting in probation or prison were significant explanatory factors in determining reported tax collections. Additionally, the individual audit rate was also statistically significant in determining reported tax collections.

The present chapter treats sentenced cases and convictions as basically identical because they are virtually synonymous in actual practice. With respect to the questions posed in this chapter, the final model is useful to address the first of these questions—what is the marginal benefit of a CI conviction? To do this, I increase (by a small amount) the total number of CI sentenced cases in my simulation rather than doubling this number. The specification selected holds constant the mix of such cases (tax and money laundering) and the percentage that receive fines versus prison or probation.

The second question—what is the marginal benefit of a CI conviction resulting in imprisonment versus probation?—may not be answered using the model from Chap. 7. That model combined prison and probation cases and compared these to fines because it was not possible to find a statistically significant difference between prison and probation cases. Here, in order to answer the question, I add a model that includes all sentenced cases that result in prison time and all sentenced cases that result in probation. Hence, I replace the total number of sentenced cases and the percentage of such cases that result in fines by these new factors. I then simulate these factors by increasing their levels by a small amount.

Finally, the third question asks "What is the marginal benefit of the three different types of convictions: legal, illegal, and narcotic sources?" Again, the model of Chap. 7 is not particularly suited to analyzing this issue because that model included factors for the percentage of all CI sentenced cases that are tax versus money laundering. Instead, I provide a new model that includes the number of tax sentenced cases and money laundering cases. I use those factors in the simulations I report below.

Results

I present the econometric models in Table 8.1. The first model (IRS1) is from Chap. 7. Model IRS2 provides a specification in which I consider tax and money laundering sentences as separate components. As I expected, the component for tax cases is not statistically significant, while the component for money laundering is statistically significant. I expected this result in the sense that it parallels the results previously found in Chap. 7. Model IRS3 separates the prison and probation components of CI sentenced cases. I proceed with the simulation based on the three models shown in Table 8.1.

As discussed above, I considered three experiments for the separate CI variables and for the audit rate (simulated for comparison purposes only). I increased a specific factor in one of three ways by: (1) doubling it; (2) increasing it marginally by five percent; or (3) increasing it absolutely by a small number of cases (200 audits per state or 10,000 audits total) and 100 CI component convictions (two per state). I selected the percentage increases to match these absolute levels to some extent, while maintaining the distribution of CI or exam activity across the states. I used the same percentages or absolute increases whether I was increasing the total of tax and money laundering sentences or some specific component such as CI sentenced cases that receive probation. For example, consider the simulation in which audit rates are doubled. The simulation results are provided in Table 8.2.

The first row of Table 8.2 (Model IRS1) shows that estimated assessed tax collections would increase to $963.3 billion (Column A) from $941.6 billion (Column B) in 2001. The $21.7 billion change (Column C) is the total revenue effect. These estimates also show that reported tax collections rise by $20.35 billion (Column F). This change is the indirect effect of doubling the audit rate. The difference between these two estimated differences is approximately $1.356 billion and represents the direct revenue effect. This amount is 93.8 percent of the total revenue effect.

Using the same model, I find that doubling CI activity (tax and money laundering cases) (Row 4) leads to $15.30 billion in increased reported taxes, $16.01 billion in increased assessed tax revenue, and a direct revenue increase of $0.713 billion.

Table 8.1 Econometric model summary

Variable	Models								
	1			2			3		
	ALR	RTR	RCAP	ALR	RTR	RCAP	ALR	RTR	RCAP
Constant	0.5101	0.5525	0.1712	0.6687	0.7181	0.1728	0.6569	0.7068	0.1687
	(1.443)	(1.567)	(4.308)	(1.805)	(1.945)	(4.410)	(1.785)	(1.926)	(4.296)
Percent of families on welfare	0.0021	0.0022	−0.0003	0.0089	0.0088	0.0000	0.0072	0.0069	0.0001
	(0.251)	(0.262)	(−0.36)	(1.069)	(1.054)	(0.006)	(0.867)	(0.842)	(0.167)
State tax rate	−0.0076	−0.0076	−0.0024	−0.0037	−0.0037	−0.0024	−0.0039	−0.0040	−0.0023
	(−1.30)	(−1.30)	(−3.08)	(−0.57)	(−0.57)	(−3.08)	(−0.62)	(−0.62)	(−2.96)
Personal income per capita	0.3216	0.3209	0.0118	0.3322	0.3314	0.0111	0.3277	0.3269	0.0112
	(18.33)	(18.34)	(6.029)	(17.82)	(17.83)	(5.713)	(17.79)	(17.79)	(5.737)
Family size	−3.2702	−3.3619	0.6035	−3.5577	−3.6645	0.5742	−3.5685	−3.6782	0.6041
	(−3.24)	(−3.34)	(5.452)	(−3.33)	(−3.45)	(5.232)	(−3.37)	(−3.49)	(5.550)
Farms per household	−0.7826	−0.6027	−0.3616	−0.0674	0.0778	−0.2430	0.3651	0.5297	−0.3122
	(−0.43)	(−0.33)	(−1.23)	(−0.03)	(0.039)	(−0.78)	(0.188)	(0.273)	(−1.02)
Percent of adults with high school diploma	−0.5224	−0.5352	0.0311	−0.6383	−0.6536	0.0372	−0.5816	−0.5960	0.0320
	(−3.73)	(−3.84)	(2.404)	(−4.46)	(−4.59)	(2.959)	(−4.19)	(−4.32)	(2.574)
Percent of pop over 65	2.8583	2.8748	−0.3649	3.2606	3.2876	−0.3773	3.0377	3.0570	−0.3667
	(2.884)	(2.903)	(−2.68)	(3.034)	(3.062)	(−2.74)	(2.854)	(2.875)	(−2.65)
Percent of employed persons in manufacturing	−0.4492	−0.4534	0.1925	−0.7492	−0.7529	0.1955	−0.7358	−0.7387	0.1963
	(−1.46)	(−1.48)	(4.982)	(−2.28)	(−2.29)	(5.092)	(−2.26)	(−2.27)	(5.109)
Percent of employed persons in service	0.3364	0.3733	−0.0092	0.2051	0.2370	0.0306	0.2678	0.3024	0.0177
	(0.839)	(0.934)	(−0.21)	(0.492)	(0.571)	(0.730)	(0.655)	(0.743)	(0.424)
Unemployment rate	−3.0195	−3.0728	−0.2194	−3.1091	−3.1753	−0.2043	−3.0767	−3.1442	−0.2087
	(−5.21)	(−5.33)	(−4.41)	(−5.41)	(−5.56)	(−4.30)	(−5.36)	(−5.52)	(−4.36)

(continued)

Table 8.1 (continued)

Variable	Models								
	1			2			3		
	ALR	RTR	RCAP	ALR	RTR	RCAP	ALR	RTR	RCAP
Audit rate	0.1980	0.1804	0.0216	0.1769	0.1610	0.0181	0.1715	0.1555	0.0183
	(4.161)	(3.811)	(5.029)	(3.995)	(3.657)	(4.727)	(3.907)	(3.564)	(4.758)
Total sentences (tax & money laun only)	0.000508	0.000490	−0.000026	–	–	–	–	–	–
	(2.073)	(2.006)	(-0.97)	–	–	–	–	–	–
Tax sentences	–	–	–	−0.000084	−0.000113	0.000040	–	–	–
	–	–	–	(−0.22)	(−0.30)	(1.100)	–	–	–
Money laundering sentences	–	–	–	0.001127	0.001122	−0.000077	–	–	–
	–	–	–	(2.831)	(2.834)	(−2.21)	–	–	–
Total prison sentences	–	–	–	–	–	–	0.000704	0.000735	−0.000036
	–	–	–	–	–	–	(1.143)	(1.201)	(−0.69)
Total probation sentences	–	–	–	–	–	–	0.000176	0.000139	−0.000011
	–	–	–	–	–	–	(0.295)	(0.233)	(−0.20)
% of Tot sent related to tax	0.0450	0.0427	0.0014	–	–	–	–	–	–
	(1.199)	(1.145)	(0.449)	–	–	–	–	–	–
% of Tot sent related to money laun	0.0400	0.0367	0.0039	–	–	–	–	–	–
	(0.915)	(0.846)	(1.056)	–	–	–	–	–	–
% of Tax sent neither prison nor probation	0.0157	0.0027	0.0120	–	–	–	–	–	–
	(0.167)	(0.029)	(1.533)	–	–	–	–	–	–
% of money laun sent neither prison nor probation	−0.3808	−0.3611	−0.0203	–	–	–	–	–	–
	(−4.66)	(−4.44)	(−2.92)	–	–	–	–	–	–

Table 8.2 Results from IRS collections revenue simulation

	Significant vars	Estimated assessed tax collections			Estimated assessed tax collections		
		Modified amount ($) (A)	Original amount ($) (B)	Difference (A-B) ($) (C)	Modified amount ($) (D)	Original amount ($) (E)	Difference (D - E) ($) (F)
IRS1 audits doubled	tottm, mnei_m, iar2	963,310.94	941,600.50	21,710.44	959,942.75	939,588.56	20,354.19
IRS1 audits increase 5%		942,679.88	941,600.50	1,079.38	940,600.69	939,588.56	1,012.13
IRS1 audits increase by 200 per state		942,611.75	941,600.50	1,011.25	940,534.63	939,588.56	946.06
IRS1 total sentences (tax, money) doubled		957,619.19	941,600.50	16,018.69	954,893.94	939,588.56	15,305.38
IRS1 total sentences (tax, money) increase 5%		942,409.69	941,600.50	809.19	940,361.81	939,588.56	773.25
IRS1 total sentences (tax, money) increase by 2 per state		942,005.50	941,600.50	405.00	939,976.00	939,588.56	387.44
IRS2 audits doubled	m, iar2	968,389.50	949,295.31	19,094.19	965,024.94	947,156.13	17,868.81
IRS2 audits increase 5%		950,245.50	949,295.31	950.19	948,045.38	947,156.13	889.25
IRS2 audits increase by 200 per state		950,184.75	949,295.31	889.44	947,986.50	947,156.13	830.38
IRS2 tax sentences doubled		951,245.81	949,295.31	1,950.50	948,499.44	947,156.13	1,343.31
IRS2 tax sentences increase 5%		949,393.38	949,295.31	98.06	947,224.00	947,156.13	67.88
IRS2 tax sentences increase by 2 per state		949,369.94	949,295.31	74.63	947,201.25	947,156.13	45.13
IRS2 money laun sentences doubled		966,114.13	949,295.31	16,818.81	963,874.94	947,156.13	16,718.81
IRS2 money laun sentences increase 5%		950,153.19	949,295.31	857.88	948,008.94	947,156.13	852.81
IRS2 money laun sentences increase by 2 per state		950,114.38	949,295.31	819.06	947,970.38	947,156.13	814.25

(continued)

Table 8.2 (continued)

	Significant vars	Estimated assessed tax collections			Estimated assessed tax collections		
		Modified amount ($) (A)	Original amount ($) (B)	Difference (A-B) ($) (C)	Modified amount ($) (D)	Original amount ($) (E)	Difference (D - E) ($) (F)
IRS3 audits doubled	iar2	967,741.19	948,999.50	18,741.69	964,548.00	947,031.13	17,516.88
IRS3 audits increase 5%		949,932.06	948,999.50	932.56	947,902.88	947,031.13	871.75
IRS3 audits increase by 200 per state		949,871.88	948,999.50	872.38	947,844.25	947,031.13	813.13
IRS3 prison sentences (tax, money) doubled		967,890.50	948,999.50	18,891.00	967,014.56	947,031.13	19,983.44
IRS3 prison sentences (tax, money) increase 5%		949,955.81	948,999.50	956.31	948,042.50	947,031.13	1,011.38
IRS3 prison sentences (tax, money) increase by 2 per state		949,559.06	948,999.50	559.56	947,621.81	947,031.13	590.69
IRS3 probation sentences (tax, money) doubled		953,609.50	948,999.50	4,610.00	950,282.38	947,031.13	3,251.25
IRS3 probation sentences (tax, money) increase 5%		949,230.94	948,999.50	231.44	947,194.50	947,031.13	163.38
IRS3 probation sentences (tax, money) increase by 2 per state		949,133.00	948,999.50	133.50	947,127.13	947,031.13	96.00

(continued)

Table 8.2 (continued)

	Actual reported collections ($) (G)	% of Estimated reported difference and actual reported tax revenue (F/G) (H)	% of Estimated reported difference and estimated reported tax revenue (F/E) (I)	% Change in estimated assessed and reported tax revenue (C – F)/F (J)	Direct revenue effect (C – F) ($) (K)	Indirect revenue effect (F) ($) (L)	Indirect revenue effect/total revenue effect (L/(K + L)) (%) (M)
IRS1 audits doubled	882,128	2.3	2.2	6.7	1,356.25	20,354.19	93.75
IRS1 audits increase 5	882,128	0.1	0.1	6.6	67.25	1,012.13	93.77
IRS1 audits increase by 200 per state	882,128	0.1	0.1	6.9	65.19	946.06	93.55
IRS1 total sentences (tax, money) doubled	882,128	1.7	1.6	4.7	713.31	15,305.38	95.55
IRS1 total sentences (tax, money) increase 5	882,128	0.1	0.1	4.6	35.94	773.25	95.56
IRS1 total sentences (tax, money) increase by 2 per state	882,128	0.0	0.0	4.5	17.56	387.44	95.66
IRS2 audits doubled	882,128	2.0	1.9	6.9	1,225.38	17,868.81	93.58
IRS2 audits increase 5	882,128	0.1	0.1	6.9	60.94	889.25	93.59

(continued)

Table 8.2 (continued)

	Actual reported collections ($) (G)	% of Estimated reported difference and actual reported tax revenue (F/G) (H)	% of Estimated reported difference and estimated reported tax revenue (F/E) (I)	% Change in estimated assessed and reported tax revenue (C – F)/F (J)	Direct revenue effect (C – F) ($) (K)	Indirect revenue effect (F) ($) (L)	Indirect revenue effect/total revenue effect (L/(K + L)) (%) (M)
IRS2 audits increase by 200 per state	882,128	0.1	0.1	7.1	59.06	830.38	93.36
IRS2 tax sentences doubled	882,128	0.2	0.1	45.2	607.19	1,343.31	68.87
IRS2 tax sentences increase 5	882,128	0.0	0.0	44.5	30.19	67.88	69.22
IRS2 tax sentences increase by 2 per state	882,128	0.0	0.0	65.4	29.50	45.13	60.47
IRS2 money laun sentences doubled	882,128	1.9	1.8	0.6	100.00	16,718.81	99.41
IRS2 money laun sentences increase 5	882,128	0.1	0.1	0.6	5.06	852.81	99.41
IRS2 money laun sentences increase by 2 per state	882,128	0.1	0.1	0.6	4.81	814.25	99.41
IRS3 audits doubled	882,128	2.0	1.8	7.0	1,224.81	17,516.88	93.46
IRS3 audits increase 5	882,128	0.1	0.1	7.0	60.81	871.75	93.48

(continued)

Table 8.2 (continued)

	Actual reported collections ($) (G)	% of Estimated reported difference and actual reported tax revenue (F/G) (H)	% of Estimated reported difference and estimated reported tax revenue (F/E) (I)	% Change in estimated assessed and reported tax revenue (C − F)/F (J)	Direct revenue effect (C − F) ($) (K)	Indirect revenue effect (F) ($) (L)	Indirect revenue effect/total revenue effect (L/(K + L)) (%) (M)
IRS3 audits increase by 200 per state	882,128	0.1	0.1	7.3	59.25	813.13	93.21
IRS3 prison sentences (tax, money) doubled	882,128	2.3	2.1	−5.5	(1,092.44)	19,983.44	105.78
IRS3 prison sentences (tax, money) increase 5	882,128	0.1	0.1	−5.4	(55.06)	1,011.38	105.76
IRS3 prison sentences (tax, money) increase by 2 per state	882,128	0.1	0.1	−5.3	(31.13)	590.69	105.56
IRS3 probation sentences (tax, money) doubled	882,129	0.4	0.3	41.8	1,358.75	3,251.25	70.53
IRS3 probation sentences (tax, money) increase 5	882,130	0.0	0.0	41.7	68.06	163.38	70.59
IRS3 probation sentences (tax, money) increase by 2 per state	882,131	0.0	0.0	39.1	37.50	96.00	71.91

Hence, I measured the spillover effect to be approximately 96 percent. Importantly, doubling CI activity or doubling the IRS audit examination rate leads to similar revenue increases and implies similar levels of increased general deterrence. The marginal analysis is reported in Table 8.3.

Table 8.3 has rows corresponding to the rows of Table 8.2. For instance, the second row of Table 8.3 shows that increasing the audit rate by five percent leads to 10,083 (Column C) additional audits and increases total revenues by $1.079 billion (Column F). Also, in row six of Table 8.3, I show the effects of increasing the number of CI sentenced cases by two per state (or 100 in total). This leads to an increase in total revenue of $405.0 million (Column F). For the first example, the marginal effect is the increase in total revenue of $1.079 billion divided by 10,083 audits, or roughly $107,044 per audit in specific and general deterrence. Using the same model and simulation (row 2), we see that the direct revenues increase by $67.25 million (Column D), or $6,669 per audit. The simulation (using model IRS1) in which the audit rate was doubled (Table 8.3, Row 1) leads to an increase of $21.7 billion (Column F) of additional total revenue and corresponded to 201,670 additional audits. This implies an average of $6,725 per audit—a figure not dissimilar from that obtained in the marginal simulation with a five percent increase. On the other hand, doubling CI sentenced cases (Table 8.3, row 4) leads to 1,732 additional cases and $16.0 billion (Column F) in additional revenue. This corresponds to $9.25 million per additional sentenced case in specific and general deterrence. From Table 8.3, row 6, we see that adding two CI sentenced cases per state (or 100 additional cases in total) leads to $405 million (Column F) additional total revenue or $4.05 million per additional sentenced case. Here, the marginal and average effects diverge.[1]

The additional simulations are shown in Tables 8.2 and 8.3. Increasing CI sentenced cases leads to $4.05 million to $9.25 million per case. Increasing CI probation cases leads to $1.33 million to $2.99 million per case. Increasing CI prison cases leads to $5.59 million to $12.66 million per case. Increasing tax cases leads to $0.746 million to $2.18 million per case. Increasing money laundering cases leads to $8.19 million to $19.54 million per case. However, neither the increases in prison or probation cases nor the increases in the tax-sentenced cases are statistically significant.

The marginal gains considered above need to be compared to the marginal costs. According to estimates reported by Plumley (1996), Table 5, pp. 41),[2] the

[1] The results show that absolute changes in audits or sentences lead to smaller marginal changes in revenue than percentage changes. Absolute changes are constant across states, whereas the percentage changes vary according to state size (i.e., California will have large changes and Rhode Island will have small changes). This difference is important when we extrapolate to form totals for the U.S. as a whole. When we simulate with absolute changes, big states have relatively smaller changes. Extrapolating by population, small changes are more heavily weighted in large states, and the overall effect is consequently lowered.

[2] Plumley, Alan H. "The Determinants of Individual Income Tax Compliance: Estimating the Impacts of Tax Policy, Enforcement, and IRS Responsiveness." Internal Revenue Service, Publication 1916 (Rev. 11-96), 1996.

Table 8.3 Estimated gains in collection revenue

	Amount before change	Amount after change	Difference (B - A)	Direct change in revenue ($)	Indirect change in revenue ($)	Total change in revenue (D + E) ($)	Direct revenue change per audit or per sentence (D/C) ($)	Indirect revenue change per audit or per sentence (E/C) ($)	Total revenue change per audit or per sentence (F/C) ($)
	(A)	(B)	(C)	(D)	(E)	(F)	(G)	(H)	(I)
IRS1 audits doubled	201,670	403,340	201,670	1,356,250,000	20,354,187,500	21,710,437,500	6,725	100,928	107,653
IRS1 audits increase 5%	201,670	211,753	10,083	67,250,000	1,012,125,000	1,079,375,000	6,669	100,375	107,044
IRS1 audits increase by 200 per state	201,670	211,670	10,000	65,187,500	946,062,500	1,011,250,000	6,519	94,606	101,125
IRS1 total sentences (tax, money) doubled	1,732	3,464	1,732	713,312,500	15,305,375,000	16,018,687,500	411,843	8,836,822	9,248,665
IRS1 total sentences (tax, money) increase 5%	1,732	1,819	87	35,937,500	773,250,000	809,187,500	414,983	8,928,999	9,343,983
IRS1 total sentences (tax, money) increase by 2 per state	1,732	1,832	100	17,562,500	387,437,500	405,000,000	175,625	3,874,375	4,050,000

(continued)

Table 8.3 (continued)

	Amount before change (A)	Amount after change (B)	Difference (B - A) (C)	Direct change in revenue ($) (D)	Indirect change in revenue ($) (E)	Total change in revenue (D + E) ($) (F)	Direct revenue change per audit or per sentence (D/C) ($) (G)	Indirect revenue change per audit or per sentence (E/C) ($) (H)	Total revenue change per audit or per sentence (F/C) ($) (I)
IRS2 audits doubled	201,670	403,340	201,670	1,225,375,000	17,868,812,500	19,094,187,500	6,076	88,604	94,680
IRS2 audits increase 5%	201,670	211,753	10,083	60,937,500	889,250,000	950,187,500	6,043	88,189	94,232
IRS2 audits increase by 200 per state	201,670	211,670	10,000	59,062,500	830,375,000	889,437,500	5,906	83,038	88,944
IRS2 tax sentences doubled	899	1,798	899	607,187,500	1,343,312,500	1,950,500,000	675,403	1,494,230	2,169,633
IRS2 tax sentences increase 5%	899	944	45	30,187,500	67,875,000	98,062,500	671,580	1,510,013	2,181,593
IRS2 tax sentences increase by 2 per state	899	999	100	29,500,000	45,125,000	74,625,000	295,000	451,250	746,250
IRS2 money laun sentences doubled	878	1,756	878	100,000,000	16,718,812,500	16,818,812,500	113,895	19,041,928	19,155,823

(continued)

Table 8.3 (continued)

	Amount before change (A)	Amount after change (B)	Difference (B - A) (C)	Direct change in revenue ($) (D)	Indirect change in revenue ($) (E)	Total change in revenue (D + E) ($) (F)	Direct revenue change per audit or per sentence (D/C) ($) (G)	Indirect revenue change per audit or per sentence (E/C) ($) (H)	Total revenue change per audit or per sentence (F/C) ($) (I)
IRS2 money laun sentences increase 5%	878	922	44	5,062,500	852,812,500	857,875,000	115,319	19,426,271	19,541,590
IRS2 money laun sentences increase by 2 per state	878	978	100	4,812,500	814,250,000	819,062,500	48,125	8,142,500	8,190,625
IRS3 audits doubled	201,670	403,340	201,670	1,224,812,500	17,516,875,000	18,741,687,500	6,073	86,859	92,932
IRS3 audits increase 5%	201,670	211,753	10,083	60,812,500	871,750,000	932,562,500	6,031	86,453	92,484
IRS3 audits increase by 200 per state	201,670	211,670	10,000	59,250,000	813,125,000	872,375,000	5,925	81,313	87,238
IRS3 prison sentences (tax, money) doubled	1,511	3,022	1,511	(1,092,437,500)	19,983,437,500	18,891,000,000	(722,990)	13,225,306	12,502,316

(continued)

Table 8.3 (continued)

	Amount before change (A)	Amount after change (B)	Difference (B - A) (C)	Direct change in revenue ($) (D)	Indirect change in revenue ($) (E)	Total change in revenue (D + E) ($) (F)	Direct revenue change per audit or per sentence (D/C) ($) (G)	Indirect revenue change per audit or per sentence (E/C) ($) (H)	Total revenue change per audit or per sentence (F/C) ($) (I)
IRS3 prison sentences (tax, money) increase 5%	1,511	1,587	76	(55,062,500)	1,011,375,000	956,312,500	(728,823)	13,386,842	12,658,020
IRS3 prison sentences (tax, money) increase by 2 per state	1,511	1,611	100	(31,125,000)	590,687,500	559,562,500	(311,250)	5,906,875	5,595,625
IRS3 probation sentences (tax, money) doubled	1,538	3,076	1,538	1,358,750,000	3,251,250,000	4,610,000,000	883,453	2,113,947	2,997,399
IRS3 probation sentences (tax, money) increase 5%	1,538	1,615	77	68,062,500	163,375,000	231,437,500	885,079	2,124,515	3,009,594
IRS3 probation sentences (tax, money) increase by 2 per state	1,538	1,638	100	37,500,000	96,000,000	133,500,000	375,000	960,000	1,335,000

cost for a CI conviction was nearly 80 times greater than the cost of an audit in 1991. In 1991, Plumley reported a unit cost of $1,298 per audit and a unit cost of $103,064 per CI conviction. After adjusting for inflation, the CI division has updated these costs to $1,597 per audit and $126,801 per conviction in 2001. The CI budget in 2001 was $445,043,278. Of this amount, roughly 30.1 percent was attributable to money laundering cases, yielding an average cost of $259 million divided by 878 money laundering cases, or $295,259 per case. Similarly, 58.3 percent of the budget was devoted to tax cases, which translates to $288,362 per case on average (based on 899 tax sentenced cases in 2001). The overall average is $227,147 per case ($393.4 million/1,732 tax or money laundering cases). CI Division can neither determine the marginal cost of a sentenced case nor can it attribute its budget to cases that led to prison versus probation versus fines. I was not able to find a significant temporal correlation between tax and money laundering cases sentenced and the CI Division's budget.[3] Nevertheless, the relative magnitude of estimates compared to Plumley's figures suggests that the incremental cost of CI activities is much lower than the average costs derived above. Comparing the average costs per case to the average total revenue gains per case from specific and general deterrence demonstrates that money laundering cases have especially large marginal benefits. The marginal benefits from money laundering cases are also statistically significant at conventional levels (the confidence interval around the estimate would not include zero dollars at the 95 percent level of confidence). Relying on the point estimates I have shown that the marginal benefits from money laundering convictions exceed those achieved from tax convictions. While not statistically significant, CI cases resulting in prison result in higher marginal benefits than cases that result in probation.

Conclusions

While I was not able to find statistically significant effects resulting from a change in prison or probation cases, prison convictions achieve larger estimated gains than probation convictions. In Chap. 7, I was able to conclude that the decreasing number of cases that result in fines was a statistically significant determinant of assessed tax liability. In other words, prison or probation outcomes are better than fines for specific and general deterrence. These results point further to larger gains from prison as compared to probation outcomes. Additional years of socioeconomic data and enforcement data help the significance of the results and resolve some of the empirical issues. We now turn to the results in the next chapter.

---

[3] This type of time-series analysis can sometimes be used to untangle marginal and average costs over time.

Chapter 9
Extensions to the Period 2002–2004

Introduction

In this Chapter, I extend the models presented in Chap. 8 to add three additional years of information (2002–2004) and to consider several new econometrics models. The addition of these three years was not straightforward. First, I observed significant structural instability in adding the years 2002 through 2004 to the econometrics models. Generally, for the specifications reported in Chaps. 7 and 8, poor results were obtained for any specifications that included media factors. More importantly, these models produced perverse outcomes for examination factors. Closer examination revealed major changes in the recent time period for the reported and assessed tax collections variables. These changes are plainly evident in Fig. 9.1, where I show the variable *PICAP* (personal income per capita) and tax revenue assessed per individual.

After 2000, changes in tax policy led to significant declines in tax collections. These tax cuts led to significant declines in Federal revenues that were subsequently reversed in 2003 with the Jobs and Growth Act of 2003. I note this reversal in Fig. 9.1 with the upward shift in individual tax revenues in 2004. These recent swings in individual tax collections require a new explanatory factor that was missing from the previous specifications and analysis. Accordingly, this Chapter provides alternative models using Federal tax rates and the simulation results from the marginal impacts using these models.

Federal Tax Rates

The original DGW study presented an empirical specification for tax collections that did not include Federal tax rates. First, the Federal marginal tax rates were not available to DGW at the state level in their study. Statutory Federal tax rates would be constant across states and would not show variation from state to state. Moreover, there was little variation in tax rates during the 1977–1987 period used

J. A. Dubin, *The Causes and Consequences of Income Tax Noncompliance*,
DOI: 10.1007/978-1-4419-0907-7_9,

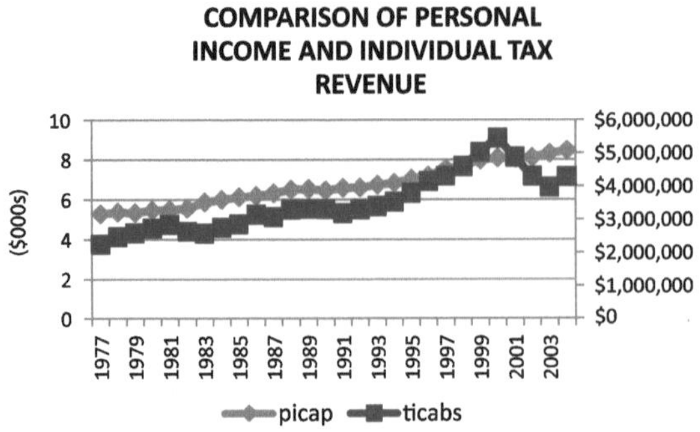

Fig. 9.1 Comparison of personal income and individual tax revenue

by DGW. For these reasons, DGW omitted Federal tax rates but included state tax rates. My analysis reported in Chap. 7 similarly omitted Federal tax rates.

Theoretically, tax rates should matter in determining tax compliance. Several theoretical studies have investigated the connection between tax rates and compliance. Competing theories preclude a definite a priori theory for tax rates and compliance, as discussed in Yitzhakie (1974) or Witte and Woodbury (1983) as well as the survey articles reviewed in Chap. 4. Empirically, Clotfelter (1983), and Crane and Nourzad (1986) have used tax rates to explain compliance. Clearly, the tax rate—and, more generally, the tax structure in combination with personal income—determines reported and assessed tax revenue. In the simplest of cases, the average tax rate multiplied by personal income should determine income tax. However, tax rates are themselves endogenous (i.e., taxpayers choose to some degree their tax bracket). An observed effect (such as noncompliance for some taxpayers) can simultaneously affect tax rates and taxable income. These issues require that tax rates be treated endogenously in micro-econometric studies and considered endogenous in some aggregate studies as well. I return to this point below.

Meanwhile, there has been significant improvement in measuring average and marginal tax rates at the Federal level. These factors are available from the National Bureau of Economic Research (NBER). NBER calculates the maximum (marginal) tax rate for an additional $1,000 of income for a married couple filing a joint return with $500,000 in annual wage income. Assuming a set of deductions, NBER uses its TAXSIM simulation model to calculate the effective maximum rate for its sample of taxpayers. These rates vary by state and time due to changes in tax law and changes in the state income tax deduction (if present) on the Federal return (this, too, varies by state and time). The maximum Federal tax rates described above are used typically as instruments because they should be exogenous but correlated with average tax rates. This factor is denoted by *FMXTAX* and is the maximum federal tax rate with cross tax deductions.[1] NBER also tabulates

[1] http://nber.org/ ~ taxmin/state-rates/maxrate.html

average marginal state income tax rates using the TAXSIM model. This factor is denoted *STAXR* and is the average state marginal income tax rate based on 1995 national income distribution and an average Federal tax rate by state and time.[2] This factor is denoted by *FAVTAX* and is the Federal and state combined income tax rate based on the national 1995 income distribution.[3]

My empirical treatments are: Model 0, State tax rate only: *STAXR* (this is the baseline model from DGW (1988) and not reported here); Model 1, State tax rate, and Federal/State top marginal rate: *STAXR*, *FMXTAX*; Model 2, State tax rate, and Federal/State average marginal rate—treated exogenously: *STAXR*, *FAVTAX*; Model 3, Federal/State top tax rate only: *FMXTAX*; Model 4, State tax rate and interaction of personal income with Federal/State top tax rate: *STAXR*, *FMX-TAX*PICAP*; Model 5, State tax rate, and Federal/State average marginal rate—treated endogenously with top marginal rate as instrument: *STAXR*, *FAVTAX*.

Generally, I expect a negative sign on the coefficient of state tax rates due to the deductibility of the latter (see also the discussion in DGW) and a positive sign on Federal/State tax rates given that their dominant role has a positive association with reported income taxes due. As tax rates increase, holding personal income constant, tax revenues rise. This effect explains the pattern of lower taxes due in 2001 through 2004.

I specified and estimated alternative models using the various tax measures as described above. In addition to marginal and average tax rates, I allowed a post-2001 effect in the model using a dummy indicator for the period 2001–2004. This dummy indicator captures additional changes in the tax code, such as changes in capital gains tax treatment, that are not measured by other factors in the model.

Alternate Econometric Models

I present the econometric models in Table 9.1 for the period ending in 2004 and in Table 9.1A for the period ending in 2001. Generally, the results are similar between the two periods, which demonstrate model stability. The additional factor for the Federal/State top marginal tax rate is statistically significant in the 1988–2001 period (Table 9.1A, Model 1) and demonstrates an improvement over the Chap. 7 models for the same period without this factor. Since results are similar, I concentrate on the full data period from 1988–2004.

Model 1 in Table 9.1 shows that the Federal/State top tax rate is statistically significant, while state tax rates have coefficients that are negative and statistically significant. These results follow standard economic theory. As I expected, the audit factor is positive. Moreover, this model shows that CI total sentences are

---

[2] http://www.nber.org/~taxsim/state-marginal/state-fix.html

[3] http://www.nber.org/~taxsim/state-marginal/avratesffx.html

Table 9.1 Econometric models for the period ending in 2004

Variable	1				2				3			
	ALR	RTR	RCAP	IAR	ALR	RTR	RCAP	IAR	ALR	RTR	RCAP	IAR
Constant	1.6998	1.7316	0.1776	2.3414	−0.2805	−0.2510	0.1568	2.1416	1.5867	1.6159	0.1767	2.2221
	(4.898)	(4.989)	(5.081)	(5.449)	(−0.83)	(−0.75)	(4.354)	(4.454)	(4.642)	(4.728)	(5.030)	(5.123)
Percent of families on welfare	0.0243	0.0243	0.0006	0.0904	0.0299	0.0298	0.0008	0.0904	0.0231	0.0231	0.0005	0.0895
	(2.677)	(2.671)	(0.857)	(8.677)	(3.721)	(3.730)	(1.068)	(8.747)	(2.559)	(2.552)	(0.628)	(8.495)
State tax rate	−0.0147	−0.0149	−0.0021	−0.0227	0.0037	0.0038	−0.0019	−0.0206	–	–	–	–
	(−2.38)	(−2.42)	(−2.82)	(−3.17)	(0.629)	(0.646)	(−2.58)	(−2.76)	–	–	–	–
Personal income per capita	0.2003	0.1978	0.0072	−0.1524	0.2426	0.2402	0.0082	−0.1515	0.2032	0.2009	0.0071	−0.1516
	(11.13)	(10.99)	(4.070)	(−8.41)	(14.62)	(14.55)	(4.648)	(−8.32)	(11.42)	(11.29)	(3.998)	(−8.26)
Federal & state top tax rate	0.0127	0.0127	0.0003	−0.0004	–	–	–	–	0.0129	0.0129	0.0002	0.0005
	(7.972)	(7.970)	(1.963)	(−0.16)	–	–	–	–	(8.099)	(8.103)	(1.852)	(0.183)
Personal income* Federal & state top tax rate	–	–	–	–	–	–	–	–	–	–	–	–
	–	–	–	–	–	–	–	–	–	–	–	–
Federal & state avg marginal tax rate	–	–	–	–	0.0898	0.0906	0.0009	0.0105	–	–	–	–
	–	–	–	–	(18.20)	(18.48)	(1.837)	(0.973)	–	–	–	–
Family size	−4.2603	−4.3048	0.7574	−0.6925	−5.3792	−5.4687	0.7244	−0.7614	−3.9687	−4.0063	0.7465	−0.1822
	(−4.43)	(−4.47)	(7.798)	(−0.54)	(−6.07)	(−6.20)	(7.479)	(−0.59)	(−4.16)	(−4.20)	(7.657)	(−0.14)
Farms per household	−2.0972	−1.9245	−0.3523	3.6203	−2.4266	−2.2203	−0.3701	3.6422	−2.1158	−1.9461	−0.3113	3.8691
	(−1.13)	(−1.04)	(−1.28)	(1.707)	(−1.38)	(−1.26)	(−1.36)	(1.709)	(−1.16)	(−1.07)	(−1.13)	(1.790)
Percent of adults with high school diploma	−0.9153	−0.9303	0.0168	−0.6873	−0.6579	−0.6756	0.0258	−0.7806	−0.9522	−0.9678	0.0152	−0.8077
	(−5.65)	(−5.74)	(1.222)	(−2.75)	(−4.88)	(−5.04)	(2.005)	(−3.35)	(−5.87)	(−5.96)	(1.095)	(−3.24)
Percent of pop over 65	0.8405	0.7996	−0.5667	−4.3910	3.3305	3.3173	−0.5012	−4.3825	0.6961	0.6530	−0.5603	−4.8393
	(0.832)	(0.792)	(−4.66)	(−3.85)	(3.506)	(3.503)	(−4.17)	(−3.82)	(0.696)	(0.653)	(−4.59)	(−4.19)
Percent of employed persons in manufacturing	1.0318	1.0566	0.1752	−0.2245	0.0980	0.1105	0.1622	−0.2969	0.9445	0.9678	0.1739	−0.3702
	(3.597)	(3.684)	(5.835)	(−0.61)	(0.358)	(0.405)	(5.109)	(−0.79)	(3.334)	(3.418)	(5.765)	(−1.00)

(continued)

Table 9.1 (continued)

Variable	1				2				3			
	ALR	RTR	RCAP	IAR	ALR	RTR	RCAP	IAR	ALR	RTR	RCAP	IAR
Percent of employed persons in service	0.8937	0.9662	−0.0034	1.6323	−0.0563	0.0087	−0.0108	1.5325	0.7611	0.8305	−0.0115	1.4676
	(2.712)	(2.929)	(−0.12)	(3.819)	(−0.18)	(0.029)	(−0.37)	(3.607)	(2.357)	(2.571)	(−0.40)	(3.435)
Unemployment rate	−6.4026	−6.4535	−0.2762	−2.0194	−2.8971	−2.9157	−0.2555	−1.6273	−6.3876	−6.4378	−0.2803	−1.9730
	(−11.6)	(−11.6)	(−5.96)	(−2.34)	(−5.37)	(−5.44)	(−5.09)	(−1.73)	(−11.5)	(−11.6)	(−6.03)	(−2.27)
Audit rate	0.0912	0.0736	0.0108	–	0.2233	0.2065	0.0135	–	0.1033	0.0859	0.0110	–
	(1.587)	(1.279)	(2.266)	–	(4.351)	(4.052)	(2.832)	–	(1.814)	(1.508)	(2.296)	–
Direct examination time	–	–	–	0.2254	–	–	–	0.3227	–	–	–	0.2275
	–	–	–	(1.742)	–	–	–	(2.050)	–	–	–	(1.752)
Budget per return	–	–	–	25.2471	–	–	–	25.2854	–	–	–	25.8897
	–	–	–	(10.85)	–	–	–	(10.90)	–	–	–	(11.14)
Total sentences	–	–	–	–	–	–	–	–	–	–	–	–
	–	–	–	–	–	–	–	–	–	–	–	–
Total sentences (tax & money laun only)	0.000857	0.000848	−0.000014	0.000142	0.000310	0.000295	−0.000017	0.000083	0.000905	0.000897	−0.000010	0.000249
	(3.360)	(3.323)	(−0.54)	(0.425)	(1.303)	(1.246)	(−0.64)	(0.245)	(3.582)	(3.548)	(−0.40)	(0.737)
% of tot sent related to tax	0.0486	0.0473	0.0035	−0.0880	0.0275	0.0261	0.0033	−0.0892	0.0478	0.0464	0.0035	−0.0914
	(1.352)	(1.312)	(1.221)	(−1.52)	(0.856)	(0.821)	(1.140)	(−1.55)	(1.321)	(1.281)	(1.186)	(−1.57)
% of tot sent related to money laun	−0.0480	−0.0503	0.0018	−0.2107	−0.0154	−0.0176	0.0028	−0.2211	−0.0498	−0.0521	0.0018	−0.2172
	(−1.18)	(−1.23)	(0.558)	(−3.32)	(−0.43)	(−0.49)	(0.879)	(−3.53)	(−1.21)	(−1.27)	(0.545)	(−3.41)
% of tax sent neither prison nor probation	0.0584	0.0472	0.0077	−0.3648	0.0215	0.0103	0.0077	−0.3655	0.0679	0.0569	0.0088	−0.3607
	(0.601)	(0.486)	(0.992)	(−2.31)	(0.248)	(0.119)	(0.974)	(−2.32)	(0.697)	(0.583)	(1.122)	(−2.28)
% of money laun sent neither prison nor probation	−0.2397	−0.2210	−0.0071	0.9023	−0.3354	−0.3168	−0.0098	0.9156	−0.2404	−0.2219	−0.0060	0.9157
	(−2.61)	(−2.40)	(−0.95)	(7.918)	(−4.11)	(−3.91)	(−1.32)	(8.063)	(−2.60)	(−2.39)	(−0.81)	(8.015)
Number of obs	850				850				850			
Years	1988–2004				1988–2004				1988–2004			

(continued)

Table 9.1 (continued)

Variable	4				5			
	ALR	RTR	RCAP	IAR	ALR	RTR	RCAP	IAR
Constant	2.1395	2.1758	0.1813	2.3413	−0.2704	−0.2418	0.1782	2.3414
	(6.297)	(6.408)	(5.147)	(5.312)	(−0.76)	(−0.68)	(4.809)	(5.449)
Percent of families on welfare	0.0190	0.0189	0.0008	0.0902	0.0295	0.0294	0.0009	0.0904
	(2.153)	(2.140)	(1.083)	(8.647)	(3.652)	(3.659)	(1.201)	(8.677)
State tax rate	−0.0138	−0.0140	−0.0021	−0.0226	0.0039	0.0040	−0.0020	−0.0227
	(−2.31)	(−2.34)	(−2.81)	(−3.15)	(0.654)	(0.672)	(−2.76)	(−3.17)
Personal income per capita	0.1184	0.1156	0.0067	−0.1519	0.2431	0.2408	0.0076	−0.1524
	(6.280)	(6.135)	(3.401)	(−6.86)	(14.26)	(14.20)	(4.229)	(−8.41)
Federal & state top tax rate	–	–	–	–	–	–	–	−0.0004
	–	–	–	–	–	–	–	(−0.16)
Personal income* Federal & state top tax rate	0.0024	0.0024	0.0000	0.0000	–	–	–	–
	(10.86)	(10.91)	(0.917)	(−0.05)	–	–	–	–
Federal & state avg marginal tax rate	–	–	–	–	0.0897	0.0905	−0.0001	–
	–	–	–	–	(13.63)	(13.85)	(−0.13)	–
Family size	−3.9132	−3.9619	0.7441	−0.6920	−5.4258	−5.5163	0.7266	−0.6925
	(−4.19)	(−4.24)	(7.623)	(−0.54)	(−6.09)	(−6.22)	(7.546)	(−0.54)
Farms per household	−2.7939	−2.6189	−0.3393	3.6181	−2.4034	−2.1965	−0.3220	3.6203
	(−1.55)	(−1.46)	(−1.25)	(1.700)	(−1.35)	(−1.23)	(−1.18)	(1.707)
Percent of adults with high school diploma	−0.9785	−0.9958	0.0230	−0.7011	−0.6552	−0.6729	0.0278	−0.6873
	(−6.35)	(−6.47)	(1.704)	(−2.84)	(−4.84)	(−5.00)	(2.163)	(−2.75)
Percent of pop over 65	0.6535	0.6123	−0.5516	−4.4031	3.3719	3.3605	−0.5269	−4.3910
	(0.667)	(0.625)	(−4.52)	(−3.84)	(3.486)	(3.486)	(−4.39)	(−3.85)
Percent of employed persons in manufacturing	0.9958	1.0206	0.1794	−0.2277	0.0956	0.1075	0.1846	−0.2245
	(3.590)	(3.682)	(6.003)	(−0.62)	(0.338)	(0.381)	(5.581)	(−0.61)
Percent of employed persons in service	0.6486	0.7187	0.0053	1.6250	−0.0617	0.0024	0.0125	1.6323
	(2.030)	(2.250)	(0.186)	(3.815)	(−0.19)	(0.007)	(0.411)	(3.819)

(continued)

Table 9.1 (continued)

Variable	4				5			
	ALR	RTR	RCAP	IAR	ALR	RTR	RCAP	IAR
Unemployment rate	−6.1521	−6.1993	−0.2869	−2.0065	−2.9069	−2.9237	−0.2983	−2.0194
	(−11.4)	(−11.5)	(−6.18)	(−2.33)	(−4.99)	(−5.05)	(−5.58)	(−2.34)
Audit rate	0.1224	0.1050	0.0105	–	0.2265	0.2099	0.0107	–
	(2.188)	(1.877)	(2.200)	–	(4.258)	(3.974)	(2.169)	–
Direct examination time	–	–	–	0.2282	–	–	–	0.2254
	–	–	–	(1.738)	–	–	–	(1.742)
Budget per return	–	–	–	25.2450	–	–	–	25.2471
	–	–	–	(10.85)	–	–	–	(10.85)
Total sentences	–	–	–	–	–	–	–	–
	–	–	–	–	–	–	–	–
Total sentences (Tax & money laun only)	0.000763	0.000753	−0.000010	0.000140	0.000310	0.000295	−0.000005	0.000142
	(3.081)	(3.042)	(−0.40)	(0.416)	(1.277)	(1.220)	(−0.20)	(0.425)
% of tot sent related to tax	0.0526	0.0514	0.0033	−0.0876	0.0279	0.0266	0.0032	−0.0880
	(1.505)	(1.470)	(1.141)	(−1.52)	(0.869)	(0.834)	(1.106)	(−1.52)
% of tot sent related to money laun	−0.0554	−0.0579	0.0023	−0.2119	−0.0143	−0.0165	0.0028	−0.2107
	(−1.40)	(−1.46)	(0.715)	(−3.34)	(−0.39)	(−0.46)	(0.873)	(−3.32)
% of tax sent neither prison nor probation	0.0706	0.0596	0.0074	−0.3641	0.0224	0.0112	0.0074	−0.3648
	(0.748)	(0.632)	(0.953)	(−2.31)	(0.258)	(0.130)	(0.940)	(−2.31)
% of money laun sent neither prison nor probation	−0.2356	−0.2168	−0.0071	0.9034	−0.3389	−0.3204	−0.0080	0.9023
	(−2.64)	(−2.42)	(−0.96)	(7.907)	(−4.12)	(−3.92)	(−1.08)	(7.918)
Number of obs	850				850			
Years	1988–2004				1988–2004			

Table 9.1A Econometric models for the period ending in 2001

Variable	1				2				3			
	ALR	RTR	RCAP	IAR	ALR	RTR	RCAP	IAR	ALR	RTR	RCAP	IAR
Constant	0.5665	0.6091	0.1718	2.0500	−0.3164	−0.2837	0.1885	2.7690	0.4944	0.5366	0.1697	1.8802
	(1.604)	(1.729)	(4.314)	(4.113)	(−0.80)	(−0.72)	(4.572)	(5.076)	(1.424)	(1.549)	(4.239)	(3.769)
Percent of families on welfare	−0.0012	−0.0011	−0.0003	0.0522	0.0123	0.0125	−0.0005	0.0391	−0.0021	−0.0020	−0.0005	0.0507
	(−0.14)	(−0.12)	(−0.38)	(4.034)	(1.414)	(1.452)	(−0.57)	(2.899)	(−0.24)	(−0.23)	(−0.68)	(3.895)
State tax rate	−0.0071	−0.0071	−0.0024	−0.0203	−0.0010	−0.0009	−0.0025	−0.0257	–	–	–	–
	(−1.21)	(−1.21)	(−3.08)	(−2.63)	(−0.16)	(−0.14)	(−3.28)	(−3.27)	–	–	–	–
Personal income per capita	0.3219	0.3212	0.0118	−0.0994	0.3130	0.3121	0.0123	−0.0915	0.3215	0.3207	0.0117	−0.0973
	(18.40)	(18.39)	(6.013)	(−4.39)	(17.90)	(17.91)	(6.285)	(−4.06)	(18.55)	(18.55)	(5.895)	(−4.26)
Federal & state top tax rate	0.0046	0.0045	0.0000	−0.0027	–	–	–	–	0.0047	0.0047	0.0000	−0.0022
	(2.756)	(2.724)	(0.165)	(−0.94)	–	–	–	–	(2.839)	(2.808)	(0.183)	(−0.74)
Personal income* Federal & state top tax rate	–	–	–	–	–	–	–	–	–	–	–	–
	–	–	–	–	–	–	–	–	–	–	–	–
Federal & state avg marginal tax rate	–	–	–	–	0.0484	0.0492	−0.0011	−0.0422	–	–	–	–
	–	–	–	–	(5.234)	(5.358)	(−1.38)	(−2.90)	–	–	–	–
Family size	−3.2020	−3.2965	0.6048	−0.6579	−3.7852	−3.8930	0.6117	−0.1497	−2.9678	−3.0609	0.6010	−0.0672
	(−3.18)	(−3.28)	(5.434)	(−0.45)	(−3.72)	(−3.84)	(5.556)	(−0.10)	(−2.99)	(−3.09)	(5.373)	(−0.04)
Farms per household	−1.3749	−1.1861	−0.3639	4.6072	−1.6232	−1.4582	−0.3458	4.5962	−1.3962	−1.2115	−0.3345	4.9097
	(−0.76)	(−0.65)	(−1.24)	(1.960)	(−0.90)	(−0.81)	(−1.20)	(1.986)	(−0.78)	(−0.68)	(−1.13)	(2.064)
Percent of adults with high school diploma	−0.6771	−0.6871	0.0304	−0.8468	−0.5978	−0.6119	0.0319	−0.8166	−0.6939	−0.7038	0.0297	−0.9518
	(−4.49)	(−4.58)	(2.234)	(−3.19)	(−4.22)	(−4.35)	(2.481)	(−3.31)	(−4.61)	(−4.70)	(2.171)	(−3.60)

(continued)

Table 9.1A (continued)

Variable	1				2				3			
	ALR	RTR	RCAP	IAR	ALR	RTR	RCAP	IAR	ALR	RTR	RCAP	IAR
Percent of pop over 65	2.8341	2.8517	–0.3678	–4.6682	3.4166	3.4463	–0.3618	–5.0091	2.6639	2.6815	–0.3675	–5.1370
	(2.870)	(2.889)	(−2.67)	(−3.72)	(3.414)	(3.450)	(−2.69)	(−4.02)	(2.729)	(2.748)	(−2.66)	(−4.07)
Percent of employed persons in manufacturing	−0.5080	−0.5124	0.1916	−0.9548	−0.4421	−0.4492	0.1896	−0.9374	−0.5198	−0.5236	0.1921	−1.1022
	(−1.66)	(−1.67)	(4.956)	(−2.27)	(−1.44)	(−1.47)	(4.962)	(−2.26)	(−1.72)	(−1.73)	(4.941)	(−2.61)
Percent of employed persons in service	−0.0530	−0.0118	−0.0124	1.1976	−0.3201	−0.2975	0.0089	1.4415	−0.1023	−0.0621	−0.0314	1.0791
	(−0.12)	(−0.02)	(−0.26)	(2.018)	(−0.75)	(−0.70)	(0.195)	(2.495)	(−0.24)	(−0.14)	(−0.67)	(1.804)
Unemployment rate	−2.9119	−2.9673	−0.2188	0.4169	−2.0689	−2.1073	−0.2436	−0.3119	−2.8777	−2.9336	−0.2249	0.5622
	(−5.01)	(−5.14)	(−4.38)	(0.399)	(−3.37)	(−3.46)	(−4.65)	(−0.29)	(−4.94)	(−5.07)	(−4.48)	(0.536)
Audit rate	0.2047	0.1869	0.0216	–	0.2439	0.2270	0.0208	–	0.2073	0.1895	0.0214	–
	(4.294)	(3.943)	(5.027)	–	(4.855)	(4.552)	(4.806)	–	(4.387)	(4.031)	(4.969)	–
Direct examination time	–	–	–	1.1857	–	–	–	1.1130	–	–	–	1.2035
	–	–	–	(6.170)	–	–	–	(5.775)	–	–	–	(6.243)
Budget per return	–	–	–	22.3488	–	–	–	21.5784	–	–	–	22.7909
	–	–	–	(9.101)	–	–	–	(8.782)	–	–	–	(9.271)
Total sentences	–	–	–	–	–	–	–	–	–	–	–	–
	–	–	–	–	–	–	–	–	–	–	–	–
Total sentences (Tax & money laun only)	0.000462	0.000445	−0.000026	−0.000023	0.000350	0.000329	−0.000022	0.000085	0.000493	0.000475	−0.000022	0.000072
	(1.889)	(1.822)	(−0.99)	(−0.06)	(1.418)	(1.337)	(−0.81)	(0.238)	(2.034)	(1.965)	(−0.83)	(0.201)
% of tot sent related to tax	0.0539	0.0515	0.0015	−0.1776	0.0422	0.0399	0.0016	−0.1653	0.0538	0.0514	0.0017	−0.1772
	(1.432)	(1.377)	(0.463)	(−2.63)	(1.114)	(1.062)	(0.501)	(−2.47)	(1.425)	(1.370)	(0.518)	(−2.61)
% of tot sent related to money laun	0.0163	0.0135	0.0038	−0.2972	0.0099	0.0064	0.0043	−0.2685	0.0149	0.0121	0.0039	−0.3034

(continued)

Table 9.1A (continued)

Variable	1				2				3			
	ALR	RTR	RCAP	IAR	ALR	RTR	RCAP	IAR	ALR	RTR	RCAP	IAR
	(0.367)	(0.306)	(1.011)	(−3.85)	(0.224)	(0.145)	(1.183)	(−3.53)	(0.334)	(0.273)	(1.045)	(−3.92)
% of tax sent neither prison nor probation	0.0241	0.0110	0.0120	−0.4621	0.0048	−0.0085	0.0125	−0.4382	0.0261	0.0130	0.0129	−0.4626
	(0.258)	(0.118)	(1.534)	(−2.72)	(0.050)	(−0.09)	(1.608)	(−2.59)	(0.278)	(0.139)	(1.635)	(−2.71)
% of money laun sent neither prison nor probation	−0.3685	−0.3490	−0.0202	0.9386	−0.3889	−0.3692	−0.0201	0.9128	−0.3676	−0.3481	−0.0188	0.9501
	(−4.50)	(−4.29)	(−2.89)	(8.033)	(−4.69)	(−4.49)	(−2.90)	(7.852)	(−4.48)	(−4.26)	(−2.69)	(8.109)
Number of obs	700				700				700			
Years	1988–2001				1988–2001				1988–2001			

(continued)

Table 9.1A (continued)

Variable	4				5			
	ALR	RTR	RCAP	IAR	ALR	RTR	RCAP	IAR
Constant	0.8118	0.8542	0.1644	1.9637	−0.2403	−0.1854	0.1814	2.0500
	(2.303)	(2.430)	(4.102)	(3.821)	(−0.53)	(−0.41)	(3.892)	(4.113)
Percent of families on welfare	−0.0040	−0.0039	0.0000	0.0522	0.0115	0.0115	−0.0004	0.0522
	(−0.46)	(−0.46)	(−0.05)	(4.029)	(1.244)	(1.247)	(−0.41)	(4.034)
State tax rate	−0.0073	−0.0073	−0.0023	−0.0202	−0.0014	−0.0015	−0.0025	−0.0203
	(−1.28)	(−1.28)	(−3.06)	(−2.61)	(−0.21)	(−0.23)	(−3.06)	(−2.63)
Personal income per capita	0.2755	0.2749	0.0133	−0.0844	0.3141	0.3134	0.0123	−0.0994
	(14.32)	(14.32)	(5.970)	(−3.10)	(17.69)	(17.72)	(5.913)	(−4.39)
Federal & state top tax rate	–	–	–	–	–	–	–	−0.0027
	–	–	–	–	–	–	–	(−0.94)
Personal income* federal & state top tax rate	0.0012	0.0012	0.0000	−0.0004	–	–	–	–
	(4.942)	(4.963)	(−1.41)	(−0.96)	–	–	–	–
Federal & state avg marginal tax rate	–	–	–	–	0.0446	0.0440	−0.0006	–
	–	–	–	–	(2.668)	(2.648)	(−0.34)	–
Family size	−2.9261	−3.0160	0.5787	−0.6765	−3.7847	−3.8727	0.6042	−0.6579
	(−2.96)	(−3.06)	(5.187)	(−0.46)	(−3.66)	(−3.77)	(5.421)	(−0.45)
Farms per household	−2.0622	−1.8874	−0.3340	4.6470	−1.5311	−1.3443	−0.3522	4.6072
	(−1.17)	(−1.07)	(−1.15)	(1.970)	(−0.84)	(−0.74)	(−1.22)	(1.960)
Percent of adults with high school diploma	−0.7517	−0.7637	0.0356	−0.8556	−0.5933	−0.6050	0.0316	−0.8468
	(−5.12)	(−5.23)	(2.669)	(−3.27)	(−4.13)	(−4.24)	(2.430)	(−3.19)
Percent of pop over 65	2.6059	2.6208	−0.3292	−4.6463	3.4021	3.4115	−0.3602	−4.6682
	(2.708)	(2.724)	(−2.39)	(−3.69)	(3.345)	(3.365)	(−2.68)	(−3.72)
Percent of employed persons in manufacturing	−0.4359	−0.4405	0.1860	−0.9673	−0.4549	−0.4605	0.1866	−0.9548
	(−1.46)	(−1.48)	(4.837)	(−2.30)	(−1.48)	(−1.50)	(4.870)	(−2.27)
Percent of employed persons in service	−0.2904	−0.2567	0.0119	1.1907	−0.2727	−0.2303	−0.0019	1.1976
	(−0.70)	(−0.62)	(0.259)	(2.015)	(−0.58)	(−0.49)	(−0.03)	(2.018)

(continued)

Table 9.1A (continued)

Variable	4				5			
	ALR	RTR	RCAP	IAR	ALR	RTR	RCAP	IAR
Unemployment rate	−2.9039	−2.9576	−0.2246	0.4440	−2.1497	−2.2145	−0.2332	0.4169
	(−5.03)	(−5.15)	(−4.51)	(0.425)	(−3.22)	(−3.34)	(−3.78)	(0.399)
Audit rate	0.2153	0.1976	0.0214	–	0.2407	0.2223	0.0214	–
	(4.536)	(4.188)	(4.996)	–	(4.727)	(4.405)	(4.872)	–
Direct examination time	–	–	–	1.1801	–	–	–	1.1857
	–	–	–	(6.142)	–	–	–	(6.170)
Budget per return	–	–	–	22.3034	–	–	–	22.3488
	–	–	–	(9.071)	–	–	–	(9.101)
Total sentences	–	–	–	–	–	–	–	–
	–	–	–	–	–	–	–	–
Total sentences (tax & money laun only)	0.000438	0.000419	−0.000023	−0.000025	0.000361	0.000345	−0.000025	−0.000023
	(1.821)	(1.747)	(−0.85)	(−0.07)	(1.435)	(1.376)	(−0.90)	(−0.06)
% of tot sent related to tax	0.0574	0.0551	0.0012	−0.1765	0.0428	0.0405	0.0016	−0.1776
	(1.531)	(1.480)	(0.367)	(−2.62)	(1.132)	(1.081)	(0.498)	(−2.63)
% of tot sent related to money laun	−0.0002	−0.0032	0.0046	−0.2972	0.0127	0.0100	0.0042	−0.2972
	(−0.00)	(−0.07)	(1.246)	(−3.86)	(0.282)	(0.223)	(1.110)	(−3.85)
% of tax sent neither prison nor probation	0.0324	0.0193	0.0118	−0.4623	0.0059	−0.0070	0.0124	−0.4621
	(0.347)	(0.208)	(1.507)	(−2.72)	(0.062)	(−0.07)	(1.570)	(−2.72)
% of money laun sent neither prison nor probation	−0.3580	−0.3384	−0.0207	0.9355	−0.3881	−0.3683	−0.0203	0.9386
	(−4.39)	(−4.18)	(−2.96)	(7.982)	(−4.70)	(−4.50)	(−2.91)	(8.033)
Number of obs	700				700			
Years	1988–2001				1988–2001			

statistically significant and positively related to tax compliance as an increase in total sentences raises tax revenues.

Turning to the percentage breakdown by CI activity, the coefficient on the percentage of total CI sentences related to tax investigations is positive. Therefore, increasing tax cases raises tax compliance. Finally, an increase in the percentage of cases that do not receive prison or probation is negatively related to compliance, at least for money laundering cases. Hence, money laundering cases that receive prison or probation outcomes as opposed to fines help deter noncompliance. I found no similar effect among tax cases. The pattern of results remains similar across the specifications (Models 1–5). This includes models that use some form of average Federal/State tax rate (whether or not it is treated exogenously), models that include income tax rate interactions, or models that use the top Federal/State top marginal rate.

On theoretical grounds, Model 2 is preferred since it uses the average Federal/ State tax rate as the explanatory factor. Models with the top rate measure the tax effect exogenously, but with error. Moreover, the second specification using average Federal/State tax rates parallels the measure of State tax rates, STAXR, used in this study. Finally, I found that in specifications where the average and top marginal rates were both used as explanatory factors, only the former was statistically significant. Therefore, the second specification is theoretically the correct specification. This model produces significant audit results but weakens the significance of the CI total sentence result. This pattern is true in all models I report below.

Media Models

Media models continue to demonstrate insignificant results even after extending the analysis to 2004 and controlling for tax rate changes. I show eight specifications of the media models in Tables 9.2 and 9.3. The models occur in pairs. Thus, the first specification has explanatory factors for total sentences and total sentences in the media. I give the results of this specification in Models 1 and 2, with the difference being the treatment of Federal/State tax rates. In Table 9.2, I present the results for the time period through 2001, while in Table 9.3, I present the results through 2004. In Table 9.3A, I present results from the media models with the 2001–2004 dummy variable used as an additional factor.

Alternative specifications of media effects used: (1) tax and money laundering sentences released in the media; (2) total sentence released in media without a factor for total sentences; and (3) tax and money laundering sentences released in the media without a factor for total sentences. However, the media results remain inconclusive because the relevant coefficients on these factors were statistically insignificant in all specifications attempted. Media models are necessarily constrained to the period after 1992 and result in losing four years of data. The resulting data period does not appear suitable for measuring IRS media outcomes.

Table 9.2 2001, Media

Variable	(2001, Media)											
	1				2				3			
	ALR	RTR	RCAP	IAR	ALR	RTR	RCAP	IAR	ALR	RTR	RCAP	IAR
Constant	1.7976	1.8456	0.1033	0.8458	1.2515	1.2952	0.0831	1.8304	1.8157	1.8652	0.1056	0.8103
	(4.395)	(4.515)	(2.080)	(1.428)	(2.868)	(2.973)	(1.613)	(2.883)	(4.390)	(4.513)	(2.120)	(1.354)
Percent of families on welfare	0.0042	0.0046	−0.0009	0.0716	0.0135	0.0140	−0.0006	0.0586	0.0045	0.0049	−0.0010	0.0731
	(0.445)	(0.492)	(−0.88)	(5.941)	(1.452)	(1.508)	(−0.53)	(4.565)	(0.471)	(0.517)	(−0.93)	(5.998)
State tax rate	−0.0212	−0.0217	−0.0005	−0.0205	−0.0159	−0.0162	−0.0003	−0.0296	−0.0210	−0.0215	−0.0005	−0.0200
	(−2.94)	(−3.00)	(−0.43)	(−2.35)	(−2.16)	(−2.21)	(−0.24)	(−3.39)	(−2.84)	(−2.91)	(−0.44)	(−2.26)
Personal income per capita	0.3026	0.3012	0.0171	−0.0906	0.2990	0.2976	0.0173	−0.0914	0.3025	0.3012	0.0171	−0.0888
	(17.39)	(17.32)	(8.005)	(−4.04)	(17.39)	(17.32)	(8.084)	(−4.15)	(17.22)	(17.16)	(7.992)	(−3.91)
Federal & state top tax rate	0.0011	0.0011	0.0000	0.0051	–	–	–	–	0.0011	0.0011	–0.0001	0.0051
	(0.505)	(0.480)	(−0.20)	(1.391)	–	–	–	–	(0.507)	(0.479)	(−0.23)	(1.379)
Federal & state avg marginal tax rate	–	–	–	–	0.0352	0.0355	0.0013	−0.0428	–	–	–	–
	–	–	–	–	(3.717)	(3.758)	(1.206)	(−3.00)	–	–	–	–
Family size	−3.1573	−3.2560	0.4736	−2.0605	−3.5437	−3.6461	0.4691	−1.7877	−3.2313	−3.3313	0.4718	−2.0395
	(−3.13)	(−3.22)	(3.838)	(−1.45)	(−3.57)	(−3.68)	(3.883)	(−1.26)	(−3.16)	(−3.26)	(3.814)	(−1.42)
Farms per household	−4.4118	−4.2471	−0.0158	5.3745	−4.2933	−4.1232	−0.0235	4.7089	−4.3429	−4.1732	−0.0096	5.4350
	(−2.15)	(−2.07)	(−0.04)	(2.105)	(−2.11)	(−2.02)	(−0.07)	(1.860)	(−2.07)	(−1.99)	(−0.02)	(2.107)
Percent of adults with high school diploma	−1.3824	−1.3897	0.1006	0.1387	−1.5162	−1.5281	0.0922	0.4141	−1.3881	−1.3956	0.0999	0.1500
	(−5.31)	(−5.34)	(3.416)	(0.354)	(−6.03)	(−6.09)	(3.194)	(1.100)	(−5.30)	(−5.34)	(3.391)	(0.381)
Percent of pop over 65	2.1428	2.1390	−0.2871	−2.6433	2.5828	2.5833	−0.2669	−3.0048	2.2026	2.1960	−0.2900	−2.6294
	(2.017)	(2.014)	(−1.77)	(−1.97)	(2.435)	(2.435)	(−1.69)	(−2.25)	(2.029)	(2.024)	(−1.78)	(−1.94)
Percent of employed persons in manufacturing	−0.1507	−0.1389	0.1319	−0.4897	−0.3023	−0.2942	0.1040	−0.3477	−0.1548	−0.1422	0.1356	−0.4884
	(−0.42)	(−0.39)	(2.569)	(−1.05)	(−0.85)	(−0.83)	(2.031)	(−0.75)	(−0.42)	(−0.39)	(2.629)	(−1.04)
Percent of employed persons in service	−0.2973	−0.2606	−0.0337	1.0904	−0.6689	−0.6378	−0.0592	1.5367	−0.2830	−0.2450	−0.0320	1.0759
	(−0.65)	(−0.57)	(−0.59)	(1.754)	(−1.44)	(−1.37)	(−1.01)	(2.474)	(−0.61)	(−0.53)	(−0.56)	(1.719)
Unemployment rate	−6.0789	−6.1126	−0.1016	2.0535	−5.0688	−5.0879	−0.0559	0.1017	−6.1019	−6.1380	−0.1045	2.1277
	(−8.74)	(−8.79)	(−1.40)	(1.765)	(−7.08)	(−7.12)	(−0.72)	(0.085)	(−8.79)	(−8.86)	(−1.44)	(1.829)
Audit rate	0.1251	0.1026	0.0368	–	0.1436	0.1211	0.0379	–	0.1253	0.1028	0.0369	–
	(2.432)	(1.995)	(6.694)	–	(2.742)	(2.318)	(6.722)	–	(2.428)	(1.993)	(6.684)	–

(continued)

Table 9.2 (continued)

Variable	(2001, Media)											
	1				2				3			
	ALR	RTR	RCAP	IAR	ALR	RTR	RCAP	IAR	ALR	RTR	RCAP	IAR
Direct examination time	–	–	–	1.3437	–	–	–	1.2983	–	–	–	1.3396
	–	–	–	(7.855)	–	–	–	(7.630)	–	–	–	(7.817)
Budget per return	–	–	–	15.8850	–	–	–	15.2974	–	–	–	15.8550
	–	–	–	(7.303)	–	–	–	(7.054)	–	–	–	(7.293)
Total sentences	–	–	–	–	–	–	–	–	–	–	–	–
	–	–	–	–	–	–	–	–	–	–	–	–
Total sentences (Tax & money laun only)	0.000349	0.000304	−0.000059	−0.000239	0.000286	0.000241	−0.000068	−0.000197	0.000351	0.000306	−0.000061	−0.000390
	(1.041)	(0.909)	(−1.50)	(−0.47)	(0.862)	(0.725)	(−1.73)	(−0.39)	(0.988)	(0.860)	(−1.47)	(−0.73)
Tax sentences	–	–	–	–	–	–	–	–	–	–	–	–
	–	–	–	–	–	–	–	–	–	–	–	–
Money laundering sentences	–	–	–	–	–	–	–	–	–	–	–	–
	–	–	–	–	–	–	–	–	–	–	–	–
Total prison sentences	–	–	–	–	–	–	–	–	–	–	–	–
	–	–	–	–	–	–	–	–	–	–	–	–
Total probation sentences	–	–	–	–	–	–	–	–	–	–	–	–
	–	–	–	–	–	–	–	–	–	–	–	–
Total sentences released in media	−0.000101	−0.000052	0.000057	0.000218	−0.000205	−0.000157	0.000054	0.000469	–	–	–	–
	(−0.33)	(−0.17)	(1.879)	(0.431)	(−0.68)	(−0.52)	(1.736)	(0.936)	–	–	–	–
Tax sentences released in media	–	–	–	–	–	–	–	–	−0.000315	−0.000249	0.000103	−0.000222
	–	–	–	–	–	–	–	–	(−0.54)	(−0.42)	(1.706)	(−0.22)
Money laundering sentences released in media	–	–	–	–	–	–	–	–	0.000117	0.000166	0.000018	0.001406
	–	–	–	–	–	–	–	–	(0.136)	(0.194)	(0.203)	(1.006)
Tax sentences resulting in prison	–	–	–	–	–	–	–	–	–	–	–	–
	–	–	–	–	–	–	–	–	–	–	–	–
Tax sentences resulting in probation	–	–	–	–	–	–	–	–	–	–	–	–
	–	–	–	–	–	–	–	–	–	–	–	–
Money laun sentences resulting in prison	–	–	–	–	–	–	–	–	–	–	–	–
	–	–	–	–	–	–	–	–	–	–	–	–
Money laun sentences resulting in probation	–	–	–	–	–	–	–	–	–	–	–	–
	–	–	–	–	–	–	–	–	–	–	–	–

(continued)

Table 9.2 (continued)

Variable	(2001, Media)											
	1				2				3			
	ALR	RTR	RCAP	IAR	ALR	RTR	RCAP	IAR	ALR	RTR	RCAP	IAR
Tax sent resulting in neither prison nor probation	–	–	–	–	–	–	–	–	–	–	–	–
	–	–	–	–	–	–	–	–	–	–	–	–
Money laun sent resulting in neither prison nor probation	–	–	–	–	–	–	–	–	–	–	–	–
	–	–	–	–	–	–	–	–	–	–	–	–
% of tot sent related to tax	0.0482	0.0477	0.0053	−0.1335	0.0437	0.0433	0.0055	−0.1321	0.0533	0.0520	0.0040	−0.1258
	(1.280)	(1.267)	(1.369)	(−2.12)	(1.174)	(1.165)	(1.413)	(−2.12)	(1.394)	(1.360)	(1.013)	(−1.97)
% of tot sent related to money laun	0.0246	0.0241	0.0057	−0.1699	0.0092	0.0087	0.0054	−0.1408	0.0245	0.0235	0.0054	−0.1826
	(0.610)	(0.600)	(1.386)	(−2.55)	(0.230)	(0.218)	(1.296)	(−2.11)	(0.600)	(0.576)	(1.306)	(−2.71)
% of total sentences not prison or prob	–	–	–	–	–	–	–	–	–	–	–	–
	–	–	–	–	–	–	–	–	–	–	–	–
% of tax sentences in prison	–	–	–	–	–	–	–	–	–	–	–	–
	–	–	–	–	–	–	–	–	–	–	–	–
% of money laun sentences in prison	–	–	–	–	–	–	–	–	–	–	–	–
	–	–	–	–	–	–	–	–	–	–	–	–
% of tax sentences in probation	–	–	–	–	–	–	–	–	–	–	–	–
	–	–	–	–	–	–	–	–	–	–	–	–
% of money laun sentences in probation	–	–	–	–	–	–	–	–	–	–	–	–
	–	–	–	–	–	–	–	–	–	–	–	–
% of tax sent neither prison nor probation	0.0947	0.0802	−0.0002	−0.2945	0.0740	0.0594	−0.0009	−0.2682	0.0972	0.0825	−0.0006	−0.2910
	(1.066)	(0.904)	(−0.02)	(−1.94)	(0.840)	(0.676)	(−0.10)	(−1.77)	(1.097)	(0.932)	(−0.06)	(−1.92)
% of money laun sent neither prison nor probation	−0.1785	−0.1801	0.0055	−0.1050	−0.1427	−0.1436	0.0072	−0.1761	−0.1772	−0.1785	0.0055	−0.0940
	(−1.50)	(−1.52)	(0.463)	(−0.52)	(−1.21)	(−1.22)	(0.592)	(−0.88)	(−1.49)	(−1.50)	(0.455)	(−0.46)
% of total sentences in media	–	–	–	–	–	–	–	–	–	–	–	–
	–	–	–	–	–	–	–	–	–	–	–	–
% of tax sentences in media	–	–	–	–	–	–	–	–	–	–	–	–
	–	–	–	–	–	–	–	–	–	–	–	–
% of money laun sentences in media	–	–	–	–	–	–	–	–	–	–	–	–
	–	–	–	–	–	–	–	–	–	–	–	–
Number of obs	500				500				500			
Years	1992–2001				1992–2001				1992–2001			

(continued)

Table 9.2 (continued)

Variable	(2001, Media)											
	4				5				6			
	ALR	RTR	RCAP	IAR	ALR	RTR	RCAP	IAR	ALR	RTR	RCAP	IAR
Constant	1.2652	1.3102	0.0856	1.7983	1.7855	1.8329	0.1027	0.8486	1.2391	1.2827	0.0838	1.8262
	(2.882)	(2.989)	(1.659)	(2.812)	(4.390)	(4.508)	(2.061)	(1.419)	(2.848)	(2.952)	(1.617)	(2.876)
Percent of families on welfare	0.0137	0.0142	−0.0006	0.0600	0.0052	0.0055	−0.0010	0.0714	0.0144	0.0148	−0.0008	0.0580
	(1.463)	(1.518)	(−0.60)	(4.646)	(0.560)	(0.593)	(−1.00)	(5.935)	(1.568)	(1.607)	(−0.73)	(4.559)
State tax rate	−0.0156	−0.0160	−0.0003	−0.0292	−0.0214	−0.0218	−0.0005	−0.0204	−0.0160	−0.0164	−0.0003	−0.0296
	(−2.08)	(−2.14)	(−0.26)	(−3.29)	(−3.01)	(−3.07)	(−0.43)	(−2.29)	(−2.20)	(−2.25)	(−0.24)	(−3.38)
Personal income per capita	0.2986	0.2973	0.0172	−0.0892	0.3042	0.3027	0.0171	−0.0922	0.3004	0.2988	0.0172	−0.0925
	(17.23)	(17.17)	(8.042)	(−4.00)	(17.62)	(17.53)	(7.961)	(−4.09)	(17.57)	(17.50)	(8.017)	(−4.23)
Federal & state top tax rate	–	–	–	–	0.0012	0.0012	−0.0001	0.0052	–	–	–	–
	–	–	–	–	(0.541)	(0.513)	(−0.31)	(1.408)	–	–	–	–
Federal & state avg marginal tax rate	0.0357	0.0360	0.0013	−0.0433	–	–	–	–	0.0353	0.0356	0.0011	−0.0430
	(3.760)	(3.802)	(1.214)	(−3.02)	–	–	–	–	(3.733)	(3.770)	(1.069)	(−3.01)
Family size	−3.6095	−3.7130	0.4685	−1.7634	−3.1320	−3.2282	0.4671	−2.0234	−3.5313	−3.6300	0.4671	−1.7645
	(−3.60)	(−3.71)	(3.870)	(−1.24)	(−3.12)	(−3.22)	(3.773)	(−1.40)	(−3.57)	(−3.68)	(3.848)	(−1.25)
Farms per household	−4.2515	−4.0762	−0.0163	4.7981	−4.6578	−4.4686	0.0386	5.4344	−4.4909	−4.2959	0.0384	4.7722
	(−2.05)	(−1.96)	(−0.04)	(1.874)	(−2.31)	(−2.22)	(0.114)	(2.089)	(−2.24)	(−2.14)	(0.117)	(1.885)
Percent of adults with high school diploma	−1.5251	−1.5375	0.0908	0.4282	−1.3925	−1.3982	0.1027	0.1490	−1.5211	−1.5314	0.0940	0.4262
	(−6.04)	(−6.10)	(3.145)	(1.132)	(−5.38)	(−5.40)	(3.477)	(0.378)	(−6.08)	(−6.13)	(3.246)	(1.135)
Percent of pop over 65	2.6363	2.6344	−0.2731	−3.0036	2.1889	2.1775	−0.2933	−2.7109	2.6267	2.6182	−0.2800	−3.0479
	(2.442)	(2.441)	(−1.72)	(−2.23)	(2.089)	(2.078)	(−1.80)	(−1.99)	(2.504)	(2.495)	(−1.77)	(−2.29)
Percent of employed persons in manufacturing	−0.3165	−0.3079	0.1089	−0.3389	−0.1733	−0.1586	0.1377	−0.4825	−0.3166	−0.3055	0.1135	−0.3394
	(−0.87)	(−0.85)	(2.110)	(−0.73)	(−0.49)	(−0.45)	(2.683)	(−1.01)	(−0.90)	(−0.87)	(2.209)	(−0.73)
Percent of employed persons in service	−0.6700	−0.6377	−0.0575	1.5337	−0.3203	−0.2821	−0.0275	1.0721	−0.6832	−0.6503	−0.0511	1.5401
	(−1.43)	(−1.36)	(−0.98)	(2.449)	(−0.70)	(−0.62)	(−0.48)	(1.699)	(−1.48)	(−1.41)	(−0.87)	(2.476)
Unemployment rate	-5.0738	-5.0949	-0.0583	0.1634	-5.9466	-5.9959	-0.1145	1.9326	-4.9639	-4.9995	-0.0733	0.0201
	(−7.10)	(−7.14)	(−0.76)	(0.137)	(−8.65)	(−8.73)	(−1.58)	(1.682)	(−7.02)	(−7.08)	(−0.95)	(0.017)
Audit rate	0.1436	0.1211	0.0379	–	0.1229	0.1007	0.0372	–	0.1420	0.1198	0.0382	–
	(2.738)	(2.315)	(6.710)	–	(2.399)	(1.967)	(6.751)	–	(2.719)	(2.300)	(6.763)	–
Direct examination time	–	–	–	1.2948	–	–	–	1.3414	–	–	–	1.3033
	–	–	–	(7.601)	–	–	–	(7.883)	–	–	–	(7.698)

(continued)

Table 9.2 (continued)

Variable	(2001, Media)											
	4				5				6			
	ALR	RTR	RCAP	IAR	ALR	RTR	RCAP	IAR	ALR	RTR	RCAP	IAR
Budget per return	–	–	–	15.2608	–	–	–	15.8579	–	–	–	15.2863
	–	–	–	(7.042)	–	–	–	(7.312)	–	–	–	(7.057)
Total sentences	–	–	–	–	–	–	–	–	–	–	–	–
	–	–	–	–	–	–	–	–	–	–	–	–
Total sentences (Tax & money laun only)	0.000299	0.000252	−0.000069	−0.000368	–	–	–	–	–	–	–	–
	(0.849)	(0.717)	(−1.67)	(−0.69)	–	–	–	–	–	–	–	–
Tax sentences	–	–	–	–	–	–	–	–	–	–	–	–
	–	–	–	–	–	–	–	–	–	–	–	–
Money laundering sentences	–	–	–	–	–	–	–	–	–	–	–	–
	–	–	–	–	–	–	–	–	–	–	–	–
Total prison sentences	–	–	–	–	–	–	–	–	–	–	–	–
	–	–	–	–	–	–	–	–	–	–	–	–
Total probation sentences	–	–	–	–	–	–	–	–	–	–	–	–
	–	–	–	–	–	–	–	–	–	–	–	–
Total sentences released in media	–	–	–	–	0.000108	0.000131	0.000030	0.000052	−0.000034	−0.000013	0.000022	0.000328
	–	–	–	–	(0.484)	(0.586)	(1.223)	(0.147)	(−0.15)	(−0.05)	(0.889)	(0.938)
Tax sentences released in media	−0.000386	−0.000323	0.000100	0.000032	–	–	–	–	–	–	–	–
	(−0.67)	(−0.56)	(1.636)	(0.033)	–	–	–	–	–	–	–	–
Money laundering sentences released in media	−0.000101	−0.000053	0.000012	0.001815	–	–	–	–	–	–	–	–
	(−0.11)	(−0.06)	(0.133)	(1.306)	–	–	–	–	–	–	–	–
Tax sentences resulting in prison	–	–	–	–	–	–	–	–	–	–	–	–
	–	–	–	–	–	–	–	–	–	–	–	–
Tax sentences resulting in probation	–	–	–	–	–	–	–	–	–	–	–	–
	–	–	–	–	–	–	–	–	–	–	–	–
Money laun sentences resulting in prison	–	–	–	–	–	–	–	–	–	–	–	–
	–	–	–	–	–	–	–	–	–	–	–	–
Money laun sentences resulting in probation	–	–	–	–	–	–	–	–	–	–	–	–
	–	–	–	–	–	–	–	–	–	–	–	–
Tax sent resulting in neither prison nor probation	–	–	–	–	–	–	–	–	–	–	–	–
	–	–	–	–	–	–	–	–	–	–	–	–

(continued)

Table 9.2 (continued)

Variable	(2001, Media)											
	4				5				6			
	ALR	RTR	RCAP	IAR	ALR	RTR	RCAP	IAR	ALR	RTR	RCAP	IAR
Money laun sent resulting in neither prison nor probation	–	–	–	–	–	–	–	–	–	–	–	–
	–	–	–	–	–	–	–	–	–	–	–	–
% of tot sent related to tax	0.0491	0.0479	0.0042	−0.1269	0.0511	0.0502	0.0046	−0.1350	0.0461	0.0452	0.0048	−0.1338
	(1.299)	(1.270)	(1.062)	(−2.01)	(1.358)	(1.335)	(1.193)	(−2.16)	(1.239)	(1.219)	(1.217)	(−2.15)
% of tot sent related to money laun	0.0111	0.0100	0.0052	−0.1577	0.0292	0.0281	0.0047	−0.1725	0.0130	0.0118	0.0043	−0.1437
	(0.273)	(0.248)	(1.229)	(−2.35)	(0.728)	(0.702)	(1.165)	(−2.62)	(0.327)	(0.298)	(1.051)	(−2.17)
% of total sentences not prison or prob	–	–	–	–	–	–	–	–	–	–	–	–
	–	–	–	–	–	–	–	–	–	–	–	–
% of tax sentences in prison	–	–	–	–	–	–	–	–	–	–	–	–
	–	–	–	–	–	–	–	–	–	–	–	–
% of money laun sentences in prison	–	–	–	–	–	–	–	–	–	–	–	–
	–	–	–	–	–	–	–	–	–	–	–	–
% of tax sentences in probation	–	–	–	–	–	–	–	–	–	–	–	–
	–	–	–	–	–	–	–	–	–	–	–	–
% of money laun sentences in probation	–	–	–	–	–	–	–	–	–	–	–	–
	–	–	–	–	–	–	–	–	–	–	–	–
% of tax sent neither prison nor probation	0.0759	0.0611	−0.0014	−0.2647	0.0976	0.0827	−0.0009	−0.2960	0.0765	0.0614	−0.0016	−0.2697
	(0.864)	(0.697)	(−0.14)	(−1.75)	(1.098)	(0.932)	(−0.09)	(−1.96)	(0.868)	(0.699)	(−0.17)	(−1.79)
% of money laun sent neither prison nor probation	−0.1424	−0.1431	0.0071	−0.1627	−0.1799	−0.1813	0.0059	−0.1052	−0.1439	−0.1447	0.0075	−0.1765
	(−1.21)	(−1.22)	(0.584)	(−0.81)	(−1.51)	(−1.52)	(0.489)	(−0.52)	(−1.22)	(−1.23)	(0.616)	(−0.88)
% of total sentences in media	–	–	–	–	–	–	–	–	–	–	–	–
	–	–	–	–	–	–	–	–	–	–	–	–
% of tax sentences in media	–	–	–	–	–	–	–	–	–	–	–	–
	–	–	–	–	–	–	–	–	–	–	–	–
% of money laun sentences in media	–	–	–	–	–	–	–	–	–	–	–	–
	–	–	–	–	–	–	–	–	–	–	–	–
Number of obs	500				500				500			
Years	1992–2001				1992–2001				1992–2001			

Table 9.2 (continued)

Variable	(2001, Media)							
	7				8			
	ALR	RTR	RCAP	IAR	ALR	RTR	RCAP	IAR
Constant	1.7904	1.8395	0.1050	0.8095	1.2456	1.2903	0.0858	1.7910
	(4.368)	(4.490)	(2.100)	(1.339)	(2.849)	(2.956)	(1.654)	(2.798)
Percent of families on welfare	0.0055	0.0058	−0.0011	0.0724	0.0147	0.0150	−0.0008	0.0590
	(0.592)	(0.623)	(−1.07)	(5.960)	(1.585)	(1.623)	(−0.80)	(4.602)
State tax rate	−0.0212	−0.0217	−0.0005	−0.0198	−0.0158	−0.0162	−0.0003	−0.0291
	(−2.94)	(−3.00)	(−0.44)	(−2.19)	(−2.15)	(−2.20)	(−0.25)	(−3.27)
Personal income per capita	0.3044	0.3029	0.0171	−0.0913	0.3003	0.2987	0.0172	−0.0914
	(17.52)	(17.44)	(7.932)	(−4.01)	(17.48)	(17.40)	(7.977)	(−4.13)
Federal & state top tax rate	0.0012	0.0011	−0.0001	0.0052	–	–	–	–
	(0.536)	(0.506)	(−0.32)	(1.406)	–	–	–	–
Federal & state avg marginal tax rate	–	–	–	–	0.0355	0.0358	0.0011	−0.0434
	–	–	–	–	(3.752)	(3.791)	(1.096)	(−3.03)
Family size	−3.1654	−3.2638	0.4645	−1.9928	−3.5690	−3.6698	0.4646	−1.7302
	(−3.13)	(−3.23)	(3.743)	(−1.37)	(−3.59)	(−3.69)	(3.820)	(−1.21)
Farms per household	−4.5982	−4.4077	0.0393	5.5136	−4.4528	−4.2568	0.0378	4.8867
	(−2.25)	(−2.15)	(0.115)	(2.094)	(−2.19)	(−2.09)	(0.114)	(1.905)
Percent of adults with high school diploma	−1.3941	−1.4003	0.1020	0.1665	−1.5263	−1.5372	0.0928	0.4494
	(−5.36)	(−5.39)	(3.449)	(0.421)	(−6.07)	(−6.13)	(3.203)	(1.191)
Percent of pop over 65	2.2200	2.2077	−0.2951	−2.7159	2.6610	2.6519	−0.2824	−3.0690
	(2.090)	(2.078)	(−1.80)	(−1.97)	(2.503)	(2.494)	(−1.77)	(−2.27)
Percent of employed persons in manufacturing	−0.1733	−0.1581	0.1408	−0.4784	−0.3250	−0.3137	0.1160	−0.3262
	(−0.48)	(−0.44)	(2.729)	(−1.00)	(−0.91)	(−0.88)	(2.244)	(−0.70)
Percent of employed persons in service	−0.3128	−0.2734	−0.0256	1.0573	−0.6846	−0.6508	−0.0498	1.5394
	(−0.68)	(−0.60)	(−0.45)	(1.662)	(−1.47)	(−1.40)	(−0.85)	(2.453)
Unemployment rate	−5.9641	−6.0158	−0.1176	1.9586	−4.9679	−5.0050	−0.0752	0.0217
	(−8.70)	(−8.79)	(−1.63)	(1.705)	(−7.03)	(−7.10)	(−0.98)	(0.018)
Audit rate	0.1234	0.1012	0.0373	–	0.1421	0.1201	0.0383	–
	(2.405)	(1.975)	(6.761)	–	(2.721)	(2.303)	(6.773)	–
Direct examination time	–	–	–	1.3411	–	–	–	1.3042
	–	–	–	(7.865)	–	–	–	(7.691)
Budget per return	–	–	–	15.8229	–	–	–	15.2443
	–	–	–	(7.298)	–	–	–	(7.041)

(continued)

Table 9.2 (continued)

Variable	(2001, Media)							
	7				8			
	ALR	RTR	RCAP	IAR	ALR	RTR	RCAP	IAR
Total sentences	–	–	–	–	–	–	–	–
	–	–	–	–	–	–	–	–
Total sentences (Tax & money laun only)	–	–	–	–	–	–	–	–
	–	–	–	–	–	–	–	–
Tax sentences	–	–	–	–	–	–	–	–
	–	–	–	–	–	–	–	–
Money laundering sentences	–	–	–	–	–	–	–	–
	–	–	–	–	–	–	–	–
Total prison sentences	–	–	–	–	–	–	–	–
	–	–	–	–	–	–	–	–
Total probation sentences	–	–	–	–	–	–	–	–
	–	–	–	–	–	–	–	–
Total sentences released in media	–	–	–	–	–	–	–	–
	–	–	–	–	–	–	–	–
Tax sentences released in media	−0.000106	−0.000067	0.000074	−0.000475	−0.000209	−0.000173	0.000066	−0.000204
	(−0.19)	(−0.12)	(1.289)	(−0.52)	(−0.38)	(−0.32)	(1.148)	(−0.22)
Money laundering sentences released in media	0.000463	0.000466	−0.000029	0.000956	0.000193	0.000193	−0.000042	0.001372
	(0.596)	(0.600)	(−0.35)	(0.771)	(0.248)	(0.249)	(−0.49)	(1.114)
Tax sentences resulting in prison	–	–	–	–	–	–	–	–
	–	–	–	–	–	–	–	–
Tax sentences resulting in probation	–	–	–	–	–	–	–	–
	–	–	–	–	–	–	–	–
Money laun sentences resulting in prison	–	–	–	–	–	–	–	–
	–	–	–	–	–	–	–	–
Money laun sentences resulting in probation	–	–	–	–	–	–	–	–
	–	–	–	–	–	–	–	–
Tax sent resulting in neither prison nor probation	–	–	–	–	–	–	–	–
	–	–	–	–	–	–	–	–
Money laun sent resulting in neither prison nor probation	–	–	–	–	–	–	–	–
	–	–	–	–	–	–	–	–
% of tot sent related to tax	0.0537	0.0523	0.0036	−0.1262	0.0496	0.0482	0.0038	−0.1277
	(1.402)	(1.365)	(0.909)	(−1.98)	(1.310)	(1.277)	(0.955)	(−2.02)

(continued)

Table 9.2 (continued)

Variable	(2001, Media)							
	7				8			
	ALR	RTR	RCAP	IAR	ALR	RTR	RCAP	IAR
% of tot sent related to money laun	0.0248	0.0237	0.0050	−0.1825	0.0115	0.0103	0.0048	−0.1583
	(0.604)	(0.577)	(1.201)	(−2.72)	(0.284)	(0.255)	(1.121)	(−2.36)
% of total sentences not prison or prob	–	–	–	–	–	–	–	–
	–	–	–	–	–	–	–	–
% of tax sentences in prison	–	–	–	–	–	–	–	–
	–	–	–	–	–	–	–	–
% of money laun sentences in prison	–	–	–	–	–	–	–	–
	–	–	–	–	–	–	–	–
% of tax sentences in probation	–	–	–	–	–	–	–	–
	–	–	–	–	–	–	–	–
% of money laun sentences in probation	–	–	–	–	–	–	–	–
	–	–	–	–	–	–	–	–
% of tax sent neither prison nor probation	0.0990	0.0840	−0.0012	−0.2929	0.0778	0.0627	−0.0019	−0.2668
	(1.114)	(0.946)	(−0.13)	(−1.93)	(0.884)	(0.714)	(−0.21)	(−1.77)
% of money laun sent neither prison nor probation	−0.1763	−0.1778	0.0055	−0.0972	−0.1419	−0.1428	0.0071	−0.1664
	(−1.48)	(−1.49)	(0.454)	(−0.48)	(−1.20)	(−1.21)	(0.578)	(−0.83)
% of total sentences in media	–	–	–	–	–	–	–	–
	–	–	–	–	–	–	–	–
% of tax sentences in media	–	–	–	–	–	–	–	–
	–	–	–	–	–	–	–	–
% of money laun sentences in media	–	–	–	–	–	–	–	–
	–	–	–	–	–	–	–	–
Number of obs	500				500			
Years	1992–2001				1992–2001			

Table 9.3 2004, Media

Variable	(2004, Media)											
	1				2				3			
	ALR	RTR	RCAP	IAR	ALR	RTR	RCAP	IAR	ALR	RTR	RCAP	IAR
Constant	2.5254	2.5413	0.1478	1.3934	0.9598	0.9826	0.1029	1.3221	2.5576	2.5755	0.1467	1.3678
	(5.742)	(5.734)	(3.295)	(2.793)	(2.512)	(2.567)	(2.209)	(2.398)	(5.777)	(5.772)	(3.270)	(2.721)
Percent of families on welfare	0.0510	0.0524	0.0010	0.1064	0.0411	0.0421	0.0012	0.1109	0.0502	0.0516	0.0010	0.1077
	(4.261)	(4.322)	(0.969)	(10.95)	(4.339)	(4.423)	(1.102)	(11.36)	(4.153)	(4.213)	(0.997)	(10.93)
State tax rate	−0.0329	−0.0334	−0.0010	−0.0225	−0.0138	−0.0143	−0.0005	−0.0234	−0.0328	−0.0333	−0.0010	−0.0221
	(−4.12)	(−4.17)	(−0.96)	(−2.81)	(−1.91)	(−1.97)	(−0.45)	(−2.90)	(−4.03)	(−4.07)	(−0.96)	(−2.72)
Personal income per capita	0.1541	0.1515	0.0098	−0.1500	0.2016	0.1985	0.0116	−0.1541	0.1518	0.1492	0.0098	−0.1496
	(7.587)	(7.406)	(4.765)	(−8.61)	(11.66)	(11.46)	(5.484)	(−8.88)	(7.441)	(7.259)	(4.778)	(−8.53)
Federal & state top tax rate	0.0149	0.0151	0.0005	0.0096	–	–	–	–	0.0149	0.0151	0.0005	0.0095
	(5.848)	(5.865)	(2.393)	(2.805)	–	–	–	–	(5.848)	(5.865)	(2.361)	(2.794)
Federal & state avg marginal tax rate	–	–	–	–	0.0790	0.0797	0.0023	0.0178	–	–	–	–
	–	–	–	–	(15.96)	(16.07)	(4.119)	(1.745)	–	–	–	–
Family size	−3.0472	−3.0970	0.6091	−1.6130	−4.1609	−4.2352	0.5448	−2.0821	−3.0883	−3.1407	0.6135	−1.5932
	(−2.84)	(−2.87)	(5.450)	(−1.32)	(−4.70)	(−4.77)	(4.975)	(−1.71)	(−2.85)	(−2.88)	(5.478)	(−1.29)
Farms per household	−4.1019	−3.8764	−0.1237	4.2083	−4.3505	−4.0985	−0.1378	4.1762	−4.1296	−3.9003	−0.1227	4.1938
	(−1.89)	(−1.78)	(−0.40)	(1.882)	(−2.24)	(−2.11)	(−0.46)	(1.864)	(−1.86)	(−1.75)	(−0.39)	(1.855)
Percent of adults with high school diploma	−1.7235	−1.7332	0.0594	−0.2650	−1.5442	−1.5592	0.0731	−0.0806	−1.7341	−1.7446	0.0593	−0.2595
	(−5.87)	(−5.85)	(2.119)	(−0.74)	(−6.67)	(−6.72)	(2.692)	(−0.23)	(−5.88)	(−5.86)	(2.118)	(−0.72)
Percent of pop over 65	−1.6244	-1.6654	-0.4550	-3.0801	1.1875	1.1401	-0.3199	-2.7654	−1.6518	-1.6929	-0.4570	-3.0671
	(−1.44)	(−1.47)	(−3.25)	(−2.59)	(1.188)	(1.140)	(−2.28)	(−2.32)	(−1.44)	(−1.47)	(−3.25)	(−2.55)
Percent of employed persons in manufacturing	1.9351	1.9539	0.1377	0.4338	0.6697	0.7007	0.0751	0.4016	1.9782	1.9978	0.1395	0.4501
	(5.569)	(5.594)	(3.636)	(1.118)	(2.140)	(2.237)	(1.819)	(1.015)	(5.621)	(5.646)	(3.674)	(1.150)
Percent of employed persons in service	1.4674	1.5529	−0.0150	1.8847	0.2999	0.3896	−0.0505	1.9008	1.4849	1.5723	−0.0154	1.8841
	(4.165)	(4.361)	(−0.47)	(5.082)	(1.024)	(1.327)	(−1.50)	(5.076)	(4.223)	(4.424)	(−0.48)	(5.074)

(continued)

Table 9.3 (continued)

Variable	(2004, Media)											
	1				2				3			
	ALR	RTR	RCAP	IAR	ALR	RTR	RCAP	IAR	ALR	RTR	RCAP	IAR
Unemployment rate	−9.0625	−9.0801	−0.2222	−1.0224	−5.4633	−5.4581	−0.1351	−1.0569	−9.0552	−9.0774	−0.2232	−1.0149
	(−12.7)	(−12.6)	(−3.53)	(−1.13)	(−8.98)	(−8.95)	(−1.97)	(−1.07)	(−12.8)	(−12.7)	(−3.56)	(−1.13)
Audit rate	−0.1901	−0.2157	0.0160	–	0.0368	0.0120	0.0230	–	−0.1924	−0.2181	0.0160	–
	(−2.46)	(−2.75)	(2.400)	–	(0.592)	(0.193)	(3.307)	–	(−2.50)	(−2.79)	(2.400)	–
Direct examination time	–	–	–	0.4032	–	–	–	0.4519	–	–	–	0.4083
	–	–	–	(3.661)	–	–	–	(3.296)	–	–	–	(3.696)
Budget per return	–	–	–	19.2628	–	–	–	19.2871	–	–	–	19.2124
	–	–	–	(9.092)	–	–	–	(9.059)	–	–	–	(9.081)
Total sentences	–	–	–	–	–	–	–	–	–	–	–	–
	–	–	–	–	–	–	–	–	–	–	–	–
Total sentences (Tax & money laun only)	0.001107	0.001082	−0.000040	−0.000092	0.000424	0.000396	−0.000059	−0.000154	0.001180	0.001160	−0.000047	−0.000172
	(2.812)	(2.725)	(−1.05)	(−0.19)	(1.316)	(1.227)	(−1.55)	(−0.31)	(2.847)	(2.774)	(−1.18)	(−0.33)
Tax sentences	–	–	–	–	–	–	–	–	–	–	–	–
	–	–	–	–	–	–	–	–	–	–	–	–
Money laundering sentences	–	–	–	–	–	–	–	–	–	–	–	–
	–	–	–	–	–	–	–	–	–	–	–	–
Total prison sentences	–	–	–	–	–	–	–	–	–	–	–	–
	–	–	–	–	–	–	–	–	–	–	–	–
Total probation sentences	–	–	–	–	–	–	–	–	–	–	–	–
	–	–	–	–	–	–	–	–	–	–	–	–

(continued)

Table 9.3 (continued)

Variable	(2004, Media)											
	1				2				3			
	ALR	RTR	RCAP	IAR	ALR	RTR	RCAP	IAR	ALR	RTR	RCAP	IAR
Total sentences released in media	−0.000663	−0.000628	0.000039	0.000141	−0.000512	−0.000472	0.000041	0.000234	–	–	–	–
	(−1.76)	(−1.65)	(1.209)	(0.285)	(−1.75)	(−1.61)	(1.289)	(0.473)	–	–	–	–
Tax sentences released in media	–	–	–	–	–	–	–	–	−0.001104	−0.001058	0.000031	−0.000508
	–	–	–	–	–	–	–	–	(−1.65)	(−1.56)	(0.540)	(−0.58)
Money laundering sentences released in media	–	–	–	–	–	–	–	–	−0.000598	−0.000580	0.000086	0.001292
	–	–	–	–	–	–	–	–	(−0.60)	(−0.57)	(0.990)	(1.035)
Tax sentences resulting in prison	–	–	–	–	–	–	–	–	–	–	–	–
	–	–	–	–	–	–	–	–	–	–	–	–
Tax sentences resulting in probation	–	–	–	–	–	–	–	–	–	–	–	–
	–	–	–	–	–	–	–	–	–	–	–	–
Money laun sentences resulting in prison	–	–	–	–	–	–	–	–	–	–	–	–
	–	–	–	–	–	–	–	–	–	–	–	–
Money laun sentences resulting in probation	–	–	–	–	–	–	–	–	–	–	–	–
	–	–	–	–	–	–	–	–	–	–	–	–
Tax sent resulting in neither prison nor probation	–	–	–	–	–	–	–	–	–	–	–	–

(continued)

Table 9.3 (continued)

Variable	(2004, Media)											
	1				2				3			
	ALR	RTR	RCAP	IAR	ALR	RTR	RCAP	IAR	ALR	RTR	RCAP	IAR
	–	–	–	–	–	–	–	–	–	–	–	–
Money laun sent resulting in neither prison nor probation	–	–	–	–	–	–	–	–	–	–	–	–
	–	–	–	–	–	–	–	–	–	–	–	–
% of tot sent related to tax	0.0129	0.0130	0.0056	−0.0421	0.0106	0.0104	0.0057	−0.0514	0.0241	0.0236	0.0055	−0.0323
	(0.318)	(0.317)	(1.616)	(−0.81)	(0.335)	(0.329)	(1.641)	(−0.99)	(0.585)	(0.566)	(1.547)	(−0.61)
% of tot sent related to money laun	−0.0433	−0.0438	0.0031	−0.0739	−0.0240	−0.0241	0.0036	−0.0762	−0.0375	−0.0382	0.0024	−0.0850
	(−1.03)	(−1.03)	(0.888)	(−1.39)	(−0.74)	(−0.74)	(1.010)	(−1.42)	(−0.88)	(−0.89)	(0.667)	(−1.58)
% of total sentences not prison or prob	–	–	–	–	–	–	–	–	–	–	–	–
	–	–	–	–	–	–	–	–	–	–	–	–
% of tax sentences in prison	–	–	–	–	–	–	–	–	–	–	–	–
	–	–	–	–	–	–	–	–	–	–	–	–
% of money laun sentences in prison	–	–	–	–	–	–	–	–	–	–	–	–
	–	–	–	–	–	–	–	–	–	–	–	–
% of tax sentences in probation	–	–	–	–	–	–	–	–	–	–	–	–
	–	–	–	–	–	–	–	–	–	–	–	–
% of money laun sentences in probation	–	–	–	–	–	–	–	–	–	–	–	–
	–	–	–	–	–	–	–	–	–	–	–	–
% of tax sent neither prison nor probation	0.1194	0.1076	−0.0005	−0.2050	0.0869	0.0743	−0.0010	−0.2250	0.1213	0.1093	−0.0005	−0.2007
	(1.090)	(0.970)	(−0.05)	(−1.44)	(1.021)	(0.870)	(−0.10)	(−1.57)	(1.113)	(0.990)	(−0.05)	(−1.41)
% of money laun sent neither prison nor probation	−0.1039	−0.1025	0.0113	−0.0488	−0.0710	−0.0705	0.0125	−0.0721	−0.1101	−0.1087	0.0119	−0.0402
	(−0.68)	(−0.66)	(0.878)	(−0.25)	(−0.60)	(−0.59)	(0.966)	(−0.36)	(−0.72)	(−0.70)	(0.921)	(−0.20)
% of total sentences in media	–	–	–	–	–	–	–	–	–	–	–	–
	–	–	–	–	–	–	–	–	–	–	–	–

(continued)

Table 9.3 (continued)

Variable	(2004, Media)											
	1				2				3			
	ALR	RTR	RCAP	IAR	ALR	RTR	RCAP	IAR	ALR	RTR	RCAP	IAR
% of tax sentences in media	–	–	–	–	–	–	–	–	–	–	–	–
	–	–	–	–	–	–	–	–	–	–	–	–
% of money laun sentences in media	–	–	–	–	–	–	–	–	–	–	–	–
	–	–	–	–	–	–	–	–	–	–	–	–
Number of obs	650				650				650			
Years	1992–2004				1992–2004				1992–2004			

(continued)

Table 9.3 (continued)

Variable	(2004, Media)											
	4				5				6			
	ALR	RTR	RCAP	IAR	ALR	RTR	RCAP	IAR	ALR	RTR	RCAP	IAR
Constant	0.9980	1.0217	0.1028	1.3027	2.5027	2.5187	0.1495	1.3956	0.9091	0.9338	0.1077	1.3149
	(2.605)	(2.662)	(2.205)	(2.349)	(5.640)	(5.634)	(3.334)	(2.796)	(2.385)	(2.445)	(2.313)	(2.389)
Percent of families on welfare	0.0402	0.0411	0.0012	0.1122	0.0580	0.0592	0.0008	0.1060	0.0437	0.0445	0.0009	0.1104
	(4.192)	(4.277)	(1.082)	(11.34)	(4.839)	(4.883)	(0.799)	(11.08)	(4.679)	(4.749)	(0.849)	(11.52)
State tax rate	−0.0137	−0.0141	−0.0005	−0.0231	−0.0340	−0.0343	−0.0010	−0.0225	−0.0141	−0.0145	−0.0004	−0.0234
	(−1.86)	(−1.92)	(−0.44)	(−2.81)	(−4.27)	(−4.31)	(−0.92)	(−2.80)	(−1.97)	(−2.03)	(−0.42)	(−2.90)
Personal income per capita	0.2000	0.1969	0.0115	−0.1538	0.1568	0.1542	0.0099	−0.1508	0.2033	0.2001	0.0116	−0.1546
	(11.55)	(11.35)	(5.473)	(−8.80)	(7.650)	(7.474)	(4.829)	(−8.70)	(11.79)	(11.58)	(5.508)	(−9.00)
Federal & state top tax rate	–	–	–	–	0.0155	0.0157	0.0005	0.0096	–	–	–	–
	–	–	–	–	(5.985)	(5.996)	(2.296)	(2.814)	–	–	–	–
Federal & state avg marginal tax rate	0.0789	0.0796	0.0023	0.0177	–	–	–	–	0.0801	0.0808	0.0022	0.0178
	(15.93)	(16.04)	(4.089)	(1.731)	–	–	–	–	(16.38)	(16.48)	(3.906)	(1.742)
Family size	−4.2125	−4.2874	0.5503	−2.0644	−3.0348	−3.0876	0.5974	−1.6008	−4.1273	−4.2025	0.5327	−2.0716
	(−4.73)	(−4.80)	(5.008)	(−1.68)	(−2.81)	(−2.84)	(5.368)	(−1.31)	(−4.67)	(−4.75)	(4.869)	(−1.70)
Farms per household	−4.3435	−4.0874	−0.1351	4.1709	−4.6211	−4.3751	−0.0943	4.2497	−4.6241	−4.3562	−0.0942	4.2297

(continued)

Table 9.3 (continued)

Variable	(2004, Media)											
	4				5				6			
	ALR	RTR	RCAP	IAR	ALR	RTR	RCAP	IAR	ALR	RTR	RCAP	IAR
	(−2.20)	(−2.07)	(−0.44)	(1.840)	(−2.14)	(−2.03)	(−0.30)	(1.899)	(−2.42)	(−2.28)	(−0.31)	(1.902)
Percent of adults with high school diploma	−1.5538	−1.5693	0.0723	−0.0753	−1.7718	−1.7800	0.0617	−0.2658	−1.5543	−1.5681	0.0758	−0.0710
	(−6.70)	(−6.75)	(2.661)	(−0.21)	(−5.98)	(−5.95)	(2.206)	(−0.75)	(−6.72)	(−6.77)	(2.790)	(−0.20)
Percent of pop over 65	1.1874	1.1397	−0.3251	−2.7557	−1.4325	−1.4776	−0.4550	−3.1164	1.2884	1.2347	−0.3280	−2.7926
	(1.172)	(1.124)	(−2.30)	(−2.28)	(−1.27)	(−1.30)	(−3.25)	(−2.62)	(1.303)	(1.247)	(−2.34)	(−2.36)
Percent of employed persons in manufacturing	0.6630	0.6945	0.0776	0.4176	1.8860	1.9051	0.1368	0.4411	0.6494	0.6818	0.0776	0.4042
	(2.095)	(2.193)	(1.870)	(1.045)	(5.408)	(5.436)	(3.614)	(1.133)	(2.091)	(2.193)	(1.882)	(1.025)
Percent of employed persons in service	0.3067	0.3973	−0.0505	1.9010	1.4717	1.5565	−0.0146	1.8915	0.2827	0.3730	−0.0479	1.9024
	(1.049)	(1.356)	(−1.51)	(5.069)	(4.114)	(4.307)	(−0.46)	(5.104)	(0.963)	(1.268)	(−1.42)	(5.089)
Unemployment rate	−5.4723	−5.4711	−0.1358	−1.0537	−8.8773	−8.8960	−0.2258	−1.0436	−5.3453	−5.3471	−0.1462	−1.0942
	(−9.04)	(−9.02)	(−1.99)	(−1.07)	(−12.3)	(−12.1)	(−3.59)	(−1.17)	(−8.82)	(−8.80)	(−2.14)	(−1.12)
Audit rate	0.0368	0.0121	0.0229	–	−0.2066	−0.2319	0.0167	–	0.0337	0.0092	0.0235	–
	(0.594)	(0.194)	(3.302)	–	(−2.63)	(−2.92)	(2.508)	–	(0.543)	(0.147)	(3.379)	–
Direct examination time	–	–	–	0.4547	–	–	–	0.4079	–	–	–	0.4582
	–	–	–	(3.314)	–	–	–	(3.789)	–	–	–	(3.378)
Budget per return	–	–	–	19.2402	–	–	–	19.2349	–	–	–	19.2783
	–	–	–	(9.051)	–	–	–	(9.095)	–	–	–	(9.061)
Total sentences	–	–	–	–	–	–	–	–	–	–	–	–
	–	–	–	–	–	–	–	–	–	–	–	–
Total sentences (Tax & money laun only)	0.000492	0.000467	−0.000066	−0.000252	–	–	–	–	–	–	–	–
	(1.453)	(1.377)	(−1.63)	(−0.49)	–	–	–	–	–	–	–	–
Tax sentences	–	–	–	–	–	–	–	–	–	–	–	–
	–	–	–	–	–	–	–	–	–	–	–	–
Money laundering sentences	–	–	–	–	–	–	–	–	–	–	–	–
	–	–	–	–	–	–	–	–	–	–	–	–
Total prison sentences	–	–	–	–	–	–	–	–	–	–	–	–
	–	–	–	–	–	–	–	–	–	–	–	–

(continued)

Table 9.3 (continued)

Variable	(2004, Media)											
	4				5				6			
	ALR	RTR	RCAP	IAR	ALR	RTR	RCAP	IAR	ALR	RTR	RCAP	IAR
Total probation sentences	–	–	–	–	–	–	–	–	–	–	–	–
	–	–	–	–	–	–	–	–	–	–	–	–
Total sentences released in media	–	–	–	–	0.000076	0.000099	0.000017	0.000072	−0.000251	−0.000228	0.000010	0.000117
	–	–	–	–	(0.275)	(0.355)	(0.693)	(0.216)	(−1.15)	(−1.05)	(0.387)	(0.350)
Tax sentences released in media	−0.000600	−0.000556	0.000049	−0.000362	–	–	–	–	–	–	–	–
	(−1.15)	(−1.06)	(0.855)	(−0.41)	–	–	–	–	–	–	–	–
Money laundering sentences released in media	−0.000833	−0.000794	0.000068	0.001419	–	–	–	–	–	–	–	–
	(−1.06)	(−1.01)	(0.780)	(1.133)	–	–	–	–	–	–	–	–
Tax sentences resulting in prison	–	–	–	–	–	–	–	–	–	–	–	–
	–	–	–	–	–	–	–	–	–	–	–	–
Tax sentences resulting in probation	–	–	–	–	–	–	–	–	–	–	–	–
	–	–	–	–	–	–	–	–	–	–	–	–
Money laun sentences resulting in prison	–	–	–	–	–	–	–	–	–	–	–	–
	–	–	–	–	–	–	–	–	–	–	–	–
Money laun sentences resulting in probation	–	–	–	–	–	–	–	–	–	–	–	–
	–	–	–	–	–	–	–	–	–	–	–	–
Tax sent resulting in neither prison nor probation	–	–	–	–	–	–	–	–	–	–	–	–
	–	–	–	–	–	–	–	–	–	–	–	–
Money laun sent resulting in neither prison nor probation	–	–	–	–	–	–	–	–	–	–	–	–
	–	–	–	–	–	–	–	–	–	–	–	–

(continued)

Table 9.3 (continued)

Variable	(2004, Media)											
	4				5				6			
	ALR	RTR	RCAP	IAR	ALR	RTR	RCAP	IAR	ALR	RTR	RCAP	IAR
% of tot sent related to tax	0.0155	0.0148	0.0053	−0.0427	0.0210	0.0209	0.0053	−0.0430	0.0136	0.0133	0.0053	−0.0525
	(0.482)	(0.460)	(1.495)	(−0.81)	(0.508)	(0.499)	(1.528)	(−0.83)	(0.431)	(0.418)	(1.512)	(−1.01)
% of tot sent related to money laun	−0.0163	−0.0168	0.0030	−0.0882	−0.0321	−0.0330	0.0027	−0.0748	−0.0196	−0.0200	0.0029	−0.0783
	(−0.49)	(−0.50)	(0.829)	(−1.63)	(−0.76)	(−0.77)	(0.762)	(−1.42)	(−0.60)	(−0.61)	(0.821)	(−1.47)
% of total sentences not prison or prob	–	–	–	–	–	–	–	–	–	–	–	–
	–	–	–	–	–	–	–	–	–	–	–	–
% of tax sentences in prison	–	–	–	–	–	–	–	–	–	–	–	–
	–	–	–	–	–	–	–	–	–	–	–	–
% of money laun sentences in prison	–	–	–	–	–	–	–	–	–	–	–	–
	–	–	–	–	–	–	–	–	–	–	–	–
% of tax sentences in probation	–	–	–	–	–	–	–	–	–	–	–	–
	–	–	–	–	–	–	–	–	–	–	–	–
% of money laun sentences in probation	–	–	–	–	–	–	–	–	–	–	–	–
	–	–	–	–	–	–	–	–	–	–	–	–
% of tax sent neither prison nor probation	0.0877	0.0749	−0.0011	−0.2208	0.1362	0.1239	−0.0011	−0.2059	0.0926	0.0796	−0.0018	−0.2269
	(1.034)	(0.881)	(−0.11)	(−1.55)	(1.220)	(1.096)	(−0.11)	(−1.45)	(1.085)	(0.930)	(−0.18)	(−1.59)
% of money laun sent neither prison nor probation	−0.0776	−0.0769	0.0130	-0.0627	-0.1025	-0.1009	0.0115	-0.0496	-0.0707	-0.0701	0.0127	-0.0722
	(−0.65)	(−0.65)	(0.999)	(−0.32)	(−0.66)	(−0.64)	(0.891)	(−0.25)	(−0.59)	(−0.59)	(0.977)	(−0.36)
% of total sentences in media	–	–	–	–	–	–	–	–	–	–	–	–
	–	–	–	–	–	–	–	–	–	–	–	–
% of tax sentences in media	–	–	–	–	–	–	–	–	–	–	–	–
	–	–	–	–	–	–	–	–	–	–	–	–
% of money laun sentences in media	–	–	–	–	–	–	–	–	–	–	–	–
	–	–	–	–	–	–	–	–	–	–	–	–
Number of obs	650				650				650			
Years	1992–2004				1992–2004				1992–2004			

(continued)

Table 9.3 (continued)

Variable	(2004, Media)							
	7				8			
	ALR	RTR	RCAP	IAR	ALR	RTR	RCAP	IAR
Constant	2.5178	2.5358	0.1490	1.3688	0.9343	0.9596	0.1080	1.2958
	(5.634)	(5.632)	(3.320)	(2.719)	(2.445)	(2.506)	(2.318)	(2.339)
Percent of families on welfare	0.0586	0.0599	0.0008	0.1068	0.0434	0.0442	0.0008	0.1112
	(4.863)	(4.907)	(0.775)	(11.08)	(4.627)	(4.698)	(0.790)	(11.51)
State tax rate	−0.0339	−0.0343	−0.0010	−0.0220	−0.0140	−0.0144	−0.0004	−0.0230
	(−4.20)	(−4.24)	(−0.90)	(−2.70)	(−1.94)	(−2.00)	(−0.41)	(−2.81)
Personal income per capita	0.1549	0.1523	0.0099	−0.1509	0.2021	0.1989	0.0116	−0.1548
	(7.524)	(7.347)	(4.847)	(−8.64)	(11.69)	(11.49)	(5.507)	(−8.94)
Federal & state top tax rate	0.0154	0.0156	0.0005	0.0096	–	–	–	–
	(5.944)	(5.956)	(2.266)	(2.814)	–	–	–	–
Federal & state avg marginal tax rate	–	–	–	–	0.0801	0.0808	0.0022	0.0176
	–	–	–	–	(16.32)	(16.42)	(3.873)	(1.729)
Family size	−3.0356	−3.0910	0.5994	−1.5787	−4.1535	−4.2299	0.5344	−2.0568
	(−2.78)	(−2.82)	(5.377)	(−1.28)	(−4.68)	(−4.76)	(4.872)	(−1.68)
Farms per household	−4.6224	−4.3762	−0.0933	4.2603	−4.6361	−4.3683	−0.0934	4.2512
	(−2.11)	(−1.99)	(−0.30)	(1.878)	(−2.39)	(−2.25)	(−0.31)	(1.886)

(continued)

Table 9.3 (continued)

Variable	(2004, Media)							
	7				8			
	ALR	RTR	RCAP	IAR	ALR	RTR	RCAP	IAR
Percent of adults with high school diploma	−1.7737	−1.7830	0.0617	−0.2592	−1.5628	−1.5771	0.0752	−0.0629
	(−5.95)	(−5.93)	(2.204)	(−0.72)	(−6.74)	(−6.79)	(2.766)	(−0.18)
Percent of pop over 65	−1.4658	−1.5104	−0.4566	−3.1202	1.2892	1.2366	−0.3308	−2.7982
	(−1.28)	(−1.31)	(−3.25)	(−2.59)	(1.289)	(1.235)	(−2.35)	(−2.33)
Percent of employed persons in manufacturing	1.9240	1.9433	0.1380	0.4596	0.6460	0.6783	0.0788	0.4223
	(5.456)	(5.482)	(3.635)	(1.170)	(2.060)	(2.161)	(1.900)	(1.060)
Percent of employed persons in service	1.4890	1.5754	−0.0151	1.8939	0.2881	0.3791	−0.0481	1.9066
	(4.161)	(4.357)	(−0.48)	(5.103)	(0.982)	(1.290)	(−1.43)	(5.092)
Unemployment rate	−8.9034	−8.9251	−0.2260	−1.0447	−5.3530	−5.3568	−0.1459	−1.1034
	(−12.3)	(−12.2)	(−3.60)	(−1.17)	(−8.85)	(−8.84)	(−2.14)	(−1.13)
Audit rate	−0.2118	−0.2372	0.0168	–	0.0326	0.0081	0.0236	–
	(−2.70)	(−2.99)	(2.540)	–	(0.526)	(0.129)	(3.404)	–
Direct examination time	–	–	–	0.4169	–	–	–	0.4649
	–	–	–	(3.867)	–	–	–	(3.429)
Budget per return	–	–	–	19.1707	–	–	–	19.2186
	–	–	–	(9.079)	–	–	–	(9.047)
Total sentences	–	–	–	–	–	–	–	–
	–	–	–	–	–	–	–	–
Total sentences (Tax & money laun only)	–	–	–	–	–	–	–	–
	–	–	–	–	–	–	–	–
Tax sentences	–	–	–	–	–	–	–	–
	–	–	–	–	–	–	–	–
Money laundering sentences	–	–	–	–	–	–	–	–
	–	–	–	–	–	–	–	–

(continued)

Table 9.3 (continued)

Variable	(2004, Media)							
	7				8			
	ALR	RTR	RCAP	IAR	ALR	RTR	RCAP	IAR
Total prison sentences	–	–	–	–	–	–	–	–
	–	–	–	–	–	–	–	–
Total probation sentences	–	–	–	–	–	–	–	–
	–	–	–	–	–	–	–	–
Total sentences released in media	–	–	–	–	–	–	–	–
	–	–	–	–	–	–	–	–
Tax sentences released in media	−0.000400	−0.000361	0.000009	−0.000632	−0.000319	−0.000289	0.000018	−0.000530
	(−0.62)	(−0.55)	(0.168)	(−0.79)	(−0.65)	(−0.58)	(0.326)	(−0.66)
Money laundering sentences released in media	0.000727	0.000729	0.000040	0.001088	−0.000326	−0.000314	0.000006	0.001098
	(0.822)	(0.815)	(0.521)	(1.016)	(−0.46)	(−0.45)	(0.075)	(1.019)
Tax sentences resulting in prison	–	–	–	–	–	–	–	–
	–	–	–	–	–	–	–	–
Tax sentences resulting in probation	–	–	–	–	–	–	–	–
	–	–	–	–	–	–	–	–
Money laun sentences resulting in prison	–	–	–	–	–	–	–	–
	–	–	–	–	–	–	–	–
Money laun sentences resulting in probation	–	–	–	–	–	–	–	–
	–	–	–	–	–	–	–	–
Tax sent resulting in neither prison nor probation	–	–	–	–	–	–	–	–
	–	–	–	–	–	–	–	–
Money laun sent resulting in neither prison nor probation	–	–	–	–	–	–	–	–
	–	–	–	–	–	–	–	–
% of tot sent related to tax	0.0273	0.0267	0.0053	−0.0327	0.0168	0.0160	0.0051	−0.0433
	(0.647)	(0.625)	(1.488)	(−0.62)	(0.520)	(0.496)	(1.421)	(−0.82)

(continued)

Table 9.3 (continued)

Variable	(2004, Media)							
	7				8			
	ALR	RTR	RCAP	IAR	ALR	RTR	RCAP	IAR
% of tot sent related to money laun	−0.0387	−0.0395	0.0023	−0.0849	−0.0161	−0.0166	0.0029	−0.0884
	(−0.89)	(−0.90)	(0.637)	(−1.58)	(−0.48)	(−0.50)	(0.784)	(−1.64)
% of total sentences not prison or prob	–	–	–	–	–	–	–	–
	–	–	–	–	–	–	–	–
% of tax sentences in prison	–	–	–	–	–	–	–	–
	–	–	–	–	–	–	–	–
% of money laun sentences in prison	–	–	–	–	–	–	–	–
	–	–	–	–	–	–	–	–
% of tax sentences in probation	–	–	–	–	–	–	–	–
	–	–	–	–	–	–	–	–
% of money laun sentences in probation	–	–	–	–	–	–	–	–
	–	–	–	–	–	–	–	–
% of tax sent neither prison nor probation	0.1375	0.1251	−0.0011	−0.2021	0.0936	0.0805	−0.0019	−0.2235
	(1.232)	(1.108)	(−0.12)	(−1.42)	(1.098)	(0.942)	(−0.19)	(−1.57)
% of money laun sent neither prison nor probation	−0.0995	−0.0981	0.0118	−0.0426	−0.0737	−0.0732	0.0127	−0.0652
	(−0.64)	(−0.62)	(0.911)	(−0.21)	(−0.62)	(−0.61)	(0.978)	(−0.33)
% of total sentences in media	–	–	–	–	–	–	–	–
	–	–	–	–	–	–	–	–
% of tax sentences in media	–	–	–	–	–	–	–	–
	–	–	–	–	–	–	–	–
% of money laun sentences in media	–	–	–	–	–	–	–	–
	–	–	–	–	–	–	–	–
Number of obs	650				650			
Years	1992–2004				1992–2004			

(continued)

Table 9.3A 2004, Media/Dummy

Variable	(2004, Media/Dummy)											
	1				2				3			
	ALR	RTR	RCAP	IAR	ALR	RTR	RCAP	IAR	ALR	RTR	RCAP	IAR
Constant	1.8062	1.8385	0.1178	0.6359	1.1928	1.2271	0.0898	1.3616	1.8189	1.8521	0.5787	0.5787
	(5.325)	(5.412)	(2.609)	(1.301)	(3.377)	(3.479)	(1.890)	(2.579)	(5.323)	(5.412)	(1.174)	(1.174)
Percent of families on welfare	0.0057	0.0064	−0.0002	0.0775	0.0126	0.0133	0.0005	0.0751	0.0061	0.0069	0.0795	0.0795
	(0.705)	(0.790)	(−0.16)	(7.745)	(1.576)	(1.671)	(0.449)	(7.234)	(0.747)	(0.834)	(7.889)	(7.889)
State tax rate	−0.0197	−0.0203	−0.0006	−0.0172	−0.0134	−0.0139	−0.0003	−0.0240	−0.0195	−0.0201	−0.0164	−0.0164
	(−2.89)	(−2.98)	(−0.51)	(−2.21)	(−1.97)	(−2.04)	(−0.24)	(−3.08)	(−2.79)	(−2.88)	(−2.09)	(−2.09)
Personal income per capita	0.2530	0.2500	0.0134	−0.1025	0.2542	0.2510	0.0133	−0.1099	0.2524	0.2495	−0.1008	−0.1008
	(17.03)	(16.80)	(6.759)	(−5.75)	(17.29)	(17.10)	(6.597)	(−6.24)	(16.90)	(16.68)	(−5.61)	(−5.61)
Federal & state top tax rate	0.0056	0.0057	0.0004	0.0087	–	–	–	–	0.0056	0.0057	0.0086	0.0086
	(2.979)	(3.010)	(1.600)	(2.667)	–	–	–	–	(2.964)	(2.994)	(2.648)	(2.648)
Federal & state avg marginal tax rate	–	–	–	–	0.0397	0.0400	0.0022	−0.0160	–	–	–	–
	–	–	–	–	(6.424)	(6.486)	(2.821)	(−1.50)	–	–	–	–
Family size	−2.9764	−3.0377	0.5961	−1.0820	−3.6189	−3.6950	0.5463	−1.2678	−3.0006	−3.0625	−1.0454	−1.0454
	(−3.51)	(−3.58)	(5.260)	(−0.92)	(−4.44)	(−4.54)	(4.905)	(−1.08)	(−3.51)	(−3.58)	(−0.88)	(−0.88)
Farms per household	−4.4546	−4.1889	−0.1892	5.2376	−4.6013	−4.3313	−0.1751	4.6957	−4.4519	−4.1817	5.2244	5.2244
	(−2.36)	(−2.22)	(−0.61)	(2.419)	(−2.51)	(−2.37)	(−0.58)	(2.172)	(−2.30)	(−2.17)	(2.386)	(2.386)
Percent of adults with high school diploma	−1.2467	−1.2604	0.0742	−0.1829	−1.2476	−1.2619	0.0773	0.0805	−1.2486	−1.2626	−0.1653	−0.1653
	(−5.55)	(−5.60)	(2.594)	(−0.53)	(−5.85)	(−5.93)	(2.770)	(0.241)	(−5.54)	(−5.59)	(−0.48)	(−0.48)
Percent of pop over 65	1.1143	1.0561	−0.3352	−2.8825	1.9632	1.9141	−0.2776	−2.8866	1.1427	1.0844	−2.8343	−2.8343
	(1.180)	(1.119)	(−2.36)	(−2.51)	(2.115)	(2.065)	(−1.97)	(−2.51)	(1.188)	(1.128)	(−2.44)	(−2.44)
Percent of employed persons in manufacturing	−0.1086	−0.0824	0.0776	−0.4885	−0.2506	−0.2274	0.0603	−0.3199	−0.1193	−0.0924	−0.4949	−0.4949
	(−0.35)	(−0.26)	(1.789)	(−1.24)	(−0.84)	(−0.76)	(1.392)	(−0.81)	(−0.38)	(−0.29)	(−1.25)	(−1.25)
Percent of employed persons in service	0.2262	0.3195	−0.0574	1.5868	−0.0670	0.0257	−0.0699	1.7697	0.2254	0.3198	1.5704	1.5704
	(0.905)	(1.274)	(−1.84)	(4.447)	(−0.26)	(0.100)	(−2.12)	(4.938)	(0.902)	(1.276)	(4.397)	(4.397)

(continued)

Table 9.3A (continued)

Variable	(2004, Media/Dummy)											
	1				2				3			
	ALR	RTR	RCAP	IAR	ALR	RTR	RCAP	IAR	ALR	RTR	RCAP	IAR
Unemployment rate	−5.0044	−4.9897	−0.1485	2.1344	−4.3805	−4.3702	−0.1176	0.7735	−5.0328	−5.0228	2.1921	2.1921
	(−8.85)	(−8.79)	(−2.14)	(2.256)	(−7.93)	(−7.92)	(−1.68)	(0.798)	(−8.94)	(−8.89)	(2.324)	(2.324)
Dummy 2002–2004	−0.2918	−0.2946	−0.0053	−0.2431	−0.2120	−0.2140	−0.0014	−0.2671	−0.2914	−0.2941	−0.2453	−0.2453
	(−18.0)	(−18.1)	(−2.60)	(−7.86)	(−9.91)	(−10.0)	(−0.53)	(−7.88)	(−17.9)	(−18.0)	(−7.91)	(−7.91)
Audit rate	0.0090	−0.0176	0.0264	–	0.0865	0.0605	0.0291	–	0.0090	−0.0176	–	–
	(0.181)	(−0.35)	(4.349)	–	(1.622)	(1.137)	(4.332)	–	(0.182)	(−0.35)	–	–
Direct examination time	–	–	–	1.0271	–	–	–	0.8522	–	–	1.0361	1.0361
	–	–	–	(7.807)	–	–	–	(6.080)	–	–	(7.865)	(7.865)
Budget per return	–	–	–	16.6495	–	–	–	16.7117	–	–	16.5906	16.5906
	–	–	–	(8.135)	–	–	–	(8.131)	–	–	(8.124)	(8.124)
Total sentences	–	–	–	–	–	–	–	–	–	–	–	–
	–	–	–	–	–	–	–	–	–	–	–	–
Total sentences (Tax & money laun only)	0.000240	0.000211	−0.000050	−0.000234	0.000155	0.000124	−0.000059	−0.000274	0.000201	0.000175	−0.000389	−0.000389
	(0.789)	(0.692)	(−1.28)	(−0.50)	(0.523)	(0.419)	(−1.50)	(−0.59)	(0.626)	(0.542)	(−0.80)	(−0.80)
Tax sentences	–	–	–	–	–	–	–	–	–	–	–	–
	–	–	–	–	–	–	–	–	–	–	–	–
Money laundering sentences	–	–	–	–	–	–	–	–	–	–	–	–
	–	–	–	–	–	–	–	–	–	–	–	–
Total prison sentences	–	–	–	–	–	–	–	–	–	–	–	–
	–	–	–	–	–	–	–	–	–	–	–	–

(continued)

Table 9.3A (continued)

Variable	(2004, Media/Dummy)											
	1				2				3			
	ALR	RTR	RCAP	IAR	ALR	RTR	RCAP	IAR	ALR	RTR	RCAP	IAR
Total probation	–	–	–	–	–	–	–	–	–	–	–	–
sentences	–	–	–	–	–	–	–	–	–	–	–	–
Total sentences	0.000044	0.000090	0.000044	0.000128	−0.000084	−0.000038	0.000040	0.000459	–	–	–	–
released in media	(0.161)	(0.327)	(1.348)	(0.272)	(−0.31)	(−0.14)	(1.193)	(0.971)	–	–	–	–
Tax sentences	–	–	–	–	–	–	–	–	−0.000215	−0.000168	−0.000801	−0.000801
released in media	–	–	–	–	–	–	–	–	(−0.44)	(−0.34)	(−0.96)	(−0.96)
Money laundering	–	–	–	–	–	–	–	–	0.000493	0.000547	0.001883	0.001883
sentences released in media	–	–	–	–	–	–	–	–	(0.679)	(0.750)	(1.580)	(1.580)
Tax sentences	–	–	–	–	–	–	–	–	–	–	–	–
resulting in prison	–	–	–	–	–	–	–	–	–	–	–	–
Tax sentences	–	–	–	–	–	–	–	–	–	–	–	–
resulting in probation	–	–	–	–	–	–	–	–	–	–	–	–
Money laun	–	–	–	–	–	–	–	–	–	–	–	–
sentences resulting in prison	–	–	–	–	–	–	–	–	–	–	–	–
Money laun	–	–	–	–	–	–	–	–	–	–	–	–
sentences resulting in probation	–	–	–	–	–	–	–	–	–	–	–	–
Tax sent resulting in	–	–	–	–	–	–	–	–	–	–	–	–
neither prison nor probation	–	–	–	–	–	–	–	–	–	–	–	–

(continued)

Table 9.3A (continued)

Variable	(2004, Media/Dummy)											
	1				2				3			
	ALR	RTR	RCAP	IAR	ALR	RTR	RCAP	IAR	ALR	RTR	RCAP	IAR
Money laun sent resulting in neither prison nor probation	–	–	–	–	–	–	–	–	–	–	–	–
	–	–	–	–	–	–	–	–	–	–	–	–
% of tot sent related to tax	0.0275	0.0273	0.0064	−0.0535	0.0230	0.0229	0.0062	−0.0543	0.0319	0.0312	−0.0377	−0.0377
	(0.938)	(0.930)	(1.809)	(−1.08)	(0.808)	(0.805)	(1.732)	(−1.09)	(1.069)	(1.044)	(−0.75)	(−0.75)
% of tot sent related to money laun	−0.0066	−0.0067	0.0040	−0.0786	−0.0068	−0.0068	0.0040	−0.0709	−0.0104	−0.0110	−0.0946	−0.0946
	(−0.22)	(−0.22)	(1.123)	(−1.55)	(−0.23)	(−0.23)	(1.115)	(−1.39)	(−0.34)	(−0.36)	(−1.85)	(−1.85)
% of total sentences not prison or prob	–	–	–	–	–	–	–	–	–	–	–	–
	–	–	–	–	–	–	–	–	–	–	–	–
% of tax sentences in prison	–	–	–	–	–	–	–	–	–	–	–	–
	–	–	–	–	–	–	–	–	–	–	–	–
% of money laun sentences in prison	–	–	–	–	–	–	–	–	–	–	–	–
	–	–	–	–	–	–	–	–	–	–	–	–
% of tax sentences in probation	–	–	–	–	–	–	–	–	–	–	–	–
	–	–	–	–	–	–	–	–	–	–	–	–
% of money laun sentences in probation	–	–	–	–	–	–	–	–	–	–	–	–
	–	–	–	–	–	–	–	–	–	–	–	–
% of tax sent neither prison nor probation	0.1032	0.0907	−0.0002	−0.1993	0.0918	0.0793	−0.0007	−0.2105	0.1053	0.0926	−0.1925	−0.1925
	(1.309)	(1.146)	(−0.02)	(−1.47)	(1.197)	(1.036)	(−0.07)	(−1.55)	(1.338)	(1.173)	(−1.42)	(−1.42)
% of money laun sent neither prison nor probation	−0.1620	−0.1625	0.0115	−0.1156	−0.1288	−0.1291	0.0129	−0.1647	−0.1583	−0.1585	−0.1019	−0.1019
	(−1.48)	(−1.48)	(0.876)	(−0.62)	(−1.20)	(−1.21)	(0.976)	(−0.88)	(−1.45)	(−1.44)	(−0.54)	(−0.54)
% of total sentences in media	–	–	–	–	–	–	–	–	–	–	–	–
	–	–	–	–	–	–	–	–	–	–	–	–

(continued)

Table 9.3A (continued)

Variable	(2004, Media/Dummy)											
	1				2				3			
	ALR	RTR	RCAP	IAR	ALR	RTR	RCAP	IAR	ALR	RTR	RCAP	IAR
% of tax sentences in media	–	–	–	–	–	–	–	–	–	–	–	–
	–	–	–	–	–	–	–	–	–	–	–	–
% of money laun sentences in media	–	–	–	–	–	–	–	–	–	–	–	–
	–	–	–	–	–	–	–	–	–	–	–	–
Number of obs	650				650				650			
Years	1992–2004				1992–2004				1992–2004			

(continued)

Table 9.3A (continued)

Variable	(2004, Media/Dummy)											
	4				5				6			
	ALR	RTR	RCAP	IAR	ALR	RTR	RCAP	IAR	ALR	RTR	RCAP	IAR
Constant	1.2087	1.2433	0.0898	1.3172	1.7785	1.8118	0.1208	0.6329	1.1669	1.2028	0.0938	1.3549
	(3.412)	(3.515)	(1.891)	(2.482)	(5.271)	(5.361)	(2.672)	(1.293)	(3.317)	(3.423)	(1.972)	(2.571)
Percent of families on welfare	0.0126	0.0133	0.0004	0.0771	0.0068	0.0074	−0.0004	0.0767	0.0132	0.0138	0.0002	0.0741
	(1.559)	(1.656)	(0.426)	(7.395)	(0.855)	(0.925)	(−0.39)	(7.766)	(1.696)	(1.775)	(0.190)	(7.230)
State tax rate	−0.0131	−0.0136	−0.0003	−0.0234	−0.0200	−0.0205	−0.0005	−0.0171	−0.0136	−0.0141	−0.0002	−0.0239
	(−1.90)	(−1.98)	(−0.23)	(−2.96)	(−2.98)	(−3.06)	(−0.47)	(−2.19)	(−2.03)	(−2.10)	(−0.20)	(−3.07)
Personal income per capita	0.2534	0.2503	0.0133	−0.1078	0.2543	0.2513	0.0134	−0.1039	0.2554	0.2521	0.0133	−0.1110
	(17.19)	(17.00)	(6.595)	(−6.07)	(17.21)	(16.98)	(6.747)	(−5.86)	(17.46)	(17.26)	(6.587)	(−6.37)
Federal & state top tax rate	–	–	–	–	0.0057	0.0057	0.0003	0.0087	–	–	–	–
	–	–	–	–	(3.009)	(3.036)	(1.514)	(2.690)	–	–	–	–
Federal & state avg marginal tax rate	0.0400	0.0403	0.0022	−0.0167	–	–	–	–	0.0397	0.0400	0.0021	−0.0161
	(6.438)	(6.501)	(2.796)	(−1.56)	–	–	–	–	(6.421)	(6.478)	(2.702)	(−1.51)
Family size	−3.6570	−3.7332	0.5510	−1.2197	−2.9262	−2.9905	0.5831	−1.0597	−3.5760	−3.6545	0.5342	−1.2512
	(−4.45)	(−4.55)	(4.929)	(−1.03)	(−3.48)	(−3.55)	(5.153)	(−0.90)	(−4.41)	(−4.51)	(4.796)	(−1.07)

(continued)

Table 9.3A (continued)

Variable	(2004, Media/Dummy)											
	4				5				6			
	ALR	RTR	RCAP	IAR	ALR	RTR	RCAP	IAR	ALR	RTR	RCAP	IAR
Farms per household	−4.5877	−4.3132	−0.1723	4.6958	−4.6220	−4.3398	−0.1523	5.3356	−4.7237	−4.4369	−0.1319	4.7947
	(−2.46)	(−2.31)	(−0.56)	(2.147)	(−2.50)	(−2.35)	(−0.49)	(2.461)	(−2.63)	(−2.47)	(−0.44)	(2.234)
Percent of adults with high school diploma	−1.2535	−1.2682	0.0764	0.0997	−1.2504	−1.2630	0.0762	−0.1771	−1.2469	−1.2601	0.0794	0.0941
	(−5.86)	(−5.94)	(2.737)	(0.298)	(−5.59)	(−5.63)	(2.657)	(−0.52)	(−5.87)	(−5.94)	(2.839)	(0.284)
Percent of pop over 65	1.9894	1.9404	−0.2824	−2.8526	1.1549	1.0916	−0.3413	−2.9473	1.9856	1.9305	−0.2868	−2.9439
	(2.112)	(2.063)	(−1.99)	(−2.45)	(1.240)	(1.172)	(−2.40)	(−2.57)	(2.168)	(2.110)	(−2.04)	(−2.58)
Percent of employed persons in manufacturing	−0.2674	−0.2436	0.0624	−0.3208	−0.1186	−0.0907	0.0811	−0.4805	−0.2493	−0.2242	0.0644	−0.3094
	(−0.88)	(−0.80)	(1.436)	(−0.81)	(−0.39)	(−0.29)	(1.872)	(−1.22)	(−0.84)	(−0.76)	(1.491)	(−0.79)
Percent of employed persons in service	−0.0677	0.0257	−0.0698	1.7565	0.2141	0.3078	−0.0555	1.5958	−0.0762	0.0172	−0.0673	1.7762
	(−0.26)	(0.100)	(−2.13)	(4.897)	(0.857)	(1.228)	(−1.78)	(4.474)	(−0.29)	(0.067)	(−2.03)	(4.965)
Unemployment rate	−4.3964	−4.3901	−0.1179	0.8066	−4.9217	−4.9143	−0.1585	2.0704	−4.3231	−4.3212	−0.1300	0.7046
	(−7.99)	(−7.99)	(−1.69)	(0.835)	(−8.77)	(−8.73)	(−2.30)	(2.204)	(−7.89)	(−7.90)	(−1.86)	(0.734)
Dummy 2002–2004	−0.2109	−0.2129	−0.0014	−0.2703	−0.2945	−0.2969	−0.0048	−0.2420	−0.2137	−0.2155	−0.0011	−0.2669
	(−9.80)	(−9.92)	(−0.53)	(−7.95)	(−18.5)	(−18.6)	(−2.42)	(−7.83)	(−10.0)	(−10.1)	(−0.40)	(−7.89)
Audit rate	0.0871	0.0612	0.0291	–	0.0067	−0.0195	0.0272	–	0.0856	0.0600	0.0298	–
	(1.635)	(1.150)	(4.332)	–	(0.136)	(−0.39)	(4.487)	–	(1.612)	(1.131)	(4.431)	–
Direct examination time	–	–	–	0.8574	–	–	–	1.0348	–	–	–	0.8630
	–	–	–	(6.121)	–	–	–	(7.951)	–	–	–	(6.206)
Budget per return	–	–	–	16.6486	–	–	–	16.6237	–	–	–	16.6869
	–	–	–	(8.120)	–	–	–	(8.132)	–	–	–	(8.123)
Total sentences	–	–	–	–	–	–	–	–	–	–	–	–
	–	–	–	–	–	–	–	–	–	–	–	–
Tax sent resulting in neither prison nor probation	–	–	–	–	–	–	–	–	–	–	–	–
	–	–	–	–	–	–	–	–	–	–	–	–

(continued)

Table 9.3A (continued)

Variable	(2004, Media/Dummy)											
	4				5				6			
	ALR	RTR	RCAP	IAR	ALR	RTR	RCAP	IAR	ALR	RTR	RCAP	IAR
Total sentences (Tax & money laun only)	0.000150	0.000121	−0.000065	−0.000465	–	–	–	–	–	–	–	–
	(0.479)	(0.387)	(−1.56)	(−0.95)	–	–	–	–	–	–	–	–
Tax sentences	–	–	–	–	–	–	–	–	–	–	–	–
	–	–	–	–	–	–	–	–	–	–	–	–
Money laundering sentences	–	–	–	–	–	–	–	–	–	–	–	–
	–	–	–	–	–	–	–	–	–	–	–	–
Total prison sentences	–	–	–	–	–	–	–	–	–	–	–	–
	–	–	–	–	–	–	–	–	–	–	–	–
Total probation sentences	–	–	–	–	–	–	–	–	–	–	–	–
	–	–	–	–	–	–	–	–	–	–	–	–
Total sentences released in media	–	–	–	–	0.000195	0.000223	0.000017	−0.000047	0.000016	0.000042	0.000008	0.000254
	–	–	–	–	(0.960)	(1.097)	(0.682)	(−0.14)	(0.078)	(0.209)	(0.297)	(0.789)
Tax sentences released in media	−0.000180	−0.000134	0.000054	−0.000412	–	–	–	–	–	–	–	–
	(−0.38)	(−0.28)	(0.914)	(−0.49)	–	–	–	–	–	–	–	–
Money laundering sentences released in media	−0.000005	0.000048	0.000056	0.002400	–	–	–	–	–	–	–	–
	(−0.00)	(0.067)	(0.620)	(2.001)	–	–	–	–	–	–	–	–
Tax sentences resulting in prison	–	–	–	–	–	–	–	–	–	–	–	–
	–	–	–	–	–	–	–	–	–	–	–	–
Tax sentences resulting in probation	–	–	–	–	–	–	–	–	–	–	–	–
	–	–	–	–	–	–	–	–	–	–	–	–
Money laun sentences resulting in prison	–	–	–	–	–	–	–	–	–	–	–	–
	–	–	–	–	–	–	–	–	–	–	–	–
Money laun sentences resulting in probation	–	–	–	–	–	–	–	–	–	–	–	–
	–	–	–	–	–	–	–	–	–	–	–	–

(continued)

Table 9.3A (continued)

Variable	(2004, Media/Dummy)											
	4				5				6			
	ALR	RTR	RCAP	IAR	ALR	RTR	RCAP	IAR	ALR	RTR	RCAP	IAR
Money laun sent resulting in neither	–	–	–	–	–	–	–	–	–	–	–	–
prison nor probation	–	–	–	–	–	–	–	–	–	–	–	–
% of tot sent related to tax	0.0255	0.0249	0.0057	−0.0415	0.0291	0.0288	0.0060	−0.0553	0.0240	0.0237	0.0057	−0.0563
	(0.880)	(0.861)	(1.562)	(−0.82)	(0.996)	(0.981)	(1.694)	(−1.12)	(0.845)	(0.834)	(1.602)	(−1.14)
% of tot sent related to money laun	−0.0063	−0.0068	0.0036	−0.0913	−0.0041	−0.0045	0.0035	−0.0813	−0.0052	−0.0055	0.0034	−0.0745
	(−0.21)	(−0.23)	(0.965)	(−1.78)	(−0.13)	(−0.15)	(0.964)	(−1.62)	(−0.18)	(−0.19)	(0.928)	(−1.47)
% of total sentences not prison or prob	–	–	–	–	–	–	–	–	–	–	–	–
	–	–	–	–	–	–	–	–	–	–	–	–
% of tax sentences in prison	–	–	–	–	–	–	–	–	–	–	–	–
	–	–	–	–	–	–	–	–	–	–	–	–
% of money laun sentences in prison	–	–	–	–	–	–	–	–	–	–	–	–
	–	–	–	–	–	–	–	–	–	–	–	–
% of tax sentences in probation	–	–	–	–	–	–	–	–	–	–	–	–
	–	–	–	–	–	–	–	–	–	–	–	–
% of money laun sentences in probation	–	–	–	–	–	–	–	–	–	–	–	–
	–	–	–	–	–	–	–	–	–	–	–	–
% of tax sent neither prison nor	0.0930	0.0803	−0.0009	−0.2040	0.1062	0.0933	−0.0009	−0.2018	0.0936	0.0807	−0.0015	−0.2138
probation	(1.214)	(1.051)	(−0.09)	(−1.50)	(1.346)	(1.179)	(−0.09)	(−1.49)	(1.220)	(1.053)	(−0.15)	(−1.57)
% of money laun sent neither prison nor	−0.1283	−0.1284	0.0133	−0.1480	−0.1630	−0.1633	0.0117	−0.1159	−0.1295	−0.1297	0.0132	−0.1652
probation	(−1.20)	(−1.20)	(1.003)	(−0.79)	(−1.48)	(−1.48)	(0.893)	(−0.62)	(−1.21)	(−1.21)	(0.993)	(−0.88)
% of total sentences in media	–	–	–	–	–	–	–	–	–	–	–	–
	–	–	–	–	–	–	–	–	–	–	–	–
% of tax sentences in media	–	–	–	–	–	–	–	–	–	–	–	–
	–	–	–	–	–	–	–	–	–	–	–	–
% of money laun sentences in media	–	–	–	–	–	–	–	–	–	–	–	–
	–	–	–	–	–	–	–	–	–	–	–	–
Number of obs	650				650				650			
Years	1992–2004				1992–2004				1992–2004			

(continued)

Table 9.3A (continued)

Variable	(2004, Media/Dummy)							
	7				8			
	ALR	RTR	RCAP	IAR	ALR	RTR	RCAP	IAR
Constant	1.7829	1.8172	0.1209	0.5755	1.1769	1.2130	0.0942	1.3094
	(5.258)	(5.350)	(2.669)	(1.165)	(3.337)	(3.444)	(1.978)	(2.469)
Percent of families on welfare	0.0071	0.0077	−0.0004	0.0781	0.0132	0.0139	0.0001	0.0754
	(0.890)	(0.963)	(−0.43)	(7.876)	(1.688)	(1.770)	(0.133)	(7.339)
State tax rate	−0.0197	−0.0203	−0.0005	−0.0163	−0.0134	−0.0139	−0.0002	−0.0233
	(−2.90)	(−2.98)	(−0.46)	(−2.06)	(−1.98)	(−2.05)	(−0.19)	(−2.95)
Personal income per capita	0.2541	0.2511	0.0134	−0.1030	0.2549	0.2517	0.0133	−0.1100
	(17.15)	(16.92)	(6.755)	(−5.76)	(17.40)	(17.20)	(6.580)	(−6.26)
Federal & state top tax rate	0.0056	0.0057	0.0003	0.0088	–	–	–	–
	(2.972)	(3.002)	(1.494)	(2.695)	–	–	–	–
Federal & state avg marginal tax rate	–	–	–	–	0.0399	0.0402	0.0021	−0.0166
	–	–	–	–	(6.405)	(6.465)	(2.701)	(−1.55)
Family size	−2.9386	−3.0037	0.5844	−1.0247	−3.5993	−3.6785	0.5352	−1.2121
	(−3.47)	(−3.54)	(5.153)	(−0.86)	(−4.42)	(−4.52)	(4.791)	(−1.02)

(continued)

Table 9.3A (continued)

Variable	(2004, Media/Dummy)							
	7				8			
	ALR	RTR	RCAP	IAR	ALR	RTR	RCAP	IAR
Farms per household	−4.5973	−4.3146	−0.1508	5.3657	−4.7095	−4.4222	−0.1311	4.8468
	(−2.45)	(−2.30)	(−0.48)	(2.442)	(−2.58)	(−2.43)	(−0.43)	(2.228)
Percent of adults with high school diploma	−1.2475	−1.2606	0.0759	−0.1570	−1.2502	−1.2639	0.0786	0.1192
	(−5.56)	(−5.60)	(2.644)	(−0.46)	(−5.87)	(−5.94)	(2.805)	(0.358)
Percent of pop over 65	1.1719	1.1094	−0.3434	−2.9257	2.0037	1.9498	−0.2897	−2.9378
	(1.242)	(1.176)	(−2.41)	(−2.51)	(2.163)	(2.106)	(−2.04)	(−2.54)
Percent of employed persons in manufacturing	−0.1220	−0.0939	0.0825	−0.4825	−0.2601	−0.2349	0.0658	−0.3039
	(−0.39)	(−0.30)	(1.899)	(−1.21)	(−0.87)	(−0.79)	(1.515)	(−0.77)
Percent of employed persons in service	0.2115	0.3061	−0.0557	1.5851	−0.0781	0.0159	−0.0674	1.7705
	(0.847)	(1.222)	(−1.78)	(4.438)	(−0.30)	(0.062)	(−2.04)	(4.943)
Unemployment rate	−4.9567	−4.9526	−0.1592	2.1031	−4.3401	−4.3409	−0.1297	0.7046
	(−8.86)	(−8.83)	(−2.31)	(2.242)	(−7.94)	(−7.95)	(−1.86)	(0.735)
Dummy 2002–2004	−0.2939	−0.2964	−0.0048	−0.2432	−0.2130	−0.2148	−0.0010	−0.2689
	(−18.4)	(−18.5)	(−2.40)	(−7.85)	(−9.99)	(−10.0)	(−0.37)	(−7.92)
Audit rate	0.0076	−0.0186	0.0273	–	0.0866	0.0609	0.0300	–
	(0.156)	(−0.37)	(4.534)	–	(1.634)	(1.152)	(4.464)	–
Direct examination time	–	–	–	1.0484	–	–	–	0.8741
	–	–	–	(8.038)	–	–	–	(6.286)
Budget per return	–	–	–	16.5546	–	–	–	16.6147
	–	–	–	(8.114)	–	–	–	(8.104)
Total sentences	–	–	–	–	–	–	–	–
	–	–	–	–	–	–	–	–
Total sentences (Tax & money laun only)	–	–	–	–	–	–	–	–
	–	–	–	–	–	–	–	–
Tax sentences	–	–	–	–	–	–	–	–
	–	–	–	–	–	–	–	–

(continued)

Table 9.3A (continued)

Variable	(2004, Media/Dummy)							
	7				8			
	ALR	RTR	RCAP	IAR	ALR	RTR	RCAP	IAR
Money laundering sentences	–	–	–	–	–	–	–	–
	–	–	–	–	–	–	–	–
Total prison sentences	–	–	–	–	–	–	–	–
	–	–	–	–	–	–	–	–
Total probation sentences	–	–	–	–	–	–	–	–
	–	–	–	–	–	–	–	–
Total sentences released in media	–	–	–	–	–	–	–	–
	–	–	–	–	–	–	–	–
Tax sentences released in media	–0.000093	–0.000060	0.000023	–0.001065	–0.000086	–0.000056	0.000022	–0.000721
	(–0.20)	(–0.13)	(0.413)	(–1.40)	(–0.19)	(–0.12)	(0.399)	(–0.94)
Money laundering sentences released in media	0.000703	0.000728	0.000021	0.001402	0.000154	0.000176	–0.000007	0.001813
	(1.099)	(1.135)	(0.267)	(1.369)	(0.243)	(0.278)	(–0.08)	(1.757)
Tax sentences resulting in prison	–	–	–	–	–	–	–	–
	–	–	–	–	–	–	–	–
Tax sentences resulting in probation	–	–	–	–	–	–	–	–
	–	–	–	–	–	–	–	–
Money laun sentences resulting in prison	–	–	–	–	–	–	–	–
	–	–	–	–	–	–	–	–
Money laun sentences resulting in probation	–	–	–	–	–	–	–	–
	–	–	–	–	–	–	–	–
Tax sent resulting in neither prison nor probation	–	–	–	–	–	–	–	–
	–	–	–	–	–	–	–	–
Money laun sent resulting in neither prison nor probation	–	–	–	–	–	–	–	–
	–	–	–	–	–	–	–	–
% of tot sent related to tax	0.0322	0.0314	0.0057	–0.0386	0.0257	0.0250	0.0054	–0.0427
	(1.078)	(1.051)	(1.591)	(–0.77)	(0.885)	(0.863)	(1.486)	(–0.85)

(continued)

Table 9.3A (continued)

Variable	(2004, Media/Dummy)							
	7				8			
	ALR	RTR	RCAP	IAR	ALR	RTR	RCAP	IAR
% of tot sent related to money laun	−0.0104	−0.0111	0.0033	−0.0946	−0.0064	−0.0069	0.0034	−0.0916
	(−0.34)	(−0.36)	(0.886)	(−1.85)	(−0.21)	(−0.23)	(0.921)	(−1.78)
% of total sentences not prison or prob	–	–	–	–	–	–	–	–
	–	–	–	–	–	–	–	–
% of tax sentences in prison	–	–	–	–	–	–	–	–
	–	–	–	–	–	–	–	–
% of money laun sentences in prison	–	–	–	–	–	–	–	–
	–	–	–	–	–	–	–	–
% of tax sentences in probation	–	–	–	–	–	–	–	–
	–	–	–	–	–	–	–	–
% of money laun sentences in probation	–	–	–	–	–	–	–	–
	–	–	–	–	–	–	–	–
% of tax sent neither prison nor probation	0.1072	0.0942	−0.0010	−0.1961	0.0943	0.0813	−0.0016	−0.2089
	(1.361)	(1.192)	(−0.10)	(−1.45)	(1.230)	(1.062)	(−0.16)	(−1.54)
% of money laun sent neither prison nor probation	−0.1577	−0.1580	0.0119	−0.1053	−0.1280	−0.1281	0.0132	−0.1525
	(−1.44)	(−1.43)	(0.902)	(−0.56)	(−1.19)	(−1.20)	(0.989)	(−0.81)
% of total sentences in media	–	–	–	–	–	–	–	–
	–	–	–	–	–	–	–	–
% of tax sentences in media	–	–	–	–	–	–	–	–
	–	–	–	–	–	–	–	–
% of money laun sentences in media	–	–	–	–	–	–	–	–
	–	–	–	–	–	–	–	–
Number of obs	650				650			
Years	1992–2004				1992–2004			

At best, I find that these media factors are statistically insignificant. Chapter 7 argued that the large spillover effect of CI activity on tax compliance implies that media plays an important role in tax compliance. Nonetheless I proceed with specifications ignoring media factors in what follows.

Marginal Impacts

I now consider the marginal impacts and compare the results for the estimation period ending in 2001 and 2004. I consider the marginal percentage increase and the "doubling" scenarios but do not further discuss the results of increasing CI or audit activity by a constant amount per state.

First, consider the simulation in which audit rates are doubled (Table 9.4). I provide the simulation results for the period ending in 2001 in Table 9.4A. The first row of Table 9.4A shows that, for Model 1, estimated assessed tax collections would increase to \$959.9 billion from \$937.7 billion in 2001. The \$22.2 billion change is the total revenue effect. These estimates also show that reported tax collections rise by \$20.8 billion. This change is the indirect effect of doubling the audit rate. The difference between these two estimated differences is approximately \$1.365 billion and represents the direct revenue effect. This amount is 93.8% of the total revenue effect.

Next, I examine the same results for the same model where the estimation period is extended to 2004. Tables 9.4 and 9.5 (row 1) show that for the period ending in 2004, doubling the audit rate leads to a direct revenue effect of \$1.37 billion, an indirect revenue effect of \$8.68 billion, and a total change in revenue of \$10.06 billion. These values are somewhat smaller than I observed in the estimation period through 2001 (approximately one-half the size). The Model 2 results for audit examinations are more comparable for the two time periods.

Using the same model for the period ending in 2001 (Table 9.1A, Model 1), I find that doubling CI activity (tax and money laundering cases) leads to \$13.38 billion in increased reported taxes, \$14.08 billion in increased assessed tax revenue, and a direct revenue increase of \$0.699 billion. For the period ending in 2004, the corresponding model shows that doubling CI activity leads to \$29.47 billion in increased reported collections, \$29.79 billion in increased assessed tax revenue, and a direct revenue increase of \$0.332 billion. By comparison, the aggregate effects are larger than I estimated for the estimation period ending in 2001, but the direct revenue effects are smaller.

I report the marginal analysis in Table 9.5. This table has rows corresponding to the rows of Table 9.4. For instance, the second row of Table 9.5 shows that increasing the audit rate by 5 percent leads to 9,708 additional audits and increases total revenues by \$0.502 billion. Using the same model and simulation (Row 2), we can see that the direct revenues rise by \$68.5 million, or \$7,056 per audit. The simulation (using model IRS1) in which the audit rate was doubled (Table 9.5, Row 1) leads to an increase of \$10.06 billion dollars of additional total revenue

Table 9.4 2004, No Media

	Estimated assessed tax collections ($Millions)			Estimated reported tax collections ($Millions)		
	Modified amount (A)	Original amount (B)	Difference (A – B) (C)	Modified amount (D)	Original amount (E)	Difference (D – E) (F)
IRS1 audits doubled	889,363.50	879,304.00	10,059.50	884,665.75	875,979.63	8,686.13
IRS1 audits increase 5%	879,805.75	879,304.00	501.75	876,412.88	875,979.63	433.25
IRS1 audits increase by 200 per state	879,797.50	879,304.00	493.50	876,403.44	875,979.63	423.81
IRS1 total sentences (tax, money) doubled	909,102.19	879,304.00	29,798.19	905,445.75	875,979.63	29,466.13
IRS1 total sentences (tax, money) increase 5%	880,799.50	879,304.00	1,495.50	877,458.44	875,979.63	1,478.81
IRS1 total sentences (tax, money) increase by 2 per state	880,171.19	879,304.00	867.19	876,837.06	875,979.63	857.44
IRS2 audits doubled	848,858.25	828,014.44	20,843.81	843,511.88	823,981.63	19,530.25
IRS2 audits increase 5%	829,052.69	828,014.44	1,038.25	824,954.50	823,981.63	972.88
IRS2 audits increase by 200 per state	829,049.81	828,014.44	1,035.38	824,950.56	823,981.63	968.94
IRS2 total sentences (tax, money) doubled	837,225.06	828,014.44	9,210.63	832,650.50	823,981.63	8,668.88
IRS2 total sentences (tax, money) increase 5%	828,477.38	828,014.44	462.94	824,417.38	823,981.63	435.75
IRS2 total sentences (tax, money) increase by 2 per state	828,287.69	828,014.44	273.25	824,239.25	823,981.63	257.63
IRS3 audits doubled	889,181.75	878,138.13	11,043.63	884,490.44	874,800.56	9,689.88
IRS3 audits increase 5%	878,688.81	878,138.13	550.69	875,283.81	874,800.56	483.25
IRS3 audits increase by 200 per state	878,681.38	878,138.13	543.25	875,275.06	874,800.56	474.50
IRS3 total sentences (tax, money) doubled	910,234.94	878,138.13	32,096.81	906,574.13	874,800.56	31,773.56
IRS3 total sentences (tax, money) increase 5%	879,747.38	878,138.13	1,609.25	876,393.63	874,800.56	1,593.06
IRS3 total sentences (tax, money) increase by 2 per state	879,068.88	878,138.13	930.75	875,721.88	874,800.56	921.31
IRS4 audits doubled	880,279.56	867,937.56	12,342.00	875,424.94	864,444.25	10,980.69
IRS4 audits increase 5%	868,553.00	867,937.56	615.44	864,991.88	864,444.25	547.63

(continued)

Table 9.4 (continued)

	Estimated assessed tax collections ($Millions)			Estimated reported tax collections ($Millions)		
	Modified amount (A)	Original amount (B)	Difference (A – B) (C)	Modified amount (D)	Original amount (E)	Difference (D – E) (F)
IRS4 audits increase by 200 per state	868,548.25	867,937.56	610.69	864,985.94	864,444.25	541.69
IRS4 total sentences (tax, money) doubled	894,867.75	867,937.56	26,930.19	891,002.19	864,444.25	26,557.94
IRS4 total sentences (tax, money) increase 5%	869,287.75	867,937.56	1,350.19	865,775.75	864,444.25	1,331.50
IRS4 total sentences (tax, money) increase by 2 per state	868,718.75	867,937.56	781.19	865,214.69	864,444.25	770.44
IRS5 audits doubled	850,728.75	830,363.50	20,365.25	845,364.69	826,295.81	19,068.88
IRS5 audits increase 5%	831,378.56	830,363.50	1,015.06	827,246.31	826,295.81	950.50
IRS5 audits increase by 200 per state	831,379.81	830,363.50	1,016.31	827,246.38	826,295.81	950.56
IRS5 total sentences (tax, money) doubled	841,210.69	830,363.50	10,847.19	836,584.06	826,295.81	10,288.25
IRS5 total sentences (tax, money) increase 5%	830,906.56	830,363.50	543.06	826,810.94	826,295.81	515.13
IRS5 total sentences (tax, money) increase by 2 per state	830,678.00	830,363.50	314.50	826,594.19	826,295.81	298.38

(continued)

Table 9.4 (continued)

	Actual reported collections ($Millions) (G)	Estimated reported difference and actual reported tax revenue (F/G) (%) (H)	Estimated reported difference and estimated reported tax revenue (F/E) (%) (I)	Change in estimated assessed and reported tax revenue (C − F)/F (%) (J)	Direct revenue effect ($Millions) (C − F) (K)	Indirect revenue effect ($Millions) (F) (L)	Indirect revenue effect/total revenue effect (L/(K + L)) (%) (M)
IRS1 audits doubled	823,876	1.1	1.0	15.8	1,373.38	8,686.13	86.35
IRS1 audits increase 5%	823,876	0.1	0.0	15.8	68.50	433.25	86.35
IRS1 audits increase by 200 per state	823,876	0.1	0.0	16.4	69.69	423.81	85.88
IRS1 total sentences (tax, money) doubled	823,876	3.6	3.4	1.1	332.06	29,466.13	98.89
IRS1 total sentences (tax, money) increase 5%	823,876	0.2	0.2	1.1	16.69	1,478.81	98.88
IRS1 total sentences (tax, money) increase by 2 per state	823,876	0.1	0.1	1.1	9.75	857.44	98.88
IRS2 audits doubled	823,876	2.4	2.4	6.7	1,313.56	19,530.25	93.70
IRS2 audits increase 5%	823,876	0.1	0.1	6.7	65.38	972.88	93.70
IRS2 audits increase by 200 per state	823,876	0.1	0.1	6.9	66.44	968.94	93.58
IRS2 total sentences (tax, money) doubled	823,876	1.1	1.1	6.2	541.75	8,668.88	94.12
IRS2 total sentences (tax, money) increase 5%	823,876	0.1	0.1	6.2	27.19	435.75	94.13
IRS2 total sentences (tax, money) increase by 2 per state	823,876	0.0	0.0	6.1	15.63	257.63	94.28
IRS3 audits doubled	823,876	1.2	1.1	14.0	1,353.75	9,689.88	87.74

(continued)

Table 9.4 (continued)

	Actual reported collections ($Millions) (G)	Estimated reported difference and actual reported tax revenue (F/G) (%) (H)	Estimated reported difference and estimated reported tax revenue (F/E) (%) (I)	Change in estimated assessed and reported tax revenue (C – F)/F (%) (J)	Direct revenue effect ($Millions) (C – F) (K)	Indirect revenue effect ($Millions) (F) (L)	Indirect revenue effect/total revenue effect (L/(K + L)) (%) (M)
IRS3 audits increase 5%	823,876	0.1	0.1	14.0	67.44	483.25	87.75
IRS3 audits increase by 200 per state	823,876	0.1	0.1	14.5	68.75	474.50	87.34
IRS3 total sentences (tax, money) doubled	823,876	3.9	3.6	1.0	323.25	31,773.56	98.99
IRS3 total sentences (tax, money) increase 5%	823,876	0.2	0.2	1.0	16.19	1,593.06	98.99
IRS3 total sentences (tax, money) increase by 2 per state	823,876	0.1	0.1	1.0	9.44	921.31	98.99
IRS4 audits doubled	823,876	1.3	1.3	12.4	1,361.31	10,980.69	88.97
IRS4 audits increase 5%	823,876	0.1	0.1	12.4	67.81	547.63	88.98
IRS4 audits increase by 200 per state	823,876	0.1	0.1	12.7	69.00	541.69	88.70
IRS4 total sentences (tax, money) doubled	823,876	3.2	3.1	1.4	372.25	26,557.94	98.62
IRS4 total sentences (tax, money) increase 5%	823,876	0.2	0.2	1.4	18.69	1,331.50	98.62
IRS4 total sentences (tax, money) increase by 2 per state	823,876	0.1	0.1	1.4	10.75	770.44	98.62

(continued)

Table 9.4 (continued)

	Actual reported collections ($Millions) (G)	Estimated reported difference and actual reported tax revenue (F/G) (%) (H)	Estimated reported difference and estimated reported tax revenue (F/E) (%) (I)	Change in estimated assessed and reported tax revenue (C − F)/F (%) (J)	Direct revenue effect ($Millions) (C − F) (K)	Indirect revenue effect ($Millions) (F) (L)	Indirect revenue effect/total revenue effect (L/(K + L)) (%) (M)
IRS5 audits doubled	823,876	2.3	2.3	6.8	1,296.38	19,068.88	93.63
IRS5 audits increase 5%	823,876	0.1	0.1	6.8	64.56	950.50	93.64
IRS5 audits increase by 200 per state	823,876	0.1	0.1	6.9	65.75	950.56	93.53
IRS5 total sentences (tax, money) doubled	823,876	1.2	1.2	5.4	558.94	10,288.25	94.85
IRS5 total sentences (tax, money) increase 5%	823,876	0.1	0.1	5.4	27.94	515.13	94.86
IRS5 total sentences (tax, money) increase by 2 per state	823,876	0.0	0.0	5.4	16.13	298.38	94.87

Table 9.4A 2001, No Media

	Estimated assessed tax collections ($Millions)			Estimated reported tax collections ($Millions)		
	Modified amount (A)	Original amount (B)	Difference (A – B) (C)	Modified amount (D)	Original amount (E)	Difference (D – E) (F)
IRS1 audits doubled	959,949.88	937,772.31	22,177.56	956,618.75	935,806.31	20,812.44
IRS1 audits increase 5%	938,874.88	937,772.31	1,102.56	936,841.19	935,806.31	1,034.88
IRS1 audits increase by 200 per state	938,807.31	937,772.31	1,035.00	936,775.63	935,806.31	969.31
IRS1 total sentences (tax, money) doubled	951,854.38	937,772.31	14,082.06	949,189.19	935,806.31	13,382.88
IRS1 total sentences (tax, money) increase 5%	938,484.13	937,772.31	711.81	936,482.88	935,806.31	676.56
IRS1 total sentences (tax, money) increase by 2 per state	938,130.06	937,772.31	357.75	936,146.88	935,806.31	340.56
IRS2 audits doubled	949,933.06	925,043.19	24,889.88	946,251.75	922,674.31	23,577.44
IRS2 audits increase 5%	926,280.31	925,043.19	1,237.13	923,846.44	922,674.31	1,172.13
IRS2 audits increase by 200 per state	926,209.63	925,043.19	1,166.44	923,777.75	922,674.31	1,103.44
IRS2 total sentences (tax, money) doubled	935,543.50	925,043.19	10,500.31	932,315.00	922,674.31	9,640.69
IRS2 total sentences (tax, money) increase 5%	925,572.94	925,043.19	529.75	923,160.81	922,674.31	486.50
IRS2 total sentences (tax, money) increase by 2 per state	925,310.00	925,043.19	266.81	922,920.19	922,674.31	245.88
IRS3 audits doubled	958,429.25	936,096.06	22,333.19	955,074.69	934,112.19	20,962.50
IRS3 audits increase 5%	937,206.31	936,096.06	1,110.25	935,154.56	934,112.19	1,042.38
IRS3 audits increase by 200 per state	937,138.69	936,096.06	1,042.63	935,088.94	934,112.19	976.75
IRS3 total sentences (tax, money) doubled	952,191.94	936,096.06	16,095.88	949,491.13	934,112.19	15,378.94
IRS3 total sentences (tax, money) increase 5%	936,907.75	936,096.06	811.69	934,887.81	934,112.19	775.63
IRS3 total sentences (tax, money) increase by 2 per state	936,499.81	936,096.06	403.75	934,498.38	934,112.19	386.19
IRS4 audits doubled	959,509.75	936,586.06	22,923.69	956,088.00	934,530.38	21,557.63
IRS4 audits increase 5%	937,725.63	936,586.06	1,139.56	935,602.13	934,530.38	1,071.75

(continued)

Table 9.4A (continued)

	Estimated assessed tax collections ($Millions)			Estimated reported tax collections ($Millions)		
	Modified amount (A)	Original amount (B)	Difference (A – B) (C)	Modified amount (D)	Original amount (E)	Difference (D – E) (F)
IRS4 audits increase by 200 per state	937,657.13	936,586.06	1,071.06	935,535.81	934,530.38	1,005.44
IRS4 total sentences (tax, money) doubled	950,468.69	936,586.06	13,882.63	947,647.94	934,530.38	13,117.56
IRS4 total sentences (tax, money) increase 5%	937,286.38	936,586.06	700.31	935,192.13	934,530.38	661.75
IRS4 total sentences (tax, money) increase by 2 per state	936,935.13	936,586.06	349.06	934,860.69	934,530.38	330.31
IRS5 audits doubled	950,240.31	925,438.88	24,801.44	947,014.50	923,624.38	23,390.13
IRS5 audits increase 5%	926,671.56	925,438.88	1,232.69	924,787.00	923,624.38	1,162.63
IRS5 audits increase by 200 per state	926,600.19	925,438.88	1,161.31	924,717.75	923,624.38	1,093.38
IRS5 total sentences (tax, money) doubled	935,799.81	925,438.88	10,360.94	933,325.31	923,624.38	9,700.94
IRS5 total sentences (tax, money) increase 5%	925,962.56	925,438.88	523.69	924,114.81	923,624.38	490.44
IRS5 total sentences (tax, money) increase by 2 per state	925,704.38	925,438.88	265.50	923,873.56	923,624.38	249.19

(continued)

Table 9.4A (continued)

	Actual reported collections ($Millions) (G)	Estimated reported difference and actual reported tax revenue (F/G) (%) (H)	Estimated reported difference and estimated reported tax revenue (F/E) (%) (I)	Change in estimated assessed and reported tax revenue (C − F)/F (%) (J)	Direct revenue effect ($Millions) (C − F) (K)	Indirect revenue effect ($Millions) (F) (L)	Indirect revenue effect/Total revenue effect (L/(K + L)) (%) (M)
IRS1 audits doubled	882,128	2.4	2.2	6.6	1,365.13	20,812.44	93.84
IRS1 audits increase 5%	882,128	0.1	0.1	6.5	67.69	1,034.88	93.86
IRS1 audits increase by 200 per state	882,128	0.1	0.1	6.8	65.69	969.31	93.65
IRS1 total sentences (tax, money) doubled	882,128	1.5	1.4	5.2	699.19	13,382.88	95.03
IRS1 total sentences (tax, money) increase 5%	882,128	0.1	0.1	5.2	35.25	676.56	95.05
IRS1 total sentences (tax, money) increase by 2 per state	882,128	0.0	0.0	5.0	17.19	340.56	95.20
IRS2 audits doubled	882,128	2.7	2.6	5.6	1,312.44	23,577.44	94.73
IRS2 audits increase 5%	882,128	0.1	0.1	5.5	65.00	1,172.13	94.75
IRS2 audits increase by 200 per state	882,128	0.1	0.1	5.7	63.00	1,103.44	94.60
IRS2 total sentences (tax, money) doubled	882,128	1.1	1.0	8.9	859.63	9,640.69	91.81
IRS2 total sentences (tax, money) increase 5%	882,128	0.1	0.1	8.9	43.25	486.50	91.84
IRS2 total sentences (tax, money) increase by 2 per state	882,128	0.0	0.0	8.5	20.94	245.88	92.15

(continued)

Table 9.4A (continued)

	Actual reported collections ($Millions) (G)	Estimated reported difference and actual reported tax revenue (F/G) (%) (H)	Estimated reported difference and estimated reported tax revenue (F/E) (%) (I)	Change in estimated assessed and reported tax revenue (C − F)/F (%) (J)	Direct revenue effect ($Millions) (C − F) (K)	Indirect revenue effect ($Millions) (F) (L)	Indirect revenue effect/Total revenue effect (L/(K + L)) (%) (M)
IRS3 audits doubled	882,128	2.4	2.2	6.5	1,370.69	20,962.50	93.86
IRS3 audits increase 5%	882,128	0.1	0.1	6.5	67.88	1,042.38	93.89
IRS3 audits increase by 200 per state	882,128	0.1	0.1	6.7	65.88	976.75	93.68
IRS3 total sentences (tax, money) doubled	882,128	1.7	1.6	4.7	716.94	15,378.94	95.55
IRS3 total sentences (tax, money) increase 5%	882,128	0.1	0.1	4.6	36.06	775.63	95.56
IRS3 total sentences (tax, money) increase by 2 per state	882,128	0.0	0.0	4.5	17.56	386.19	95.65
IRS4 audits doubled	882,128	2.4	2.3	6.3	1,366.06	21,557.63	94.04
IRS4 audits increase 5%	882,128	0.1	0.1	6.3	67.81	1,071.75	94.05
IRS4 audits increase by 200 per state	882,128	0.1	0.1	6.5	65.63	1,005.44	93.87
IRS4 total sentences (tax, money) doubled	882,128	1.5	1.4	5.8	765.06	13,117.56	94.49
IRS4 total sentences (tax, money) increase 5%	882,128	0.1	0.1	5.8	38.56	661.75	94.49
IRS4 total sentences (tax, money) increase by 2 per state	882,128	0.0	0.0	5.7	18.75	330.31	94.63

(continued)

Table 9.4A (continued)

	Actual reported collections ($Millions) (G)	Estimated reported difference and actual reported tax revenue (F/G) (%) (H)	Estimated reported difference and estimated reported tax revenue (F/E) (%) (I)	Change in estimated assessed and reported tax revenue (C – F)/F (%) (J)	Direct revenue effect ($Millions) (C – F) (K)	Indirect revenue effect ($Millions) (F) (L)	Indirect revenue effect/Total revenue effect (L/(K + L)) (%) (M)
IRS5 audits doubled	882,128	2.7	2.5	6.0	1,411.31	23,390.13	94.31
IRS5 audits increase 5%	882,128	0.1	0.1	6.0	70.06	1,162.63	94.32
IRS5 audits increase by 200 per state	882,128	0.1	0.1	6.2	67.94	1,093.38	94.15
IRS5 total sentences (tax, money) doubled	882,128	1.1	1.1	6.8	660.00	9,700.94	93.63
IRS5 total sentences (tax, money) increase 5%	882,128	0.1	0.1	6.8	33.25	490.44	93.65
IRS5 total sentences (tax, money) increase by 2 per state	882,128	0.0	0.0	6.5	16.31	249.19	93.86

(continued)

Table 9.5 2004, No Media

	Amount before change (A)	Amount after change (B)	Difference (B − A) (C)	Direct change in revenue ($) (D)	Indirect change in revenue ($) (E)	Total change in revenue (D + E) ($) (F)
IRS1 audits doubled	194,160	388,320	194,160	1,373,375,000	8,686,125,000	10,059,500,000
IRS1 audits increase 5%	194,160	203,868	9,708	68,500,000	433,250,000	501,750,000
IRS1 audits increase by 200 per state	194,160	204,160	10,000	69,687,500	423,812,500	493,500,000
IRS1 total sentences (tax, money) doubled	1,502	3,004	1,502	332,062,500	29,466,125,000	29,798,187,500
IRS1 total sentences (tax, money) increase 5%	1,502	1,577	75	16,687,500	1,478,812,500	1,495,500,000
IRS1 total sentences (tax, money) increase by 2 per state	1,502	1,602	100	9,750,000	857,437,500	867,187,500
IRS2 audits doubled	194,160	388,320	194,160	1,313,562,500	19,530,250,000	20,843,812,500
IRS2 audits increase 5%	194,160	203,868	9,708	65,375,000	972,875,000	1,038,250,000
IRS2 audits increase by 200 per state	194,160	204,160	10,000	66,437,500	968,937,500	1,035,375,000
IRS2 total sentences (tax, money) doubled	1,502	3,004	1,502	541,750,000	8,668,875,000	9,210,625,000
IRS2 total sentences (tax, money) increase 5%	1,502	1,577	75	27,187,500	435,750,000	462,937,500
IRS2 total sentences (tax, money) increase by 2 per state	1,502	1,602	100	15,625,000	257,625,000	273,250,000
IRS3 audits doubled	194,160	388,320	194,160	1,353,750,000	9,689,875,000	11,043,625,000
IRS3 audits increase 5%	194,160	203,868	9,708	67,437,500	483,250,000	550,687,500
IRS3 audits increase by 200 per state	194,160	204,160	10,000	68,750,000	474,500,000	543,250,000
IRS3 total sentences (tax, money) doubled	1,502	3,004	1,502	323,250,000	31,773,562,500	32,096,812,500

(continued)

Table 9.5 (continued)

	Amount before change (A)	Amount after change (B)	Difference (B − A) (C)	Direct change in revenue ($) (D)	Indirect change in revenue ($) (E)	Total change in revenue (D + E) ($) (F)
IRS3 total sentences (tax, money) increase 5%	1,502	1,577	75	16,187,500	1,593,062,500	1,609,250,000
IRS3 total sentences (tax, money) increase by 2 per state	1,502	1,602	100	9,437,500	921,312,500	930,750,000
IRS4 audits doubled	194,160	388,320	194,160	1,361,312,500	10,980,687,500	12,342,000,000
IRS4 audits increase 5%	194,160	203,868	9,708	67,812,500	547,625,000	615,437,500
IRS4 audits increase by 200 per state	194,160	204,160	10,000	69,000,000	541,687,500	610,687,500
IRS4 total sentences (tax, money) doubled	1,502	3,004	1,502	372,250,000	26,557,937,500	26,930,187,500
IRS4 total sentences (tax, money) increase 5%	1,502	1,577	75	18,687,500	1,331,500,000	1,350,187,500
IRS4 total sentences (tax, money) increase by 2 per state	1,502	1,602	100	10,750,000	770,437,500	781,187,500
IRS5 audits doubled	194,160	388,320	194,160	1,296,375,000	19,068,875,000	20,365,250,000
IRS5 audits increase 5%	194,160	203,868	9,708	64,562,500	950,500,000	1,015,062,500
IRS5 audits increase by 200 per state	194,160	204,160	10,000	65,750,000	950,562,500	1,016,312,500
IRS5 total sentences (tax, money) doubled	1,502	3,004	1,502	558,937,500	10,288,250,000	10,847,187,500
IRS5 total sentences (tax, money) increase 5%	1,502	1,577	75	27,937,500	515,125,000	543,062,500
IRS5 total sentences (tax, money) increase by 2 per state	1,502	1,602	100	16,125,000	298,375,000	314,500,000

(continued)

Table 9.5 (continued)

	Direct revenue change per audit or per sentence (D/C) ($) (G)	Indirect revenue change per audit or per sentence (E/C) ($) (H)	Total revenue change per audit or per sentence (F/C) ($) (I)
IRS1 audits doubled	7,073	44,737	51,810
IRS1 audits increase 5%	7,056	44,628	51,684
IRS1 audits increase by 200 per state	6,969	42,381	49,350
IRS1 total sentences (tax, money) doubled	221,080	19,617,926	19,839,006
IRS1 total sentences (tax, money) increase 5%	222,204	19,691,250	19,913,454
IRS1 total sentences (tax, money) increase by 2 per state	97,500	8,574,375	8,671,875
IRS2 audits doubled	6,765	100,588	107,354
IRS2 audits increase 5%	6,734	100,214	106,948
IRS2 audits increase by 200 per state	6,644	96,894	103,538
IRS2 total sentences (tax, money) doubled	360,686	5,771,555	6,132,240
IRS2 total sentences (tax, money) increase 5%	362,017	5,802,265	6,164,283
IRS2 total sentences (tax, money) increase by 2 per state	156,250	2,576,250	2,732,500
IRS3 audits doubled	6,972	49,907	56,879
IRS3 audits increase 5%	6,947	49,779	56,725
IRS3 audits increase by 200 per state	6,875	47,450	54,325
IRS3 total sentences (tax, money) doubled	215,213	21,154,169	21,369,382
IRS3 total sentences (tax, money) increase 5%	215,546	21,212,556	21,428,102

(continued)

Table 9.5 (continued)

	Direct revenue change per audit or per sentence (D/C) ($) (G)	Indirect revenue change per audit or per sentence (E/C) ($) (H)	Total revenue change per audit or per sentence (F/C) ($) (I)
IRS3 total sentences (tax, money) increase by 2 per state	94,375	9,213,125	9,307,500
IRS4 audits doubled	7,011	56,555	63,566
IRS4 audits increase 5%	6,985	56,410	63,395
IRS4 audits increase by 200 per state	6,900	54,169	61,069
IRS4 total sentences (tax, money) doubled	247,836	17,681,716	17,929,552
IRS4 total sentences (tax, money) increase 5%	248,835	17,729,698	17,978,533
IRS4 total sentences (tax, money) increase by 2 per state	107,500	7,704,375	7,811,875
IRS5 audits doubled	6,677	98,212	104,889
IRS5 audits increase 5%	6,650	97,909	104,559
IRS5 audits increase by 200 per state	6,575	95,056	101,631
IRS5 total sentences (tax, money) doubled	372,129	6,849,700	7,221,829
IRS5 total sentences (tax, money) increase 5%	372,004	6,859,190	7,231,194
IRS5 total sentences (tax, money) increase by 2 per state	161,250	2,983,750	3,145,000

* All Dollar amounts shown are in the correct denomination.

and corresponds to 194,160 additional audits. This result implies an average of $7,073 per audit (direct revenue change per audit)—a figure not dissimilar from that obtained in the marginal simulation with a 5 percent increase.

The corresponding marginal audit effects for the period ending in 2004 are much smaller for total revenue generated per audit than those determined in the period ending in 2001. In Table 9.5A, I show that the increase in collections per audit from specific and general deterrence was $109,970 per audit for the period ending in 2001 (Table 9.5A, Column I, Row 1), but was approximately $51,810 per audit using data through 2004 (Table 9.5, Column I, Row 1).

Doubling CI sentenced cases (Table 9.5A, Row 4) leads to 1,732 additional cases and $14.08 billion in additional revenue for 2001. This corresponds to $8.13 million per additional sentenced case in specific and general deterrence. The estimates using data through 2004 are much larger. From Table 9.5, row 4, we see that doubling CI tax and money laundering cases lead to an increase of $29.8 billion from an additional 1,502-sentenced cases. This result corresponds to $19.8 million per case.

The results vary by marginal and average tax treatment to some degree. Comparing Table 9.5 for Models 1–2 shows that doubling CI sentences raises specific and general deterrence revenues by $19.8 million per case (Model IRS1) and raises specific and general deterrence by $6.1 million (Model IRS2). Conversely, Model IRS2 has larger per audit effects than does model IRS1. The difference in these two models is the tax treatments. IRS1 is based on the top Federal/State marginal rate, while IRS2 is based on the average Federal/State tax rate. As I stated previously, model IRS2 is the theoretically correct specification because reported tax collections are primarily determined by average tax rates and personal income, not by the top marginal tax rate. In this instance, I report the range of outcomes rather than picking one model over the other.

In Tables 9.6, 9.7, and 9.8, I present the simulations using the period through 2004 with the addition of a dummy variable for the period 2001–2004. The dummy variable for this period is highly significant and indicates a large drop in reported and assessed collection above that measured by changes in Federal/State tax rate changes. The pattern of results is similar to that reported for the models without this dummy variable. However, the magnitudes of the simulated audit and CI enforcement consequences are changed. As seen in Table 9.8, the effect of doubling the audit rate ranges from $83,022 to $112,464 in the first two models (different in treatment of taxes), while the effect of doubling CI sentences ranges from $6.506 million per sentence to $10.476 million per case. Generally, these effects are somewhat larger for audit and somewhat smaller for CI sentences compared to the results presented in Table 9.5 for the period ending in 2004.

I have also estimated models for prison and probation specific effects and for tax versus money laundering effects. I present these models in Tables 9.9, 9.10, and 9.11. Again, the results occur in pairs with the first pair a baseline case (IRS1, IRS2), the second pair (IRS3, IRS4) showing the breakdown between tax and money laundering cases, and the last pair (IRS5, IRS6) showing the prison and probation breakdown. Within each pair, the first model uses the top Federal/State

Table 9.5A 2001, No Media

	Amount before change	Amount after change	Difference (B − A)	Direct change in revenue ($)	Indirect change in revenue ($)	Total change in revenue (D + E) ($)
	(A)	(B)	(C)	(D)	(E)	(F)
IRS1 audits doubled	201,670	403,340	201,670	1,365,125,000	20,812,437,500	22,177,562,500
IRS1 audits increase 5%	201,670	211,753	10,083	67,687,500	1,034,875,000	1,102,562,500
IRS1 audits increase by 200 per state	201,670	211,670	10,000	65,687,500	969,312,500	1,035,000,000
IRS1 total sentences (tax, money) doubled	1,732	3,464	1,732	699,187,500	13,382,875,000	14,082,062,500
IRS1 total sentences (tax, money) increase 5%	1,732	1,819	87	35,250,000	676,562,500	711,812,500
IRS1 total sentences (tax, money) increase by 2 per state	1,732	1,832	100	17,187,500	340,562,500	357,750,000
IRS2 audits doubled	201,670	403,340	201,670	1,312,437,500	23,577,437,500	24,889,875,000
IRS2 audits increase 5%	201,670	211,753	10,083	65,000,000	1,172,125,000	1,237,125,000
IRS2 audits increase by 200 per state	201,670	211,670	10,000	63,000,000	1,103,437,500	1,166,437,500
IRS2 total sentences (tax, money) doubled	1,732	3,464	1,732	859,625,000	9,640,687,500	10,500,312,500
IRS2 total sentences (tax, money) increase 5%	1,732	1,819	87	43,250,000	486,500,000	529,750,000
IRS2 total sentences (tax, money) increase by 2 per state	1,732	1,832	100	20,937,500	245,875,000	266,812,500
IRS3 audits doubled	201,670	403,340	201,670	1,370,687,500	20,962,500,000	22,333,187,500
IRS3 audits increase 5%	201,670	211,753	10,083	67,875,000	1,042,375,000	1,110,250,000
IRS3 audits increase by 200 per state	201,670	211,670	10,000	65,875,000	976,750,000	1,042,625,000
IRS3 total sentences (tax, money) doubled	1,732	3,464	1,732	716,937,500	15,378,937,500	16,095,875,000
IRS3 total sentences (tax, money) increase 5%	1,732	1,819	87	36,062,500	775,625,000	811,687,500

(continued)

Table 9.5A (continued)

	Amount before change	Amount after change	Difference (B − A)	Direct change in revenue ($)	Indirect change in revenue ($)	Total change in revenue (D + E) ($)
	(A)	(B)	(C)	(D)	(E)	(F)
IRS3 total sentences (tax, money) increase by 2 per state	1,732	1,832	100	17,562,500	386,187,500	403,750,000
IRS4 audits doubled	201,670	403,340	201,670	1,366,062,500	21,557,625,000	22,923,687,500
IRS4 audits increase 5%	201,670	211,753	10,083	67,812,500	1,071,750,000	1,139,562,500
IRS4 audits increase by 200 per state	201,670	211,670	10,000	65,625,000	1,005,437,500	1,071,062,500
IRS4 total sentences (tax, money) doubled	1,732	3,464	1,732	765,062,500	13,117,562,500	13,882,625,000
IRS4 total sentences (tax, money) increase 5%	1,732	1,819	87	38,562,500	661,750,000	700,312,500
IRS4 total sentences (tax, money) increase by 2 per state	1,732	1,832	100	18,750,000	330,312,500	349,062,500
IRS5 audits doubled	201,670	403,340	201,670	1,411,312,500	23,390,125,000	24,801,437,500
IRS5 audits increase 5%	201,670	211,753	10,083	70,062,500	1,162,625,000	1,232,687,500
IRS5 audits increase by 200 per state	201,670	211,670	10,000	67,937,500	1,093,375,000	1,161,312,500
IRS5 total sentences (tax, money) doubled	1,732	3,464	1,732	660,000,000	9,700,937,500	10,360,937,500
IRS5 total sentences (tax, money) increase 5%	1,732	1,819	87	33,250,000	490,437,500	523,687,500
IRS5 total sentences (tax, money) increase by 2 per state	1,732	1,832	100	16,312,500	249,187,500	265,500,000

(continued)

Table 9.5A (continued)

	Direct revenue change per audit or per sentence (D/C) ($) (G)	Indirect revenue change per audit or per sentence (E/C) ($) (H)	Total revenue change per audit or per sentence (F/C) ($) (I)
IRS1 audits doubled	6,769	103,200	109,970
IRS1 audits increase 5%	6,713	102,631	109,343
IRS1 audits increase by 200 per state	6,569	96,931	103,500
IRS1 total sentences (tax, money) doubled	403,688	7,726,833	8,130,521
IRS1 total sentences (tax, money) increase 5%	407,045	7,812,514	8,219,558
IRS1 total sentences (tax, money) increase by 2 per state	171,875	3,405,625	3,577,500
IRS2 audits doubled	6,508	116,911	123,419
IRS2 audits increase 5%	6,446	116,242	122,688
IRS2 audits increase by 200 per state	6,300	110,344	116,644
IRS2 total sentences (tax, money) doubled	496,319	5,566,217	6,062,536
IRS2 total sentences (tax, money) increase 5%	499,423	5,617,793	6,117,216
IRS2 total sentences (tax, money) increase by 2 per state	209,375	2,458,750	2,668,125
IRS3 audits doubled	6,797	103,945	110,741
IRS3 audits increase 5%	6,731	103,374	110,106

(continued)

Table 9.5A (continued)

	Direct revenue change per audit or per sentence (D/C) ($) (G)	Indirect revenue change per audit or per sentence (E/C) ($) (H)	Total revenue change per audit or per sentence (F/C) ($) (I)
IRS3 audits increase by 200 per state	6,588	97,675	104,263
IRS3 total sentences (tax, money) doubled	413,936	8,879,294	9,293,230
	(G)	(H)	(I)
IRS3 total sentences (tax, money) increase 5%	416,427	8,956,424	9,372,851
IRS3 total sentences (tax, money) increase by 2 per state	175,625	3,861,875	4,037,500
IRS4 audits doubled	6,774	106,896	113,669
IRS4 audits increase 5%	6,725	106,288	113,013
IRS4 audits increase by 200 per state	6,563	100,544	107,106
IRS4 total sentences (tax, money) doubled	441,722	7,573,650	8,015,372
IRS4 total sentences (tax, money) increase 5%	445,295	7,641,468	8,086,763
IRS4 total sentences (tax, money) increase by 2 per state	187,500	3,303,125	3,490,625
IRS5 audits doubled	6,998	115,982	122,980
IRS5 audits increase 5%	6,948	115,300	122,248
IRS5 audits increase by 200 per state	6,794	109,338	116,131
IRS5 total sentences (tax, money) doubled	381,062	5,601,003	5,982,066
IRS5 total sentences (tax, money) increase 5%	383,950	5,663,260	6,047,210
IRS5 total sentences (tax, money) increase by 2 per state	163,125	2,491,875	2,655,000

Table 9.6 Dummy 2002–2004

Variable	(2004, Dummy)											
	1				2				3			
	ALR	RTR	RCAP	IAR	ALR	RTR	RCAP	IAR	ALR	RTR	RCAP	IAR
Constant	1.1498	1.1944	0.1599	1.8843	0.1547	0.1904	0.1542	2.4326	1.0995	1.1430	0.1591	1.7804
	(3.845)	(4.008)	(4.519)	(4.465)	(0.469)	(0.581)	(4.134)	(5.213)	(3.718)	(3.878)	(4.474)	(4.191)
Percent of families on welfare	−0.0044	−0.0045	0.0000	0.0554	0.0069	0.0069	0.0003	0.0479	−0.0051	−0.0052	−0.0001	0.0541
	(−0.61)	(−0.62)	(0.061)	(5.000)	(0.945)	(0.952)	(0.411)	(4.229)	(−0.70)	(−0.72)	(−0.15)	(4.853)
State tax rate	–0.0058	–0.0060	–0.0020	–0.0177	0.0013	0.0013	–0.0019	–0.0217	–	–	–	–
	(−1.04)	(−1.07)	(−2.71)	(−2.53)	(0.225)	(0.235)	(−2.60)	(−3.00)	–	–	–	–
Personal income per capita	0.2939	0.2916	0.0098	–0.1044	0.2920	0.2896	0.0099	–0.1010	0.2941	0.2918	0.0097	–0.1025
	(19.76)	(19.66)	(5.623)	(−5.58)	(19.56)	(19.51)	(5.754)	(−5.38)	(19.95)	(19.86)	(5.526)	(−5.42)
Federal & state top tax rate	0.0058	0.0057	0.0002	−0.0030	–	–	–	–	0.0058	0.0058	0.0002	−0.0024
	(4.147)	(4.127)	(1.343)	(−1.19)	–	–	–	–	(4.203)	(4.184)	(1.257)	(−0.94)
Personal income* Federal & state top tax rate	–	–	–	–	–	–	–	–	–	–	–	–
	–	–	–	–	–	–	–	–	–	–	–	–
Federal & State avg marginal tax rate	–	–	–	–	0.0495	0.0501	0.0004	−0.0297	–	–	–	–
	–	–	–	–	(7.442)	(7.613)	(0.531)	(−2.55)	–	–	–	–
Family size	−4.1780	−4.2530	0.7419	−0.1329	−4.8061	−4.9007	0.7218	0.1714	−4.0353	−4.1078	0.7318	0.2885
	(−4.93)	(−5.04)	(7.468)	(−0.10)	(−5.62)	(−5.77)	(7.314)	(0.138)	(−4.80)	(−4.90)	(7.340)	(0.233)
Farms per household	−1.7600	−1.5296	−0.4198	4.3293	−2.1811	−1.9643	−0.4067	4.2502	−1.7773	−1.5495	−0.3800	4.5341
	(−1.02)	(−0.88)	(−1.51)	(2.092)	(−1.27)	(−1.15)	(−1.49)	(2.054)	(−1.04)	(−0.91)	(−1.36)	(2.153)
Percent of adults with high school diploma	−0.6839	−0.6993	0.0230	−0.8754	−0.5564	−0.5751	0.0292	−0.8524	−0.6965	−0.7120	0.0212	−0.9737
	(−5.05)	(−5.19)	(1.638)	(−3.60)	(−4.39)	(−4.58)	(2.242)	(−3.79)	(−5.15)	(−5.29)	(1.505)	(−4.02)
Percent of pop over 65	2.7750	2.7410	−0.4814	−4.6178	3.6955	3.6824	−0.4557	−4.8204	2.6733	2.6386	−0.4767	−4.9776
	(3.080)	(3.049)	(−3.94)	(−4.15)	(4.068)	(4.071)	(−3.79)	(−4.33)	(3.002)	(2.970)	(−3.88)	(−4.43)

(continued)

Table 9.6 (continued)

Variable	(2004, Dummy)											
	1				2				3			
	ALR	RTR	RCAP	IAR	ALR	RTR	RCAP	IAR	ALR	RTR	RCAP	IAR
Percent of employed persons in manufacturing	−0.6399	−0.6302	0.1498	−0.9312	−0.5833	−0.5785	0.1476	−0.8937	−0.6387	−0.6292	0.1490	−1.0734
	(−2.34)	(−2.31)	(4.409)	(−2.53)	(−2.13)	(−2.12)	(4.359)	(−2.42)	(−2.36)	(−2.33)	(4.364)	(−2.90)
Percent of employed persons in service	0.0715	0.1515	−0.0308	1.4279	−0.2077	−0.1395	−0.0248	1.5205	0.0294	0.1081	−0.0384	1.2914
	(0.265)	(0.566)	(−1.09)	(3.440)	(−0.75)	(−0.50)	(−0.86)	(3.705)	(0.111)	(0.410)	(−1.36)	(3.119)
Unemployment rate	−2.9992	−3.0333	−0.2450	0.6274	−2.1954	−2.2185	−0.2445	0.0769	−2.9748	−3.0088	−0.2495	0.7170
	(−6.15)	(−6.25)	(−4.94)	(0.695)	(−4.31)	(−4.39)	(−4.79)	(0.082)	(−6.09)	(−6.19)	(−5.01)	(0.793)
Dummy 2002−2004	−0.3216	−0.3240	−0.0029	−0.2789	−0.2172	−0.2177	−0.0029	−0.3170	−0.3216	−0.3240	−0.0029	−0.2851
	(−18.3)	(−18.5)	(−1.62)	(−7.69)	(−8.92)	(−9.02)	(−1.19)	(−7.96)	(−18.2)	(−18.5)	(−1.58)	(−7.86)
Audit rate	0.1486	0.1289	0.0173	–	0.2238	0.2059	0.0171	–	0.1512	0.1315	0.0175	–
	(3.352)	(2.922)	(3.819)	–	(4.673)	(4.337)	(3.589)	–	(3.434)	(3.002)	(3.835)	–
Direct examination time	–	–	–	0.9092	–	–	–	0.7815	–	–	–	0.9251
	–	–	–	(5.934)	–	–	–	(4.817)	–	–	–	(6.031)
Budget per return	–	–	–	22.5571	–	–	–	22.2270	–	–	–	22.9877
	–	–	–	(9.924)	–	–	–	(9.801)	–	–	–	(10.12)
Total sentences	–	–	–	–	–	–	–	–	–	–	–	–
	–	–	–	–	–	–	–	–	–	–	–	–

(continued)

Table 9.6 (continued)

Variable	(2004, Dummy)											
	1				2				3			
	ALR	RTR	RCAP	IAR	ALR	RTR	RCAP	IAR	ALR	RTR	RCAP	IAR
Total sentences (Tax & money laun only)	0.000493 (2.195)	0.000485 (2.165)	−0.000019 (−0.71)	−0.000011 (−0.03)	0.000326 (1.434)	0.000312 (1.378)	−0.000017 (−0.65)	0.000081 (0.247)	0.000513 (2.305)	0.000505 (2.275)	−0.000015 (−0.57)	0.000065 (0.198)
% of tot sent related to tax	0.0337 (1.133)	0.0321 (1.084)	0.0040 (1.347)	−0.1039 (−1.86)	0.0268 (0.888)	0.0255 (0.851)	0.0037 (1.244)	−0.0964 (−1.73)	0.0331 (1.106)	0.0314 (1.057)	0.0039 (1.313)	−0.1069 (−1.91)
% of tot sent related to money laun	−0.0095 (−0.28)	−0.0119 (−0.35)	0.0031 (0.936)	−0.2056 (−3.35)	0.0044 (0.130)	0.0018 (0.055)	0.0036 (1.098)	−0.1977 (−3.27)	−0.0102 (−0.30)	−0.0126 (−0.37)	0.0030 (0.918)	−0.2105 (−3.43)
% of tax sent neither prison nor probation	0.0334 (0.417)	0.0218 (0.273)	0.0091 (1.142)	−0.3728 (−2.45)	0.0230 (0.281)	0.0118 (0.146)	0.0087 (1.084)	−0.3605 (−2.38)	0.0358 (0.446)	0.0242 (0.303)	0.0101 (1.266)	−0.3695 (−2.42)
% of money laun sent neither prison nor probation	−0.3013 (−4.10)	−0.2805 (−3.84)	−0.0134 (−1.82)	0.9014 (8.191)	−0.3618 (−4.78)	−0.3418 (−4.56)	−0.0135 (−1.81)	0.8868 (8.100)	−0.3007 (−4.08)	−0.2798 (−3.81)	−0.0123 (−1.67)	0.9123 (8.281)
Number of obs	850				850				850			
Years	1988–2004				1988–2004				1988–2004			

(continued)

Table 9.6 (continued)

Variable	(2004, Dummy)							
	4				5			
	ALR	RTR	RCAP	IAR	ALR	RTR	RCAP	IAR
Constant	1.3786	1.4241	0.1602	1.7927	0.3048	0.3497	0.1672	1.8843
	(4.629)	(4.802)	(4.503)	(4.128)	(0.854)	(0.987)	(4.222)	(4.465)
Percent of families on welfare	−0.0073	−0.0074	0.0002	0.0554	0.0060	0.0059	0.0002	0.0554
	(−1.00)	(−1.02)	(0.288)	(4.997)	(0.809)	(0.807)	(0.224)	(5.000)
State tax rate	−0.0061	−0.0062	−0.0020	−0.0177	0.0005	0.0004	−0.0021	−0.0177
	(−1.12)	(−1.14)	(−2.69)	(−2.52)	(0.080)	(0.074)	(−2.73)	(−2.53)
Personal income per capita	0.2447	0.2423	0.0100	−0.0886	0.2928	0.2904	0.0103	−0.1044
	(14.79)	(14.71)	(4.999)	(−3.84)	(19.58)	(19.54)	(5.919)	(−5.58)
Federal & state top tax rate	–	–	–	–	–	–	–	−0.0030
	–	–	–	–	–	–	–	(−1.19)
Personal income* Federal & state top tax rate	0.0013	0.0013	0.0000	−0.0004	–	–	–	–
	(6.462)	(6.507)	(0.138)	(−1.20)	–	–	–	–
Federal & State avg marginal tax rate	–	–	–	–	0.0427	0.0429	−0.0004	–
	–	–	–	–	(4.203)	(4.261)	(−0.42)	–
Family size	−3.8538	−3.9273	0.7263	−0.1499	−4.8092	−4.8992	0.7260	−0.1329
	(−4.61)	(−4.72)	(7.301)	(−0.12)	(−5.61)	(−5.75)	(7.372)	(−0.10)
Farms per household	−2.3376	−2.1156	−0.4054	4.3646	−2.0122	−1.7835	−0.3968	4.3293
	(−1.39)	(−1.26)	(−1.48)	(2.103)	(−1.16)	(−1.03)	(−1.46)	(2.092)
Percent of adults with high school diploma	−0.7522	−0.7698	0.0294	−0.8856	−0.5440	−0.5620	0.0310	−0.8754
	(−5.71)	(−5.88)	(2.145)	(−3.70)	(−4.28)	(−4.46)	(2.370)	(−3.60)

(continued)

Table 9.6 (continued)

Variable	(2004, Dummy)							
	4				5			
	ALR	RTR	RCAP	IAR	ALR	RTR	RCAP	IAR
Percent of pop over 65	2.4713	2.4350	−0.4590	−4.5951	3.6450	3.6234	−0.4560	−4.6178
	(2.804)	(2.770)	(−3.76)	(−4.12)	(3.974)	(3.968)	(−3.81)	(−4.15)
Percent of employed persons in manufacturing	−0.5405	−0.5320	0.1488	−0.9430	−0.6047	−0.5997	0.1482	−0.9312
	(−2.01)	(−1.99)	(4.396)	(−2.56)	(−2.20)	(−2.20)	(4.393)	(−2.53)
Percent of employed persons in service	−0.0745	0.0015	−0.0225	1.4216	−0.1326	−0.0583	−0.0174	1.4279
	(−0.27)	(0.005)	(−0.80)	(3.437)	(−0.46)	(−0.20)	(−0.58)	(3.440)
Unemployment rate	−2.9791	−3.0126	−0.2505	0.6495	−2.3379	−2.3696	−0.2595	0.6274
	(−6.14)	(−6.25)	(−5.06)	(0.721)	(−4.45)	(−4.55)	(−4.89)	(0.695)
Dummy 2002–2004	−0.3022	−0.3044	−0.0036	−0.2793	−0.2344	−0.2361	−0.0049	−0.2789
	(−16.9)	(−17.1)	(−1.96)	(−7.68)	(−7.60)	(−7.72)	(−1.54)	(−7.69)
Audit rate	0.1704	0.1509	0.0168	–	0.2112	0.1923	0.0162	–
	(3.840)	(3.423)	(3.700)	–	(4.302)	(3.951)	(3.320)	–
Direct examination time	–	–	–	0.9008	–	–	–	0.9092
	–	–	–	(5.849)	–	–	–	(5.934)
Budget per return	–	–	–	22.5260	–	–	–	22.5571
	–	–	–	(9.905)	–	–	–	(9.924)
Total sentences	–	–	–	–	–	–	–	–
	–	–	–	–	–	–	–	–
Total sentences (Tax & money laun only)	0.000444	0.000433	−0.000015	−0.000014	0.000360	0.000349	−0.000012	−0.000011
	(2.003)	(1.963)	(−0.58)	(−0.04)	(1.556)	(1.516)	(−0.44)	(−0.03)
% of tot sent related to tax	0.0381	0.0366	0.0037	−0.1032	0.0266	0.0252	0.0037	−0.1039
	(1.283)	(1.241)	(1.253)	(−1.85)	(0.888)	(0.848)	(1.249)	(−1.86)

(continued)

Table 9.6 (continued)

Variable	(2004, Dummy)							
	4				5			
	ALR	RTR	RCAP	IAR	ALR	RTR	RCAP	IAR
% of tot sent related to money laun	−0.0169	−0.0194	0.0036	−0.2060	0.0056	0.0031	0.0037	−0.2056
	(−0.51)	(−0.59)	(1.100)	(−3.36)	(0.169)	(0.094)	(1.146)	(−3.35)
% of tax sent neither prison nor probation	0.0431	0.0317	0.0087	−0.3726	0.0227	0.0114	0.0088	−0.3728
	(0.539)	(0.398)	(1.095)	(−2.45)	(0.280)	(0.142)	(1.098)	(−2.45)
% of money laun sent neither prison nor probation	−0.3027	−0.2818	−0.0134	0.8983	−0.3542	−0.3335	−0.0132	0.9014
	(−4.13)	(−3.87)	(−1.82)	(8.141)	(−4.71)	(−4.47)	(−1.77)	(8.191)
Number of obs	850				850			
Years	1988–2004				1988–2004			

Table 9.7 Dummy 2002–2004

	Estimated assessed tax collections ($Millions)			Estimated reported tax collections ($Millions)		
	Modified amount (A)	Original amount (B)	Difference (A − B) (C)	Modified amount (D)	Original amount (E)	Difference (D − E) (F)
IRS1 audits doubled	850,854.69	834,735.06	16,119.63	845,668.56	831,094.44	14,574.13
IRS1 audits increase 5%	835,537.69	834,735.06	802.63	831,820.25	831,094.44	725.81
IRS1 audits increase by 200 per state	835,522.50	834,735.06	787.44	831,803.75	831,094.44	709.31
IRS1 total sentences (tax, money) doubled	850,470.38	834,735.06	15,735.31	846,531.69	831,094.44	15,437.25
IRS1 total sentences (tax, money) increase 5%	835,526.06	834,735.06	791.00	831,870.56	831,094.44	776.13
IRS1 total sentences (tax, money) increase by 2 per state	835,198.06	834,735.06	463.00	831,548.75	831,094.44	454.31
IRS2 audits doubled	845,748.56	823,912.50	21,836.06	840,374.88	819,947.38	20,427.50
IRS2 audits increase 5%	824,999.38	823,912.50	1,086.88	820,964.19	819,947.38	1,016.81
IRS2 audits increase by 200 per state	824,989.56	823,912.50	1,077.06	820,953.25	819,947.38	1,005.88
IRS2 total sentences (tax, money) doubled	833,685.38	823,912.50	9,772.88	829,197.94	819,947.38	9,250.56
IRS2 total sentences (tax, money) increase 5%	824,403.81	823,912.50	491.31	820,412.44	819,947.38	465.06
IRS2 total sentences (tax, money) increase by 2 per state	824,202.25	823,912.50	289.75	820,221.94	819,947.38	274.56
IRS3 audits doubled	849,886.81	833,529.31	16,357.50	844,684.25	829,870.50	14,813.75
IRS3 audits increase 5%	834,343.75	833,529.31	814.44	830,608.19	829,870.50	737.69
IRS3 audits increase by 200 per state	834,328.75	833,529.31	799.44	830,591.88	829,870.50	721.38
IRS3 total sentences (tax, money) doubled	850,509.69	833,529.31	16,980.38	846,544.75	829,870.50	16,674.25
IRS3 total sentences (tax, money) increase 5%	834,381.94	833,529.31	852.63	830,707.75	829,870.50	837.25
IRS3 total sentences (tax, money) increase by 2 per state	834,025.81	833,529.31	496.50	830,358.13	829,870.50	487.63
IRS4 audits doubled	847,718.81	830,073.00	17,645.81	842,447.06	826,328.19	16,118.88

(continued)

Table 9.7 (continued)

	Estimated assessed tax collections ($Millions)			Estimated reported tax collections ($Millions)		
	Modified amount (A)	Original amount (B)	Difference (A – B) (C)	Modified amount (D)	Original amount (E)	Difference (D – E) (F)
IRS4 audits increase 5%	830,951.56	830,073.00	878.56	827,130.81	826,328.19	802.63
IRS4 audits increase by 200 per state	830,939.25	830,073.00	866.25	827,117.38	826,328.19	789.19
IRS4 total sentences (tax, money) doubled	844,505.19	830,073.00	14,432.19	840,378.50	826,328.19	14,050.31
IRS4 total sentences (tax, money) increase 5%	830,797.75	830,073.00	724.75	827,033.75	826,328.19	705.56
IRS4 total sentences (tax, money) increase by 2 per state	830,495.56	830,073.00	422.56	826,739.75	826,328.19	411.56
IRS5 audits doubled	848,600.88	827,936.69	20,664.19	843,315.88	824,141.56	19,174.31
IRS5 audits increase 5%	828,965.44	827,936.69	1,028.75	825,096.25	824,141.56	954.69
IRS5 audits increase by 200 per state	828,955.38	827,936.69	1,018.69	825,085.00	824,141.56	943.44
IRS5 total sentences (tax, money) doubled	839,714.81	827,936.69	11,778.13	835,505.13	824,141.56	11,363.56
IRS5 total sentences (tax, money) increase 5%	828,527.63	827,936.69	590.94	824,711.69	824,141.56	570.13
IRS5 total sentences (tax, money) increase by 2 per state	828,281.25	827,936.69	344.56	824,474.06	824,141.56	332.50

(continued)

Table 9.7 (continued)

	Actual reported collections ($Millions) (G)	Estimated reported difference and actual reported tax revenue (F/G) (%) (H)	Estimated reported difference and estimated reported tax revenue (F/E) (%) (I)	Change in estimated assessed and reported Tax revenue (C − F)/F (%) (J)	Direct revenue effect ($Millions) (C – F) (K)	Indirect revenue effect ($Millions) (F) (L)	Indirect revenue effect/ total revenue effect (L/(K + L)) (%) (M)
IRS1 audits doubled	823,876	1.8	1.8	10.6	1,545.50	14,574.13	90.41
IRS1 audits increase 5%	823,876	0.1	0.1	10.6	76.81	725.81	90.43
IRS1 audits increase by 200 per state	823,876	0.1	0.1	11.0	78.13	709.31	90.08
IRS1 total sentences (tax, money) doubled	823,876	1.9	1.9	1.9	298.06	15,437.25	98.11
IRS1 total sentences (tax, money) increase 5%	823,876	0.1	0.1	1.9	14.88	776.13	98.12
IRS1 total sentences (tax, money) increase by 2 per state	823,876	0.1	0.1	1.9	8.69	454.31	98.12
IRS2 audits doubled	823,876	2.5	2.5	6.9	1,408.56	20,427.50	93.55

(continued)

Table 9.7 (continued)

	Actual reported collections ($Millions) (G)	Estimated reported difference and actual reported tax revenue (F/G) (%) (H)	Estimated reported difference and estimated reported tax revenue (F/E) (%) (I)	Change in estimated assessed and reported Tax revenue (C − F)/F (%) (J)	Direct revenue effect ($Millions) (C – F) (K)	Indirect revenue effect ($Millions) (F) (L)	Indirect revenue effect/ total revenue effect (L/(K + L)) (%) (M)
IRS2 audits increase 5%	823,876	0.1	0.1	6.9	70.06	1,016.81	93.55
IRS2 audits increase by 200 per state	823,876	0.1	0.1	7.1	71.19	1,005.88	93.39
IRS2 total sentences (tax, money) doubled	823,876	1.1	1.1	5.6	522.31	9,250.56	94.66
IRS2 total sentences (tax, money) increase 5%	823,876	0.1	0.1	5.6	26.25	465.06	94.66
IRS2 total sentences (tax, money) increase by 2 per state	823,876	0.0	0.0	5.5	15.19	274.56	94.76
IRS3 audits doubled	823,876	1.8	1.8	10.4	1,543.75	14,813.75	90.56

(continued)

Table 9.7 (continued)

	Actual reported collections ($Millions) (G)	Estimated reported difference and actual reported tax revenue (F/G) (%) (H)	Estimated reported difference and estimated reported tax revenue (F/E) (%) (I)	Change in estimated assessed and reported Tax revenue (C − F)/F (%) (J)	Direct revenue effect ($Millions) (C – F) (K)	Indirect revenue effect ($Millions) (F) (L)	Indirect revenue effect/ total revenue effect (L/(K + L)) (%) (M)
IRS3 audits increase 5%	823,876	0.1	0.1	10.4	76.75	737.69	90.58
IRS3 audits increase by 200 per state	823,876	0.1	0.1	10.8	78.06	721.38	90.24
IRS3 total sentences (tax, money) doubled	823,876	2.0	2.0	1.8	306.13	16,674.25	98.20
IRS3 total sentences (tax, money) increase 5%	823,876	0.1	0.1	1.8	15.38	837.25	98.20
IRS3 total sentences (tax, money) increase by 2 per state	823,876	0.1	0.1	1.8	8.88	487.63	98.21
IRS4 audits doubled	823,876	2.0	2.0	9.5	1,526.94	16,118.88	91.35
IRS4 audits increase 5%	823,876	0.1	0.1	9.5	75.94	802.63	91.36

(continued)

Table 9.7 (continued)

	Actual reported collections ($Millions) (G)	Estimated reported difference and actual reported tax revenue (F/G) (%) (H)	Estimated reported difference and estimated reported tax revenue (F/E) (%) (I)	Change in estimated assessed and reported Tax revenue (C − F)/F (%) (J)	Direct revenue effect ($Millions) (C – F) (K)	Indirect revenue effect ($Millions) (F) (L)	Indirect revenue effect/ total revenue effect (L/(K + L)) (%) (M)
IRS4 audits increase by 200 per state	823,876	0.1	0.1	9.8	77.06	789.19	91.10
IRS4 total sentences (tax, money) doubled	823,876	1.7	1.7	2.7	381.88	14,050.31	97.35
IRS4 total sentences (tax, money) increase 5%	823,876	0.1	0.1	2.7	19.19	705.56	97.35
IRS4 total sentences (tax, money) increase by 2 per state	823,876	0.0	0.0	2.7	11.00	411.56	97.40
IRS5 audits doubled	823,876	2.3	2.3	7.8	1,489.88	19,174.31	92.79
IRS5 audits increase 5%	823,876	0.1	0.1	7.8	74.06	954.69	92.80
IRS5 audits increase by 200 per state	823,876	0.1	0.1	8.0	75.25	943.44	92.61

(continued)

Table 9.7 (continued)

	Actual reported collections ($Millions) (G)	Estimated reported difference and actual reported tax revenue (F/G) (%) (H)	Estimated reported difference and estimated reported tax revenue (F/E) (%) (I)	Change in estimated assessed and reported Tax revenue (C – F)/F (%) (J)	Direct revenue effect ($Millions) (C – F) (K)	Indirect revenue effect ($Millions) (F) (L)	Indirect revenue effect/ total revenue effect (L/(K + L)) (%) (M)
IRS5 total sentences (tax, money) doubled	823,876	1.4	1.4	3.6	414.56	11,363.56	96.48
IRS5 total sentences (tax, money) increase 5%	823,876	0.1	0.1	3.7	20.81	570.13	96.48
IRS5 total sentences (tax, money) increase by 2 per state	823,876	0.0	0.0	3.6	12.06	332.50	96.50

Table 9.8 Dummy 2002–2004

	Amount before change (A)	Amount after change (B)	Difference (B − A) (C)	Direct change in revenue ($) (D)	Indirect change in revenue ($) (E)	Total change in revenue (D + E) ($) (F)
IRS1 audits doubled	194,160	388,320	194,160	1,545,500,000	14,574,125,000	16,119,625,000
IRS1 audits increase 5%	194,160	203,868	9,708	76,812,500	725,812,500	802,625,000
IRS1 audits increase by 200 per state	194,160	204,160	10,000	78,125,000	709,312,500	787,437,500
IRS1 total sentences (tax, money) doubled	1,502	3,004	1,502	298,062,500	15,437,250,000	15,735,312,500
IRS1 total sentences (tax, money) increase 5%	1,502	1,577	75	14,875,000	776,125,000	791,000,000
IRS1 total sentences (tax, money) increase by 2 per state	1,502	1,602	100	8,687,500	454,312,500	463,000,000
IRS2 audits doubled	194,160	388,320	194,160	1,408,562,500	20,427,500,000	21,836,062,500
IRS2 audits increase 5%	194,160	203,868	9,708	70,062,500	1,016,812,500	1,086,875,000
IRS2 audits increase by 200 per state	194,160	204,160	10,000	71,187,500	1,005,875,000	1,077,062,500
IRS2 total sentences (tax, money) doubled	1,502	3,004	1,502	522,312,500	9,250,562,500	9,772,875,000
IRS2 total sentences (tax, money) increase 5%	1,502	1,577	75	26,250,000	465,062,500	491,312,500
IRS2 total sentences (tax, money) increase by 2 per state	1,502	1,602	100	15,187,500	274,562,500	289,750,000
IRS3 audits doubled	194,160	388,320	194,160	1,543,750,000	14,813,750,000	16,357,500,000
IRS3 audits increase 5%	194,160	203,868	9,708	76,750,000	737,687,500	814,437,500
IRS3 audits increase by 200 per state	194,160	204,160	10,000	78,062,500	721,375,000	799,437,500
IRS3 total sentences (tax, money) doubled	1,502	3,004	1,502	306,125,000	16,674,250,000	16,980,375,000

(continued)

Table 9.8 (continued)

	Amount before change (A)	Amount after change (B)	Difference (B – A) (C)	Direct change in revenue ($) (D)	Indirect change in revenue ($) (E)	Total change in revenue (D + E) ($) (F)
IRS3 total sentences (tax, money) increase 5%	1,502	1,577	75	15,375,000	837,250,000	852,625,000
IRS3 total sentences (tax, money) increase by 2 per state	1,502	1,602	100	8,875,000	487,625,000	496,500,000
IRS4 audits doubled	194,160	388,320	194,160	1,526,937,500	16,118,875,000	17,645,812,500
IRS4 audits increase 5%	194,160	203,868	9,708	75,937,500	802,625,000	878,562,500
IRS4 audits increase by 200 per state	194,160	204,160	10,000	77,062,500	789,187,500	866,250,000
IRS4 total sentences (tax, money) doubled	1,502	3,004	1,502	381,875,000	14,050,312,500	14,432,187,500
IRS4 total sentences (tax, money) increase 5%	1,502	1,577	75	19,187,500	705,562,500	724,750,000
IRS4 total sentences (tax, money) increase by 2 per state	1,502	1,602	100	11,000,000	411,562,500	422,562,500
IRS5 audits doubled	194,160	388,320	194,160	1,489,875,000	19,174,312,500	20,664,187,500
IRS5 audits increase 5%	194,160	203,868	9,708	74,062,500	954,687,500	1,028,750,000
IRS5 audits increase by 200 per state	194,160	204,160	10,000	75,250,000	943,437,500	1,018,687,500
IRS5 total sentences (tax, money) doubled	1,502	3,004	1,502	414,562,500	11,363,562,500	11,778,125,000
IRS5 total sentences (tax, money) increase 5%	1,502	1,577	75	20,812,500	570,125,000	590,937,500
IRS5 total sentences (tax, money) increase by 2 per state	1,502	1,602	100	12,062,500	332,500,000	344,562,500

(continued)

Table 9.8 (continued)

	Direct revenue change per audit or per sentence (D/C) ($) (G)	Indirect revenue change per audit or per sentence (E/C) ($) (H)	Total revenue change per audit or per sentence (F/C) ($) (I)
IRS1 audits doubled	7,960	75,062	83,022
IRS1 audits increase 5%	7,912	74,764	82,677
IRS1 audits increase by 200 per state	7,813	70,931	78,744
IRS1 total sentences (tax, money) doubled	198,444	10,277,796	10,476,240
IRS1 total sentences (tax, money) increase 5%	198,069	10,334,557	10,532,626
IRS1 total sentences (tax, money) increase by 2 per state	86,875	4,543,125	4,630,000
IRS2 audits doubled	7,255	105,210	112,464
IRS2 audits increase 5%	7,217	104,740	111,957
IRS2 audits increase by 200 per state	7,119	100,588	107,706
IRS2 total sentences (tax, money) doubled	347,745	6,158,830	6,506,575
IRS2 total sentences (tax, money) increase 5%	349,534	6,192,578	6,542,112
IRS2 total sentences (tax, money) increase by 2 per state	151,875	2,745,625	2,897,500
IRS3 audits doubled	7,951	76,297	84,248
IRS3 audits increase 5%	7,906	75,988	83,893
IRS3 audits increase by 200 per state	7,806	72,138	79,944
IRS3 total sentences (tax, money) doubled	203,812	11,101,365	11,305,176

(continued)

Table 9.8 (continued)

	Direct revenue change per audit or per sentence (D/C) ($) (G)	Indirect revenue change per audit or per sentence (E/C) ($) (H)	Total revenue change per audit or per sentence (F/C) ($) (I)
IRS3 total sentences (tax, money) increase 5%	204,727	11,148,472	11,353,199
IRS3 total sentences (tax, money) increase by 2 per state	88,750	4,876,250	4,965,000
IRS4 audits doubled	7,864	83,019	90,883
IRS4 audits increase 5%	7,822	82,677	90,499
IRS4 audits increase by 200 per state	7,706	78,919	86,625
IRS4 total sentences (tax, money) doubled	254,244	9,354,402	9,608,647
IRS4 total sentences (tax, money) increase 5%	255,493	9,394,976	9,650,469
IRS4 total sentences (tax, money) increase by 2 per state	110,000	4,115,625	4,225,625
IRS5 audits doubled	7,673	98,755	106,429
IRS5 audits increase 5%	7,629	98,340	105,969
IRS5 audits increase by 200 per state	7,525	94,344	101,869
IRS5 total sentences (tax, money) doubled	276,007	7,565,621	7,841,628
IRS5 total sentences (tax, money) increase 5%	277,131	7,591,547	7,868,677
IRS5 total sentences (tax, money) increase by 2 per state	120,625	3,325,000	3,445,625

Table 9.9 Alternative specifications

Variable	(2004 Models)							
	1				2			
	ALR	RTR	RCAP	IAR	ALR	RTR	RCAP	IAR
Constant	1.1498	1.1944	0.1599	1.8843	0.1547	0.1904	0.1542	2.4326
	(3.845)	(4.008)	(4.519)	(4.465)	(0.469)	(0.581)	(4.134)	(5.213)
Percent of families on welfare	−0.0044	−0.0045	0.0000	0.0554	0.0069	0.0069	0.0003	0.0479
	(−0.61)	(−0.62)	(0.061)	(5.000)	(0.945)	(0.952)	(0.411)	(4.229)
State tax rate	−0.0058	−0.0060	−0.0020	−0.0177	0.0013	0.0013	−0.0019	−0.0217
	(−1.04)	(−1.07)	(−2.71)	(−2.53)	(0.225)	(0.235)	(−2.60)	(−3.00)
Personal income per capita	0.2939	0.2916	0.0098	−0.1044	0.2920	0.2896	0.0099	−0.1010
	(19.76)	(19.66)	(5.623)	(−5.58)	(19.56)	(19.51)	(5.754)	(−5.38)
Federal & state top tax rate	0.0058	0.0057	0.0002	−0.0030	–	–	–	–
	(4.147)	(4.127)	(1.343)	(−1.19)	–	–	–	–
Personal income* Federal & state top tax rate	–	–	–	–	–	–	–	–
	–	–	–	–	–	–	–	–
Federal & State avg marginal tax rate	–	–	–	–	0.0495	0.0501	0.0004	−0.0297
	–	–	–	–	(7.442)	(7.613)	(0.531)	(−2.55)
Family size	−4.1780	−4.2530	0.7419	−0.1329	−4.8061	−4.9007	0.7218	0.1714
	(−4.93)	(−5.04)	(7.468)	(−0.10)	(−5.62)	(−5.77)	(7.314)	(0.138)
Farms per household	−1.7600	−1.5296	−0.4198	4.3293	−2.1811	−1.9643	−0.4067	4.2502
	(−1.02)	(−0.88)	(−1.51)	(2.092)	(−1.27)	(−1.15)	(−1.49)	(2.054)
Percent of adults with high school diploma	−0.6839	−0.6993	0.0230	−0.8754	−0.5564	−0.5751	0.0292	−0.8524
	(−5.05)	(−5.19)	(1.638)	(−3.60)	(−4.39)	(−4.58)	(2.242)	(−3.79)
Percent of pop over 65	2.7750	2.7410	−0.4814	−4.6178	3.6955	3.6824	−0.4557	−4.8204
	(3.080)	(3.049)	(−3.94)	(−4.15)	(4.068)	(4.071)	(−3.79)	(−4.33)

(continued)

Table 9.9 (continued)

Variable	(2004 Models)							
	1				2			
	ALR	RTR	RCAP	IAR	ALR	RTR	RCAP	IAR
Percent of employed persons in manufacturing	−0.6399	−0.6302	0.1498	−0.9312	−0.5833	−0.5785	0.1476	−0.8937
	(−2.34)	(−2.31)	(4.409)	(−2.53)	(−2.13)	(−2.12)	(4.359)	(−2.42)
Percent of employed persons in service	0.0715	0.1515	−0.0308	1.4279	−0.2077	−0.1395	−0.0248	1.5205
	(0.265)	(0.566)	(−1.09)	(3.440)	(−0.75)	(−0.50)	(−0.86)	(3.705)
Unemployment rate	−2.9992	−3.0333	−0.2450	0.6274	−2.1954	−2.2185	−0.2445	0.0769
	(−6.15)	(−6.25)	(−4.94)	(0.695)	(−4.31)	(−4.39)	(−4.79)	(0.082)
Dummy 2002−2004	−0.3216	−0.3240	−0.0029	−0.2789	−0.2172	−0.2177	−0.0029	−0.3170
	(−18.3)	(−18.5)	(−1.62)	(−7.69)	(−8.92)	(−9.02)	(−1.19)	(−7.96)
Audit rate	0.1486	0.1289	0.0173	–	0.2238	0.2059	0.0171	–
	(3.352)	(2.922)	(3.819)	–	(4.673)	(4.337)	(3.589)	–
Direct examination time	–	–	–	0.9092	–	–	–	0.7815
	–	–	–	(5.934)	–	–	–	(4.817)
Budget per return	–	–	–	22.5571	–	–	–	22.2270
	–	–	–	(9.924)	–	–	–	(9.801)
Total sentences	–	–	–	–	–	–	–	–
	–	–	–	–	–	–	–	–
Total sentences (tax & money laun only)	0.000493	0.000485	−0.000019	−0.000011	0.000326	0.000312	−0.000017	0.000081
	(2.195)	(2.165)	(−0.71)	(−0.03)	(1.434)	(1.378)	(−0.65)	(0.247)
Tax sentences	–	–	–	–	–	–	–	–
	–	–	–	–	–	–	–	–
Money laundering sentences	–	–	–	–	–	–	–	–
	–	–	–	–	–	–	–	–

(continued)

Table 9.9 (continued)

Variable	(2004 Models)							
	1				2			
	ALR	RTR	RCAP	IAR	ALR	RTR	RCAP	IAR
Total prison sentences	–	–	–	–	–	–	–	–
	–	–	–	–	–	–	–	–
Total probation sentences	–	–	–	–	–	–	–	–
	–	–	–	–	–	–	–	–
% of tot sent related to tax	0.0337	0.0321	0.0040	−0.1039	0.0268	0.0255	0.0037	−0.0964
	(1.133)	(1.084)	(1.347)	(−1.86)	(0.888)	(0.851)	(1.244)	(−1.73)
% of tot sent related to money laun	−0.0095	−0.0119	0.0031	−0.2056	0.0044	0.0018	0.0036	−0.1977
	(−0.28)	(−0.35)	(0.936)	(−3.35)	(0.130)	(0.055)	(1.098)	(−3.27)
% of tax sent neither prison nor probation	0.0334	0.0218	0.0091	−0.3728	0.0230	0.0118	0.0087	−0.3605
	(0.417)	(0.273)	(1.142)	(−2.45)	(0.281)	(0.146)	(1.084)	(−2.38)
% of money laun sent neither prison nor probation	−0.3013	−0.2805	−0.0134	0.9014	−0.3618	−0.3418	−0.0135	0.8868
	(−4.10)	(−3.84)	(−1.82)	(8.191)	(−4.78)	(−4.56)	(−1.81)	(8.100)
% of total sentences in Media	–	–	–	–	–	–	–	–
	–	–	–	–	–	–	–	–
% of tax sentences in Media	–	–	–	–	–	–	–	–
	–	–	–	–	–	–	–	–
% of money laun sentences in media	–	–	–	–	–	–	–	–
	–	–	–	–	–	–	–	–
Number of obs	850				850			
Years	1988–2004				1988–2004			

(continued)

Table 9.9 (continued)

Variable	(2004 Models)							
	3				4			
	ALR	RTR	RCAP	IAR	ALR	RTR	RCAP	IAR
Constant	1.2379	1.2850	0.1671	1.9480	0.2705	0.3109	0.1562	2.6472
	(4.040)	(4.208)	(4.697)	(4.687)	(0.806)	(0.932)	(4.178)	(5.764)
Percent of families on welfare	−0.0026	−0.0026	−0.0001	0.0572	0.0077	0.0076	0.0002	0.0480
	(−0.35)	(−0.35)	(−0.14)	(5.096)	(1.045)	(1.049)	(0.306)	(4.194)
State tax rate	−0.0042	−0.0043	−0.0021	−0.0188	0.0028	0.0029	−0.0020	−0.0231
	(−0.72)	(−0.74)	(−2.81)	(−2.69)	(0.480)	(0.493)	(−2.64)	(−3.16)
Personal income per capita	0.2980	0.2956	0.0097	−0.1041	0.2946	0.2921	0.0098	−0.1008
	(19.58)	(19.48)	(5.564)	(−5.55)	(19.26)	(19.21)	(5.657)	(−5.31)
Federal & state top tax rate	0.0045	0.0044	0.0002	−0.0050	–	–	–	–
	(3.273)	(3.233)	(1.756)	(−2.01)	–	–	–	–
Personal income* Federal & state top tax rate	–	–	–	–	–	–	–	–
	–	–	–	–	–	–	–	–
Federal & State avg marginal tax rate	–	–	–	–	0.0483	0.0490	0.0005	−0.0355
	–	–	–	–	(7.202)	(7.368)	(0.765)	(−3.03)
Family size	−4.2117	−4.2938	0.7172	−0.3086	−4.8367	−4.9407	0.6970	0.0571
	(−4.80)	(−4.91)	(7.097)	(−0.25)	(−5.44)	(−5.59)	(6.900)	(0.045)
Farms per household	−1.7364	−1.4999	−0.3541	4.1920	−2.2173	−1.9908	−0.3500	4.0621
	(−0.95)	(−0.82)	(−1.25)	(2.032)	(−1.22)	(−1.09)	(−1.25)	(1.938)
Percent of adults with high school diploma	−0.7404	−0.7566	0.0255	−0.8880	−0.6376	−0.6579	0.0337	−0.9356
	(−5.41)	(−5.56)	(1.811)	(−3.63)	(−4.96)	(−5.16)	(2.574)	(−4.13)
Percent of pop over 65	2.9445	2.9121	−0.4849	−4.5937	3.8315	3.8174	−0.4497	−4.8970
	(3.132)	(3.103)	(−3.94)	(−4.15)	(4.037)	(4.036)	(−3.70)	(−4.36)

(continued)

Table 9.9 (continued)

Variable	(2004 Models)							
	3				4			
	ALR	RTR	RCAP	IAR	ALR	RTR	RCAP	IAR
Percent of employed persons in manufacturing	−0.7073	−0.6986	0.1495	−0.9225	−0.6692	−0.6660	0.1484	−0.8973
	(−2.51)	(−2.48)	(4.400)	(−2.51)	(−2.37)	(−2.36)	(4.376)	(−2.41)
Percent of employed persons in service	0.0128	0.0932	−0.0243	1.3749	−0.2878	−0.2198	−0.0166	1.4372
	(0.047)	(0.345)	(−0.86)	(3.298)	(−1.03)	(−0.79)	(−0.58)	(3.473)
Unemployment rate	−3.1222	−3.1625	−0.2311	0.3270	−2.2999	−2.3282	−0.2294	−0.3110
	(−6.42)	(−6.53)	(−4.70)	(0.361)	(−4.51)	(−4.61)	(−4.53)	(−0.33)
Dummy 2002−2004	−0.3257	−0.3281	−0.0029	−0.2821	−0.2200	−0.2205	−0.0026	−0.3232
	(−18.5)	(−18.7)	(−1.60)	(−7.74)	(−9.00)	(−9.11)	(−1.07)	(−8.06)
Audit rate	0.1530	0.1335	0.0168	–	0.2277	0.2100	0.0165	–
	(3.445)	(3.021)	(3.732)	–	(4.761)	(4.431)	(3.502)	–
Direct examination time	–	–	–	0.8813	–	–	–	0.7330
	–	–	–	(5.724)	–	–	–	(4.505)
Budget per return	–	–	–	22.9392	–	–	–	22.6284
	–	–	–	(10.02)	–	–	–	(9.927)
Total sentences	–	–	–	–	–	–	–	–
	–	–	–	–	–	–	–	–
Total Sentences (Tax & money laun only)	–	–	–	–	–	–	–	–
	–	–	–	–	–	–	–	–
Tax sentences	0.000126	0.000111	0.000032	−0.000003	−0.000026	−0.000041	0.000028	0.000097
	(0.381)	(0.336)	(0.884)	(−0.00)	(−0.07)	(−0.12)	(0.768)	(0.184)
Money laundering sentences	0.000858	0.000858	−0.000067	−0.000156	0.000669	0.000655	−0.000057	−0.000085
	(2.406)	(2.417)	(−1.81)	(−0.25)	(1.884)	(1.858)	(−1.56)	(−0.14)

(continued)

Table 9.9 (continued)

Variable	(2004 Models)							
	3				4			
	ALR	RTR	RCAP	IAR	ALR	RTR	RCAP	IAR
Total Prison Sentences	–	–	–	–	–	–	–	–
	–	–	–	–	–	–	–	–
Total probation sentences	–	–	–	–	–	–	–	–
	–	–	–	–	–	–	–	–
% of tot sent related to tax	–	–	–	–	–	–	–	–
	–	–	–	–	–	–	–	–
% of tot sent related to money laun	–	–	–	–	–	–	–	–
	–	–	–	–	–	–	–	–
% of tax sent neither prison nor probation	0.0539	0.0427	0.0081	−0.3591	0.0420	0.0313	0.0074	−0.3389
	(0.674)	(0.537)	(1.025)	(−2.34)	(0.518)	(0.390)	(0.930)	(−2.22)
% of money laun sent neither prison nor probation	−0.3045	−0.2839	−0.0129	0.8884	−0.3601	−0.3403	−0.0130	0.8779
	(−4.17)	(−3.91)	(−1.78)	(8.021)	(−4.79)	(−4.56)	(−1.77)	(7.974)
% of total sentences in Media	–	–	–	–	–	–	–	–
	–	–	–	–	–	–	–	–
% of tax sentences in Media	–	–	–	–	–	–	–	–
	–	–	–	–	–	–	–	–
% of money laun sentences in media	–	–	–	–	–	–	–	–
	–	–	–	–	–	–	–	–
Number of obs	850				850			
Years	1988–2004				1988–2004			

(continued)

Table 9.9 (continued)

Variable	(2004 Models)							
	5				6			
	ALR	RTR	RCAP	IAR	ALR	RTR	RCAP	IAR
Constant	1.1273	1.1694	0.1640	1.9504	0.1691	0.2058	0.1558	2.7122
	(3.786)	(3.942)	(4.678)	(4.455)	(0.514)	(0.630)	(4.212)	(5.639)
Percent of families on welfare	−0.0026	−0.0029	0.0003	0.0549	0.0101	0.0098	0.0006	0.0441
	(−0.36)	(−0.41)	(0.388)	(4.785)	(1.435)	(1.402)	(0.864)	(3.763)
State tax rate	−0.0040	−0.0041	−0.0020	−0.0198	0.0033	0.0033	−0.0019	−0.0249
	(−0.71)	(−0.74)	(−2.69)	(−2.73)	(0.579)	(0.583)	(−2.54)	(−3.34)
Personal income per capita	0.2920	0.2896	0.0097	−0.1099	0.2892	0.2868	0.0097	−0.1047
	(19.64)	(19.55)	(5.559)	(−5.65)	(19.41)	(19.37)	(5.634)	(−5.40)
Federal & state top tax rate	0.0060	0.0059	0.0002	−0.0053	–	–	–	–
	(4.278)	(4.230)	(1.665)	(−2.03)	–	–	–	–
Personal income* Federal & state top tax rate	–	–	–	–	–	–	–	–
	–	–	–	–	–	–	–	–
Federal & State avg marginal tax rate	–	–	–	–	0.0497	0.0502	0.0005	−0.0409
	–	–	–	–	(7.349)	(7.491)	(0.779)	(−3.38)
Family size	−4.0098	−4.0800	0.7354	−0.0730	−4.7309	−4.8186	0.7125	0.3527
	(−4.72)	(−4.83)	(7.432)	(−0.05)	(−5.51)	(−5.65)	(7.224)	(0.276)
Farms per household	−1.2263	−1.0163	−0.3887	3.5105	−1.4261	−1.2266	−0.3740	3.3531
	(−0.72)	(−0.60)	(−1.41)	(1.647)	(−0.84)	(−0.72)	(−1.38)	(1.583)
Percent of adults with high school diploma	−0.6999	−0.7136	0.0210	−0.8592	−0.5654	−0.5839	0.0283	−0.8764
	(−5.19)	(−5.32)	(1.511)	(−3.39)	(−4.48)	(−4.67)	(2.193)	(−3.75)
Percent of pop over 65	2.5402	2.5023	−0.4790	−4.5994	3.4479	3.4269	−0.4514	−4.8784
	(2.845)	(2.809)	(−3.94)	(−4.02)	(3.808)	(3.801)	(−3.75)	(−4.28)

(continued)

Table 9.9 (continued)

Variable	(2004 Models)							
	5				6			
	ALR	RTR	RCAP	IAR	ALR	RTR	RCAP	IAR
Percent of employed persons in manufacturing	−0.7260	−0.7093	0.1436	−0.7969	−0.7090	−0.6975	0.1417	−0.7620
	(−2.69)	(−2.64)	(4.289)	(−2.09)	(−2.62)	(−2.59)	(4.246)	(−2.01)
Percent of employed persons in service	0.0373	0.1183	−0.0280	1.5400	−0.1996	−0.1303	−0.0206	1.6064
	(0.137)	(0.439)	(−0.99)	(3.562)	(−0.72)	(−0.47)	(−0.72)	(3.768)
Unemployment rate	−2.9446	−2.9855	−0.2423	0.3736	−2.1671	−2.1988	−0.2400	−0.3410
	(−6.05)	(−6.16)	(−4.94)	(0.398)	(−4.28)	(−4.38)	(−4.76)	(−0.35)
Dummy 2002–2004	−0.3225	−0.3245	−0.0033	−0.2795	−0.2206	−0.2210	−0.0030	−0.3300
	(−18.5)	(−18.7)	(−1.85)	(−7.39)	(−9.11)	(−9.20)	(−1.24)	(−7.97)
Audit rate	0.1263	0.1084	0.0156	–	0.1899	0.1736	0.0151	–
	(3.071)	(2.650)	(3.728)	–	(4.279)	(3.947)	(3.436)	–
Direct examination time	–	–	–	0.8915	–	–	–	0.7229
	–	–	–	(5.582)	–	–	–	(4.275)
Budget per return	–	–	–	24.8474	–	–	–	24.5107
	–	–	–	(10.65)	–	–	–	(10.55)
Total sentences	–	–	–	–	–	–	–	–
	–	–	–	–	–	–	–	–
Total sentences (Tax & money laun only)	–	–	–	–	–	–	–	–
	–	–	–	–	–	–	–	–
Tax sentences	–	–	–	–	–	–	–	–
	–	–	–	–	–	–	–	–
Money laundering sentences	–	–	–	–	–	–	–	–
	–	–	–	–	–	–	–	–
Total Prison Sentences	0.000503	0.000538	−0.000014	0.000269	0.000405	0.000439	−0.000015	0.000344
	(1.009)	(1.086)	(−0.27)	(0.286)	(0.803)	(0.878)	(−0.30)	(0.368)

(continued)

Table 9.9 (continued)

Variable	(2004 Models)							
	5				6			
	ALR	RTR	RCAP	IAR	ALR	RTR	RCAP	IAR
Total probation sentences	0.000251	0.000222	−0.000024	−0.000240	0.000164	0.000131	−0.000020	−0.000180
	(0.522)	(0.466)	(−0.48)	(−0.26)	(0.338)	(0.271)	(−0.40)	(−0.20)
% of tot sent related to tax	0.0407	0.0394	0.0035	−0.1033	0.0294	0.0283	0.0031	−0.0888
	(1.363)	(1.325)	(1.175)	(−1.76)	(0.975)	(0.946)	(1.039)	(−1.52)
% of tot sent related to money laun	−0.0129	−0.0146	0.0022	−0.1859	−0.0019	−0.0040	0.0028	−0.1809
	(−0.39)	(−0.44)	(0.675)	(−2.91)	(−0.05)	(−0.12)	(0.871)	(−2.88)
% of tax sent neither prison nor probation	–	–	–	–	–	–	–	–
	–	–	–	–	–	–	–	–
% of money laun sent neither prison nor probation	–	–	–	–	–	–	–	–
	–	–	–	–	–	–	–	–
% of total sentences in Media	–	–	–	–	–	–	–	–
	–	–	–	–	–	–	–	–
% of tax sentences in Media	–	–	–	–	–	–	–	–
	–	–	–	–	–	–	–	–
% of money laun sentences in media	–	–	–	–	–	–	–	–
	–	–	–	–	–	–	–	–
Number of obs	850				850			
Years	1988–2004				1988–2004			

Table 9.10

	Estimated assessed tax collections ($Millions)			Estimated reported tax collections ($Millions)		
	Modified amount (A)	Original amount (B)	Difference (A – B) (C)	Modified amount (D)	Original amount (E)	Difference (D – E) (F)
IRS1 audits doubled	850,854.69	834,735.06	16,119.63	845,668.56	831,094.44	14,574.13
IRS1 audits increase 5%	835,537.69	834,735.06	802.63	831,820.25	831,094.44	725.81
IRS1 audits increase by 200 per state	835,522.50	834,735.06	787.44	831,803.75	831,094.44	709.31
IRS1 total sentences (tax, money) doubled	850,470.38	834,735.06	15,735.31	846,531.69	831,094.44	15,437.25
IRS1 total sentences (tax, money) increase 5%	835,526.06	834,735.06	791.00	831,870.56	831,094.44	776.13
IRS1 total sentences (tax, money) increase by 2 per state	835,198.06	834,735.06	463.00	831,548.75	831,094.44	454.31
IRS2 audits doubled	845,748.56	823,912.50	21,836.06	840,374.88	819,947.38	20,427.50
IRS2 audits increase 5%	824,999.38	823,912.50	1,086.88	820,964.19	819,947.38	1,016.81
IRS2 audits increase by 200 per state	824,989.56	823,912.50	1,077.06	820,953.25	819,947.38	1,005.88
IRS2 total sentences (tax, money) doubled	833,685.38	823,912.50	9,772.88	829,197.94	819,947.38	9,250.56
IRS2 total sentences (tax, money) increase 5%	824,403.81	823,912.50	491.31	820,412.44	819,947.38	465.06
IRS2 total sentences (tax, money) increase by 2 per state	824,202.25	823,912.50	289.75	820,221.94	819,947.38	274.56
IRS3 audits doubled	852,545.69	836,208.88	16,336.81	847,392.69	832,586.06	14,806.63
IRS3 audits increase 5%	837,022.38	836,208.88	813.50	833,323.50	832,586.06	737.44
IRS3 audits increase by 200 per state	837,007.63	836,208.88	798.75	833,307.44	832,586.06	721.38
IRS3 tax sentences doubled	841,321.19	836,208.88	5,112.31	837,369.31	832,586.06	4,783.25
IRS3 tax sentences increase 5%	836,463.88	836,208.88	255.00	832,824.75	832,586.06	238.69
IRS3 tax sentences increase by 2 per state	836,458.25	836,208.88	249.38	832,818.63	832,586.06	232.56
IRS3 money laun sentences doubled	846,776.00	836,208.88	10,567.13	843,165.81	832,586.06	10,579.75
IRS3 money laun sentences increase 5%	836,743.50	836,208.88	534.63	833,121.38	832,586.06	535.31
IRS3 money laun sentences increase by 2 per state	836,891.13	836,208.88	682.25	833,269.00	832,586.06	682.94
IRS4 audits doubled	846,397.75	824,396.88	22,000.88	841,022.88	820,413.56	20,609.31

(continued)

Table 9.10 (continued)

	Estimated assessed tax collections ($Millions)			Estimated reported tax collections ($Millions)		
	Modified amount (A)	Original amount (B)	Difference (A – B) (C)	Modified amount (D)	Original amount (E)	Difference (D – E) (F)
IRS4 audits increase 5%	825,492.00	824,396.88	1,095.13	821,439.50	820,413.56	1,025.94
IRS4 audits increase by 200 per state	825,482.56	824,396.88	1,085.69	821,429.00	820,413.56	1,015.44
IRS4 tax sentences doubled	825,988.13	824,396.88	1,591.25	821,669.81	820,413.56	1,256.25
IRS4 tax sentences increase 5%	824,476.50	824,396.88	79.63	820,476.56	820,413.56	63.00
IRS4 tax sentences increase by 2 per state	824,466.81	824,396.88	69.94	820,466.38	820,413.56	52.81
IRS4 money laun sentences doubled	832,404.94	824,396.88	8,008.06	828,188.06	820,413.56	7,774.50
IRS4 money laun sentences increase 5%	824,801.44	824,396.88	404.56	820,806.31	820,413.56	392.75
IRS4 money laun sentences increase by 2 per state	824,915.00	824,396.88	518.13	820,917.25	820,413.56	503.69
IRS5 audits doubled	849,561.19	835,635.56	13,925.63	844,853.81	832,326.81	12,527.00
IRS5 audits increase 5%	836,329.31	835,635.56	693.75	832,950.94	832,326.81	624.13
IRS5 audits increase by 200 per state	836,314.69	835,635.56	679.13	832,934.94	832,326.81	608.13
IRS5 prison sentences doubled	851,827.75	835,635.56	16,192.19	849,809.44	832,326.81	17,482.63
IRS5 prison sentences increase 5%	836,448.25	835,635.56	812.69	833,204.25	832,326.81	877.44
IRS5 prison sentences increase by 2 per state	836,123.75	835,635.56	488.19	832,853.38	832,326.81	526.56
IRS5 probation sentences doubled	841,718.00	835,635.56	6,082.44	837,353.69	832,326.81	5,026.88
IRS5 probation sentences increase 5%	835,942.69	835,635.56	307.13	832,580.81	832,326.81	254.00
IRS5 probation sentences increase by 2 per state	835,819.81	835,635.56	184.25	832,481.06	832,326.81	154.25
IRS6 audits doubled	843,204.25	824,535.31	18,668.94	838,294.56	820,896.94	17,397.63
IRS6 audits increase 5%	825,465.00	824,535.31	929.69	821,763.38	820,896.94	866.44
IRS6 audits increase by 200 per state	825,455.81	824,535.31	920.50	821,753.00	820,896.94	856.06
IRS6 prison sentences doubled	837,088.44	824,535.31	12,553.13	834,675.19	820,896.94	13,778.25

(continued)

Table 9.10 (continued)

	Estimated assessed tax collections ($Millions)			Estimated reported tax collections ($Millions)		
	Modified amount (A)	Original amount (B)	Difference (A – B) (C)	Modified amount (D)	Original amount (E)	Difference (D – E) (F)
IRS6 prison sentences increase 5%	825,165.63	824,535.31	630.31	821,588.75	820,896.94	691.81
IRS6 prison sentences increase by 2 per state	824,915.50	824,535.31	380.19	821,313.50	820,896.94	416.56
IRS6 probation sentences doubled	827,934.69	824,535.31	3,399.38	823,052.69	820,896.94	2,155.75
IRS6 probation sentences increase 5%	824,706.94	824,535.31	171.63	821,006.00	820,896.94	109.06
IRS6 probation sentences increase by 2 per state	824,641.31	824,535.31	106.00	820,967.69	820,896.94	70.75

(continued)

Table 9.10 (continued)

	Actual reported collections ($Millions) (G)	Estimated reported difference and actual reported tax revenue (F/G) (%) (H)	Estimated reported difference and estimated reported tax revenue (F/E) (%) (I)	Change in estimated assessed and reported tax revenue (C – F)/F (%) (J)	Direct revenue effect ($Millions) (C – F) (K)	Indirect revenue effect ($Millions) (F) (L)	Indirect revenue effect/Total revenue effect (L/(K + L)) (%) (M)
IRS1 audits doubled	823,876	1.8	1.8	10.6	1,545.50	14,574.13	90.41
IRS1 audits increase 5%	823,876	0.1	0.1	10.6	76.81	725.81	90.43
IRS1 audits increase by 200 per state	823,876	0.1	0.1	11.0	78.13	709.31	90.08
IRS1 total sentences (tax, money) doubled	823,876	1.9	1.9	1.9	298.06	15,437.25	98.11
IRS1 total sentences (tax, money) increase 5%	823,876	0.1	0.1	1.9	14.88	776.13	98.12
IRS1 total sentences (tax, money) increase by 2 per state	823,876	0.1	0.1	1.9	8.69	454.31	98.12
IRS2 audits doubled	823,876	2.5	2.5	6.9	1,408.56	20,427.50	93.55
IRS2 audits increase 5%	823,876	0.1	0.1	6.9	70.06	1,016.81	93.55
IRS2 audits increase by 200 per state	823,876	0.1	0.1	7.1	71.19	1,005.88	93.39
IRS2 total sentences (tax, money) doubled	823,876	1.1	1.1	5.6	522.31	9,250.56	94.66

(continued)

Table 9.10 (continued)

	Actual reported collections ($Millions) (G)	Estimated reported difference and actual reported tax revenue (F/G) (%) (H)	Estimated reported difference and estimated reported tax revenue (F/E) (%) (I)	Change in estimated assessed and reported tax revenue (C − F)/F (%) (J)	Direct revenue effect ($Millions) (C − F) (K)	Indirect revenue effect ($Millions) (F) (L)	Indirect revenue effect/Total revenue effect (L/(K + L)) (%) (M)
IRS2 total sentences (tax, money) increase 5%	823,876	0.1	0.1	5.6	26.25	465.06	94.66
IRS2 total sentences (tax, money) increase by 2 per state	823,876	0.0	0.0	5.5	15.19	274.56	94.76
IRS3 audits doubled	823,876	1.8	1.8	10.3	1,530.19	14,806.63	90.63
IRS3 audits increase 5%	823,876	0.1	0.1	10.3	76.06	737.44	90.65
IRS3 audits increase by 200 per state	823,876	0.1	0.1	10.7	77.38	721.38	90.31
IRS3 tax sentences doubled	823,876	0.6	0.6	6.9	329.06	4,783.25	93.56
IRS3 tax sentences increase 5%	823,876	0.0	0.0	6.8	16.31	238.69	93.60
IRS3 tax sentences increase by 2 per state	823,876	0.0	0.0	7.2	16.81	232.56	93.26
IRS3 money laun sentences doubled	823,876	1.3	1.3	−0.1	(12.63)	10,579.75	100.12
IRS3 money laun sentences increase 5%	823,876	0.1	0.1	−0.1	(0.69)	535.31	100.13
IRS3 money laun sentences increase by 2 per state	823,876	0.1	0.1	−0.1	(0.69)	682.94	100.10
IRS4 audits doubled	823,876	2.5	2.5	6.8	1,391.56	20,609.31	93.67

(continued)

Table 9.10 (continued)

	Actual reported collections ($Millions) (G)	Estimated reported difference and actual reported tax revenue (F/G) (%) (H)	Estimated reported difference and estimated reported tax revenue (F/E) (%) (I)	Change in estimated assessed and reported tax revenue (C – F)/F (%) (J)	Direct revenue effect ($Millions) (C – F) (K)	Indirect revenue effect ($Millions) (F) (L)	Indirect revenue effect/Total revenue effect (L/(K + L)) (%) (M)
IRS4 audits increase 5%	823,876	0.1	0.1	6.7	69.19	1,025.94	93.68
IRS4 audits increase by 200 per state	823,876	0.1	0.1	6.9	70.25	1,015.44	93.53
IRS4 tax sentences doubled	823,876	0.2	0.2	26.7	335.00	1,256.25	78.95
IRS4 tax sentences increase 5%	823,876	0.0	0.0	26.4	16.63	63.00	79.12
IRS4 tax sentences increase by 2 per state	823,876	0.0	0.0	32.4	17.13	52.81	75.51
IRS4 money laun sentences doubled	823,876	0.9	0.9	3.0	233.56	7,774.50	97.08
IRS4 money laun sentences increase 5%	823,876	0.0	0.0	3.0	11.81	392.75	97.08
IRS4 money laun sentences increase by 2 per state	823,876	0.1	0.1	2.9	14.44	503.69	97.21
IRS5 audits doubled	823,876	1.5	1.5	11.2	1,398.63	12,527.00	89.96
IRS5 audits increase 5%	823,876	0.1	0.1	11.2	69.63	624.13	89.96
IRS5 audits increase by 200 per state	823,876	0.1	0.1	11.7	71.00	608.13	89.55
IRS5 prison sentences doubled	823,876	2.1	2.1	–7.4	(1,290.44)	17,482.63	107.97
IRS5 prison sentences increase 5%	823,876	0.1	0.1	–7.4	(64.75)	877.44	107.97
IRS5 prison sentences increase by 2 per state	823,876	0.1	0.1	–7.3	(38.38)	526.56	107.86

(continued)

Table 9.10 (continued)

	Actual reported collections ($Millions)	Estimated reported difference and actual reported tax revenue (F/G) (%)	Estimated reported difference and estimated reported tax revenue (F/E) (%)	Change in estimated assessed and reported tax revenue (C – F)/F (%)	Direct revenue effect ($Millions) (C – F)	Indirect revenue effect ($Millions) (F)	Indirect revenue effect/Total revenue effect (L/(K + L)) (%)
	(G)	(H)	(I)	(J)	(K)	(L)	(M)
IRS5 probation sentences doubled	823,876	0.6	0.6	21.0	1,055.56	5,026.88	82.65
IRS5 probation sentences increase 5%	823,876	0.0	0.0	20.9	53.13	254.00	82.70
IRS5 probation sentences increase by 2 per state	823,876	0.0	0.0	19.4	30.00	154.25	83.72
IRS6 audits doubled	823,876	2.1	2.1	7.3	1,271.31	17,397.63	93.19
IRS6 audits increase 5%	823,876	0.1	0.1	7.3	63.25	866.44	93.20
IRS6 audits increase by 200 per state	823,876	0.1	0.1	7.5	64.44	856.06	93.00
IRS6 prison sentences doubled	823,876	1.7	1.7	−8.9	(1,225.13)	13,778.25	109.76
IRS6 prison sentences increase 5%	823,876	0.1	0.1	−8.9	(61.50)	691.81	109.76
IRS6 prison sentences increase by 2 per state	823,876	0.1	0.1	−8.7	(36.38)	416.56	109.57
IRS6 probation sentences doubled	823,876	0.3	0.3	57.7	1,243.63	2,155.75	63.42
IRS6 probation sentences increase 5%	823,876	0.0	0.0	57.4	62.56	109.06	63.55
IRS6 probation sentences increase by 2 per state	823,876	0.0	0.0	49.8	35.25	70.75	66.75

Table 9.11

	Amount before change (A)	Amount after change (B)	Difference (B − A) (C)	Direct change in revenue ($) (D)	Indirect change in revenue ($) (E)	Total change in revenue (D + E) ($) (F)
IRS1 audits doubled	194,160	388,320	194,160	1,545,500,000	14,574,125,000	16,119,625,000
IRS1 audits increase 5%	194,160	203,868	9,708	76,812,500	725,812,500	802,625,000
IRS1 audits increase by 200 per state	194,160	204,160	10,000	78,125,000	709,312,500	787,437,500
IRS1 total sentences (tax, money) doubled	1,502	3,004	1,502	298,062,500	15,437,250,000	15,735,312,500
IRS1 total sentences (tax, money) increase 5%	1,502	1,577	75	14,875,000	776,125,000	791,000,000
IRS1 total sentences (tax, money) increase by 2 per state	1,502	1,602	100	8,687,500	454,312,500	463,000,000
IRS2 audits doubled	194,160	388,320	194,160	1,408,562,500	20,427,500,000	21,836,062,500
IRS2 audits increase 5%	194,160	203,868	9,708	70,062,500	1,016,812,500	1,086,875,000
IRS2 audits increase by 200 per state	194,160	204,160	10,000	71,187,500	1,005,875,000	1,077,062,500
IRS2 total sentences (tax, money) doubled	1,502	3,004	1,502	522,312,500	9,250,562,500	9,772,875,000
IRS2 total sentences (tax, money) increase 5%	1,502	1,577	75	26,250,000	465,062,500	491,312,500
IRS2 total sentences (tax, money) increase by 2 per state	1,502	1,602	100	15,187,500	274,562,500	289,750,000
IRS3 audits doubled	194,160	388,320	194,160	1,530,187,500	14,806,625,000	16,336,812,500
IRS3 audits increase 5%	194,160	203,868	9,708	76,062,500	737,437,500	813,500,000
IRS3 audits increase by 200 per state	194,160	204,160	10,000	77,375,000	721,375,000	798,750,000
IRS3 tax sentences doubled	845	1,690	845	329,062,500	4,783,250,000	5,112,312,500
IRS3 tax sentences increase 5%	845	887	42	16,312,500	238,687,500	255,000,000

(continued)

Table 9.11 (continued)

	Amount before change (A)	Amount after change (B)	Difference (B − A) (C)	Direct change in revenue ($) (D)	Indirect change in revenue ($) (E)	Total change in revenue (D + E) ($) (F)
IRS3 tax sentences increase by 2 per state	845	945	100	16,812,500	232,562,500	249,375,000
IRS3 money laun sentences doubled	693	1,386	693	(12,625,000)	10,579,750,000	10,567,125,000
IRS3 money laun sentences increase 5%	693	728	35	(687,500)	535,312,500	534,625,000
IRS3 money laun sentences increase by 2 per state	693	793	100	(687,500)	682,937,500	682,250,000
IRS4 audits doubled	194,160	388,320	194,160	1,391,562,500	20,609,312,500	22,000,875,000
IRS4 audits increase 5%	194,160	203,868	9,708	69,187,500	1,025,937,500	1,095,125,000
IRS4 audits increase by 200 per state	194,160	204,160	10,000	70,250,000	1,015,437,500	1,085,687,500
IRS4 tax sentences doubled	845	1,690	845	335,000,000	1,256,250,000	1,591,250,000
IRS4 tax sentences increase 5%	845	887	42	16,625,000	63,000,000	79,625,000
IRS4 tax sentences increase by 2 per state	845	945	100	17,125,000	52,812,500	69,937,500
IRS4 money laun sentences doubled	693	1,386	693	233,562,500	7,774,500,000	8,008,062,500
IRS4 money laun sentences increase 5%	693	728	35	11,812,500	392,750,000	404,562,500
IRS4 money laun sentences increase by 2 per state	693	793	100	14,437,500	503,687,500	518,125,000
IRS5 audits doubled	194,160	388,320	194,160	1,398,625,000	12,527,000,000	13,925,625,000
IRS5 audits increase 5%	194,160	203,868	9,708	69,625,000	624,125,000	693,750,000
IRS5 audits increase by 200 per state	194,160	204,160	10,000	71,000,000	608,125,000	679,125,000

(continued)

Table 9.11 (continued)

	Amount before change (A)	Amount after change (B)	Difference (B − A) (C)	Direct change in revenue ($) (D)	Indirect change in revenue ($) (E)	Total change in revenue (D + E) ($) (F)
IRS5 prison sentences doubled	1,451	2,902	1,451	(1,290,437,500)	17,482,625,000	16,192,187,500
IRS5 prison sentences increase 5%	1,451	1,524	73	(64,750,000)	877,437,500	812,687,500
IRS5 prison sentences increase by 2 per state	1,451	1,551	100	(38,375,000)	526,562,500	488,187,500
IRS5 probation sentences doubled	1,535	3,070	1,535	1,055,562,500	5,026,875,000	6,082,437,500
IRS5 probation sentences increase 5%	1,535	1,612	77	53,125,000	254,000,000	307,125,000
IRS5 probation sentences increase by 2 per state	1,535	1,635	100	30,000,000	154,250,000	184,250,000
IRS6 audits doubled	194,160	388,320	194,160	1,271,312,500	17,397,625,000	18,668,937,500
IRS6 audits increase 5%	194,160	203,868	9,708	63,250,000	866,437,500	929,687,500
IRS6 audits increase by 200 per state	194,160	204,160	10,000	64,437,500	856,062,500	920,500,000
IRS6 prison sentences doubled	1,451	2,902	1,451	(1,225,125,000)	13,778,250,000	12,553,125,000
IRS6 prison sentences increase 5%	1,451	1,524	73	(61,500,000)	691,812,500	630,312,500
IRS6 prison sentences increase by 2 per state	1,451	1,551	100	(36,375,000)	416,562,500	380,187,500
IRS6 probation sentences doubled	1,535	3,070	1,535	1,243,625,000	2,155,750,000	3,399,375,000
IRS6 probation sentences increase 5%	1,535	1,612	77	62,562,500	109,062,500	171,625,000
IRS6 probation sentences increase by 2 per state	1,535	1,635	100	35,250,000	70,750,000	106,000,000

(continued)

Table 9.11

	Direct revenue change per audit or per sentence (D/C) ($) (G)	Indirect revenue change per audit or per sentence (E/C) ($) (H)	Total revenue change per audit or per sentence (F/C) ($) (I)
IRS1 audits doubled	7,960	75,062	83,022
IRS1 audits increase 5%	7,912	74,764	82,677
IRS1 audits increase by 200 per state	7,813	70,931	78,744
IRS1 total sentences (tax, money) doubled	198,444	10,277,796	10,476,240
IRS1 total sentences (tax, money) increase 5%	198,069	10,334,557	10,532,626
IRS1 total sentences (tax, money) increase by 2 per state	86,875	4,543,125	4,630,000
IRS2 audits doubled	7,255	105,210	112,464
IRS2 audits increase 5%	7,217	104,740	111,957
IRS2 audits increase by 200 per state	7,119	100,588	107,706
IRS2 total sentences (tax, money) doubled	347,745	6,158,830	6,506,575
IRS2 total sentences (tax, money) increase 5%	349,534	6,192,578	6,542,112
IRS2 total sentences (tax, money) increase by 2 per state	151,875	2,745,625	2,897,500
IRS3 audits doubled	7,881	76,260	84,141
IRS3 audits increase 5%	7,835	75,962	83,797
IRS3 audits increase by 200 per state	7,738	72,138	79,875
IRS3 tax sentences doubled	389,423	5,660,651	6,050,074
IRS3 tax sentences increase 5%	386,095	5,649,416	6,035,512

(continued)

Table 9.11 (continued)

	Direct revenue change per audit or per sentence (D/C) ($) (G)	Indirect revenue change per audit or per sentence (E/C) ($) (H)	Total revenue change per audit or per sentence (F/C) ($) (I)
IRS3 tax sentences increase by 2 per state	168,125	2,325,625	2,493,750
IRS3 money laun sentences doubled	(18,218)	15,266,595	15,248,377
IRS3 money laun sentences increase 5%	(19,841)	15,449,152	15,429,311
IRS3 money laun sentences increase by 2 per state	(6,875)	6,829,375	6,822,500
IRS4 audits doubled	7,167	106,146	113,313
IRS4 audits increase 5%	7,127	105,680	112,806
IRS4 audits increase by 200 per state	7,025	101,544	108,569
IRS4 tax sentences doubled	396,450	1,486,686	1,883,136
IRS4 tax sentences increase 5%	393,492	1,491,126	1,884,618
IRS4 tax sentences increase by 2 per state	171,250	528,125	699,375
IRS4 money laun sentences doubled	337,031	11,218,615	11,555,646
IRS4 money laun sentences increase 5%	340,909	11,334,789	11,675,699
IRS4 money laun sentences increase by 2 per state	144,375	5,036,875	5,181,250
IRS5 audits doubled	7,203	64,519	71,722
IRS5 audits increase 5%	7,172	64,290	71,462
IRS5 audits increase by 200 per state	7,100	60,813	67,913

(continued)

Table 9.11 (continued)

	Direct revenue change per audit or per sentence (D/C) ($) (G)	Indirect revenue change per audit or per sentence (E/C) ($) (H)	Total revenue change per audit or per sentence (F/C) ($) (I)
IRS5 prison sentences doubled	(889,344)	12,048,673	11,159,330
IRS5 prison sentences increase 5%	(892,489)	12,094,257	11,201,768
IRS5 prison sentences increase by 2 per state	(383,750)	5,265,625	4,881,875
IRS5 probation sentences doubled	687,663	3,274,837	3,962,500
IRS5 probation sentences increase 5%	692,183	3,309,451	4,001,635
IRS5 probation sentences increase by 2 per state	300,000	1,542,500	1,842,500
IRS6 audits doubled	6,548	89,605	96,152
IRS6 audits increase 5%	6,515	89,250	95,765
IRS6 audits increase by 200 per state	6,444	85,606	92,050
IRS6 prison sentences doubled	(844,331)	9,495,693	8,651,361
IRS6 prison sentences increase 5%	(847,692)	9,535,674	8,687,982
IRS6 prison sentences increase by 2 per state	(363,750)	4,165,625	3,801,875
IRS6 probation sentences doubled	810,179	1,404,397	2,214,577
IRS6 probation sentences increase 5%	815,148	1,421,012	2,236,160
IRS6 probation sentences increase by 2 per state	352,500	707,500	1,060,000

Table 9.12 Alternative tax rate treatments

Variable	Models			
	1			
	ALR	RTR	RCAP	IAR
Constant	4.9754	5.0702	0.0551	2.1954
	(8.672)	(8.945)	(0.920)	(2.128)
Percent of families on welfare	−0.0047	−0.0047	0.0004	0.0463
	(−0.63)	(−0.63)	(0.478)	(3.930)
State tax rate	0.0007	0.0009	−0.0020	−0.0222
	(0.131)	(0.164)	(−2.70)	(−3.11)
Personal income per capita	−0.4007	−0.4129	0.0255	−0.0519
	(−5.92)	(−6.18)	(3.699)	(−0.41)
Federal & state top tax rate	0.0024	0.0022	0.0001	0.0015
	(1.376)	(1.291)	(0.723)	(0.459)
Personal income* Federal & State Marginal Avg Tax Rate	0.0294	0.0298	−0.0007	−0.0020
	(10.44)	(10.72)	(−2.36)	(−0.37)
Federal & State avg marginal tax rate	−0.1761	−0.1779	0.0050	−0.0199
	(−7.60)	(−7.78)	(2.142)	(−0.46)
Family size	−3.9814	−4.0852	0.7161	0.1808
	(−4.74)	(−4.90)	(7.147)	(0.147)
Farms per household	−3.2427	−3.0328	−0.3871	4.1910
	(−1.96)	(−1.84)	(−1.41)	(2.062)
Percent of adults with high school diploma	−0.3868	−0.3954	0.0184	−0.8911
	(−2.80)	(−2.90)	(1.296)	(−3.68)
Percent of pop over 65	3.0733	3.0672	−0.4551	−4.7817
	(3.447)	(3.458)	(−3.68)	(−4.34)

(continued)

Table 9.12 (continued)

Variable	Models			
	1			
	ALR	RTR	RCAP	IAR
Percent of employed persons in manufacturing	−0.3335	−0.3275	0.1424	−0.9051
	(−1.25)	(−1.24)	(4.226)	(−2.49)
Percent of employed persons in service	−0.1660	−0.0947	−0.0280	1.4640
	(−0.61)	(−0.35)	(−0.98)	(3.539)
Unemployment rate	−2.4086	−2.4323	−0.2432	0.0358
	(−4.80)	(−4.91)	(−4.81)	(0.038)
Dummy 2002–2004	−0.1766	−0.1758	−0.0043	−0.3250
	(−7.07)	(−7.13)	(−1.74)	(−8.02)
Audit rate	0.2799	0.2633	0.0153	–
	(5.883)	(5.605)	(3.224)	–
Direct examination time	–	–	–	0.7602
	–	–	–	(4.557)
Budget per return	–	–	–	22.2874
	–	–	–	(9.804)
Total sentences	–	–	–	–
	–	–	–	–
Total sentences (Tax & money laun only)	0.000396	0.000380	−0.000017	0.000075
	(1.79)	(1.732)	(−0.66)	(0.231)
Tax sentences	–	–	–	–
	–	–	–	–
Money laundering sentences	–	–	–	–
	–	–	–	–

(continued)

Table 9.12 (continued)

Variable	Models			
	1			
	ALR	RTR	RCAP	IAR
Total Prison Sentences	–	–	–	–
	–	–	–	–
Total probation sentences	–	–	–	–
	–	–	–	–
% of tot sent related to tax	0.0332	0.0317	0.0038	−0.0932
	(1.115)	(1.078)	(1.283)	(−1.66)
% of tot sent related to money laun	0.0169	0.0154	0.0027	−0.2035
	(0.506)	(0.466)	(0.813)	(−3.32)
% of tax sent neither prison nor probation	0.0274	0.0158	0.0089	−0.3551
	(0.341)	(0.199)	(1.132)	(−2.33)
% of money laun sent neither prison nor probation	−0.4096	−0.3912	−0.0115	0.8902
	(−5.47)	(−5.29)	(−1.56)	(8.085)
% of total sentences in Media	–	–	–	–
	–	–	–	–
% of tax sentences in Media	–	–	–	–
	–	–	–	–
% of money laun sentences in media	–	–	–	–
	–	–	–	–
Number of obs	850			
Years	1988–2004			

Table 9.13 Results from IRS collections revenue simulation (1988–2004)

	Estimated assessed tax collections ($Millions)			Estimated reported tax collections ($Millions)		
	Modified amount (A)	Original amount (B)	Difference (A − B) (C)	Modified amount (D)	Original amount (E)	Difference (D − E) (F)
IRS1 audits doubled	832,885.19	807,251.56	25,633.63	827,293.44	802,971.81	24,321.63
IRS1 audits increase 5%	808,527.69	807,251.56	1,276.13	804,182.69	802,971.81	1,210.88
IRS1 audits increase by 200 per state	808,527.19	807,251.56	1,275.63	804,181.25	802,971.81	1,209.44
IRS1 total sentences (tax, money) doubled	819,730.75	807,251.56	12,479.19	814,875.63	802,971.81	11,903.81
IRS1 total sentences (tax, money) increase 5%	807,878.75	807,251.56	627.19	803,570.13	802,971.81	598.31
IRS1 total sentences (tax, money) increase by 2 per state	807,617.63	807,251.56	366.06	803,321.19	802,971.81	349.38

(continued)

Table 9.13 (continued)

	Actual reported collections ($Millions) (G)	Estimated reported difference and actual reported tax revenue (F/G) (%) (H)	Estimated reported difference and estimated reported tax revenue (F/E) (%) (I)	Change in estimated assessed and reported tax revenue (C − F)/F (%) (J)	Direct revenue effect ($Millions) (C – F) (K)	Indirect revenue effect ($Millions) (F) (L)	Indirect revenue effect/Total revenue effect (L/(K + L)) (%) (M)
IRS1 audits doubled	823,876	3.0	3.0	5.4	1,312.00	24,321.63	94.88
IRS1 audits increase 5%	823,876	0.1	0.2	5.4	65.25	1,210.88	94.89
IRS1 audits increase by 200 per state	823,876	0.1	0.2	5.5	66.19	1,209.44	94.81
IRS1 total sentences (tax, money) doubled	823,876	1.4	1.5	4.8	575.38	11,903.81	95.39
IRS1 total sentences (tax, money) increase 5%	823,876	0.1	0.1	4.8	28.88	598.31	95.40
IRS1 total sentences (tax, money) increase by 2 per state	823,876	0.0	0.0	4.8	16.69	349.38	95.44

Table 9.14 Estimated gains In collection revenue (1988–2004)

	Amount before change (A)	Amount after change (B)	Difference (B – A) (C)	Direct change in revenue (D) ($)	Indirect change in revenue (E) ($)	Total change in revenue (D + E) (F) ($)
IRS1 audits doubled	194,160	388,320	194,160	1,312,000,000	24,321,625,000	25,633,625,000
IRS1 audits increase 5%	194,160	203,868	9,708	65,250,000	1,210,875,000	1,276,125,000
IRS1 audits increase by 200 per state	194,160	204,160	10,000	66,187,500	1,209,437,500	1,275,625,000
IRS1 total sentences (tax, money) doubled	1,502	3,004	1,502	575,375,000	11,903,812,500	12,479,187,500
IRS1 total sentences (tax, money) increase 5%	1,502	1,577	75	28,875,000	598,312,500	627,187,500
IRS1 total sentences (tax, money) increase by 2 per state	1,502	1,602	100	16,687,500	349,375,000	366,062,500

(continued)

Table 9.14 (continued)

	Direct revenue change per audit or per sentence (D/C) (G) ($)	Indirect revenue change per audit or per sentence (E/C) (H) ($)	Total revenue change per audit or per sentence (F/C) (I) ($)
IRS1 audits doubled	6,757	125,266	132,023
IRS1 audits increase 5%	6,721	124,730	131,451
IRS1 audits increase by 200 per state	6,619	120,944	127,563
IRS1 total sentences (tax, money) doubled	383,073	7,925,308	8,308,380
IRS1 total sentences (tax, money) increase 5%	384,487	7,966,880	8,351,367
IRS1 total sentences (tax, money) increase by 2 per state	166,875	3,493,750	3,660,625

tax rate while the second model uses the average Federal/State tax rate. The first model in the pair produces generally larger CI impacts in each case. Doubling CI tax cases leads to $1.8–6.0 million dollars of general deterrence tax gain per case. Doubling CI money laundering cases leads to $11.5–15.2 million dollars of benefit per case sentenced. As shown in the last pair of models (specifically Table 9.11, IRS5 and IRS6), doubling CI prison sentences leads to $8.6–11.2 million in deterrence, whereas doubling CI probation cases leads to $2.2–3.9 million in deterrence per case sentenced. These are point estimates for models with generally low significance levels on the relevant coefficients. The t-statistics for the key coefficients in the prison/probation experiment were generally not statistically significant, whereas those for the tax/money laundering experiment were significant for the money laundering component only.

It is apparent that significant structural change in tax policy and revenue collection occurred in the last three years. The inclusion of average and top marginal tax rates, in these models of reported tax collection, is only a limited approximation to the complexity of the tax code. For instance, suppose that actual taxes due are given by the highly nonlinear function $f(t, y)$ where t is the tax rate and y is personal income. A first-order Taylor's series expansion of this function would include terms in t, y, and $t*y$. With this in mind, I adopted another specification based on the Taylor's series expansion to more accurately capture tax effects. This specification includes the average Federal tax rate, the product of the average Federal tax rate and personal income, and personal income as explanatory variables. To further capture nonlinearity in the tax code, I include the top Federal marginal rate. This specification is reported in Tables 9.12, 9.13, and 9.14. Notably, the CI factor for total sentences increases in significance to over 90% (t-statistic = 1.79). Importantly, the marginal effect of doubling CI sentences is estimated at $8.31 million per sentence, which is in the range of results reported for the other models in this Chapter. I conclude from this result that proper approximation of the tax shift in the 2002–2004 period is important to determine significant CI and examination effects. Nonetheless, the magnitude of the results reported using the point estimates remains virtually unchanged.

Conclusions

Extending the analysis through 2004 has resulted in some new insights. Previous analysis through 2001 occurred during a period of relatively stable tax policy. The recent changes that occurred in the post-2001 period demonstrated that additional factors are needed in the model to account for these structural changes. In this Chapter, I considered several versions of Federal/State marginal and average tax rates. These variables were highly significant in the models, as was a dummy variable for the 2002–2004 period. After controlling for these shifts in tax policy, I find the empirical results to be similar between previously reported results ending in 2001 and for the period ending in 2004. Previously, I reported that doubling CI tax and money laundering cases leads to approximately $9.25 million in deterrence. The results through 2004 show this figure to be in the range of $6.5–10.5 million for models including both Federal/State tax rates and a dummy variable for the recent three-year period. These estimates far exceed the incremental costs of an additional sentenced case (roughly $300,000). Additionally, we find that increasing tax cases results in roughly $1.8–6.0 million in deterrence, while increasing money laundering cases results in $11.5–15.2 million in deterrence (per case). Additional prison cases produces $8.6–11.1 million in deterrence, while additional probation cases results in $2.2–3.9 million per case.

In sum, I find that the addition of the recent data from 2002 to 2004 has produced results that are consistent with those we found for the period ending in 2001. However, the statistical significance of some results is now weaker. Specifically, the factor for CI sentences loses statistical significance with the addition of the most recent three years of data for the model using average Federal/State tax rates, while such results remain significant for the model using the top marginal rate. Generally, the results remain significant at lower levels of statistical significance, which implies a larger confidence interval (less precision) around these results. Nevertheless, I have reported the point estimates of these effects, as they remain our best estimates. It is apparent, in this analysis, that significant structural change in tax policy and revenue collection occurred in the last three years. These structural changes are captured to a degree using tax rates and dummy variables for the change in tax policy. It remains likely that some of these structural changes are still being worked through the tax system and additional years of information will likely result in more precise models.

Chapter 10
State Income Tax Compliance

Introduction

In this chapter I extend previous results on specific and general deterrence of IRS enforcement on federal individual income tax to the specific and general deterrence effects of enforcement on state income taxes. The possibility that increased enforcement of the federal income tax through audit or criminal investigation could spill over to state income tax compliance was initially recognized in DGW (1988). This proposition has not previously been tested empirically. The preponderance of states have state income taxes in one form or another and there is typically an explicit relationship between taxation at the federal and state levels. In some cases this connection may be as simple as a state using the federal income tax base as its measure of state taxable income. In other cases, only some income items are subject to taxation and the federal adjusted gross income is specifically adjusted before state taxes are applied. In almost all cases there is an overlap between the federal and state income tax computation including assembling information required to prepare the return. Finally, as discussed in DGW taxpayers will generally presume an enforcement connection between state and federal returns and that there is a relationship between the probability of audit at the federal and state level.

These taxpayer expectations are largely correct. Following an audit at the federal level, the IRS will issue a "revenue agent report" to the appropriate state authority noting the tax deficiency. This report will subsequently and routinely trigger an assessment by the state agency. Revenue agent reports are a result of the linkage among the state and federal agencies to coordinate enforcement activities. Congress and state legislators explicitly provide for the exchange of information in order to increase tax revenue and compliance and to reduce duplication of tax collection effects. Most states rely exclusively on revenue agent reports issued by the IRS or at least use them as a basis for their further audit investigations. To the extent that states initiate their own independent audit activities they do so at much lower frequency as compared with relying on the IRS to locate tax noncompliance.

J. A. Dubin, *The Causes and Consequences of Income Tax Noncompliance*,
DOI: 10.1007/978-1-4419-0907-7_10,

When a state does initiate an audit they will in turn report the results to the IRS. Specific data on state initiated audits i.e. state audit rates is virtually nonexistent. Mikesell (1985) developed such a measure for 42 states in 1981 presumably by directly contacting the state authorities. My approach is similar to the extent that I assemble state-by-state information on additional taxes and penalties collected by audit and state government expenditures on tax collection using published state reports. However, my approach differs from the method of Mikesell because it focuses on the effects of the federal audit rate and CI enforcement factors on state tax collections rather than attempt to measure the secondary role of state initiated audits. In other words my purpose is specifically to measure the potential spillover effect of federal enforcement on state tax collections. Given the close relationship between federal and state enforcement this approach seems sensible. Moreover, the federal state spillover effects have not been previously reported in the tax noncompliance literature. A positive finding in this area furthers the case for increased IRS enforcement as the spillover benefits are larger than previously measured.

Data Sources

The analysis in this chapter relies on several new data sources. First I assembled historical information on reported state tax collections from the U.S. Census for the period 1988–2008. The data cover all state governments with an income tax. Local government taxes are excluded. Specifically, I relied on the Annual Survey of Government Tax Collections (STC) for my measure of state individual income tax. The data were then converted to real 1972 dollars using the implicit price consumption deflator and expressed on a "per returns filed" basis by dividing by the number of individual returns filed. As the number of state tax returns was not available, I make the assumption that the number of federal individual tax returns is closely related to the number of state individual tax returns in states with an income tax. These data transformations mimic the treatment used to express federal individual income tax reported on a real per return basis.

Next, I collected detailed information on the cost of state tax collections and the additional taxes and penalties from audit by assembling annual reports from individual state agencies where available. Table 10.1 summarizes the agencies contacted and the source of information where present.

Data on state tax collections costs and state additional taxes and penalties are inconsistent. As discussed in Mikesell (1985), there are various definitional and reporting inconsistencies in this type of data. Consistent information for roughly 8–9 years was obtained on state's additional taxes and penalties for 12 states: California, Alaska, Arizona, Colorado, Hawaii, Idaho, Iowa, Montana, Nevada, New Hampshire, South Dakota, and Vermont. State expenditures on tax collections were more difficult to assemble. Consistent data was available only for roughly 6 years for 5 states: Nevada, Kentucky, Ohio, Iowa, and California.

Table 10.1 State tax collections data

State	Availability	How much is spent on collection?	Additional taxes/penalties collected by audit
Alabama	2002–2008	NA	Audit and Assessment Activity: includes number of audits conducted by tax type and revenue generated by each audit
Alaska	1999–2008	NA	Revenue collected from assessment
Arizona	2000–2008	NA	Additional revenue generated by audit and gross collection of audit assessments and delinquent tax
Arkansas	1999–2007	NA	NA
California	1980–2007	Expenditure analysis Program/process cost	Tax Collection Activities contain how much is available for collection and how much has been collected.
Colorado	1998–2008	NA	Taxation Business Group Activities contain assessment by field audit and delinquent collections
Connecticut	2001–2008	NA	NA
Delaware	2000–2008	NA	NA
District of Columbia	NA	NA	NA
Georgia	2008	Cost of collection fees collected	Revenue from collection initiatives compliance results
Hawaii	1995–2008	NA	Compliance division's summary
Idaho	1998–2008	NA	Total audit recoveries
		Total revenue versus Cost to collect (not cost to audit)	
Illinois	2000–2008	NA	NA
Indiana	1997–2008	NA	Amount of tax assessed
Iowa	1996–2008	Return on investment dollars spent on enforcement versus dollars collected	Enforcement program summary

(continued)

Table 10.1 (continued)

State	Availability	How much is spent on collection?	Additional taxes/penalties collected by audit
Kansas	2004–2008	Operating expenses (return on investment) by compliance enforcement program	NA
Kentucky	1997–2008	Expenditure for auditing services	NA
Louisiana	2002–2008	NA	NA
Maine		NA	NA
Maryland	1997–2008	NA	NA
Massachusetts	2005–2007	NA	NA
		Fees paid to collection agencies	Revenue collected by collection agencies
Michigan	1998–2007	NA	NA
Minnesota	2004–2008	Tax compliance expenditure	Compliance initiative revenue
Mississippi	1998–2008	NA	NA
Missouri	2002–2008	Fees to collection agencies (discontinued in 2005)	NA
		Fees to contract auditors	
Montana	1998–2008	Audit collections ROI ratio	NA
Nebraska	1996–2006	NA	NA
Nevada	2006–2008	Department financial statement contains expenditures on audit activities	Net collections from audit billings
New Hampshire	2002–2008	NA	Enforcement compliance section contains the revenue raised by audit and collection activities
New Jersey	1996–2007	NA	NA
New Mexico	2008	Compliance enforcement department budget	NA
New York	1997–2008	NA	Delinquency collection

(continued)

Table 10.1 (continued)

State	Availability	How much is spent on collection?	Additional taxes/penalties collected by audit
North Carolina	2004–2008	NA	NA
North Dakota	1999–2007	NA	NA
Ohio	1998–2007	Expenditure of the Ohio department of taxation by division: audit and compliance	NA
Oklahoma	1999–2006	NA	NA
Oregon	1999–2009	NA	NA
Pennsylvania	2000–2008	NA	General fund delinquent tax collection
Rhode Island	2008	NA	NA
South Carolina	2000–2008	NA	NA
South Dakota	1998–2008	NA	Additional revenue from audit division
Tennessee		NA	NA
Texas	2008	NA	NA
Utah	1995–2008	NA	NA
Vermont	1998–2008	NA	Compliance department summary
Virginia	1999–2008	NA	NA
Washington	1997–2008	NA	NA
West Virginia	2007–2009	State auditor's office expenditure	NA
Wisconsin	1999–2007	NA	NA
Wyoming	1989–2008	NA	NA

Empirical Findings

The analysis in this section focuses on the relationship between federal audit rates and state income tax collections. The econometric model specifies that state tax income taxes depend on state tax rates, personal income per capita, socio-economic factors to control the tax base and factors to control state-specific difference in IRS enforcement. Clearly state income taxes will increase with either increases in personal or increases in the average state tax rate. As state income tax increases in a multiplicative fashion with the product of average tax rates and personal income, it is natural to specify these relationships using a logarithmic transformation. Hence the logarithm of state income tax becomes the dependent variable and independent variables include the logarithms of personal income and average state tax rates. We similarly transform the IRS enforcement factors to logarithmic form. Following the discussion and rational in earlier chapters, we continue to treat the enforcement variables as endogenous factors but similarly transform the instruments with logarithms.

I show the results for the log–log specification in Table 10.2[1], for the period 1988–2004. Table 10.3 presents the results for the estimation period 1988–2001. Here, state income taxes per return filed and other explanatory variables such as the individual audit rate are converted to logarithms. For either estimation period the Hausman specification test found that the federal audit rate was endogenous. Similarly, the federal audit rate was found to be endogenous in Chap. 7. Hence the tables report estimates based on instrumental variables and generalized least squares to account for the panel structure of the data. After instrumenting the audit rate, I determined that the elasticity of the state income tax per return filed with respect to the federal audit rate is 0.128–0.155 depending on the time employed in the estimation. This implies that a 10% increase in the audit rate leads to a 1.3–1.5% increase in state income tax collections. The result is statistically significant.

I conclude that the federal audit rate does induce general deterrence at the state level. However, neither model found a spillover effect from CI enforcement that was statistically significant. This may be a result of the differences in the types of evasion that audits and criminal enforcement typically target or the lower likelihood that CI investigations lead to revenue agent reports. The data available to us at this level cannot discern this. Meanwhile, the pattern of socioeconomic effects is sensible. Clearly the most important factors are personal income per capita and state tax collections. We also see that an increase in the percent of families on welfare lowers state income tax per return filed. This is to be expected as the tax base is reduced when greater numbers of families are on welfare.

[1] A purely linear specification provided similar results.

Table 10.2 State income tax (reported, 1972$, 1000s, per return filed)

Variable	
Constant	−4.68 (−9.766)
Percent of families on welfare	−0.03 (−4.76)
Family size	−0.12 (−0.13)
Farms per household	10.48 (2.58)
Percent of adults with high school diploma	0.14 (1.22)
Unemployment rate	−0.53 (−1.24)
Personal income per capita	1.26 (8.11)
Percent of employed persons in manufacturing	−1.04 (−3.18)
Percent of employed persons in service	0.37 (1.82)
Percent of pop over 65	2.04 (1.68)
State tax rate (log)	0.37 (29.00)
Federal and state average marginal tax rate (log)	0.17 (1.58)
Federal and state maximum tax rate (log)	0.02 (0.35)
Total sentences (tax and money Laun only) (log)	0.00 (−0.22)
Audit rate (log)	0.15 6.24
Number of observations	850
R-squared	71.50%
Time period	1988–2004

We can compare these results to those obtained by Mikesell (1985) with the caveat that Mikesell's analysis focuses on sales tax and not state income tax.[2] The logic of the calculation is nonetheless identical. First, Mikesell concludes that an increase in audit coverage of one percent leads to a change in the sales tax base of 7%. This is related to a general deterrence result by converting changes in the tax base to changes in sales tax collections. Using a an average sales tax rate of roughly 4.59 for 1981 (the year of the Mikesell analysis) among states with a

[2] There exists the possibility that federal enforcement effects spillover further to other revenue streams such as sales tax or property tax. This relationship is potentially measurable using the approach developed in this chapter.

Table 10.3 State income tax (reported, 1972$, 1000s, per return filed)

Variable	
Constant	−5.12
	(−8.71)
Percent of families on welfare	−0.02
	(−2.77)
Family size	0.85
	(0.88)
Farms per household	10.65
	(2.34)
Percent of adults with high school diploma	−0.04
	(−0.35)
Unemployment rate	−0.18
	(−0.43)
Personal income per capita	0.82
	(5.27)
Percent of employed persons in manufacturing	−1.77
	(−4.41)
Percent of employed persons in service	1.27
	(3.23)
Percent of pop over 65	−0.38
	(−0.28)
State tax rate (log)	0.35
	(28.49)
Federal and state average marginal tax rate (log)	0.58
	(3.45)
Federal and state maximum tax rate (log)	−0.01
	(−0.30)
Total sentences (tax and money Laun only) (log)	−0.03
	(−1.18)
Audit rate (log)	0.13
	6.40
Number of observations	700
R-squared	76.50%
Time period (t-statistics in parenthesis)	1988–2001

non-zero sales tax, the implied elasticity of sales tax with respect to audit is (7)(4.5%) = (7)(0.045) = 0.32%. This is nearly one-third of the elasticity determined for the effect of the federal audit rate on state income tax we have determined and sustainability smaller than the 4.6% elasticity of the reported federal taxable income with respect to the federal audit rate reported in Chap. 7.

State Additional Taxes and Penalties

While the data for state additional taxes and penalties is not complete we rely on the partial data collected to analyze the relationship between state additional taxes and penalties through audit and examination and other factors in this section.

Table 10.4 State additional taxes and penalties (real 1972$) (log)

Variable	
Constant	6.64
	(6.69)
Federal additional taxes and penalties (per return filed) real 1972 $ (log)	0.61
	(9.69)
Number of observations	114
R-squared	0.46
(t-statistics in parenthesis)	

Table 10.5 State additional taxes and penalties (real 1972$) (log)

Variable	
Constant	2.01
	(16.63)
Federal additional taxes and penalties (per return filed) real 1972 $ (log)	0.30
	(5.72)
State expenditure on tax collection	0.34
	(15.56)
Number of observations	23
R-squared	0.92
(t-statistics in parenthesis)	

The data for states not reporting this information occurs presumably at random. With this caveat we present the econometric analysis of two models for state additional taxes and penalties. Table 10.4 shows the relationship between state additional taxes and penalties and federal additional taxes and penalties.

Earlier I argued that there should be a close connection between these two factors due to the reciprocity between state and federal tax agencies. The simple correlation between these two factors (expressed in real terms) is 0.87. Hence there is a high correlation between real federal and state additional taxes and penalties as one would expect.

As shown in Table 10.4, the elasticity of state additional taxes and penalties with respect to federal additional taxes and penalties is 0.61. However, as it is likely that state additional taxes and penalties are affected by budget resources allocated at the state level to collections, we consider a model in Table 10.5 which adds a state level cost of state income tax collections.

In a way this specification acts as a reduced form for a structural specification of this model in which state enforcement levels would be measured directly. In this sense we use the instrument for state enforcement (enforcement expenditures) as a proxy for the unavailable enforcement measures. As discussed above, measuring enforcement costs at the state level was difficult and further reduced the number of available states and time periods present in the regression model. Table 10.5 shows that state additional taxes and penalties increase with federal additional taxes and penalties (elasticity = 0.29) and with state expenditures for tax collections (elasticity = 0.34). These results are important in of themselves since they demonstrate that state tax collection efforts raise additional revenues at the margin i.e. holding constant the amounts reported to state agencies through revenue agent reports.

To gauge the magnitude of these effects, we combine the elasticity of federal additional taxes and penalties with respect to federal audit rates with the elasticity of state additional taxes and penalties with respect to federal additional taxes and penalties. I combine these elasticity results by multiplying the two (elasticity is the ratio of the derivatives of logarithms). I find that the elasticity of state additional taxes and penalties with respect to a change in federal audit rate is $(0.85)(0.29) = 0.25$ where I have used the elasticity of federal additional taxes and penalties with respect to the individual audit rate determined in Chap. 8 (roughly 0.85) and the elasticity of state additional taxes and penalties with respect to federal additional taxes and penalties reported above of 0.29. Hence, a 10% income in federal individual audit rates would result in a 2.5% income state additional taxes and penalties

Finally, I calculate the spillover effect of federal initiated enforcement on state tax collections. First, I combine the result presented above for the change in reported state income tax that result from a change in the federal audit rate. This effect is approximately 2.85–4.62% depending on the estimation period (ending in 2004 or 2001, respectively). Second, I use the change in state initiated additional taxes and penalties due to a change in the federal audit rate. The latter is determined as the product of the change in state additional tax and penalties with respect to a change in federal additional taxes and penalties with the change in federal additional taxes and penalties with respect to the audit rate. It is straightforward to express this with a few equations. We have:

$$\text{Spillover} = \frac{\text{dRTR}}{\text{dIAR}} \Big/ \frac{\text{dALR}}{\text{dIAR}} = \frac{\text{dRTR}}{\text{dIAR}} \Big/ \left(\frac{\text{dRTR}}{\text{dIAR}} + \frac{\text{dATP}}{\text{dIAR}} \right)$$

where:

RTR Reported state tax liability per return,

ALR Adjusted state tax liability per return (reported state tax liability per return plus state additional taxes and penalties per return),

IAR Federal individual audit rate,

FATP Federal additional taxes and penalties (federal adjusted tax liability per return—federal reported tax liability per return)

By the chain rule:

$$\frac{\text{dATP}}{\text{dIAR}} = \frac{\text{dATP}}{\text{dFATP}} \times \frac{\text{dFATP}}{\text{dIAR}}.$$

Again relying on data for the period 1988–2004, I determined that:

$$\frac{\text{dFATP}}{\text{dIAR}} = (0.00817)\,(0.148) = 0.00121.$$

Also, as I reported above,

$$\frac{\mathrm{dRTR}}{\mathrm{dIAR}} = 0.0285.$$

Combining these results, we have find that the spillover at the state level is 0.0285/(0.0285 + 0.00121) = 96%.

Conclusions

The spillover effect of federal enforcement on state income tax collections is large. Hence we see that the general deterrence effects are substantially larger than the specific deterrence effects for the state income tax case. This result parallels findings for federal audit rates. We were not able to measure the spillover effect from state initiated audits but as argued above the preponderance of state audit and enforcement activity is directly related to federal revenue reports. Nonetheless this chapter furthers the case for increased federal enforcement.

Chapter 11
Conclusions

Summary

Fifteen years since the publication of the original DGW study, the message still remains the same: increases in IRS enforcement can go a long way to increasing taxpayer compliance through general deterrence. However, the IRS should not rely solely on correspondence audits of enforcement. While much less expensive, these audits are not as effective as either-face-to-face audits or CI investigations. Meanwhile, the marginal effectiveness of IRS audits has declined since the 1977–1986 period and the amount of direct enforcement has simultaneously declined. In conjunction, these findings help explain why the tax gap continues to grow with time.

I reach several conclusions. First, a significant structural change in tax administration occurred since the original DGW study due to the Tax Reform Act of 1986. Second, focusing on the last 18 years, I find that IRS audits continue to have a measurable and statistically significant effect on taxpayer compliance. However, the individual audit rate has continued to decline since DGW first published their findings and is now only 35% of its level in 1977–1986. Of equal importance, the marginal effectiveness of audits has declined so that those audits that are now completed are not as effective in promoting general deterrence as they were nearly 20 years ago. I do not find support for the proposition that correspondence audits are an effective substitute for face-to-face audits. Third, I find marginally significant results from CI sentenced cases on general tax deterrence. I performed simulations to determine the direct revenue (spillover) effect of audits and CI activities. I find that the direct effect of doubling the audit rate on assessed tax collections (reported amounts and additional taxes and penalties) is an increase in assessed collections of $22.0 billion. Further, doubling CI tax and money laundering sentences could increase assessed collections by $11.2 billion. I estimate the spillover effects from both audit and CI activities to be approximately 95%. Doubling the audit rate or CI sentenced cases produced similar increases in

J. A. Dubin, *The Causes and Consequences of Income Tax Noncompliance*,
DOI: 10.1007/978-1-4419-0907-7_11, © Springer Science+Business Media, LLC 2012

total collections. IRS enforcement is found to be extremely cost effective but underutilized.

I find that the spillover effect of audits and CI enforcement is quite large and generally estimated to be 95%. I also find that federal audit enforcement has spillover effects on state income tax collections at similar or even higher rates. I find that an increase in IRS examination activity could have important fiscal impacts and make a large contribution toward reducing the tax gap. Doubling tax and money laundering sentences would cost $203 million (at these unit cost estimates), while doubling the audit rate would cost $330 million. However, doubling the audit rate is estimated to result in a $22.0 billion increase in per annum reported collections, while doubling tax and money laundering cases was predicted to increase reported tax collection by $11.2 billion per annum. Hence, an additional dollar allocated to audit would return $67 in general deterrence while an additional dollar allocated to CI would result in $55. The return to IRS enforcement is evidently quite large.

The policy prescription is a healthy dose of increased IRS enforcement. While the message is unpleasant this appears to be one of the only ways to decrease tax noncompliance without tax simplification.

Directions for Further Research

IRS Service

The IRS provides services to taxpayers. These services include assistance in tax return preparation, answering questions, providing ombudsmen service, taxpayer advocacy, fielding taxpayer contacts through call centers, and Web-based assistance. While the present study has concentrated on the role of enforcement, a natural extension to this research would consider IRS services as positive inducements to taxpayer voluntary compliance.

International Compliance

The methods and results presented in this monograph could be extended to other countries. The DGW approach to measuring audit and enforcement effects requires measures of taxable income, socioeconomic explanatory factors, and measures of marginal and average tax rates as well as measures of enforcement i.e. measures of audits and criminal investigations. Attempts to measure general deterrence in the international setting are nascent. A proper dataset that combines multiple countries or countries over time must be assembled to attempt this analysis.

Extensions to Other Revenue Streams

The methods presented for federal and state income tax at the individual taxpayer level could be extended to other revenue streams (sales tax) or for other taxpayer entities (corporations, sole proprietorships) in an analogous manner. Measures of specific and general deterrence could be defined and measured in an analogous fashion.

Media Coverage

This monograph starts the integration of media factors into the time-series cross-section framework. Unfortunately, the time period of media coverage was insufficient to demonstrate conclusive results. I expect that additional years of data regarding media coverage of IRS activities in print and non-print sources will reveal how information about tax rates and non-compliance is disseminated to taxpayers. The econometric studies could be augmented by statistical comparisons of treatment and control areas where media exposure to IRS activities was demonstrated to be unequal. A demonstration of the role of media coverage in tax compliance is a necessary next step in the understanding of the pathways by which taxpayers learn about audit and penalty rates as well as IRS services. Additionally, the role of social interaction must be understood so that the mechanism by which taxpayers and tax preparers share information and tax strategies become clear. A third component of voluntary compliance comes from the theories of fairness and morality. Media coverage, social interaction, and notions of fairness are important components of indirect effects because by definitions there must be some mechanism by which the experiences of a few taxpayers who have direct contact with the service potentially influence a great many taxpayers. At this point in time, these mechanisms are not fully understood and have never been measured. Historical attitudinal surveys and new surveys of social interaction have the potential to develop relevant explanatory factors that may further refine the DGW method.

Specific Policy Recommendation

Reducing the tax gap is a desirable goal and socially optimal produced that the marginal benefits exceed the marginal costs of tax collection. The former must include both specific and general deterrence influences on revenue streams while the latter must include increased IRS resource costs and taxpayer compliance costs through a third party and return preparation and record-keeping. While a theme of this book has been that increased enforcement will yield higher specific and general deterrence, such outcomes could also be achieved by simplification of the existing tax code. Tax return complexity not only increases return preparation costs but also fosters ambiguity and makes it difficult for taxpayers to comply with the tax code even if that is the sole intent. Of equal importance is that tax complexity leaves room for interpretation, "gray areas" and the like, that potentially allow for tax noncompliance. Consequently, tax code simplification should be considered at the same time and in conjunction with increased enforcement and increased taxpayer service.

Similarly, withholding at income source and third-party information matching can eliminate opportunities to evade while making return preparation easier. If this monograph is reduced to a call for increased enforcement it must simultaneously be understood as a call for tax simplification, increased withholding and reporting, and the elimination of opportunities for tax evasion.

Appendix
Variable Glossary

Variable	Category	Description	Source	Years
dir_exam or dextm	Budget (IRS)	Direct examination time	Provided by IRS	1977–2002
b	Criminal investigation	Total number of both tax and money sentences	Provided by IRS CI	1988–2002
bmd	Criminal investigation	Total number of both tax and money sentences that were released in the media	Provided by IRS CI	1992–2002
bmd_b	Criminal investigation	Percent of both tax and money laundering sentences in the media	Provided by IRS CI	1992–2002
bot_neit	Criminal investigation	Both tax and laundering sentences neither prison nor probation	Provided by IRS CI	1988–2002
bot_none	Criminal investigation	Both tax and laundering sentences not released in the media	Provided by IRS CI	1992–2002
bp	Criminal investigation	Total number of prosecutions for both tax and money laundering	Provided by IRS CI	1988–2002
bpr_b	Criminal investigation	Pct of both tax and money sentences that were released in print	Provided by IRS CI	1992–2002

(continued)

DOI: 10.1007/978-1-4419-0907-7,

(continued)

Variable	Category	Description	Source	Years
bprl	Criminal investigation	Both tax and laundering sentences released in print	Provided by IRS CI	1992–2002
bpri	Criminal investigation	Both tax and laundering prison sentences	Provided by IRS CI	1988–2002
bpri_b	Criminal investigation	Pct of both tax and money sentences that were prison sentences	Provided by IRS CI	1988–2002
bpro	Criminal investigation	Both tax and laundering probation sentences	Provided by IRS CI	1988–2002
bpro_b	Criminal investigation	Pct of both tax and money sentences that were probation sentences	Provided by IRS CI	1988–2002
brd	Criminal investigation	Both tax and laundering sentences released on radio	Provided by IRS CI	1992–2002
brd_b	Criminal investigation	Pct of both tax and money sentences that were released on radio	Provided by IRS CI	1992–2002
btv	Criminal investigation	Both tax and laundering sentences released on tv	Provided by IRS CI	1992–2002
btv_b	Criminal investigation	Pct of both tax and money sentences that were released on tv	Provided by IRS CI	1992–2002
m	Criminal investigation	Total number of money laundering sentences	Provided by IRS CI	1988–2002
m_mp	Criminal investigation	Total number of money laundering sentences/total number of money laundering prosecutions	Provided by IRS CI	1988–2002

(continued)

(continued)

Variable	Category	Description	Source	Years
md	Criminal investigation	Total sentences that were released in the media	Provided by IRS CI	1992–2002
md_tot	Criminal investigation	Pct of total sentences that were released in the media	Provided by IRS CI	1992–2002
mmd	Criminal investigation	Total money laundering sentences that were released in the media	Provided by IRS CI	1992–2002
mmd_m	Criminal investigation	Percent of total money laundering sentences in the media	Provided by IRS CI	1992–2002
mo	Criminal investigation	Total sentences for money laundering only cases	Provided by IRS CI	1988–2002
mon_neit	Criminal investigation	Money laundering sentences neither prison nor probation	Provided by IRS CI	1988–2002
mon_none	Criminal investigation	Money laundering sentences not released in the media	Provided by IRS CI	1992–2002
mon_not	Criminal investigation	Prosecuted for money laundering but not sentenced	Provided by IRS CI	1988–2002
mp	Criminal investigation	Total number of money laundering prosecutions	Provided by IRS CI	1988–2002
mpr	Criminal investigation	Money laundering sentences released in print	Provided by IRS CI	1992–2002
mpr_m	Criminal investigation	Pct of money laundering sentences that were released in print	Provided by IRS CI	1992–2002
mpri	Criminal investigation	Money laundering prison sentences	Provided by IRS CI	1988–2002
mpri_m	Criminal investigation	Pct of money laundering sentences that were prison sentences	Provided by IRS CI	1988–2002

(continued)

(continued)

Variable	Category	Description	Source	Years
mpro	Criminal investigation	Money laundering probation sentences	Provided by IRS CI	1988–2002
mpro_m	Criminal investigation	Pct of money laundering sentences that were probation sentences	Provided by IRS CI	1988–2002
mrd	Criminal investigation	Money laundering sentences released on radio	Provided by IRS CI	1992–2002
mrd_m	Criminal investigation	Pct of money laundering sentences that were released on radio	Provided by IRS CI	1992–2002
ms	Criminal investigation	Subject Criminal investigation initiations for money laundering	Provided by IRS CI	1988–2002
mtv	Criminal investigation	Money laundering sentences released on tv	Provided by IRS CI	1992–2002
mtv_m	Criminal investigation	Pct of money laundering sentences that were released on tv	Provided by IRS CI	1992–2002
na_tot	Criminal investigation	Total sentences where no media data exists	Provided by IRS CI	1988–2002
neit_tot	Criminal investigation	Total sentences neither prison nor probation	Provided by IRS CI	1988–2002
none_tot	Criminal investigation	Total sentences not released in the media	Provided by IRS CI	1988–2002
np	Criminal investigation	Total number of prosecutions neither tax or money laundering related	Provided by IRS CI	1988–2002
ns	Criminal investigation	Subject Criminal investigation initiations for neither money or tax	Provided by IRS CI	1988–2002

(continued)

(continued)

Variable	Category	Description	Source	Years
pr	Criminal investigation	Total sentences released in print	Provided by IRS CI	1992–2002
pri	Criminal investigation	Total prison sentences	Provided by IRS CI	1988–2002
pri_tot	Criminal investigation	Number of prison sentences divided by total sentences	Provided by IRS CI	1992–2002
pro	Criminal investigation	Total probation sentences	Provided by IRS CI	1988–2002
pro_tot	Criminal investigation	Number of probation sentences divided by total sentences	Provided by IRS CI	1992–2002
rd	Criminal investigation	Total sentences released on radio	Provided by IRS CI	1992–2002
t	Criminal investigation	Total number of tax sentences	Provided by IRS CI	1988–2002
t_tp	Criminal investigation	Total number of tax sentences/total number of tax prosecutions	Provided by IRS CI	1988–2002
tax_na	Criminal investigation	Tax sentences where no media data exists	Provided by IRS CI	1992–2002
tax_neit	Criminal investigation	Tax sentences neither prison nor probation	Provided by IRS CI	1988–2002
tax_none	Criminal investigation	Tax sentences not released in the media	Provided by IRS CI	1992–2002
tax_not	Criminal investigation	Prosecuted for tax crimes but not sentenced	Provided by IRS CI	1988–2002
tmd	Criminal investigation	Total tax sentences that were released in the media	Provided by IRS CI	1992–2002
tmd_t	Criminal investigation	Percent of total tax sentences in the media	Provided by IRS CI	1992–2002
to	Criminal investigation	Total sentences for tax only cases	Provided by IRS CI	1988–2002
tot or total	Criminal investigation	Total sentences, includes all factors	Provided by IRS CI	1988–2002
totp	Criminal investigation	Total prosecutions, includes all factors	Provided by IRS CI	1988–2002

(continued)

(continued)

Variable	Category	Description	Source	Years
tp	Criminal investigation	Total number of tax prosecutions	Provided by IRS CI	1988–2002
tpr	Criminal investigation	Tax sentences released in print	Provided by IRS CI	1992–2002
tpr_t	Criminal investigation	Pct of tax sentences that were released in print	Provided by IRS CI	1992–2002
tpri	Criminal investigation	Tax prison sentences	Provided by IRS CI	1988–2002
tpri_t	Criminal investigation	Pct of tax sentences that were prison sentences	Provided by IRS CI	1988–2002
tpro	Criminal investigation	Tax probation sentences	Provided by IRS CI	1988–2002
tpro_t	Criminal investigation	Pct of tax sentences that were probation sentences	Provided by IRS CI	1988–2002
trd	Criminal investigation	Tax sentences released on radio	Provided by IRS CI	1992–2002
trd_t	Criminal investigation	Pct of tax sentences that were released on radio	Provided by IRS CI	1992–2002
ts	Criminal investigation	Subject Criminal investigation initiations for tax	Provided by IRS CI	1988–2002
ttv	Criminal investigation	Tax sentences released on tv	Provided by IRS CI	1992–2002
ttv_t	Criminal investigation	Pct of tax sentences that were released on tv	Provided by IRS CI	1992–2002
tv	Criminal investigation	Total sentences released on tv	Provided by IRS CI	1992–2002
addt_aa	ERIS/TDI examinations	Additional taxes assessed after audit (ERIS) (real 1972 dollars in thousands)	Provided by IRS ERIS	1992–2003
addt_aa1	ERIS/TDI examinations	Additional taxes assessed after audit by revenue agents (ERIS) (real 1972 dollars in thousands)	Provided by IRS ERIS	1992–2003

(continued)

(continued)

Variable	Category	Description	Source	Years
addt_aa2	ERIS/TDI examinations	Additional taxes assessed after audit by tax auditors (ERIS) (real 1972 dollars in thousands)	Provided by IRS ERIS	1992–2003
addt_aa5	ERIS/TDI examinations	Additional taxes assessed after audit by service centers (ERIS) (real 1972 dollars in thousands)	Provided by IRS ERIS	1992–2003
addt_at	ERIS/TDI examinations	Additional taxes assessed after audit (TDI) (real 1972 dollars in thousands)	Provided by IRS ERIS	1992–2003
addt_at1	ERIS/TDI examinations	Additional taxes assessed after audit by revenue agents (TDI) (real 1972 dollars in thousands)	Provided by IRS ERIS	1992–2003
addt_at2	ERIS/TDI examinations	Additional taxes assessed after audit by tax auditors (TDI) (real 1972 dollars in thousands)	Provided by IRS ERIS	1992–2003
addt_at5	ERIS/TDI examinations	Additional taxes assessed after audit by service centers (TDI) (real 1972 dollars in thousands)	Provided by IRS ERIS	1992–2003
addt_ca	ERIS/TDI examinations	Additional taxes collected after audit (ERIS) (real 1972 dollars in thousands)	Provided by IRS ERIS	1992–2003
addt_ca1	ERIS/TDI examinations	Additional taxes collected after audit by revenue agents (ERIS) (real 1972 dollars in thousands)	Provided by IRS ERIS	1992–2003

(continued)

(continued)

Variable	Category	Description	Source	Years
addt_ca2	ERIS/TDI examinations	Additional taxes collected after audit by tax auditors (ERIS) (real 1972 dollars in thousands)	Provided by IRS ERIS	1992–2003
addt_ca5	ERIS/TDI examinations	Additional taxes collected after audit by service centers (ERIS) (real 1972 dollars in thousands)	Provided by IRS ERIS	1992–2003
addt_ct	ERIS/TDI examinations	Additional taxes collected after audit (TDI) (real 1972 dollars in thousands)	Provided by IRS ERIS	1992–2003
addt_ct1	ERIS/TDI examinations	Additional taxes collected after audit by revenue agents (TDI) (real 1972 dollars in thousands)	Provided by IRS ERIS	1992–2003
addt_ct2	ERIS/TDI examinations	Additional taxes collected after audit by tax auditors (TDI) (real 1972 dollars in thousands)	Provided by IRS ERIS	1992–2003
addt_ct5	ERIS/TDI examinations	Additional taxes collected after audit by service centers (TDI) (real 1972 dollars in thousands)	Provided by IRS ERIS	1992–2003
addt_ra	ERIS/TDI examinations	Additional taxes recommended after audit (ERIS) (real 1972 dollars in thousands)	Provided by IRS ERIS	1992–2003
addt_ra1	ERIS/TDI examinations	Additional taxes recommended after audit by revenue agents (ERIS) (real 1972 dollars in thousands)	Provided by IRS ERIS	1992–2003

(continued)

(continued)

Variable	Category	Description	Source	Years
addt_ra2	ERIS/TDI examinations	Additional taxes recommended after audit by tax auditors (ERIS) (real 1972 dollars in thousands)	Provided by IRS ERIS	1992–2003
addt_ra5	ERIS/TDI examinations	Additional taxes recommended after audit by service centers (ERIS) (real 1972 dollars in thousands)	Provided by IRS ERIS	1992–2003
addt_rt	ERIS/TDI examinations	Additional taxes recommended after audit (TDI) (real 1972 dollars in thousands)	Provided by IRS ERIS	1992–2003
addt_rt1	ERIS/TDI examinations	Additional taxes recommended after audit by revenue agents (TDI) (real 1972 dollars in thousands)	Provided by IRS ERIS	1992–2003
addt_rt2	ERIS/TDI examinations	Additional taxes recommended after audit by tax auditors (TDI) (real 1972 dollars in thousands)	Provided by IRS ERIS	1992–2003
addt_rt5	ERIS/TDI examinations	Additional taxes recommended after audit by service centers (TDI) (real 1972 dollars in thousands)	Provided by IRS ERIS	1992–2003
ear1	ERIS/TDI examinations	Cases of recommended adjustments by revenue agents divided by indiv returns filed (ERIS) (expressed as %)	Provided by IRS ERIS	1992–2003

(continued)

(continued)

Variable	Category	Description	Source	Years
ear12	ERIS/TDI examinations	Cases of recommended adjustments by tax auditors & revenue agents divided by indiv returns filed (ERIS) (expressed as %)	Provided by IRS ERIS	1992–2003
ear125	ERIS/TDI examinations	Total cases of recommended adjustments divided by indiv returns filed (ERIS) (expressed as %)	Provided by IRS ERIS	1992–2003
ear2	ERIS/TDI examinations	Cases of recommended adjustments by tax auditors divided by indiv returns filed (ERIS) (expressed as %)	Provided by IRS ERIS	1992–2003
ear5	ERIS/TDI examinations	Cases of recommended adjustments by service centers divided by indiv returns filed (ERIS) (expressed as %)	Provided by IRS ERIS	1992–2003
iar3	ERIS/TDI examinations	Individual audit rate (expressed as %)	Provided by IRS ERIS	1977–2002
iar4	ERIS/TDI examinations	Individual audit rate (expressed as %)	Provided by IRS ERIS	1977–2002
iat3a	ERIS/TDI examinations	Additional taxes recommended after exam (real 1972 dollars in thousands) (ind + fid); ERIS assessed taxes and penalties	Provided by IRS ERIS	1977–2002

(continued)

(continued)

Variable	Category	Description	Source	Years
iat3c	ERIS/TDI examinations	Additional taxes recommended after exam (real 1972 dollars in thousands) (ind + fid); ERIS collected taxes and penalties	Provided by IRS ERIS	1977–2002
iat3r	ERIS/TDI examinations	Additional taxes recommended after exam (real 1972 dollars in thousands) (ind + fid); ERIS recommended adjustments	Provided by IRS ERIS	1977–2002
iat4a	ERIS/TDI examinations	Additional taxes recommended after exam (real 1972 dollars in thousands) (ind + fid); TDI assessed taxes and penalties	Provided by IRS ERIS	1977–2002
iat4c	ERIS/TDI examinations	Additional taxes recommended after exam (real 1972 dollars in thousands) (ind + fid); TDI collected taxes and penalties	Provided by IRS ERIS	1977–2002
iat4r	ERIS/TDI examinations	Additional taxes recommended after exam (real 1972 dollars in thousands) (ind + fid); TDI recommended adjustments	Provided by IRS ERIS	1977–2002
tar1	ERIS/TDI examinations	Cases of recommended adjustments by revenue agents divided by indiv returns filed (TDI) (expressed as %)	Provided by IRS ERIS	1992–2003

(continued)

(continued)

Variable	Category	Description	Source	Years
tar12	ERIS/TDI examinations	Cases of recommended adjustments by tax auditors & revenue agents divided by indiv returns filed (TDI) (expressed as %)	Provided by IRS ERIS	1992–2003
tar125	ERIS/TDI examinations	Total cases of recommended adjustments divided by indiv returns filed (TDI) (expressed as %)	Provided by IRS ERIS	1992–2003
tar2	ERIS/TDI examinations	Cases of recommended adjustments by tax auditors divided by indiv returns filed (TDI) (expressed as %)	Provided by IRS ERIS	1992–2003
tar5	ERIS/TDI examinations	Cases of recommended adjustments by service centers divided by indiv returns filed (TDI) (expressed as %)	Provided by IRS ERIS	1992–2003
addt	Examinations (IRS)	Total additional taxes recommended	Provided by IRS	1993–2002
addt1	Examinations (IRS)	Additional taxes rec after audit by revenue agents (real 1972 dollars in thousands)	Provided by IRS	1993–2002
addt12	Examinations (IRS)	Additional taxes rec after audit by both tax auditors and revenue agents (real 1972 dollars in thousands)	Provided by IRS	1993–2002
addt2	Examinations (IRS)	Additional taxes rec after audit by tax auditors (real 1972 dollars in thousands)	Provided by IRS	1993–2002

(continued)

(continued)

Variable	Category	Description	Source	Years
addt5	Examinations (IRS)	Additional taxes rec after audit by service centers (real 1972 dollars in thousands)	Provided by IRS	1993–2002
audr	Examinations (IRS)	Audit Rate using total audits (expressed as %)	Provided by IRS	1993–2002
audr1	Examinations (IRS)	Audit Rate using audits by revenue agents (expressed as %)	Provided by IRS	1993–2002
audr12	Examinations (IRS)	Audit Rate using audits by both tax auditors and revenue agents (expressed as %)	Provided by IRS	1993–2002
audr2	Examinations (IRS)	Audit Rate using audits by tax auditors (expressed as %)	Provided by IRS	1993–2002
audr5	Examinations (IRS)	Audit Rate using audits by service centers (expressed as %)	Provided by IRS	1993–2002
irfsc	Information Returns (IRS)	Information returns filed by service center	Provided by IRS	1977–1988
scirp	Information Returns (IRS)	Number of info returns not W2 filed/total number of info returns filed	Provided by IRS	1977–1988
dum80	Misc	Dummy variable; 1 if time>=1980, 0 otherwise		
one	Misc	Constant term		
citido	Political science	Measure of state citizen liberalism, 100 most liberal	Dataset retrieved from homepage of Prof. William Berry, Florida State Univ.	1977–2000

(continued)

(continued)

Variable	Category	Description	Source	Years
govido	Political science	Measure of state govt liberalism, 100 most liberal	Dataset retrieved from homepage of Prof. William Berry, Florida State Univ.	1977–2000
govr	Political science	Political party of State Governor, 1 Dem 0 Rep	U.S. Congressional Almanac	1977–2002
h_app	Political science	Avg political ideology score for members of House Appropriations Committee, 100 is most liberal	U.S. Congressional Almanac; Americans for Democratic Action: www.adaction.org	1977–2000
h_wm	Political science	Avg political ideology score for members of House Ways and Means Committee, 100 is most liberal	U.S. Congressional Almanac; Americans for Democratic Action: www.adaction.org	1977–2000
house	Political science	Number of households by state	U.S. Census	1977–2001
hratio	Political science	Ratio of Democrats to Republicans in the House	clerk.house.gov	1977–2001
pres	Political science	Political party of US President, 1 Dem 0 Rep	U.S. Congressional Almanac	1977–2000
s_app	Political science	Avg political ideology score for members of Senate Appropriations Committee, 100 is most liberal	U.S. Congressional Almanac; Americans for Democratic Action: www.adaction.org	1977–2000
s_fin	Political science	Avg political ideology score for members of Senate Finance Committee, 100 is most liberal	U.S. Congressional Almanac; Americans for Democratic Action: www.adaction.org	1977–2000

(continued)

(continued)

Variable	Category	Description	Source	Years
sratio	Political science	Ratio of Democrats to Republicans in the Senate	www.senate.gov	1977–2001
stdemh	Political science	Percentage of state representatives (lower house) that are Democrat	Dataset retrieved from homepage of Prof. William Berry, Florida State Univ.	1993–2000
stdems	Political science	Percentage of state senators (upper house) that are Democrat	Dataset retrieved from homepage of Prof. William Berry, Florida State Univ.	1993–2000
alr	Returns, collections and exams (databook)	Assessed income tax liability per individual returns filed (real 1972 in thousands)	Annual Report of the Commissioner of Internal Revenue, IRS Data Book; IRS SOI Bulletin	1977–2001
bang	Returns, collections and exams (databook)	Additional taxes recommended after exam per individual returns examined (real 1972 in thousands)	Annual Report of the Commissioner of Internal Revenue, IRS Data Book	1977–2000
bpr	Returns, collections and exams (databook)	Budget per total returns filed (real 1972 in thousands)	Annual Report of the Commissioner of Internal Revenue, IRS Data Book (2000 & 2001 BPR same as '99)	1977–2001
eorf	Returns, collections and exams (databook)	Tax–exempt organizations income tax returns filed	Annual Report of the Commissioner of Internal Revenue, IRS Data Book	1977–2002
esttax	Returns, collections and exams (databook)	Estimated tax returns filed	Annual Report of the Commissioner of Internal Revenue, IRS Data Book	1977–2002
iar	Returns, collections and exams (databook)	Individual audit rate (expressed as %)	Annual Report of the Commissioner of Internal Revenue, IRS Data Book	1977–1999
iar2	Returns, collections and exams (databook)	Individual audit rate (expressed as %)	iar (1977–1992); audr12 (1993–2002)	1977–2002

(continued)

(continued)

Variable	Category	Description	Source	Years
iat	Returns, collections and exams (databook)	Additional taxes recommended after exam (real 1972 dollars in thousands) (ind + fid)	Annual Report of the Commissioner of Internal Revenue, IRS Data Book; total addl tax by year state and organization.xls	1977–1997
iat2	Returns, collections and exams (databook)	Additional taxes recommended after exam (real 1972 dollars in thousands) (ind + fid)	iat (1977–1992); addt12 (1993–2002)	1977–2002
icr	Returns, collections and exams (databook)	Individual income tax collected per individual returns filed (real 1972 in thousands)	Annual Report of the Commissioner of Internal Revenue, IRS Data Book	1977–2002
ina	Returns, collections and exams (databook)	Number of individual tax returns examined by state ind + fid + part	Annual Report of the Commissioner of Internal Revenue, IRS Data Book	1977–2000
iref1	Returns, collections and exams (databook)	Refunds for individual tax returns (real 1972 dollars in thousands)	Annual Report of the Commissioner of Internal Revenue, IRS Data Book	1977–2002
iref2	Returns, collections and exams (databook)	Refunds for employment tax returns (real 1972 dollars in thousands)	Annual Report of the Commissioner of Internal Revenue, IRS Data Book	1977–2002
irf	Returns, collections and exams (databook)	Number of individual tax returns filed by state ind + fid + part	Annual Report of the Commissioner of Internal Revenue, IRS Data Book	1977–2002

(continued)

(continued)

Variable	Category	Description	Source	Years
rcap	Returns, collections and exams (databook)	Individual income tax returns filed per capita * 1000	Annual Report of the Commissioner of Internal Revenue, IRS Data Book	1977–2002
rtr	Returns, collections and exams (databook)	Reported income tax liability per individual returns filed (real 1972 dollars in thousands)	Annual Report of the Commissioner of Internal Revenue, IRS Data Book; IRS SOI Bulletin	1977–2001
tcst	Returns, collections and exams (databook)	Total costs incurred by IRS, district offices only (real 1972 dollars in thousands)	Annual Report of the Commissioner of Internal Revenue, IRS Data Book	1977–1999
tic	Returns, collections and exams (databook)	Total individual IRS collections (real 1972 dollars in thousands)	Annual Report of the Commissioner of Internal Revenue, IRS Data Book	1977–2000
tic1	Returns, collections and exams (databook)	Total individual IRS collections (real 1972 dollars in thousands)	Annual Report of the Commissioner of Internal Revenue, IRS Data Book	1977–2000
trf	Returns, collections and exams (databook)	Total income tax returns filed	Annual Report of the Commissioner of Internal Revenue, IRS Data Book	1977–2002
icrabs	Returns, collections and exams (SOI Bulletin)	Federal individual income tax revenue per individual returns filed (real 1972 dollars in thousands)	IRS, Statistics of Income Bulletin	1977–2002
inc	Returns, collections and exams (SOI Bulletin)	Federal income tax revenue by state (real 1972 dollars in thousands)	IRS, Statistics of Income Bulletin	1977–2002
ticabs	Returns, collections and exams (SOI Bulletin)	Federal individual income tax revenue by state, lagged one year (real 1972 dollars in thousands)	IRS, Statistics of Income Bulletin	1977–2002

(continued)

(continued)

Variable	Category	Description	Source	Years
emp	Socioeconomic	Number of employed persons by state	Bureau of Labor Statistics	1977–2001
famsiz	Socioeconomic	Number of households divided by population	U.S. Census	1977–2001
farms	Socioeconomic	Number of farms by state	U.S. Dept of Agriculture	1977–2000
frmfam	Socioeconomic	Number of farms divided by number of households	U.S. Dept of Agriculture	1977–2000
ipce	Socioeconomic	National personal consumption expenditure price deflator (1972 dollars)	Bureau of Labor Statistics	1977–2002
manu	Socioeconomic	Number of people employed in manufacturing industry	Bureau of Labor Statistics	1977–2001
newed	Socioeconomic	Percent of pop over 25 who graduated high school	U.S. Census	1977–2000
per65	Socioeconomic	Percent of pop age 65 or older	U.S. Census	1977–2000
pgovt	Socioeconomic	Percent of employed persons working for govt by state	Bureau of Labor Statistics	1977–2001
picap	Socioeconomic	Total personal income per capita by state (real 1972 dollars in thousands)	Bureau of Economic Analysis	1977–2001
picap2	Socioeconomic	PICAP squared	Bureau of Economic Analysis	1977–2001
pman	Socioeconomic	Percent of employed persons in manufacturing	Bureau of Labor Statistics	1977–2001
pop	Socioeconomic	Population by state	U.S. Census	1977–2002
pop65	Socioeconomic	Number of people age 65 or older by state	U.S. Census	1977–2000

(continued)

(continued)

Variable	Category	Description	Source	Years
pserv	Socioeconomic	Percent of employed persons in service	Bureau of Labor Statistics	1977–2001
serv	Socioeconomic	Number of people employed in service industry	Bureau of Labor Statistics	1977–2001
staxr	Socioeconomic	Average state tax rate assuming fixed income distribution across states	National Bureau of Economic Research http://www.nber.org/~taxsim/state-marginal/state-fix.html	1977–2000
stgini	Socioeconomic	State Gini coefficient	U.S. Census	1977–2000
ui	Socioeconomic	Unemployment rate by state	Bureau of Labor Statistics	1977–2001
welfam	Socioeconomic	Number of families on welfare by state	U.S. Dept of Health and Human Services	1977–2000

Bibliography

Ali MM, Wayne Cecil H, Knoblett JA (2001) The effects of tax rates and enforcement policies on taxpayer compliance: a study of self-employed taxpayers. Atl Econ J 29(2):186–202

Allingham M, Sandmo A (1972) Income tax evasion: a theoretical analysis. J Public Econ 1:323–328

Alm J, Blackwell C, McKee M (2004) Audit selection and firm compliance with a Brand-Based Sales Tax. Nat Tax J 57(2):209–227 June

Anderson TW, Hsiao C (1981) Estimation of dynamic models with error components. J Am Stat Assoc 76:598–606

Anderson TW, Hsiao C (1982) Formulation and estimation of dynamic models using panel data. J Econometrics 18:47–82

Andreoni J, Erard B, Feinstein J (1998) Tax compliance. J Econ Lit 36(2):818–860

Arellano M (1989) A note on the Anderson–Hsiao estimator for panel data. Econ Lett 31:337–341

Arellano M, Bond S (1991) Some tests of specification for panel data: Monte Carlo evidence and its application to employment equations. Rev Econ Stud 58:277–297

Balestra P, Nerlove M (1966) Pooling cross-section and time-series data in the estimation of a dynamic model the demand for natural gas. Econometrica 34:585–612

Beron K, Tauchen H, Witte A (1992) Tax compliance: an investigation using individual tax compliance measurement program (TCMP) data. J Quant Criminol 9(2):177–202

Border K, Sobel J (1987) Samurai accountant: a theory of auditing and plunder. Rev Econ Stud 54(4): 525–540

Clotfelter C (1983) Tax evasion and tax rates: an analysis of individual returns. Rev Econ Stat 65:363–373

Cowell F (1985) Tax evasion with labour income. J Public Econ 26:19–34

Crane S, Nourzad F (1986) Inflation and tax evasion: an empirical analysis. Rev Econ Stat 68:217–223

Dubin JA (2007) Criminal investigation enforcement activities and taxpayer noncompliance. Publ Finan Rev 35(4):500–529 July

Dubin JA, Wilde LL (1988) An empirical analysis of federal income tax auditing and compliance. Natl Tax J 41:61–74

Dubin JA, Graetz MJ, Udell MA, Wilde LL (1992a) The demand for tax return preparation services. Rev Econ Stat 74(1):75–82

Dubin JA, Graetz MJ, Udell MA, Wilde LL (1992b) The demand for tax return preparation services. Rev Econ Stat 74(1):75–82

Dubin JA, Graetz MJ, Wilde LL (1990a) The changing face of tax enforcement, 1978–1988. Tax Lawyer 43: 893–914. (Reprinted in Westin R, Hishon R, Green B (eds) (1991) Criminal tax prosecutions. Anderson Publishing Company)

DOI: 10.1007/978-1-4419-0907-7,

Dubin JA, Graetz MJ, Wilde LL (1990b) The effect of audit rates on the federal individual income tax, 1977–1986. Natl Tax J 43:395–409

Dubin JA, Graetz MJ, Wilde LL (1987) Are we a nation of tax cheaters? New econometric evidence on tax compliance. Am Econ Rev Pap Proc 77:240–245

Durlauf S, Peyton Young H (2001) Social dynamics. The MIT Press, Cambridge

Giles DEA, Caragata PJ (2001) The learning path of the hidden economy: the tax burden and tax evasion in New Zealand. Appl Econ 33:1857–1867

Graetz MJ, Reinganum JF, Wilde LL (1986) The tax compliance game: toward an interactive theory of law enforcement. J Law Econ Organiz 2(1):1–32 (Oxford University Press, Spring)

Hausman JA (1978) Specification tests in econometrics. Econometrica 46(6):1251–1271

Internal Revenue Service (1990) Net tax gap and remittance tax gap estimates, Publication 1415 (Washington, D.C.: Research Division, Compliance Estimates Group, April)

Internal Revenue Service (1996) Federal tax compliance research: individual income tax gap estimates for 1985, 1988, and 1992. Technical Report 1415, IRS, Washington, DC

Joel S, Yitzhaki S (2002) Tax avoidance, evasion, and administration. Handb Public Econ 3:1425–1470

Kiviet J (1995) On bias, inconsistency, and efficiency of various estimators in dynamic panel data models. J Econometrics 68:53–78

Manski C (1993) Identification of endogenous social effects: the reflection problem. Rev Econ Stud 60:531–542

Manski C (1995) Identification problems in the social sciences. Harvard University Press, Cambridge

Mete M (2002) Bureaucratic behavior in strategic environments: politicians, taxpayers, and the IRS. J Politics 64(2):384–407

Mikesell J (1985) Audits and the tax base: evidence of induced sales tax compliance. West Tax Rev 6(2):86–114

Plumley AH (1996) The determinants of individual income tax compliance: estimating the impacts of tax policy, enforcement, and irs responsiveness. Internal Revenue Service, Publication 1916 (Rev. pp 11–96)

Reinganum JF, Wilde LL (1985) Income tax compliance in a principal-agent framework. J Publ Econ Elsevier 26(1):1–18 (February)

Roth J, Scholz J, Witte A (1989) Taxpayer compliance: an agenda for research. A national research council report. University of Pennsylvania Press, Philadelphia

Sandmo A (1981) Income tax evasion, labour supply, and the equity-effeciency trade off. J Public Econ 16:265–288

Scholz J (1998) Trusting government: fear, duty and trust in tax compliance. Trust and governance. Russell Sage Foundation, New York

Scholz J, Lubell M (1998a) Trust and taxpaying: testing the heuristic approach to collective action. Am J Political Sci 42:398–417

Scholz J, Lubell M (1998b) Adaptive political attitudes: duty, trust, and fear as monitors of tax policy. Am J Political Sci 42:903–920

Slemrod J (1985) An empirical test for tax evasion. Rev Econ Stat 67(2):232–238

Slemrod J (1989) The return to tax simplification: an econometric analysis. Public Finan Quart 17:3–27

Slemrod J (ed) (1992) Why people pay taxes: tax compliance and enforcement. The University of Michigan Press, Michigan, Ann Arbor

Srinivasan T (1973) Tax evasion: a model. J Public Econ 2(4): 339–346

Witte AD, Woodbury DF (1985) The effect of tax laws and tax administration on tax compliance: the case of the U.S. individual income tax. Natl Tax J 38:1–14

Witte AD, Woodbury DF (1983) What we know about factors affecting compliance with the tax laws. In: Phillip Sawicki (ed) Income tax compliance, pp 133–148

Yitzhaki S (1974) A note on income tax evasion: a theoretical analysis. J Public Econ 3:201–202

About the Author

Jeffrey A. Dubin, Ph.D. is an Adjunct Professor of Economics and Statistics in Global Economy and Management at the UCLA Anderson School of Management. Dr. Dubin left the California Institute of Technology (Caltech) in 2007 where he was tenured Professor of Economics. Dr. Dubin joined Caltech in 1982. Dr. Dubin earned his undergraduate degree in Economics with highest honors and great distinction from the University of California, Berkeley, and received a Ph.D. in Economics from the Massachusetts Institute of Technology.

Dr. Dubin is the author of four books: Consumer Durable Choice and the Demand for Electricity: Elsevier North-Holland, 1985, Studies in Consumer Demand-Econometric Methods Applied to Market Data, Kluwer Academic Publishers, 1998, Empirical Studies in Applied Economics, Kluwer Academic Publishers, 2001, and The California Energy Crisis: What, Why, and What's Next, Springer-Kluwer Academic Publishers, 2004. Dr. Dubin received the Econometric Society Frisch Medal in 1986 with Professor Daniel McFadden (Nobel 2000).

Dr. Dubin is also co-founding member and Director of Statistical and Economic Analysis at Pacific Economics Group in Pasadena. Dr. Dubin frequently provides expert testimony and consults in matters of statistics and applied economics.

J. A. Dubin, *The Causes and Consequences of Income Tax Noncompliance*,
DOI: 10.1007/978-1-4419-0907-7,

MIX
Papier aus verantwortungsvollen Quellen
Paper from responsible sources
FSC® C105338

If you have any concerns about our products,
you can contact us on
ProductSafety@springernature.com

In case Publisher is established outside the EU,
the EU authorized representative is:
Springer Nature Customer Service Center GmbH
Europaplatz 3, 69115 Heidelberg, Germany

Printed by Libri Plureos GmbH
in Hamburg, Germany